HeavenWord Daily

Other books by David Servant

Christ's Incredible Cross

Forgive Me for Waiting so Long to Tell You This

God's Tests

Modern Myths About Satan and Spiritual Warfare

The Disciple-Making Minister

The Great Gospel Deception

Through the Needle's Eye

HeavenWord Daily

A Year of Growth Through the New Testament

David Servant

ETHNOS PRESS
Pittsburgh, Pennsylvania

HeavenWord Daily
A Year of Growth Through the New Testament
First Printing: November 2010

Copyright © 2009 by David Servant. All rights reserved. No portion of this book may be reproduced in any form without the written permission of the copyright owner, except for brief excerpts quoted in critical reviews.

All Scripture quotations in this book, except those noted otherwise, are from the *New American Standard Bible* ®, Copyright © 1960, 1962, 1963, 1968, 1971, 1972, 1973, 1975, 1977, and 1995 by The Lockman Foundation, and are used by permission. (www.Lockman.org)

Printed in the United States of America
International Standard Book Number: 978-0-9827656-0-9

To all who pray with the psalmist:
"Let my cry come before You, O Lord;
Give me understanding according to Your word."
(Psalm 119:169)

Acknowledgements

As with every book project, I'm always so happy for those people who find my misteaks and make me lock even more intelligant than I actually am. Who knows how might this book be without there help? My sinceer thanks to LaVerne Kirkwood, Charity McDaniel, Emily Growden, Chris Posti, Anne Witham, David Warnock and Becky Servant for all that you all did to keep the truth hidden about my writing skils. You've saved me alot of embarasment. (I didn't ask any of you to edit this Acknowledgment because I wanted you to be surprized when you saw saw you're names in the book!)

Contents

Chronological Order

Introduction	i
Matthew	13
Acts 1:1 – 11:18	69
James	91
Acts 11:19 – 14:28	101
Galatians	107
Acts 15:1 – 18:17	119
1 Thessalonians	127
2 Thessalonians	137
Mark	143
Acts 18:18 – 19:41	175
1 Corinthians	177
Acts 20:1-6	209
2 Corinthians	209
Romans	235
Acts 20:7 – 28:31	267
Luke	285
Ephesians	333
Colossians	345
Philemon	353
Philippians	355
1 Timothy	363
Titus	375
1 Peter	381
Jude	391
2 Peter	393
2 Timothy	399
John	407
Hebrews	449
1 John	475
2 John	485
3 John	487
Revelation	489
Congratulations!	533

Alphabetical Order

Introduction	i
Acts 1:1 – 11:18	69
Acts 11:19 – 14:28	101
Acts 15:1 – 18:17	119
Acts 18:18 – 19:41	175
Acts 20:1-6	209
Acts 20:7 – 28:31	267
Colossians	345
1 Corinthians	177
2 Corinthians	209
Ephesians	333
Galatians	107
Hebrews	449
James	91
John	407
1 John	475
2 John	485
3 John	487
Jude	391
Luke	285
Mark	143
Matthew	13
1 Peter	381
2 Peter	393
Philemon	353
Philippians	355
Revelation	489
Romans	235
1 Thessalonians	127
2 Thessalonians	137
1 Timothy	363
2 Timothy	399
Titus	375
Congratulations!	533

Introduction

I was surprised when I first learned that a person with an average reading speed—who reads an average of three minutes a day, five days a week—can read through the entire New Testament in one year. That was very good news for a busy person like me. I checked the math just to make sure it was true. It is.

Dividing the 181,253 words of the New Testament by 260 weekdays results in an average daily read of 697 words. The average person's reading speed is about 230 words per minute. So it takes the average person three minutes to read 697 words—the average number of words in a New Testament chapter.

Armed with that knowledge, I set out to write a daily commentary and devotional that would not exceed 700 words per day. That way, you would only need to invest an average of six minutes each day, five days each week, to read through the New Testament and this book in one year. And who can't spare six minutes? Add four minutes for meditational pauses, and you've still used only ten minutes of your day. You can do this!

I also decided to use a special reading plan to make your daily reading even more interesting and enriching. With this unique reading plan, one of the four Gospels is read each quarter, while the epistles and book of Acts are read chronologically. That is, as you read through the book of Acts, you'll read each epistle at the time it was written in relationship to the book of Acts. That will help you to understand the historical context of each epistle. You may already know that the order of the epistles in most Bibles follows Martin Luther's arrangement, from the longest epistle to the shortest. It was the epistles of James and Galatians, however, that were written first, not Romans. So we'll be reading James and Galatians first.

Finally, I didn't think the Christian world needed any more "fluff devotionals." The New Testament is not a book of fluff. Rather, it is often more like a two-edged sword. So I did my best, with

God's help, to write a truth-filled "motivational devotional" for true disciples of Jesus. My goal was your spiritual growth, reflected by your obedience to the commandments of Christ. The result is what I prefer to call a "do-votional" rather than a "devotional." I hope you will be challenged as you read each day.

May the Lord complete the good work He has begun in you (Phil. 1:6)!

David Servant

Day 1, Matthew 1

All those names listed in Jesus' genealogy are meaningless apart from the Old Testament. So let me state at the outset that we're not focusing on the New Testament during this one-year study because the Old Testament is irrelevant! Jesus and the New Testament authors quoted from the Old Testament at least 700 times. If you add the New Testament allusions to the Old Testament, that number increases into the thousands. God gave us one continuing revelation, not two separate revelations with the older being completely supplanted by the new. That is why Christian Bibles contain both Old and New Testaments. Those designations, by the way, would have been completely foreign to Peter and Paul.

It is true, of course, that some of what was written in the Old Testament has limited relevance to New Covenant Christians. But every bit of the Old Testament still has some relevance, as all of it reveals to us something about God and His will. Moreover, the Old Testament contains predictive prophecies that are still waiting to be fulfilled. If you toss out the book of Isaiah, for example, you might as well toss out the book of Revelation.

So don't forget this. As we start reading Matthew's Gospel today, we're breaking into the middle of the story. What we read about today—the arrival of the Messiah—had been anticipated in the Old Testament from its very first pages. And from reading Jesus' genealogy, it is clear that Matthew wanted his targeted Jewish readership to know that Jesus was thoroughly Jewish and qualified by His lineage to be the Messiah, a descendant of Abraham, Isaac, Jacob, Judah and David. All those men were promised that the Messiah would be their descendant.

If the Mosaic Law stipulated that adulteresses should be put to death (see Lev. 20:10), why does Matthew state that Joseph, upon discovery that Mary was pregnant, "being a righteous man," intended to dissolve their engagement secretly? Should not a righteous man uphold the Law?

This is an important question, and perhaps it will provoke us to consider what makes someone truly righteous in the light of this scripture.

God is the perfect example of righteousness, but He is also very merciful. He gives sinners time to repent, rarely judging them immediately. Jesus certainly demonstrated such mercy towards the woman caught in the act of adultery (see John 8:1-11). Matthew wrote that Joseph did not want to disgrace Mary, calling attention to what she had done. Although he naturally assumed the worst about her pregnancy and was hurt because of it, he continued to act with love towards the one who offended him. Joseph was a righteous man indeed, imitating a righteous God.

Notice, however, that righteous Joseph intended not to marry his betrothed once he learned of her pregnancy. Some would want us to believe that love tolerates any behavior. Not so.

I'm so glad that an angel cleared everything up for Joseph. What a switch! Mary's pregnancy was not a tragedy, but the most wonderful event of human history! She was carrying "God with us."

Notice the angel declared that Jesus would save His people "from their sins," implying not only the forgiveness of sins, but also deliverance from sinning. Praise God that is part of our salvation. Jesus saved us from our sins by bearing them on the cross, so we see a foreshadowing of His sacrificial death even at His conception. He was born to die—for us.

Day 2, Matthew 2

Today we can glean two very important lessons about God's guidance. By means of a star, God led the wise men from the East. They likely traveled for months as the star led them westward towards Jerusalem, the logical place to find the newborn "King of the Jews." At some point they apparently lost sight of the star (2:10), either because it disappeared or because they didn't pay close enough attention, having made the assumption that Jerusalem was their final destination. But after conferring with Herod—who himself conferred with chief priests and scribes—they headed towards Bethlehem, just six miles south of Jerusalem, once again following the star that had led them for months. It guided them directly to Jesus.

The point is this: Keep watching the star, and never make assumptions about God's guidance. Many of us have been like the wise men, following God's guidance for a while, but making an assumption along the way, and thus missing His specific direction. We get near to God's perfect will, but not as close as He wants us to be, and miss out on His greatest blessings that are waiting for us. The Holy Spirit is God's star in our hearts, leading us to walk in the specific good works that He has prepared beforehand (see Eph. 2:10). To stay on course we must continue seeking God. AMEN

In the case of Joseph, an angel of the Lord told him to return to Israel from Egypt with Jesus and Mary. When Joseph obeyed those instructions, he then received more specific guidance to go to Galilee rather than Judea. Here is the second lesson: Don't expect God to lay out the entire plan before you start. He leads us one step at a time, and we must walk by faith. Once we obey His first step, then He will reveal the next step. If you refuse to budge until God has revealed His entire plan to you, you will miss out on His blessings that are waiting. We must prove to God that we trust Him and walk by faith.

Take note that, contrary to what we see in movies about Jesus' birth, the wise men didn't visit Jesus when He was a newborn, but probably when He was closer to two years old. They visited Him when He was in a house, but we know Jesus was born in a stable or a cave and that He was laid in a feeding trough right after His birth (see Luke 2:7). Additionally, we read today that Herod had all of the male children of Bethlehem and its environs murdered who "were from two years old and under, according to the time which he had ascertained" from the wise men (2:16).

Why did God prevent Jesus' death at the hand of Herod's soldiers but not prevent the deaths of so many other children in Bethlehem? We don't know because the Bible doesn't say. But one truth becomes very clear to us as we read this tragic story: Jesus was special. His life was of much greater importance than the life of any other child in Bethlehem. In fact, if we compared the value of Jesus with the value of all other human beings combined, His value would infinitely exceed their combined value, as He is God.

Finally, take note that the wise men traveled for months (and perhaps even years) with the intention of finding and worshiping the King of the Jews (2:2). When they finally beheld the tiny king, "They fell down and worshiped Him" (2:11) and gave Him precious gifts. They knew Jesus was no ordinary baby—He was God in the flesh, a person who was worthy of worship. Jesus cannot be just our "buddy" or "pal." He must be our God, who deserves our devotion and obedience. Is that how you relate to Him?

Day 3, Matthew 3

John the Baptist preached repentance, as did Jesus and the apostles. It is through repentance that we begin a relationship with God. There is no other way to be saved. Repentance simply means turning away from sin and turning to obedience. A gospel that does not include the concept of repentance is not a biblical gospel.

Tragically, repentance is often edited from the modern "gospel." It seems old-fashioned to some and contrary to the principle of grace to others. Yet the Word of God has not changed. If we truly believe in Jesus, the Son of God, we will naturally turn from sin and begin to serve Him. The grace that God offers humanity is not a license to sin, but a temporary opportunity to repent of sin and receive forgiveness.

If people must repent to be saved, then we need to help them see their need for repentance. John set a great example. His gospel included the two foundational elements: (1) the sinfulness of humanity, and (2) the wrath of God against sin. Unless people are convinced of those facts, they will have no reason to repent. Unlike many modern preachers, John didn't consider it inappropriate to mention God's wrath (3:7), or hell (3:10-12), or to address his audience as sinners (3:7-8).

John also very skillfully exposed the lies that propped up the false spiritual security of his hearers. He knew that before they could be saved, he had to convince them that they were unsaved. Nothing has changed since then. Most folks today think they are good people who are on their way to heaven. They need to see themselves in the light of God's holy commandments so that they will realize that they are actually hell-bound rebels.

John proclaimed that, just because one could trace his lineage from Abraham, it was no guarantee of salvation. Similarly, many modern people think their salvation is certain because they had a grandfather who was a preacher or because their parents are Christians. The truth is, however, that God has no grandchildren, just children, and we must come to Him on our own.

John was also very concerned that some of those who were coming to be baptized were not sincere. So he warned them that just a claim of repentance was not enough. Those who have truly repented "bring forth fruit in keeping with [their] repentance" (3:8). Faith without works is dead, useless, and cannot save us (see Jas. 2:14-26).

Notice that John did not introduce the soon-to-come Messiah as someone "who loves you and has a wonderful plan for your life." Such a message would not have led people to repent, and thus would not have led them to salvation. Rather, John spoke of Jesus as one who would separate the wheat from the chaff, and who would "burn up the chaff with unquenchable fire" (3:12). Hardly sounds like "American Jesus," does it?

An interesting note: John's declaration of his unworthiness to baptize Jesus was not based on the fact that Jesus was the Son of God or the Messiah. John did not know that Jesus was the Messiah until after he baptized Him (see John 1:29-34). John's declaration must have been based on Jesus' reputation as a holy man. Remember, Jesus never sinned even once in His life. He always loved God with all His heart, and He always loved His neighbor as Himself. His sinless life was one of the things that qualified Him to atone for our sins. A man on death row can't volunteer to pay the death penalty for someone else.

Jesus received baptism from John to identify with humanity, and not because He needed to repent or have His sins washed away. His baptism was a foreshadowing of His taking upon Himself the sins of the world. Perhaps it would help us to imagine His baptism in this way: Everyone who went in before Him had his dirty sins washed into the water. When Jesus went down into the water, those sins clung to Him. They went down dirty and came up clean; He went down clean and came up dirty. That is a picture of what happened on the cross.

Day 4, Matthew 4

It is interesting that Jesus was led by the Spirit into the wilderness specifically to be tempted by the devil (4:1). It was God's plan. Had Jesus faced no temptation, it could not be truly said that He was sinless, and as I mentioned yesterday, He had to be sinless to atone for our sins.

God does not tempt anyone (see Jas. 1:14), but He tests *everyone* (see Ps. 11:5; Prov. 17:3). One way He tests us is by watching what we do when Satan tempts us, just as He did with Jesus. Thankfully, God limits the degree that Satan may tempt us. Scripture promises, "God is faithful, who will not allow you to be tempted beyond what you are able, but with the temptation will provide the way of escape also, that you may be able to endure it" (1 Cor. 10:13). Good to remember!

Jesus was tempted in every way that we are (see Heb. 4:15), so His wilderness temptation was not His only or final temptation. In fact, Luke wrote in his Gospel that after this incident Satan "departed from Him until an opportune time" (Luke 4:13). Satan looks for opportunities to tempt us when we are vulnerable, which is why we are admonished in the New Testament to "be on the alert," knowing that our "adversary, the devil, prowls about like a roaring lion, seeking someone to devour" (1 Pet. 5:8). We should, however, "resist him, firm in [our] faith" (1 Pet. 5:9). Faith in God's Word is our primary defense against Satan, because he is the father of lies (see John 8:44), and he would have us doubt the truth. That was his strategy against Jesus, but Jesus overcame him by faith, quoting scriptures that contradicted Satan's lies. We should follow His example.

Notice that Satan quoted God's Word in his second temptation. He quoted it, however, out of its biblical context, trying to make it mean something that it really didn't. God promised protection in Psalm 91 (a verse from which Satan quoted to Jesus), but not when we intentionally do something foolish, like jumping from a roof!

This is why it is so important to study the *entire* Bible, so that we can interpret every scripture in the light of every other scripture.

The most common error in Bible interpretation is ignoring context. The Bible can be made to say just about anything by isolating scriptures. This is the chief reason people embrace false teaching and are lulled into cults. They don't know enough of the Bible, and so they are easily deceived by those who can quote a few verses.

Does Satan actually have, as he claimed, dominion over "all the kingdoms of the world and their glory" (4:8), and can he "give it to whomever" he wishes (Luke 4:6)? Only in one sense. From reading other scriptures, we know that Satan is the chief ruler over the kingdom of darkness. He only rules those who are submitted to him, being "the god of this world" (2 Cor. 4:4). He was offering Jesus the number two position over his evil realm, an opportunity to rule over every rank of evil spirit and every rebel human, which would have required that He commit treason against His Father.

Some, who ignore the biblical context of Satan's claims, ascribe Satan much more authority than he actually has, and make God less than all-powerful. Remember, the Bible affirms that God "is ruler over the realm of mankind, and bestows it on whomever He wishes" (Dan 4:25, 32). Jesus and Paul both referred to God as "Lord of heaven and earth" (Luke 10:21; Acts 17:24).

The very first word of Jesus' very first sermon was "Repent!" It is through repentance that people escape Satan's dominion (see Acts 26:17-18). The call to repentance is part of the gospel (see Luke 24:47), and God confirmed Jesus' message with miracles of healing and deliverance. Doubtless one reason we see so few genuine and convincing miracles through today's evangelists is because God will not confirm a "gospel" that omits the call to repentance.

Day 5, Matthew 5

Today is one of those days that I wish I was allotted more than 700 words! If you are interested in learning more about the Sermon on the Mount, I've written much more extensively about it in chapter 8 of my book titled, *The Disciple-Making Minister*. You can access it on the Internet at: www.heavensfamily.org/ss/pdf/ pdF dmm/dmm_08.pdf.

In the Beatitudes, as they're called, Jesus lists the identifying characteristics of the blessed and the blessings they can anticipate. If you look at those blessings closely, you'll notice that they are all various aspects of what the blessed will enjoy in the kingdom of heaven. Thus, by examining ourselves in the light of the identifying characteristics of the blessed, we can determine if we are on the road to heaven or not.

Have you recognized your spiritual poverty, mourned over your sins, and humbled yourself in repentance, now longing for righteousness (5:3-6)? Having received God's mercy, have you become merciful towards others (5:7)? Is your heart pure, so that your holiness is not just a thin veneer of religiosity like the Pharisees (5:8)? Are you working to help others make peace with God through repentance, even those who may persecute you for your righteousness (5:9-11)? If you can answer in the affirmative to those questions, you are on the road to heaven, blessedly transformed by God's grace.

The fact that holiness is the mark of true believers is further affirmed in 5:17-20, pivotal verses in this sermon. Jesus declared that unless our righteousness exceeds that of the scribes and Pharisees, we will not enter the kingdom of heaven. He elaborated on that theme in much of the remainder of His sermon, repeatedly exposing the unrighteous doctrine and practice of the scribes and Pharisees so that His followers would know how to do better.

The Pharisees were contentious, murderers at heart, and focused more on rituals than relationships; Jesus expects His followers to love each other dearly and reconcile when there is division, as love is the important thing (5:21-24). The Pharisees kept the letter of the law prohibiting adultery, but lustfully ignored the spirit of it, and divorce was rampant among them. Jesus expects much more from us (5:27-32). The scribes and Pharisees had invented elaborate means to justify lying (for more on this, see 23:1-36); Jesus expects us to always speak simple truth (5:33-37). By misapplying scriptures meant for judges in Israel's court system, the Pharisees justified taking personal revenge for the pettiest of offenses. Jesus expects us to be merciful even to our enemies, displaying a love that is superior to the world's, imitating our merciful Father (5:38-47).

Don't make the error that so many do when they read Jesus' oft-repeated statements, "You have heard that it was said...but I say to you…" Jesus was not correcting and contradicting Old Testament statements of His Father. He was not altering moral law. Remember, He declared early in His sermon that He had not come "to abolish the Law or the Prophets," but to fill them to the full (5:17). What Jesus was correcting was the false teaching of the scribes and Pharisees, who had twisted God's commandments for their own convenience. This is especially clear, for example, in Jesus' words, "You have heard that it was said, 'You shall love your neighbor, and hate your enemy'" (5:43). The second half of that statement was obviously the teaching of the scribes and Pharisees.

Do you want to be great in the kingdom of heaven? Jesus revealed the secret: Obey and teach the commandments (5:19). We will learn as we continue to study the New Testament that, under the New Covenant, we are to obey the law of Christ (which consists of all His commandments), rather than the Law of Moses, which was given to Israel alone (see 1 Cor. 9:19-21). This is not to say, however, that there isn't plenty of overlap between those two laws. Lust was a sin under the Old Covenant (see Ex. 20:17), and it remains so under the new covenant (5:28). Incidentally, loving one's enemies is not a new concept under the new covenant (see Ex. 23:5 and Prov. 25:21-22).

Clearly we see from today's reading that there is a relationship between holiness and heaven. Those who truly believe in Jesus obey Him.

Day 6, Matthew 6

Everyone knew who Jesus was referring to when He spoke of those who blew trumpets in the marketplaces prior to their distributions to the poor, who prayed on street corners, and who advertised their fastings—it was the scribes and Pharisees. Remember, Jesus requires that our righteousness surpass theirs (5:20). His true followers are motivated by love for God and love for others. They are conscious that, even when people aren't watching, God is, and they're striving for His praise rather than the praise of men.

Tragically, many professing Christians give nothing to the poor, much less give secretly to them. Does their righteousness surpass that of the scribes and Pharisees, who *did* give to the poor, albeit for the wrong motives?

It is a good exercise to compare our regular prayers with the prayer Jesus taught His disciples to pray. Notice that the first requests are for our Father's name to be hallowed, for His kingdom to come, and for His will to be done. How can anyone but a true and devoted disciple of Christ make such requests without being hypocritical? Yet millions of false believers whose lives dishonor God's name and don't reflect kingdom priorities regularly pray the "Lord's prayer."

In this "disciple's prayer," our material needs are minimized to daily bread, reflecting submissive trust and a contentment that stands in contrast to the world's greed. This prayer also elaborates on the fourth beatitude, our "hunger and thirst for righteousness," as we request forgiveness for our sins (we haven't reached perfection yet) and ask that God will not lead us where we will be tempted lest we fail, but rather will deliver us from evil. All of these requests make perfect sense, because God's kingdom, power and glory are eternal (6:13). We want to please Him!

Everyone in Jesus' audience also knew what He meant when He spoke of the "evil eye." It was a common expression for a "greedy heart." Proverbs 28:22 says, "A man with an evil eye hastens after wealth," and Jesus also used the same expression in Matthew 20:15. Those with greedy hearts are "full of darkness" (6:23), that is, void of truth. A "clear eye" (or "good eye" in 6:22) is the opposite of the "evil eye," and thus represents a heart that is not greedy, and one that is "full of light" (6:22), that is, filled with the truth.

What characterizes a greedy person? He lays up his treasures on earth, where his heart is also. Money is his master because he loves and serves it, and he actually hates God. He is full of darkness. This is obviously not the description of a heaven-bound follower of Jesus, but of an unsaved person. True followers of Christ, those who are focused on God's coming kingdom, are laying up their treasure in heaven where their hearts are, keeping their earthly pile as small as possible. They are full of the light of the truth. They aren't tithing as a means to grow rich on earth, something commonly taught in apostate churches today.

But notice Jesus' warning about the great darkness of those whose light is really darkness (6:23). He can only be speaking of those who *think* they are full of light, while their actions reveal that they are actually full of darkness. No doubt Jesus once again had the scribes and Pharisees in mind, men who were "lovers of money" (Luke 16:14), and whose earthly treasure piles testified of their great darkness and hatred of God. Yet had you asked any of them, they would have testified that they loved God! Thinking they were full of truth, they were actually full of darkness, which was their doom. "Prosperity preachers" take note! You are no different!

Finally, note that Jesus told His followers not to worry specifically about food, drink or clothing (6:25-34) something that most of us are never tempted to worry about because we are so wealthy (by the world's standards). Our material worries usually revolve around the fear of becoming less wealthy. May God help us to see our great wealth, as well as our great responsibility before Him because of it.

Day 7, Matthew 7

Jesus' prohibition against judging was not what many think it is. He was not forbidding the moral appraisal of other people. We absolutely must appraise other people morally if we are going to obey Jesus' commandments not to "give what is holy to dogs" and not "throw our pearls before swine" (7:6). And we must appraise people if we are going to identify and avoid false prophets (7:15). Jesus does not want us to waste our time trying to persuade people who are resistant to the truth, and He does not want us to be misled by those who are void of the truth. But both require that we make moral appraisals.

As we consider the context of Jesus' words about judging (7:1-5), it becomes clear that He was condemning the practice of pointing out small faults of others when we are personally guilty of greater faults. That, of course, is hypocrisy. Notice, however, that Jesus did not disapprove of taking the speck out of a brother's eye once we have removed the log from our own eye (7:5). Rather, He endorsed it. And that also requires that we make a spiritual appraisal of another person. I've written a much longer teaching on this subject titled, "Judge Not!", which can be read on the Internet at: www.heavensfamily.org/ss/e_teachings/2005_10.

You'll be hard-pressed to find more encouraging words regarding prayer than Jesus' words in 7:7-11. But are they true? Does "every one who asks receive"? They do when they ask for "what is good," as Jesus said (7:11). Just as most earthly parents will not give something to their children that would harm them, neither will our Father. And we should be able to determine something about what He considers to be good or bad for us by studying His Word. Every request, for example, found in the "Lord's Prayer" (that we read yesterday) is asking for something that is good. But compare those requests with the carnal and selfish prayer requests so often uttered. In Luke's account of this same promise by Jesus, he indicates that one of the "good gifts" Jesus had in mind for us is the Holy Spirit (Luke 11:13). The Holy Spirit helps us be holy. That is good!

"Therefore whatever you want others to do for you, do so for them, for this is the Law and the Prophets" (7:12). That is obviously a summarizing statement (it begins with the word *therefore*). But what does it have to do with the prayer promises that immediately precede it (7:7-11)? Very little. Actually, it is an end-of-sermon statement that summarizes everything Jesus said since 5:17: "Do not think that I came to abolish the Law or the Prophets; I did not come to abolish, but to fulfill." Notice His mention of the *Law and Prophets* in both 5:17 and 7:12. Since 5:17, Jesus had been fulfilling (or "filling to the full") the Law and Prophets, which can be summed up in the Golden Rule. I love it when Jesus makes things simple!

Since the way is narrow that leads to eternal life, Jesus warned His followers of those who might lead them astray. They are false prophets and teachers, and they can be identified by their fruit, that is, their deeds and actions. Unholy teachers are *false* teachers, even if they perform miracles. If they "practice lawlessness" (7:23), they are wolves in sheep's clothing who will one day be eternally condemned. Unholy leaders cannot lead anyone on the narrow way of holiness. In light of this, why is it that millions of professing Christians follow spiritual leaders who blatantly ignore so much of what Jesus commanded in the Sermon on the Mount?

Jesus underscored the central theme of this sermon—eternal life belongs only to the holy—three times in His closing statements (7:13-14, 21-22, 24-27). Calling Jesus Lord is not enough. Only those who do the will of the Father will enter heaven (7:21). Where's the grace in that, some ask? It is found in understanding that the only people who are doing God's will are those who have repented and been born again. God's grace is not a license to sin, but a temporary opportunity to repent and receive forgiveness.

Day 8, Matthew 8

About one-tenth of all the verses in the four Gospels tell us something about Jesus' healing ministry. That's significant! Those many records of Jesus' healings all demonstrate His divinity. No historical figure has ever come close to Him when it comes to miracles. He claimed to be God, and He proved He was.

Yet the healing stories serve another purpose as well. They reveal God's will regarding healing and encourage those who are in need of healing to look to Him. This point cannot be disputed due to the fact that Jesus often told those whom He healed, "Your faith has healed you." Clearly, had they not had faith they would not have been healed—even though it was obviously His will for them to be healed, made evident by the fact that He *did* heal them! Faith is obviously the key that opens the healing door.

Most every Christian believes, like the leper we read about today, that Jesus *can* heal them. He said, "Lord, if You are willing, You can make me clean" (8:2). But like the leper, they don't know if Jesus *wants* to heal them. They hope He does, but they aren't sure. And that is their problem, because Jesus never told anyone, "Your hope has healed you." Hope is not the same as faith. Scripture says that "Faith is the assurance of things hoped for" (Heb. 11:1). Notice what Jesus said to the leper to change his hope to faith: "I am willing; be cleansed" (8:3). To be healed, we need to change our hope to faith.

The Gentile centurion, a Roman commander, certainly demonstrated faith in Jesus (8:10, 13), and as a result, his servant was healed. Incidentally, the Greek word translated *servant* in 8:6 (*pais*) literally means "boy," indicating that the centurion was his legal guardian, or perhaps his father. This is important to understand, as we can find no example in the four Gospels of Jesus healing an adult solely in response to another adult's faith. We do, however, find several examples, like this one, of children being healed by Jesus in response to his or her parent's faith. Jesus most often told the sick, "*Your* faith has healed *you*." We can, like the men who brought their paralyzed friend to Jesus, encourage the sick to look to Jesus, and we can join our faith with theirs. But our faith can't overpower their unbelief. Healing, like salvation, must be appropriated by each person's own faith.

Matthew indicated that when Jesus healed "all who were ill" (8:16) in Capernaum, it fulfilled Isaiah's messianic prophecy, "He Himself took our infirmities, and carried away our diseases" (8:17). But surely the healings of the people of Capernaum that one evening were not the *complete* fulfillment of Isaiah's prophecy. Isaiah declared just one verse later in the very same prophecy that the Messiah would be "pierced through for *our* transgressions," and "crushed for *our* iniquities" (Is. 53:5). Those words have obvious universal application. The "our" of Isaiah 53:5 is no different than the "our" in Isaiah 53:4. Just as Jesus carried our sins in His body on the cross (1 Pet. 2:24), so He also "took our infirmities, and carried away our diseases." That is good news, and faith-building news! And when Jesus healed the people of Capernaum, it was proof to Matthew's Jewish readership that Jesus was obviously the promised Messiah of Isaiah 53, as evidenced by His incredible healing ministry there (and elsewhere).

To those who expressed their intentions to follow Him, Jesus conveyed that there would be hardship and a demand for devotion. I think it is unlikely, however, that the man who requested to bury his father first was saying that his father had just died. Jesus would have wanted him to honor his parents, and a funeral would not have caused him much delay. More likely, the man was indicating that he didn't want to miss being near his father during his final years. But Jesus said to everyone, "He who loves father or mother more than Me is not worthy of Me" (Matt. 10:37). Only God has the right to expect such allegiance. Only God deserves it.

Day 9, Matthew 9

It is so obvious only a theologian could miss it! Today we read four major stories about people who were healed by Jesus, and all were healed through *faith* (Matt. 9:2, 22, 29; Luke 8:50). Apart from faith they would not have been healed, even though it was clearly Jesus' will for them to be healed due to the fact that He healed them. So when people piously say, "God is sovereign, and so if it's His will for me to be healed, He'll heal me, regardless of what I do," they display their ignorance of simple biblical truth, even if they hold doctorates in theology. Had the people we read about today adopted that same attitude, none of them would have been healed. They were healed because they believed that Jesus would heal them.

Additionally, they didn't believe Jesus would heal them "someday, in His time, when it was His will." They believed He would heal them very soon. The paralytic man believed Jesus would heal him when he was lowered into the room with Jesus. The woman with the hemorrhage believed she would be healed when she touched Jesus. The two blind men believed they would be healed when Jesus touched them. The synagogue official believed Jesus would resurrect and heal his daughter when He laid His hand on her. We should learn from their examples. Jesus said, "All things for which you pray and ask, *believe that you have received them*, and they will be granted you" (Mark 11:24, emphasis added).

I stated yesterday that there is no example in the four Gospels of Jesus healing an adult solely in response to another adult's faith. What about today's story of the paralytic lowered though the roof by four of his friends? We read, "Jesus, seeing their faith..." (9:2).

Certainly, all four men, as well as the paralytic, had faith, as demonstrated by their actions. If the paralytic had not had faith, he would not have cooperated with his four friends, and when Jesus told him, "Rise, take up your bed, and go home," he would have laid there, not believing such a thing was possible. So we see that his four friends believed *with* him, but not *for* him, that is, apart from his own faith. You and I cannot overpower another person's unbelief by our faith. For example, what if I said to an atheist, "I know that you don't believe in Jesus, but I'm going to have faith for you so you'll be forgiven and go to heaven"? Would my faith save him? No, he must believe for himself. So it is with divine healing.

But notice that the faith of the synagogue official (see Luke 8:50) brought his daughter back to life and cured her of what killed her. Thus we see that parents can use their faith on behalf of their children for healing, at least up to a certain age.

Why did Jesus first tell the paralytic man that his sins were forgiven? Perhaps because he was doubting Jesus would heal him due to his sins. Once you know God has forgiven you, it is much easier to believe that He'll heal you (see Jas. 5:14-15). Another good lesson.

When I read the brief story of Jesus calling Matthew, I often wonder how many other people heard Jesus say to them as He walked by, "Follow Me!", but who watched Him walk off into the distance. Luke's Gospel tells us that Matthew "left everything behind, and rose up and began to follow Him" (Luke 5:28). That gives us some understanding of why Matthew was later chosen to be among the twelve. He said goodbye to his dishonest and greedy lifestyle.

When Jesus made the statement that the harvest is plentiful, there were an estimated 200 million people living on planet Earth. Today there are thirty-five times that many, close to seven billion people. Truly the harvest is even more plentiful than ever before, and the need for workers is much greater than ever before. Perhaps one-third of the world's people have never heard Jesus' name a single time! Pray that the Lord will send more laborers, adding, "Lord, send me!"

Day 10, Matthew 10

When we consider the twelve men whom Jesus chose to be His apostles, we realize that it is God who qualifies people for ministry. Four of the twelve were unschooled fishermen, one was a former tax collector, and one was a former right-wing revolutionary (Simon the Zealot). On the other hand, there is little doubt that these men were chosen because of what God saw in their hearts. Eleven had a sincere love for Jesus, while one possessed the seeds of betrayal.

Jesus sent them out, not just to preach the gospel, but to heal the sick and cast out demons (Matt. 11:7-8). Those supernatural signs would validate their message of repentance. We see the same pattern in the book of Acts. Why then do so many of us believe that God has changed His methods for building His kingdom? We need God's supernatural power just as much as the original apostles did. This is the reason to be baptized in His Spirit (Acts 1:8).

Jesus' instructions to the twelve are certainly applicable to modern ministers whom He also sends. Reading and *heeding* Matthew 10 would likely do more good for modern Bible school and seminary students than years of sitting in classrooms. This is a message from the Head of the Church!

The apostles were not to go out laden with money, but were to trust God for provision as they went (10:9-10). Theirs was a journey of faith. Tragically, many modern ministers are not only laden with money, but they strangely claim that this is the evidence of their great faith!

The twelve were not to waste their time on unreceptive villages. People who would not repent after hearing their message and seeing their miracles were doomed (10:15). The apostles were to shake the dust off their feet and head towards the next town. If this one spiritual principle was followed by modern ministers, we would not have 95% of the world's preachers endlessly preaching to 5% of the world's people.

Why should anyone hear the gospel twice until everyone has heard it once? You've probably noticed that most of the reports of modern, *genuine* miracles are coming from places where everyone hasn't heard the gospel twice. What is the difference? God is trying to reach those people who have never heard, whereas He has shaken the dust off *His* feet long ago where everyone has already rejected the gospel multiple times.

The twelve were to expect hardship that would test their devotion. Notice that the large majority of what Jesus told them fell under this category (10:16-39), and His words obviously have application to all true disciples (10:24-25). Following Jesus always results in slander, persecution and rejection, at the minimum. It could result in worse--hatred from one's own family, or even martyrdom, which has been experienced by millions of believers throughout the centuries. Jesus never promised exemption from these things. But He did promise that His Spirit would be with us (10:20), that God greatly values us (10:29-31), that we would find our lives in losing them for His sake (10:39), and that we will be rewarded (10:41-42).

Most sobering are Jesus' warnings, not about the world, but about God. We should not fear those who can only kill our bodies; rather, we should fear the One who "is able to destroy both soul and body in hell" (10:28). Jesus spoke those words to His devoted disciples, one more indication that the modern theory of "once saved, always saved" ought to be questioned.

Jesus had other warnings. If we deny Him before others, He will deny us before His Father (10:33), not exactly another promise of unconditional eternal security. Thus our persecutions serve as tests of our true devotion, and this is why so many true believers have refused to deny Christ in the face of death. If we love mother, father, son, or daughter more than Jesus, we are not worthy of Him (10:37). If we do not take up our cross—an obvious analogy for embracing the suffering that comes with following Christ—we are not worthy of Him (10:38). In light of such words we must ask: *Is modern Western Christianity Christianity at all?*

Day 11, Matthew 11

Even though he had witnessed the Holy Spirit descend upon Jesus at His baptism, John the Baptist—a prophet and the greatest man who ever lived according to Jesus (11:11)—had some doubts as he sat in a prison cell contemplating his possible execution. That makes me feel better, as I've had similar doubts about Jesus, particularly when I've begun to question why He allows His people to suffer. Notice, however, that Jesus didn't explain to John why He didn't deliver him from prison. Rather, He reminded John of His miraculous credentials (11:4-5). The reasons to believe in Jesus are substantially greater than the reasons not to believe. One might, for example, keep his eyes continually focused downward in order to deny that there is a sun, moon or stars, but such a person would only be fooling himself, as are all unbelievers. Thus all who make excuses for their unbelief are rightfully condemned along with those who rejected Christ in Chorazin, Bethsaida and Capernaum (11:20-24). It was not that they *could* not believe, but that they *would* not believe.

Jesus' words about violent men taking the kingdom of heaven by force must be metaphorical, as they make no sense taken literally. Similar words of Jesus recorded by Luke help our understanding: "The Law and the Prophets were proclaimed until John; since that time the gospel of the kingdom of God has been preached, and everyone is forcing his way into it. But it is easier for heaven and earth to pass away than for one stroke of a letter of the Law to fail" (Luke 16:16-17).

Up until the time of John the Baptist, all preaching (in the synagogues, for example) had been based on the Law and Prophets, of which the major theme was holiness. John preached the good news that the kingdom of heaven was at hand, but he found that too few paid attention to his call to repentance (Matt. 3:7-12). They only went through the motions, "forcing their way into the kingdom" as it were, which certainly implies the idea of an illegitimate entrance. Thus Jesus reminded everyone that nothing in the Law or Prophets had been superseded by John's wonderful announcement of the soon-coming kingdom. Holiness was still required. As we read in the Sermon on the Mount, Jesus declared that it is only those who do the will of God who will enter the kingdom of heaven (Matt. 7:21).

Similarly, many today suppose that they've gained their ticket to heaven because they've jumped on the born-again bandwagon, having prayed a quick prayer without ever truly repenting. In God's eyes these are violent people who attempt to force their way into heaven illegitimately. Those who have truly entered, however, have not come forcefully, but with humble repentance.

Jesus invites all who are weary from sin and heavy-laden with guilt to come to Him (11:28). But they must take His yoke—symbolic of submitting to His lordship—in order to receive "rest" for their souls. This underscores Jesus' consistent message of repentance and holiness, for there is no relationship with Him apart from them. When we do take His yoke upon ourselves, Jesus empowers us to live righteously so that His load is light. We can say with John, "His commandments are not burdensome" (1 John 5:3).

Do Jesus' words, "Nor does anyone know the Father, except the Son, and anyone to whom the Son wills to reveal Him" (11:27), prove the Calvinistic idea that God wills that only some be saved? In light of Jesus' *very next words* in which He invites *all* who are weary to come to Him (11:28), certainly not. God has not chosen *certain individuals* to be saved. Rather, He has chosen to save *certain kinds of individuals*, as made so clear by what we just read. God has willed to hide the saving truth from those who are "wise and intelligent," but to reveal it to "babes" (11:25). God resists the proud but gives grace to the humble (Jas. 4:6). Being proud or humble is the choice of every free moral agent. God has chosen to save all who will believe with a living faith—one that reveals itself through obedience.

Day 12, Matthew 12

Jesus did what the Pharisees would not, harvesting a little grain to eat on the Sabbath. He did not have a lower standard than them, but rather, a better understanding of what was actually His own law. I'm so glad for this story, because it reminds us that God has reasons for His commandments, and He is motivated by love. Religious people generally don't understand that, and thus they are susceptible to misinterpret what God requires, piling burdens on people that God never intended them to carry.

Matthew obviously highlighted this flaw of the Pharisees by stringing two stories together, as Jesus both worked and healed on the Sabbath while under their critical watch. They found fault with *God*, just as they did with so many others who transgressed their twisted versions of God's commandments, "condemning the innocent" to borrow Jesus' words (12:7). This they would not have done, according to Jesus, if they had just understood one verse from Hosea, "I desire compassion, and not sacrifice; and the knowledge of God more than burnt offerings" (Hos. 6:6). Like so many modern professing Christians, they were fixated on secondary things and ignoring what was really important, listed by Jesus as "compassion" and "the knowledge of God." I am reminded of God's words spoken through Jeremiah: "Your father...pled the cause of the afflicted and needy; then it was well. *Is not that what it means to know Me*?" (Jer. 22:15-16). Jesus' two Sabbath deeds met human needs—for food and health.

Be encouraged today if you need healing. We read in 12:15, "Many followed Him, and He healed them all." If you would have been there, you would have been healed. That can't be intelligently argued against. So why would Jesus have healed you then, but not now? Believe it!

Today we read one simple, short analogy from Jesus' lips—meant to help the Pharisees understand that He was casting out demons by a power greater than Satan's—that has spawned a modern practice that has no real scriptural basis. How frequently we hear of people "doing spiritual warfare" by "binding the strong man," a phrase which allegedly incapacitates evil spirits in the atmosphere. This is a practice that is never once mentioned or even remotely endorsed in the book of Acts or any of the epistles, yet it is promoted around the world today as an essential spiritual exercise. One wonders why some of Jesus' other analogies in Matthew 12 haven't become regular practices as well. Why don't we hear anyone saying, "I lift up those sheep from the pit on the Sabbath in Jesus' name!" or "I divide the city so it will not stand in Jesus' name!"? These declarations would make just as much sense (and do just as much good) as saying, "I bind the strong man over Cincinnati!"

What does it mean to blaspheme the Holy Spirit? Considering the context, it would seem logical to conclude that those who witness a miracle by the power of the Holy Spirit and call it Satan's work are guilty of this unforgivable sin. There is no grace available to those whose hearts have become that hard. Incidentally, the idea of an unforgivable sin exposes the fallacy of those who believe that eventually everyone, no matter how evil they might be, will be redeemed. This is known theologically as *universalism*.

What are we to expect when we stand before Jesus? Today's reading gives us some idea. Because our words reveal our character, we will give an account for every careless word we've spoken (12:36). This reminds us once more that, although we are saved through faith (Eph. 2:8), saving faith changes our behavior. More specifically, there is a marked difference between the speech of unbelievers and believers, so much so that one's speech can rightfully be the criteria whereby God judges us as being worthy of heaven or hell. That is a sobering truth, but it only underscores the fact that Jesus' true family are those who do the will of His heavenly Father (12:50). He couldn't have made it more clear.

Day 13, Matthew 13

How blessed we are to gain understanding of some of the "mysteries of the kingdom of heaven" (13:11) from Jesus' parables. Sadly, the mysteries He revealed remain mysteries to two kinds of people—those who do not believe in Him (13:11-15), and more tragically, those who profess to believe in Him but reject His simple teaching. Many of the latter are teachers and theologians.

For example, while Jesus clearly revealed in the parable of the sower and the soils that it is the condition of people's hearts that determines if they will be saved or not, some theologians would have us believe that God has sovereignly predetermined the salvation or damnation of every individual. While Jesus revealed in that same parable that it is possible to believe, experience new life, begin to grow, but ultimately disbelieve and die—represented by the plants that sprouted and died—some theologians want us to believe that salvation can never be forfeited once possessed. And while Jesus made it plain in that same parable that fruit always accompanies true faith, some claim that it is possible to believe in Jesus and yet be indistinguishable from those who don't believe in Jesus!

Those of us who actually believe what Jesus said in the parable of the sower and soils must guard our hearts when persecution and affliction arise, and from the "worry of the world and the deceitfulness of wealth" (13:22), knowing that those things can rob us of faith and fruitfulness and cause us to fall away. Regarding the "deceitfulness of wealth," Paul wrote to Timothy, "Some by longing for [money] have wandered away from the faith, and pierced themselves with many a pang" (1 Tim. 6:10).

The parable of the wheat and tares is another that has suffered its share of misinterpretation. I once heard a man teach that, just as wheat and tare plants are indistinguishable, so also believers and unbelievers are often indistinguishable, and we should leave judgment to God who will sort them out in the end. Notice, however, that as soon as the wheat bore grain, "the tares became evident also" (13:26). There was a marked difference between them--only the wheat produced fruit. For this reason, the apostle John wrote, "By this the children of God and the children of the devil are *obvious*: anyone who does not practice righteousness is not of God, nor the one who does not love his brother" (1 John 3:10; emphasis added).

The parables of the treasure in a field and the pearl of great price both teach us that true believers are willing to pay a high price to gain the kingdom of heaven, because they know it to be of immeasurable value. While others may scoff at us for our costly devotion—just as they would have scoffed at the man who sold everything to purchase an "overpriced field"—in the end they'll know we actually made the wise decision. We possess a wisdom and a treasure that is hidden from unbelievers.

When we interpret any of Jesus' parables, we need to keep in mind that they are metaphors, that is, comparisons of two things that are basically dissimilar but which share some similarities. If we try to attach spiritual significance to every detail of every parable, we're liable to error. For example, when reading the parable of the dragnet, it is safe to conclude that there is coming a separation of the righteous from the wicked, that the angels will be involved in that process, and that the wicked will be cast into hell. It would be wrong to conclude, however, that the final judgment will take place on a beach or that the righteous will be placed in containers just like fish! Don't search for secret spiritual truths in the insignificant details of Jesus' parables!

Finally, take note that the people represented by the fish in today's final parable were judged by their behavior. They were either righteous or wicked. Does this contradict salvation by faith? No, because true believers repent of their wickedness and live righteously.

Day 14, Matthew 14

Once again, evil had triumphed over good. Herodias, who had divorced Herod's brother to marry him, and her dazzling dancing daughter, succeeding in silencing John by having him beheaded. When John's friend, relative, and ministry associate, Jesus, learned of the tragic news, He "withdrew from there in a boat, to a lonely place by Himself" (14:13). If I'm reading that correctly, John's death affected Jesus emotionally, and He reacted emotionally, needing some time to Himself. I wonder if He wondered why His all-powerful Father hadn't prevented John's martyrdom. Why, once again, had the bad guys succeeded when they could have been stopped? Had John's life been preserved, would he not have been enabled to lead more people to repentance?

I think it is quite possible that Jesus, who obviously stripped Himself of omniscience when He took on human flesh, and who was tempted in every way as we have been tempted (Heb. 4:15), did not have the answers to those questions, just as we don't have the answers to so many similar questions. Perhaps He could only trust, just as we must do at times. One of the best pieces of advice I've ever heard is this: When you face something that you don't understand, fall back on what you do understand. Nothing can happen to us that changes the fact that Jesus died for us. Nothing can separate us from the love of God (Rom. 8:39).

Jesus' retreat on the water was apparently short-lived, as He found a "great multitude" who had traveled from surrounding cities waiting for Him at a desolate spot along the shore. He "felt compassion for them, and healed their sick" (14:14). If you had been sick and had been among that multitude, Jesus would have felt compassion for you and healed you. If He would have healed you 2,000 years ago, why would He not heal you now? Has His compassion or power waned? No! Have faith! (And look for the same lesson in 14:34-36.)

Speaking of having faith, Jesus expected it of His disciples, and today we read a classic faith story. Surely God the Father knew that a contrary wind would descend on the Sea of Galilee the evening that the disciples would try to row to the other side. But He didn't prevent their fateful trial. Troubles may come even when we are in the center of God's perfect will. They are opportunities to trust Him and persevere. AMEN

Jesus sent the twelve on their crossing before evening (14:22-23), and He came walking to them on the water during the "fourth watch of the night" (14:25), between 3 and 6 AM. He apparently left them in their predicament to row against the wind for quite a few hours. Finally He came to them, walking on the water, a very unusual sight indeed. WALKING ON WATER

I have never understood Peter's logic when he said, "Lord, if it is You, command me to come to You on the water" (14:28). A ghost could have commanded him to come just as easily as Jesus! Good thing it was Jesus, and Peter proceeded to walk on the water—until he looked around and doubted. Keep in mind that Jesus didn't say to Peter, "Walk part way and sink!" No, it was clearly Jesus' will for Peter to stay on top of the water. No one can debate that it wasn't Peter's doubts that were the reason for his sinking. I wonder how Jesus would have reacted had He heard Peter, back in the boat, say to the other disciples, "Obviously it was God's will that I only make it so far across the water."

This is a good lesson for us to learn. God's will does not always come to pass apart from our faith. We shouldn't blame Him for failures that are actually the result of our own doubts. So trust Him and keep on trusting Him. I'm so glad that even when we doubt, however, God's mercy is still there to rescue us, just as it was for Peter.

Day 15, Matthew 15

According to Jesus, honoring one's father and mother could involve providing for their needs in their old age. Keep in mind that, even today, most people around the world depend on their children to take care of them in their old age, as saving money for retirement is impossible in poor nations. It was in this context that the Pharisees taught that one was not obligated to take care of his parents if he had given his money to God. (We can't help but wonder if "giving to God" was the same as "giving to the Pharisees.") So they invalidated God's commandment for the sake of their tradition.

When leaders in the church today teach "as their doctrines the precepts of men" (15:9), it similarly reveals that their hearts are far away from God, as Jesus said (15:8). Love for God produces a love for His Word, and neither traditions, "new revelations," or pop psychology (which all enamor large segments of the modern church) have any attraction to the lover of God. They are, in fact, repulsive to him, because they are actually an assault on the One whom they love so much.

Modern Pharisees, just like their ancient counterparts, are often fixated on their petty practices while ignoring what is truly important, and they are quick to separate themselves from anyone who is not similarly obsessed. While multitudes are starving and millions wait to hear the gospel for the first time, you'll find them deriding those who don't subscribe to their peculiarities. We read today that in Jesus' time, the big concern of the Pharisees and scribes was that His disciples were defiling themselves by eating with unwashed hands, a rule not exactly found among the Ten Commandments!

The Syrophoenician woman who came to Jesus on behalf of her demon-possessed daughter was a descendant of the Canaanites, whom God had commanded the Israelites of Joshua's day to exterminate, and for justifiable reasons. They had a reputation for idolatry, child sacrifice, gross sexual perversion, and a hardness of heart that put them beyond redemption. With such a legacy, it is quite possible that the descendants of those who survived were not exactly paragons of virtue, and Jesus' treatment of the Syrophoenician woman seems to verify this. Many are troubled by His treatment of her, but don't forget that the New Testament declares that "the eyes of the Lord are upon the righteous, and His ears attend to their prayer, but the face of the Lord is against those who do evil" (1 Pet. 3:12). Jesus was God and played the part perfectly. He ignored the initial cries of the Syrophoencian, just as God ignores the prayers of unrepentant sinners.

What is missed by readers is how this desperate Syrophoenician woman was changed as she pursued her daughter's deliverance. When Jesus completely ignored her at first, even as she kept shouting at Him, what message did that send to her? When His disciples asked that she be sent away, He declared that He was only sent to the lost sheep of Israel, another commentary on her unworthy status. She then came to Him and bowed before Him. He told her in so many words that she was an undeserving dog! She didn't debate Him, but rather begged for crumbs, confessing Him as her master. Only then did Jesus grant her request and commend her for her great faith. She had been humbled and repented. (I've written more extensively on this story on the Internet at: www.heavensfamily.org/ss/e_teachings/2008/surprised-by-jesus.)

Let us learn a lesson from this story about Jesus. His Word tells us, "The Lord is far from the wicked, but He hears the prayer of the righteous" (Prov. 15:29). The apostle John similarly penned, "Whatever we ask we receive from Him, because we keep His commandments and do the things that are pleasing in His sight" (1 John 3:22; see also Prov. 28:9; Ps. 66:18). There is an undeniable relationship between holiness and answered prayer.

For the second time in Matthew's Gospel we read of Jesus feeding thousands of hungry people. Take note they were not just physically hungry, but also very spiritually hungry. God meets the needs of those who seek Him.

Day 16, Matthew 16

Jesus is not only the Messiah, Son of God, and Savior. He is also "Mr. Metaphor." It seems He hardly spoke a sentence that didn't include at least one figurative word, and when He did, even His closest disciples sometimes misunderstood Him. People have been misunderstanding Him for 2,000 years, and it is often due to the error of interpreting literally what was meant to be understood figuratively. Today we read of such an instance.

"Beware of the leaven of the Pharisees and Sadducees" (16:6). Only one word, *leaven*, was figurative, and the disciples should have realized that, as it would make little sense for Jesus to warn them about the Pharisees' yeast. They began discussing, however, that they had forgotten to take bread with them! Let us learn a lesson from their error. And let us also realize that we, too, need to beware of false teaching that seems insignificant and harmless at first, but then permeates everything it touches, just like leaven. *Every false doctrine that is poisoning the church around the world began as a single sermon.*

One such global false doctrine has been spawned by a wrong interpretation of Jesus' words to Peter in 16:18: "You are Peter, and upon this rock I will build My church; and the gates of Hades will not overpower it."

Peter, or literally *Petros* in Greek, means "stone." The word translated "rock" is *petra*, which means "large rock," or "bedrock." The rock of which Jesus spoke as being the future foundation of His church was not Peter, who, incidentally, Jesus was figuratively calling "Satan" just seconds later (16:23). Rather, the foundation rock of the church is God's revelation that Jesus is the Son of God, the revelation that Peter believed and confessed. Everything in true Christianity is built upon that. When a person believes that Jesus is the Son of God, he repents, is born again, and becomes a member of Jesus' church.

Jesus follows His rock metaphor with three more figurative expressions that, when interpreted literally, have resulted in some strange doctrines. The first of those three is Jesus' statement about the gates of Hades not overpowering His church. Within their context, they simply tell us that the church is comprised of people who have believed that Jesus is the Son of God, and when they do, they escape their destiny in Hades/hell. Jesus' words have nothing to do with the church "doing spiritual warfare" by "attacking the gates of the enemy" and so on.

Jesus next told Peter that He would give him "the keys of the kingdom of heaven," another obvious metaphorical expression. His words simply indicated that Peter would have the means (the "keys") for people to get into heaven. Surely this was fulfilled when Peter preached the gospel, effectively opening the way to heaven to believers and closing it to unbelievers. This interpretation is underscored by the fact that Jesus told Peter—in the third metaphorical expression—that whatever he would bind (also translated as "imprison") on earth would be bound in heaven, and whatever he loosed on earth would be loosed in heaven. That is, Peter's "keys to *heaven*" (the gospel) would work on the *earth*. Unfortunately, those "binding" and "loosing" words have not only been interpreted literally, but have been also imaginatively enhanced, so that we have folks verbally "binding" and "loosing" angels, demons, favor, circumstances, and thousands of other things, even though there isn't a shred of evidence from the New Testament that anyone in the early church practiced such things.

There are still more metaphors in today's reading, such as "take up your cross" (embrace inevitable suffering), "save your life by losing it for Jesus' sake" (gain salvation by exchanging your personal agenda for Jesus' agenda), and "gain the whole world and forfeit your soul" (pursue selfish gratification at the expense of salvation). These are followed, however, by a statement we should interpret literally: "For the Son of Man is going to come in the glory of His Father with His angels; and will then recompense every man according to his deeds" (16:27). Sobering words. We will reap as we have sown. Are you ready?

Day 17, Matthew 17

Jesus' promise in Matthew 16:28 that some of His disciples would not taste death until they saw "the Son of Man coming in His kingdom" was fulfilled just six days later when He was transfigured before Peter, James and John. They saw Him as we one day will—in His glorified state—His face shining like the sun. Those three disciples were also blessed to see Moses, who had died about 1,500 years earlier, and Elijah, who never died, but was raptured 900 years earlier. Both were alive and doing well, and according to Luke's Gospel, both were extremely interested in Jesus' "departure which He was about to accomplish in Jerusalem" (Luke 9:31).

In the second-to-last verse of the Old Testament, God promised: "I am going to send you Elijah the prophet before the coming of the great and terrible day of the Lord" (Mal. 4:5). For this reason, the scribes were anticipating the return of Elijah prior to the coming of the Messiah (17:10), which was one of their excuses for rejecting Jesus as Messiah. They missed it on two counts. First, Elijah had already come, according to Jesus, in the form of John the Baptist, and as a forerunner of Jesus. Second, the Messiah would be coming to earth more than once, and His first appearance would not be at "the great and terrible day of the Lord" (Mal. 4:5). Interestingly, Jesus revealed that Elijah would also return more than once, and thus we can anticipate his return before Jesus' second coming. I'm assuming that Elijah will not *personally* return, but that Elijah's ministry will be embodied in a representative like John the Baptist. Jesus said that Elijah would "restore all things" (17:11), which although vague, certainly sounds encouraging.

Jesus had already given the twelve apostles authority to cast out demons (Matt. 10:1). So why did they fail to deliver this one young boy whose father entreated them? Clearly, their unbelief was the reason (17:17, 19-20). Once again we see the vital importance of faith. If the disciples had exercised the necessary faith, the boy would have been delivered. But they didn't, so he was left in his demonized condition. I'm glad Jesus had faith! Whenever I read these kinds of stories it makes me wonder how many blessings we are living without because of our lack of faith. Help us, Lord!

We note that Jesus also mentioned that the particular kind of demon that oppressed the boy could only come out through prayer and fasting (17:21). A note in the margin of my Bible indicates that this verse is not found in many ancient manuscripts, which means that it's questionable whether Jesus actually said those words. Regardless, Jesus' statement about the necessity of prayer and fasting do not nullify what He said about the necessity of faith. If 17:21 contains authentic words of Jesus, then the reason for the apostle's failure was not *either* lack of faith *or* lack of prayer and fasting. Rather, it was both. Therefore, prayer and fasting must be tools for increasing faith, which should not surprise us. Naturally, those who spend extended time in prayer—to the point of skipping meals—are going to have greater faith than those who don't, just as those who spend extended time meditating in God's Word will have more faith in God than those who don't.

In any case, Jesus indicated that prayer and fasting was not necessary to be successful at casting out every kind of demon, but only for the particular kind that afflicted this boy. You don't need to fast to gain personal victory over Satan's attacks. But you absolutely *must* have faith to resist him (1 Pet. 5:8-9).

Think of the string of miracles needed for Peter to pay his and Jesus' temple tax! Someone had to lose a certain coin in the Sea of Galilee, a fish had to get that coin stuck in its mouth, and that same fish had to be caught by Peter at a certain location and time! God wants us to pay our taxes, and He'll help us do it!

Day 18, Matthew 18

Children are generally not proud, but humble. Because God promises to resist and humble the proud, and because He promises to exalt and give grace to the humble (Luke 18:14; 1 Pet. 5:5), children serve as excellent examples of the kind of people who are going to heaven—and who are considered great in God's eyes. There are no proud people on the way to heaven, because those who are truly saved have humbled themselves, acknowledged their sins, repented, and now live in submission to God, conscious of His grace.

Incidentally, it is from scriptures such as these that we derive the conviction that all children who die go to heaven. If children serve as God's example of heaven-bound people, then it stands to reason that all of them are heaven-bound. They must all eventually reach an age, however, when they too must "be converted and become like children" (18:3) if they are to enter heaven. Obviously that would be when they are no longer children, but adults, the time that theologians refer to as "the age of accountability."

According to Jesus, children can indeed believe in Him (18:6) and because God wants none of them to perish (18:14), anyone who causes a believing child to stumble, that is, to doubt or disbelieve in Him, faces dire consequences. Being tied to a millstone and tossed into the ocean is a precursor of what lies beyond death for such a person. Imagine quickly descending past the cold depth of 3,280 feet—where surface light no longer penetrates—and where the pressure of the water is 1,474 pounds per square inch. Not a pleasant experience.

True believers would never cause a believing child to stumble. But unbelievers and hypocrites are guilty of it all the time, as they set sinful examples before children and sow Satan's lies in little minds. How tragic it is when, through their words or deeds, parents cause their own children to stumble into sin. What an awesome responsibility it is to raise children whose "angels in heaven continually behold the face of God" (18:10).

Perhaps the first two steps of church discipline that Jesus outlined in 18:15-17 can be followed in modern institutional churches, but everyone knows that the final step—when the entire church gets involved—is impossible. Jesus envisioned churches like those we find in the book of Acts—small groups that regularly met in houses. Only in those small settings is the third step possible, where everyone knows and loves both the offender and the offended. Notice that Jesus' words about being in the midst of a gathering of just two or three persons (18:20) are found just three verses after His words about the church (18:17).

Some groups have certainly gone overboard attempting to follow Jesus' instructions to treat unrepentant members as "Gentiles and tax-gathers," forgetting that Jesus reached out to such folks with love and the gospel. Certainly those who shun members who refuse to submit to their man-made rules and traditions are greatly missing the mark, especially when their members continue to serve the Lord in other churches.

It is unlikely that Peter, after just hearing Jesus' instruction about confronting offending brothers and excommunicating those who don't repent, was wondering how many times he should forgive an *unrepentant* brother. Certainly mercy can be offered to anyone, but forgiveness can only be given to those who ask for it, because forgiveness is the erasing of a debt that results in restoration of the broken relationship. God offers mercy to all, but only forgives those who repent. He does not expect of us what He does not practice Himself.

In the parable of the unforgiving servant, notice that the first servant *asked* for forgiveness and received it. The second servant then *asked* the first servant for forgiveness and was refused. That angered his master and resulted in the reinstatement of the first servant's formerly-forgiven debt and consequent punishment. Jesus promised the same for those of us who refuse to forgive a brother in Christ. I wish I could write more about this, and I have on the Internet at: www.heavensfamily.org/ss/pdf/dmm/dmm_24.pdf. If you have questions, take a look!

Day 19, Matthew 19

In Jesus' time, many Pharisees believed that it was lawful for a man to divorce his wife for just about any reason, all based on a very liberal interpretation of what was meant by the word "indecency" found in Deuteronomy 24:1-4. Among other things, finding a woman who was more attractive than your own wife could make her "indecent," and so as you might imagine, sudden divorce followed by quick remarriage was commonplace. But that, of course, is really no different than adultery, as Jesus pointed out. What He said has no application, however, to a person who divorces prior to coming to Christ, and who remarries years later as a believer. Such a person is not "committing adultery" and is not "still married to their former spouse in God's eyes," in spite of what some would like us to believe.

Of course, God never intended for any marriage to end in divorce, thus He never intended that anyone would ever remarry. God hates divorce (see Mal 2:16). Divorce always involves sin. But God has not been surprised about any sins, including millions of divorces, and He made grace available under the Law of Moses as well as under the Law of Christ (see 1 Cor. 7:27-28) for those who divorce, just as He has made grace available for just about every other kind of sin. For example, under the Old Covenant, it was only unlawful for priests to marry divorced women. For all other men, marrying a divorced woman was lawful, an obvious concession of grace.

To ignore historical context, as well as everything else that God said in Scripture about divorce and remarriage, and to treat Matthew 19:3-9 as if it is all that God has said, results in a flawed understanding. This subject deserves more attention than I have space for in this daily devotional. I have, however, written much more extensively on the subject at www.heavensfamily.org/ss/dmm/dmm_13.

Jesus' encounter with the rich, young ruler certainly raises evangelical eyebrows, as it seems as if Jesus said that one must keep the commandments to enter heaven, and if one is rich, he must give liberally to the poor, ideas which are contrary to the false grace that is promoted by most evangelicals. Nevertheless, Jesus said what He said, and we simply need to face up to it. Many try to wiggle out of the obvious truth by telling us that Jesus only ever told one rich man to sell his possessions. The truth, however, is that Jesus told all His followers to sell their possessions and give to charity (see Luke 12:33). And what Jesus said in this particular passage has obvious application to all wealthy people, as He spoke twice of the challenges facing "a rich man," not "that rich man" (19:23-24).

The reason, of course, that it is difficult for rich people to enter heaven is because God requires that they love their neighbor as themselves, which requires that they share with the poor. They, however, like the rich man in this story, don't want to give up any of their possessions. They thus prove that they love money rather than God. And let us not fool ourselves that God only requires that we "relinquish our possessions in our hearts" but not in actuality, or that it is only our attitudes about our possessions that God is concerned about, and not our ownership of them. Actions reveal attitudes. Jesus plainly said, "Where your treasure is, there your heart will be also" (Luke 12:34). If all that God required was an alleged "relinquishment in our hearts" and not any actual relinquishment, it would not be difficult for any rich person to enter heaven. Rich people who truly want to please God will find that He helps them do what would be impossible for them to do otherwise (19:26).

I can't resist mentioning one thing more: Jesus' words about all things being possible with God—which are often quoted by unscrupulous "ministers" to encourage people to trust God for more wealth—were actually spoken to encourage wealthy people to trust God to help them unload their possessions!

Day 20, Matthew 20

At first, it might seem unfair that the laborers who worked twelve hours were paid the same as those who worked only one hour. But several important facts need to be considered. First, those who worked all day were paid a fair wage, and a wage they agreed on before they began. They weren't cheated and had no legitimate reason to gripe. Those who worked just one hour and received a full-day's wage, however, had good reason to rejoice.

Jesus wasn't teaching that the thief on the cross, who repented during the last hours of his wasted life, and the prophet Jeremiah, who faithfully served God under persecution for decades, will both receive the same reward in the end. Notice that the one-hour laborers only worked for the final hour of the day because no one hired them until then (20:7). They would have gladly worked a full day had they been given the chance. So we learn that God will reward us based upon how faithfully we take advantage of the opportunities He gives us. To whom much is given, much is required (Luke 12:48). Perhaps you have not been given the supernatural gifts that God gives to evangelists. Perhaps you don't have the opportunity to speak to stadiums full of people. Yet you can receive the same reward in the end as any evangelist if you will be faithful with the gifts and opportunities to serve that God gives to you. That is what Jesus is teaching in the parable of the laborers.

As Jesus ascended from Jericho towards Jerusalem, the apostles believed that He was about to establish His kingdom there (see Luke 19:11), even though He plainly told them that He would die there (20:17-19). He had very recently promised the twelve that, when He would sit on His "glorious throne," they would also "sit upon twelve thrones, judging the twelve tribes of Israel" (Matt. 19:28). They apparently assumed that their exaltation was just a matter of days or hours away, and the mother of James and John was not satisfied that her two boys would be seated on two random thrones among twelve. She wanted them to be second and third in command under Jesus, helping Him rule over all of Israel! Opportunity was knocking for the ambitious!

It is quite possible that James and John put their mother up to her request (see Mark 10:35), which certainly revealed their spiritual state at that point. I'm amazed that Jesus didn't explode with anger or weep with discouragement. Rather, He patiently taught the twelve about the upside-down order of His kingdom, where the great ones are not those who are served, but those who serve. Jesus certainly preached what He practiced, setting a perfect example by humbly dying for us, the ultimate act of service. The Servant-King never ceases to amaze and inspire us every day.

Pastors, be encouraged that even the Great Shepherd had to deal with strife in His little flock! After word leaked of James and John's request to be their bosses, the 10 resented them. I'm sure they were glad that Jesus dealt with the problem immediately, a great lesson for all leaders to learn. Don't avoid confrontation that is needful, as neglecting it only makes the inevitable worse.

Here's some encouragement for those who need healing: Jesus opened the eyes of two blind beggars because they would not be discouraged by those who told them to be quiet, and because He "was moved with compassion" (Matt. 19:34). Has Jesus' compassion waned since then? Certainly not. He cares about you! So just like those two beggars, don't let anyone discourage you either!

Day 21, Matthew 21

We're certainly not reading about American Jesus today. American Jesus is never angry. He's full of love and patience for everyone. Not true, however, of Bible Jesus. What Matthew recorded was actually Jesus' second cleansing of the Jerusalem temple, the first being three years earlier as recorded by John (see John 2:14-17). John describes a veritable stampede, with Jesus using a scourge of cords to zealously drive out people, doves, sheep and oxen, while pouring out coins and overturning tables. That is Bible Jesus.

Why, exactly, was Jesus so angry? It was not simply because there was buying and selling going on. God is not opposed to commerce, as long as it is fair and honest. Jesus was offended primarily because the temple was supposed to be a sacred sanctuary of prayer, not a market place. What the merchants and money changers were doing was dishonorable to God. It was sacrilegious. It also appears that the commerce being conducted was not honest in light of Jesus' statement about the robbers' den.

Bible Jesus also revealed Himself in today's reading as being divine. When the chief priests and scribes complained that He didn't restrain the praises of the children, He quoted from Psalm 8, where David wrote that God had prepared praise for *Himself* out of the mouths of infants and nursing babes. Jesus' reply can only be considered a claim to be equal with God. For such claims He was ultimately crucified (see John 5:18; 10:33; 19:7; Mark 14:61-64).

Notice that in both the parable of the two sons and the parable of the vine-growers there is a consistent theme: *God is looking for obedience.* He's not interested in insincere verbal professions of faith. He's interested in a faith that is lived out in action. He is expecting to receive fruit from His vineyard, and judgment will fall upon those who don't produce it. Tax collectors and prostitutes will be in heaven, according to Jesus, because they repented, producing fruit, while scribes and Pharisees, who all possessed "the assurance of salvation" but no fruit, would be denied entrance. This same idea may have also been the primary lesson behind Jesus' cursing of the fruitless fig tree that we also read today. Fruitlessness invites God's curse and destruction.

Of course, the incident of the withered fig tree carries a second lesson about faith in God. Some, however, have taken it to an extreme, teaching that our words have creative supernatural power, and that we can create good and bad circumstances in our lives by the words we speak. Notice, however, that it isn't words by themselves that contain power, but faith-filled words. You cannot kill a fig tree or move a mountain by your words unless you believe what you say will happen. *And the only way you could have faith for either is if God revealed it was His will for a certain fig tree to die or a certain mountain to move.* Otherwise, all you could do is hope that your words would come to pass.

If you don't believe me, try cursing one of your house plants and watch what happens. Once you do, you'll no longer be troubled by the "confession police" who lurk in church lobbies ready to pounce on you for your "negative confessions that are bringing curses on your life!" If you read the Psalms of David, you'll read many "negative confessions" that were simply factual statements describing His trials. He wasn't creating negative circumstances with his words. But notice that he always ended his complaints with a confession of faith in God!

So the application of what Jesus said works in prayer that is based on God's promises. When you have a promise, you can pray with faith, and speak faith-filled words that will bring the answer.

Finally, Bible Jesus also revealed Himself in our reading today as an unbreakable cornerstone—foolishly rejected by the builders—a huge stone that everyone should fear (21:42-44). If anyone tries to break it (falling upon it), he will be broken to pieces. And if this stone falls upon anyone, representing Jesus' judgment on those who reject Him, they will be scattered like dust. That's Bible Jesus.

Day 22, Matthew 22

If the parable of the wedding feast teaches us anything, it teaches us that it isn't God who determines who will be in heaven, but rather, it is people themselves. The king in the parable sincerely invited scores of people to his son's wedding feast, but they ignored his invitation. Only those who ultimately responded enjoyed the feast.

Amazingly, some who suppose that God predestines some to be saved (and thus predestines some to be damned) exploit Jesus' words found at the end of this parable to support their strange doctrines, completely ignoring their context. "Many are called, but few are chosen," they quip, "which means that many hear the call of the gospel, but only those who are predestined by God, the 'chosen,' are ultimately saved." Yet the parable that precedes those words completely contradicts such an interpretation.

Notice that the king calls those who have *already been invited* to the wedding feast, telling them the feast is ready. They were a limited group, and they ignored the call. So the king destroyed them in his wrath and then sent his slaves to invite those who had not been previously invited, the "evil and good" (22:10). This can only represent the Jew's general rejection of Christ, the Jewish holocaust of A.D. 70, and the salvation invitation being extended to all the Gentiles.

In the parable, the "chosen" are those who responded to the invitation. They are chosen because God, like the parable's king, chose to welcome those who responded—even Gentiles, a horrific idea among the Jews of Jesus' day who considered themselves to be solely "God's chosen." God's choices, like all choices, are conditional. He has chosen to save all who repent and believe in Jesus. If you do that, you are among the chosen.

Wealthy wedding hosts in Christ's day provided wedding garments for their guests, and so the man caught without a wedding garment had no excuse. He represents a person who attempts to enter God's kingdom without something the King sees as vital.

Perhaps the wedding clothes in the parable represent the same as the wedding clothes at the marriage feast of the Lamb spoken of in Revelation 19:7-9: "And it was given to [the bride] to clothe herself in fine linen, bright and clean; for the fine linen is the righteous acts of the saints." Only the holy will inherit heaven, because only they are the true believers.

Pity the modern Sadducees who, like their ancient counterparts, are consumed with proving their pet doctrines, and whose faulty logic is obvious to everyone but themselves. They make the error of exalting a few scriptures at the expense of many others, and come to incorrect conclusions. Notice that Jesus answered the Sadducees with a balancing scripture they could have read themselves (22:29-32). Similarly, He sent the Pharisees to Scripture to help them understand what they did not, that the Christ was not only the son of David, but God in the flesh (22:41-46). Scripture is where we need to abide as well. Sometimes when I have scrutinized modern "Christian" teaching or practice in light of the Bible, I've been accused of "putting God in a box." I take that as a compliment, since God has put Himself in a box—the Bible box!

The most important lesson today? The two greatest commandments are, "You shall love the Lord your God with all your heart, and with all your soul, and with all your mind," and, "You shall love your neighbor as yourself." Those two summarize the moral and ethical teaching of the entire Old Testament. We have no evidence that those two commandments have been removed from the #1 and #2 position. Interestingly, the second-greatest commandment is only mentioned once in the Old Testament, but seven times in the New Testament. These two commandments should be continually emphasized by those who are making disciples, and obeying them ought to be the consuming daily goal of every true follower of Christ. Let's guard ourselves from being sidetracked.

Day 23, Matthew 23

The scribes and Pharisees were Israel's spiritual leaders, having "seated themselves in the chair of Moses," a special seat in each synagogue from which the Old Testament scrolls were read. That is why Jesus told His audience to do all that the scribes and Pharisees told them to do. He was speaking only of those times when the scribes or Pharisees were publicly reading from the Law and Prophets.

It is good for all of us, but especially leaders, to examine ourselves in the light of Jesus' denunciation of the scribes and Pharisees. Are we like them in any way? If so, we need to repent, because Jesus thrice affirmed in this chapter that unrepentant scribes and Pharisees go to hell (23:13, 15, 33).

What were some of the characteristics of the scribes and Pharisees?

Foremost, they were motivated by a desire for the praise of people. So they made themselves appear very religious in public by broadening their phylacteries, small leather boxes containing scripture texts worn on the forehead and left arm. It would be akin to our carrying a big Bible to church just to make people think we are really studious in Scripture. The Pharisees also lengthened the tassels on their garments for the sake of appearance. God had commanded the people of Israel to make tassels on the corners of their garments as reminders of His commandments (see Num. 15:38-40). So the Pharisees sent a subtle message with their longer tassels: "I'm really serious about keeping God's commandments." The trouble was, they were only serious about appearing to be serious about keeping God's commandments.

The scribes and Pharisees also loved the public respect they received, and their common titles of *Teacher*, *Father*, and *Leader* were the proof. Jesus told His disciples not to call anyone but God their *Father*, and He also forbade the titles of *Teacher* or *Leader*. In that regard, many modern ministers follow the letter of the law, yet require those underneath them always to address them as *Pastor*, *Reverend*,

Doctor, *Bishop*, or even *Apostle*. How is that any different from what the Pharisees did? And those letters that you often see behind their names are just like tail feathers on a peacock. Get ready, title-loving ministers, to ultimately be humbled to the same degree that you've exalted yourself, because Jesus promised it. The highest title in God's kingdom is *servant*. There is no pyramid. We're all brothers.

I must mention that modern ministers who proclaim a false grace gospel "shut off the kingdom of heaven from men" just as did the scribes and Pharisees.

The Pharisees were lovers of money (see Luke 16:14), thus they used their "ministries" to gain all they could, to the point of praying long prayers for gullible widows in order to dislodge some coins from some widows' purses. Modern Pharisees teach their followers "prosperity principles" to the benefit of their *own* bank accounts.

The Pharisees were zealous missionaries because they wanted to be known as such. But their disciples became "twice the sons of hell" as they were.

The Pharisees were professional scripture-twisters, and they focused, for their own advantage, on what was of lesser importance in Scripture. Topics such as tithing (23:23), which resulted in more money in their pockets, were more frequently the focus of their sermons than were the "weightier provisions of the law" such as "justice and mercy and faithfulness." (When was the last time one of those was a sermon topic at your church?)

Bible Jesus is not afraid to denounce false spiritual leaders publicly, even calling them derogatory names, while American Jesus "walks in love," keeping quiet, not wanting to offend anyone.

Bible Jesus was not a Calvinist by the way, because He wanted to "gather Jerusalem's children together, the way a hen gathers her chicks under her wings" (23:37). But why didn't He? Was it because the Father had not predestined salvation for those chicks whom the Son wanted to gather (setting Jesus against His Father, incidentally)? No, it was because those chicks were "unwilling." Consequently, the wrath of Bible Jesus would fall upon Jerusalem some forty years later in the form of a Roman army.

Day 24, Matthew 24

Although the idea of Jesus returning to rapture God's children to heaven *prior* to worldwide tribulation is popular among many modern professing Christians, there isn't a hint of that in Jesus' Olivet Discourse, half of which we read today. Quite the opposite, in fact. Jesus foretold His disciples that they would be persecuted and hated "by all nations," and that many would be killed during a tribulation that would precede His return. When they witnessed the "abomination of desolation" spoken of by the prophet Daniel—when the antichrist enters into the Jerusalem temple (see 2 Thes. 2:3-4)—they should flee to uninhabited places, as that event would mark the beginning of the worst tribulation of human history.

Jesus spoke of these things so that His disciples would not be deceived but prepared during a time when false prophets and false messiahs will abound. Sadly, many modern professing Christians aren't the least bit prepared, convinced that they will be raptured in advance of the perilous times Jesus foretold. If, however, you had asked any of the disciples who were present during Jesus' Olivet Discourse if they had such a hope, how would they have responded?

Popular preachers also attempt to pin a pre-tribulational rapture on the apostle Paul. But he concurred 100% with Jesus:

> Now we request you, brethren, *with regard to the coming of our Lord Jesus Christ and our gathering together to Him*....Let no one in any way deceive you, for *it will not come unless the apostasy comes first, and the man of lawlessness is revealed*, the son of destruction, who opposes and exalts himself above every so-called god or object of worship, so that he takes his seat in the temple of God, displaying himself as being God (2 Thes. 1-4, emphasis added).

There is going to be a generation of Christians who will be alive when everything we read today occurs. You could be among them, so it is wise to be prepared. The antichrist will be extremely popular among the world's masses. He will perform signs and wonders (2 Thes. 2:9). Surely most true Christians will have him pegged long before he enters the Jerusalem temple and declares himself to be God, what will doubtlessly be broadcast worldwide. If you haven't already fled to the wilderness by then, don't wait another minute!

And as you hide in the wilderness, don't be deceived by radio reports that Christ has returned to a certain location. His return will be unmistakable, preceded by the sun and moon going dark and stars falling, culminating with His own lightning-like appearance in the sky, an event which will be witnessed worldwide. A great trumpet will sound, and then the saints alive on earth will be raptured (24:31), just as Paul also wrote (see 1 Thes. 4:16).

Although Jesus' disciples will not know the *day* or the *hour* (24:36), He wants them to know when "He is near, right at the door"(24:33), which is why He told them exactly what would precede His return. As He stated so clearly, He will not return until many fall away (24:10), what Paul referred to as "the apostasy;" nor will He return until the antichrist is revealed. This scuttles the modern myth that Jesus could come at any time.

Jesus clearly spoke of a post-tribulation rapture in today's reading, giving several examples of people being side-by-side when He returns, with one being taken and one being left behind (24:40-41). This also indicates that not every believer will be killed during the time of great tribulation.

One other modern theological myth is exposed by what we read today. Since Jesus warned His closest disciples (see Mark 13:3) of the danger of being deceived, falling away, and not being ready for His return, that is a clear indication that such a possibility existed. Jesus' disciples were certainly saved by this point in His ministry, but notice that He warned them that hell would be the fate of those who were not ready at His return. It was possible they could forfeit their salvation. Thus the doctrine of "once-saved-always-saved" is revealed for what it is, as a very false security, a man-made doctrine. People believe it only because they want to believe it.

Day 25, Matthew 25

The two parables found in the second half of Jesus' Olivet Discourse underscore the primary and repeated theme found in the first half. Obviously, Jesus wanted His disciples to be ready at His coming. If there were no possibility of them not being ready—if they were "unconditionally eternally secure" as so many today think they are—there would have been no reason to warn them of the consequences of being unready. The heightened deception during the final days warrants His almost redundant admonitions in this regard.

There are, actually, three parables contained in the Olivet Discourse that generally all emphasize the need to be prepared for what lies ahead. The first, that of the unfaithful servant, we read yesterday. Remember that the unfaithful slave, who believed that his master would not return for a long time, found himself unprepared, and he was cast into hell (24:51). That parable, like the other two, was not spoken to the unregenerate multitudes in order to motivate them to repent and be saved. Rather, it was directed to the already saved (see Mark 13:3) in order to motivate them to remain faithful.

The parable of the ten virgins teaches essentially the same truth. The five foolish virgins do not represent non-believers. Notice that they were waiting for the bridegroom, just like the other five. Initially, they were ready, but they became unready and were thus excluded from the wedding feast. More specifically, they were not prepared if the bridegroom, who clearly represents Christ, was delayed. Had he come earlier, they would have been ready.

How applicable this is to many modern professing Christians. They are not prepared to wait for Christ during tribulation and persecution, expecting to be raptured long before. I wonder how many will fall away during dire circumstances?

The parable of the talents is also a story about believers. Keep in mind once again that Jesus spoke this parable to Peter, Andrew, James and John. The slave who was given one talent was just as much a slave of the master as were the slaves who were given two and five talents. He was entrusted with something that belonged to his master, and he was required to give an account when his master returned, just like the others. Yet, because of his unfaithfulness, he was cast into hell. He was unprepared, having no return to show on his master's investment.

Again, how applicable this is to many modern professing Christians who have all been entrusted with time and treasure by God, but who give their time only for a weekly church service, and who only contribute their treasure to what benefits themselves. But you won't find giving towards church buildings and sanctuary carpeting in Jesus' list of sacrifices that separate the sheep from the goats. Rather, true sheep meet the pressing needs of the most disadvantaged among Jesus' family, providing food, water, clothing, shelter, comfort and compassion. Every good work Jesus mentioned requires time or money. Those who have not invested their time and treasure in such good works are goats, and they will be exposed as goats and cast into hell when Jesus returns. Thus Jesus' foretelling of the judgment of the sheep and the goats is His ultimate lesson, and a very specific lesson, on being ready for His return.

Finally, notice that the goats were quite surprised at their judgment. Their questioning Jesus implied that they would surely have come to His assistance had they seen Him suffering. But those who love Bible Jesus love His suffering brothers and sisters. American Jesus has no such expectations of His followers—who will certainly be among those future goats.

A final thought: In the parable of the talents, the master agreed with the one-talent slave that he was "a hard man, reaping where [he] did not sow and gathering where [he] scattered no seed" (25:24, 26), a tacit admission of being a bandit of sorts. Thus, as in most parables, here is a detail with no spiritual counterpart, as God does not expect a return where He does not invest. The parable of the talents makes that ever so clear.

Day 26, Matthew 26

According to Mark, the value of the perfume which that particular woman poured over Jesus' head was equivalent to about 300 days' wages for a common laborer (see Mark 14:3-4). To bring it into some perspective, imagine a perfume worth fourteen months of your labor, working five days a week for fifty weeks each year. It was "very costly" (26:7) indeed.

Had she poured her perfume upon anyone other than Jesus, the disciples would have had a valid complaint. But she realized, as they should have, that Jesus, being God, was of greater importance and value than all the people of the world combined. If Jesus wasn't God, His rebuke of His disciples and His praise for the woman would expose Him as being an egomaniac of the highest degree. God, however, can't be guilty of pride, as it is impossible for Him to think more highly of Himself than He should.

Jesus instituted the Lord's Supper during a Passover meal in a home, and it seems obvious that the Lord's Supper was eaten as part of a full meal in the homes of Christians in the early church (see 1 Cor. 11:20-34). The ritualistic snack consumed in most modern Protestant churches is a tradition inherited from Roman Catholicism. How wonderful it is, however, to practice the Lord's Supper as part of a meal with true brothers and sisters in Christ! That is true Communion!

At the close of a Jewish Passover meal, the head of the household would take a thin, unleavened loaf of bread and divide it among all at the table. After that, he drank from what was called "the cup of thanksgiving" and then passed it to all the guests. It was apparently that bread and cup which Jesus consecrated to be a continual memorial of His sacrificial death. He, the "Lamb of God," was about to fulfill what every other Passover lamb, for hundreds of years, had only symbolized.

There is no need to speculate about Judas' reason for betraying Jesus. He had no higher motive than the love of money (26:15). Amazingly, Judas had heard Jesus' warnings about the lure of wealth, but perhaps he was tired of a life of self-denial. Mammon, the god who competes for the hearts of people more than any other false god, enticed and deceived him. What a sobering warning to us of the powerful seduction of riches! Even one who literally lives with Jesus is not beyond its temptation.

When Jesus prayed that if it were possible, to let "this cup pass from Me," it reminds us of Jeremiah 25:15: "Take this cup of the wine of wrath from My hand." Jesus suffered more than the pain of crucifixion; He suffered God's wrath. On the cross, God treated Him as if He were the vilest of sinners, as He had taken upon Himself all the sins and guilt of the world. It's no wonder Jesus recoiled from the thought. But thankfully He also prayed: "Not as I will, but as Thou wilt." There was no other way to procure salvation for sinners. An innocent man had to die, and only Jesus was qualified. It was not the nails that held Him to the cross, but His great love.

Christ's confession before Caiaphas, "You will see the Son of Man sitting at the right hand of power, and coming on the clouds of heaven," was a quote from Daniel 7:13, recognized by all present as a messianic prophecy. Tragically, they found the Son of God guilty of blasphemy. It is painful to read how they abused Him then. Yet it is very possible that some of the very men who so cruelly beat Him and spat in His face eventually repented and were born again, as we read in Acts 6:7, "And the number of the disciples continued to increase greatly in Jerusalem, and a great many of the priests were becoming obedient to the faith." How great is God's mercy! And even the bruises Jesus received at their hands worked towards *our* redemption, as He was "bruised for our iniquities" (Isaiah 53:5). Amazing grace!

Day 27, Matthew 27

Although Judas was remorseful for betraying Jesus, he wasn't repentant. Had he repented, he would not have hung himself. Rather, he would have used the remainder of his life to bear fruit for the glory of God. Keep in mind that it really wasn't Judas alone who was responsible for Jesus' death; it was you and me also. Our sins killed Him. But unlike Judas, we repented and now live for God.

The chief priests and elders wouldn't place Judas' returned money in the Temple treasury because it was unlawful to accept donations that were gained by doing what they had just paid Judas to do! What hypocrisy! More amazingly, after they'd condemned an innocent man—God in the flesh—they wanted to do the right thing before God with the returned betrayal money! So they purchased a potter's field as a place to bury foreigners. In doing so, they unwittingly helped prove that Jesus was indeed the Messiah by fulfilling Jeremiah's prophecy that the 30 pieces of silver used to betray the Messiah would be used to purchase a potter's field!

Cowardly Pilate thought he could extricate himself from having to condemn Jesus by offering the Jews a choice of whom he would release—Jesus, or a known murderer and insurrectionist named Barabbas. Surely the people, when offered such a choice, would vote for the release of Jesus. To Pilate's horror, however, they shouted for Barabbas' release. I wonder how Barabbas felt as he walked free that day? What a picture of the purpose of Christ's coming in this one incident: Innocent Jesus was condemned, and because of it the guilty one was pardoned. *Barabbas represents you and me.*

According to John's Gospel, Pilate had Jesus whipped 39 times in hopes of saving Him from crucifixion. Surely after seeing him scourged the Jews would say He had suffered enough. A Roman scourging was sometimes enough to kill its victim, as sharp bone fragments were attached to the ends of the whip's lashes so that the scourging ripped the flesh from its victim. Even after seeing

Jesus' lacerated back, however, the mob still demanded his crucifixion.

Had Jesus accepted the wine mingled with gall offered to Him on Golgotha, it would have relieved the pain of the nails ripping through His flesh considerably. He was willing, however, to suffer to the full extent, and He didn't want His senses to be dulled as He endured God's wrath. Amazing love! And how little did His mockers, who shouted, "He saved others; He cannot save Himself" (27:42), realize the accuracy of their words. If Jesus was going to save others, He couldn't save Himself.

Matthew's targeted Jewish readership would have recognized five direct Old Testament references in today's reading, four from Psalm 22 and one from Psalm 69. It had been prophesied that Jesus would be offered wine mixed with gall, that lots would be cast for His clothing, and that He would be mocked by the spectators. Jesus Himself directed the onlookers to His prophetic connection to Psalm 22 when He quoted its first verse: "My God, My God, why hast Thou forsaken Me?"

Immediately after Jesus died, the curtain in the temple that separated the holy place from the holy of holies was ripped in half from top to bottom. The significance is obvious. Jesus paved the way for every person to have access to God. Incidentally, the tearing of the temple curtain also proves that Jesus did not continue suffering in hell after His death in order to pay for our redemption there (as some teach). Our sins were paid for in full on the cross. Jesus cried out with His final breath, "It is finished!" (John 19:30), a phrase that can also be translated, "It has been paid in full!" Paul wrote, "He has now reconciled you in His fleshly body through death" (Col. 1:22).

I'm glad the chief priests and Pharisees decided to make Jesus' grave as secure as possible, because that makes Jesus' resurrection even more believable. The resurrection of Jesus is a well-attested historical fact, and anyone who examines the evidence will have to conclude that Jesus is indeed alive.

Day 28, Matthew 28

I'm afraid this part of Jesus' story has become so familiar to us that it loses its impact when we read it. But try to imagine the surprise and joy of the women who visited His grave that Sunday morning. Imagine, for example, going to the gravesite of one of your departed loved ones and seeing that person sitting on his tombstone, alive and well! That would be a real shocker!

We have to appreciate the fact that Jesus first appeared to women rather than men after His resurrection. It is troubling to Christianity's "men-only club" that those women were commissioned by an angel to teach men something they didn't know. And to add insult to injury, Jesus Himself entrusted those women with instructions for some men to go to Galilee (28:7, 10)! Perhaps we should keep these incidents in mind when we come to the New Testament verses that are so often used to keep women "in their places" in the church!

The story that the Roman soldiers spread about Jesus resurrection would have raised more questions than it answered in the minds of thinking people. First, why were they sleeping when Roman law demanded the execution of soldiers caught sleeping while on guard duty? If they were sleeping when Jesus' body was stolen, why weren't they executed? How is it that they were not awakened when the disciples supposedly moved the heavy grave stone? If they were sleeping (eyes closed and unconscious), how did they know it was the disciples who stole Jesus' body?

Jesus declared that He had been given "all authority in heaven and on earth" (28:18). If Jesus has it all, that means the devil doesn't have any. This destroys the modern theory that Satan has the authority that God once gave to Adam, and because of that, God can't stop Satan from doing what he wants. Tragically, that nonsensical theory is a foundation within several streams of the modern church. And when the foundation is faulty, everything built upon it is unsound.

Note that very important word—*therefore*—found within the Great Commission. It tells us that what is about to be said is based on what was just said. It is because Jesus has all authority that He can *command* His disciples to *go* and *make disciples*, and it is because Jesus has all authority that every disciple should obey all of His commandments. Clearly, what Jesus wants is a people who obey Him. That should be our goal—to obey Him and to lead others into an obedient relationship with Him. The value of everything that is done under the banner of Christendom should be judged by this criterion.

That being so, we quickly see that the very gospel that is so often proclaimed falls short. If we only call people to "accept Jesus as Savior," if we tell them that salvation is by a grace that makes works of no effect, then we're not making disciples. Tragically, it is commonly believed within many evangelical circles that one can be a believer in Christ without being a disciple of Christ.

The truth is, however, that the call to salvation is a call to discipleship. If you study the book of Acts, it becomes clear that the word *disciple* does not describe a Christian who has a higher level of commitment than the ordinary Christian. No, the word *disciple* is synonymous with the word *Christian*. If you aren't a disciple, you aren't a Christian. If you aren't a disciple of Christ, you aren't truly born again.

Finally, notice that Jesus wants disciples to be made of all nations. The word translated *nations* is the Greek word *ethne*. From it we derive our modern word ethnic. *Ethne* does not refer to geopolitical nations, but rather to ethnic groups that are distinguished from each other by language, culture, geography and so on. It has been estimated that there are as many as 16,000 different *ethne* in the world today, of which at least 6,000 have no witnessing church within their culture to reach them. Making disciples within every ethnic group in the world is something in which we should all be involved.

Day 29, Acts 1

The book of Acts was authored by Luke, the physician, who accurately recorded the first 30 or so years of the early church's history, particularly highlighting the ministries of Peter and Paul. God's purpose for preserving the historical account of the early church is so that each generation of Christians will not deviate from the pattern revealed there. It is still God's intention that the same methods be followed to make disciples of all nations. As we read through this amazing book, I encourage you to compare your Christian experience with that of the first believers.

Foremost, the church of the book of Acts is one that took *orders* from the church's Head (1:2). I cringe when I hear preachers talk about what Jesus "is *asking* us to do." Perhaps American Jesus *asks* His followers to do some things, but Bible Jesus doesn't ask anyone to do anything. Bible Jesus *commands* people. He is Lord, and His true followers obey Him.

Second, the book of Acts shows us that the church of Jesus Christ is one that is focused on expanding God's kingdom around the world. Inward-focused social clubs that meet for an hour each week in a special building do not resemble the church Jesus started. The New Testament believers were intent on obeying the Lord and fulfilling His commission to make disciples of all nations. Any church that is not vitally involved in the Great Commission is falling short of God's will. The book of Acts is a missionary story.

Third, it is apparent that the early church was supernaturally empowered to fulfill the Great Commission. We read of miracles in almost every chapter. According to Acts 1:1, Luke's Gospel was a record of "all that Jesus *began* to do and teach." The book of Acts is simply the continuation of Jesus' supernatural ministry through the church, His body according to the New Testament epistles. Jesus lives in all of us who are born again, and we should be wholly dependent on Him to work through us to build His kingdom. Apart from Him we can do nothing (see John 15:5). We certainly have a whole lot of "nothing" happening in many modern churches. As two Christians from China said after a tour of American churches, "It is amazing how much they can do without the Holy Spirit!"

Jesus considered the help of the Holy Spirit to be so essential that He commanded His disciples not to leave Jerusalem until they were baptized in the Holy Spirit (1:4-5). Similarly, Jesus did not begin His ministry until He was baptized in the Holy Spirit (see Matt. 3:16). Certainly we also need to be "clothed with power from on high" (Luke 24:49). If we removed the miracles and their effects from the book of Acts, there would be no book of Acts.

What is "a Sabbath day's journey" (1:12)? It's about two-thirds of a mile, the maximum Jews were permitted to travel on the Sabbath according to their tradition.

Today is the only time in the New Testament that you'll read of anyone determining God's will by drawing lots. Although it may have worked for the apostles on that occasion (and who can say with certainty that it actually did?), I would not recommend trying to determine God's will in that manner or any similar manner. You might get fleeced when you "put out a fleece," a phrase that is often borrowed from the story of Gideon as he sought assurance about God's direction (see Judg. 6:36-40)!

God has not promised to guide us by fleeces or by drawing straws. Most mature Christians have discovered that God leads them by less spectacular means, what is often referred to as "the inward witness." It takes practice to discern that inward witness, and it is particularly difficult to discern when you are not wholly submitted to the Lord. How many of us have thought that God was leading us and later discovered that we were actually following our own desires? That is a common error that seems to be part of the universal learning process as we grow in Christ. When it happens, we should just admit it and keep trying!

Day 30, Acts 2

God baptized the disciples in the Holy Spirit to empower them to take the gospel to all the nations, or more specifically, to all peoples, tribes and tongues. As those 120 disciples spoke supernaturally in languages they had never learned, it was a sign to them of the purpose of their Spirit baptism. They knew they were speaking in languages of people somewhere in the world whom God wanted to reach. Those who speak in other tongues today must be careful not to place so much emphasis on the supernatural sign that they forget that the sign is designed to point them to a world dying without Christ.

Speaking in tongues has become, unfortunately, a divisive issue. Some believe that speaking in other tongues can be experienced by every believer. Others believe it is only for some. Still others believe it was only for the first-century Christians.

I happen to be in the first category, but I do not think that those who speak in other tongues are superior to those who do not speak in other tongues. In fact, I sometimes think the opposite! As Paul later wrote, "If I speak with the tongues of men and of angels, but do not have love, I have become a noisy gong or a clanging cymbal" (1 Cor. 13:1). Love is much more important than speaking in other tongues. It is, in fact, the first fruit of the Spirit (see Gal. 5:22).

Notice that at the outpouring of the Holy Spirit on the day of Pentecost, *all* the believers who were present spoke in other tongues. God did not differentiate between them. Notice also that Peter told the astonished observers, "Repent...and you will receive the gift of the Holy Spirit. For the promise [the promise he had just quoted—'I will pour forth of My Spirit on all mankind'] is for you and your children and for all who are far off, as many as the Lord our God will call to Himself" (2:38-39).

Peter believed that God wanted to pour His Spirit upon everyone who would repent. Did Peter believe that those in his audience, unlike the 120 in the upper room, would receive the Spirit without any supernatural evidence? No, he believed that the Spirit's outpouring would result in gifts of prophecy and visions and dreams (2:17-18). Certainly everyone's speaking in tongues fell under the category of prophecy, as each believer was heard "speaking of the mighty deeds of God" (2:11) in known languages. Peter believed Joel's prophecy was being fulfilled before them.

Some claim that God gave the disciples the ability to speak in foreign languages so they could preach the gospel to foreign people in their native tongues. They argue that the modern tongue-talkers do not proclaim the gospel to foreign people with their unintelligible languages. The fact is, however, that nothing is said anywhere in the book of Acts about speaking in tongues being used to proclaim the gospel. No one heard the gospel on the day of Pentecost until Peter started preaching.

Notice that during his Pentecost sermon Peter never asked anyone to "invite Jesus into his heart" or "accept Jesus as her personal Savior." His formula for receiving salvation was simple: repent and be baptized. There is no salvation without repentance. When you repent, you turn from your sin and start following Jesus, your new Lord. Your first act of faith is to be baptized in obedience to His command, as were the 3,000 new believers of which we read today (2:41).

One of the characteristics of the early Christians is that they "had all things in common," and were "selling their property and possessions and were sharing them with all, as anyone might have need" (2:44-45). This was nothing more than simple obedience to what Christ told all His followers to do (see Luke 12:33). It stands in stark contrast to what is being pandered today by prosperity preachers, who tell already-rich people to gather more, while the Lord Jesus told relatively poor people to liquidate what they already had accumulated. Someday we must all give an account.

Day 31, Acts 3

He asked for alms, but got legs! This healing of the crippled man at the Beautiful Gate didn't occur because of Peter's faith. That is, Peter didn't see the crippled man and say to himself, "I'm going to have faith for that man to be healed, and so I'll lift him up and tell him to walk!" If that had been the case, Peter would have healed many others besides this one man. Rather, the crippled man was healed because Peter was suddenly anointed by the Holy Spirit with a special gift of faith (3:16) and a gift of healing (see 1 Cor. 12:1-11). It takes more than ordinary faith to seize a crippled person by the arm, lift him up, and expect him to stand and walk. If you don't believe me, try it sometime and see what happens!

The miracle occurred not only for the crippled man's sake, but also for the benefit of everyone who would be attracted to hear Peter preach the gospel. Those who are called as apostles and evangelists today should expect that God will miraculously use them in order to attract listeners to hear the gospel. As a result of one miracle and one sermon, 5,000 men came to believe in Jesus, not counting the women and children (Acts 4:4). At this point in the church's history, the Jerusalem church had at least 8,120 members, and it was only a few days old. And it was all due to the demonstration of the Holy Spirit's power. As I've previously said, if we removed the miracles and their effects from the book of Acts, there would be no book of Acts. Oh how we need the Holy Spirit's power!

Peter's sermon is a good example of how the gospel should always be proclaimed. He spoke of his audience's guilt before God (3:13-15, 19, 26) and of God's wrath (3:23). He told them about Christ's crucifixion, sufferings and resurrection (3:15, 18, 26). Also notice that Peter invited no one to "accept Christ" or "invite Jesus into their hearts," but rather told his listeners to repent because God wanted them to turn from their "wicked ways" (3:19, 26). If they would, they would be blessed, according to Peter. The chief benefit of believing in Jesus was not gaining better self-esteem or more material possessions, but receiving forgiveness of sins (3:19). How the gospel has been altered today!

Peter concluded with a quotation from Genesis in which God told Abraham that in his seed all the families (tribes or culture groups) of the earth would be blessed. We know, of course, that the seed was Jesus (see Gal. 3:16). God desires to bless every tongue, tribe and people group in the world through His Son. In Revelation 5:9 we read of a future scene in heaven where the Lord will be worshipped with a new song: "Worthy art Thou...for Thou wast slain, and didst purchase for God with Thy blood men from every tribe and tongue and people and nation." Thus we see that God's plan from the time of Abraham was to purchase people from every people group on the earth, and according to Revelation 5:9, God's plan will succeed.

Some ethnologists estimate that, although there are about 200 nations in the world today, there are about 16,000 different culture groups. As of this writing (late 2008), there are at least 6,000 people groups who have no indigenous community of believing Christians with adequate numbers and resources to evangelize them, and those people groups make up 40% of the world's population. For example, there is not a single known Christian among the 55 million Yadava people in India. They are an unreached people group.

Imagine living in a place where most of the people have never heard anything about Jesus, where it is next to impossible to find a Bible, where no Christians live. Jesus wants us to make disciples of all the nations, or literally, among every people group in the world. The task is still before us! For more information about the world's unreached people groups, visit JoshuaProject.net.

Day 32, Acts 4

Jesus had foretold His disciples that they would be delivered up to the courts and synagogues. He also told them that they shouldn't concern themselves with planning a defense, because the Holy Spirit would give them words that none of their opponents could refute (Matt. 10:17-20). Today we read one fulfillment of Jesus' promise. Notice that just prior to Peter's defense before the Sanhedrin, he was "filled with the Holy Spirit" (4:8). His hearers marveled because an "uneducated and untrained" man spoke with such power and confidence. It was God speaking through Peter, and they didn't even realize it.

Even more amazing is the fact that every member of the Sanhedrin was convinced that a forty-year-old man who had been crippled since birth had been healed (4:16), and yet not one of them came to believe in Jesus as a result. Rather, they tried to silence the apostles. Their hearts were so hard.

Although they were released, Peter and John knew that greater persecution was looming. Trouble has a way of motivating us to pray, and so they went to their companions and had a prayer meeting.

Like so many good prayers, much of what they said served to encourage themselves. They started by reminding God that He had "made the heaven and the earth and sea" (4:24), something He probably hadn't forgotten! It reminded the disciples, however, that they were talking to the One who had unlimited power.

They also quoted to the Lord Psalm 2:1-2, a few more verses He probably hadn't forgotten. Yet those verses surely comforted them.

Then they recounted the persecution Jesus had suffered in Jerusalem, something else God had not forgotten! It reminded them that what they were facing was under God's control.

Finally, after reminding themselves of these things, they were able to make their requests confidently. They didn't ask God to stop the persecution, but that He would grant them opportunities to speak boldly (just as Peter had done before the Sanhedrin), and that He would continue to confirm their message with signs and wonders. (Notice, incidentally, that one person didn't lead them in prayer while the rest were quiet. They all prayed together at the same time.)

The Lord answered their prayers, as we read, "they were all filled with the Holy Spirit and began to speak the word of God with boldness" (4:31). From this we can learn two things. First, we can experience additional fillings of the Spirit, and second, the Holy Spirit can make us bold to speak God's Word. If you are timid about that, now you know what to pray!

For a second time in Acts we read about the disciples' sharing of material things. They did not practice communism, where there is no private ownership. Rather, we read, "they held everything they owned in common" (4:32). Everyone shared what *they* owned. And those who had much sacrificed to supply the essential needs of others, so there was not one needy person among them (4:34). This was nothing more than simple obedience to what Jesus told all His followers to do: "Sell your possessions and give to charity; make yourselves money belts which do not wear out, an unfailing treasure in heaven, where no thief comes near nor moth destroys" (Luke 12:33). Their love for one another identified them as being true disciples of Christ (John 13:35). Where are the disciples today?

Luke wrote that all who owned houses or lands were selling them in order to meet the needs of the poor among them (4:34). As we continue to read the book of Acts, it will become clear that the early Christians lived in houses, and so it seems that it was those who owned more than one house, or lands that they didn't need, who sold them to relieve the poor. If farmers sold all their land, they would soon need someone to feed them. If people sold their only home, they would have to move into someone else's home. Thus it is safe to conclude that all the early disciples did not sell their primary homes.

Day 33, Acts 5

We are told that the sudden deaths of Ananias and Sapphira brought fear upon the church and everyone else (5:11). Clearly, that was God's intention. There was such an obvious cause-and-effect relationship between Ananias' and Sapphira's hypocrisy and their demise that the divine message was unmistakable.

God's disapproval of sin isn't always so obvious because He generally chooses to be more merciful with people than He was with Ananias and Sapphira. Yet we are informed by Paul that, even within the church, divine discipline by means of death is not as rare as some might suppose (see 1 Cor. 11:27-32). However, as Paul also points out, discipline by death is often not sudden, but preceded by sickness, which serves as a merciful warning and provides opportunity for repentance and healing (see also Jas. 5:14-15). Serious sickness has a way of motivating us to examine ourselves, and so we should. (It is not our responsibility, however, to pass judgment on other Christians who are suffering sickness.) To enjoy God's fullest blessing in our lives, we must give Him our fullest devotion (see 1 Pet. 3:10-12).

The sin of Ananias and Sapphira was hypocrisy. They attempted to appear to be what they were not. They wanted everyone to believe that they were giving the full sale price of their land to benefit the poor. God, however, was not fooled. We should keep that in mind whenever we are tempted to appear to be what we are not. If Ananias and Sapphira had simply told the truth that they were giving only a portion of the proceeds, they would not have died. But they "lied to the Holy Spirit" (5:3).

Peter's knowledge of their hypocrisy was a manifestation of the gift of the "word of knowledge" (1 Cor. 12:1-11), a sudden revelation of a little bit of what God knows.

I'm going to have to say it again today: If we removed all the miracles and their effects from the book of Acts, there would be no book of Acts. In a single chapter we've read about Peter being given supernatural knowledge, hypocrites falling dead, signs and wonders taking place at the hands of the apostles, multitudes of people being healed, unclean spirits being cast out, and angels releasing apostles from prison. Lord, grant us more of you and less of us!

It is obvious that the revival in Jerusalem revolved around the healings that were taking place, particularly through Peter's ministry (5:12-16). Healing of the sick is part and parcel of the church of Jesus Christ. Where divine healing is emphasized, the church is growing. For example, when I was in Nepal last year, I heard from several reliable sources that the amazing growth of Christianity in that Hindu nation has been, in large part, due to believers healing the sick. It has become common belief among non-Christians in Nepal that, if you, or even one of your animals, is sick, the thing to do is call for a Christian to come and pray. God has honored His promise to those who have taken Him at His Word.

Peter's defense before the Sanhedrin was another Holy Spirit-inspired word. Notice how he, in just four sentences, once again mentioned the key elements of the gospel: Jesus' death on the cross, His resurrection, the need for repentance, and the primary benefit being the forgiveness of sins (5:30-32). Those elements should always be included in the gospel. Jesus commanded His disciples to preach "repentance for forgiveness of sins...in His name to all the nations" (Luke 24:47). If you haven't heard about repentance and forgiveness of sins, you haven't heard the gospel.

Grumps take note! After the apostles were flogged, it didn't dishearten them but rather caused them to rejoice! They were sincerely glad to be considered worthy to suffer for Jesus' cause. Counterfeit Christians can't understand that because their "relationship" with Jesus is one-sided. In their minds Jesus exists only to serve them. The truth is, Jesus has served us by dying for our sins, and those who believe in Him now live to serve Him!

Day 34, Acts 6

Not only did the early believers generously meet the material needs of the poor among them, but they also provided daily food for a good number of Jewish widows who were apparently not part of the church. In the early church, the poor were given greater priority than they seem to be in the modern church. Doubtless one of the reasons for this is that in developed nations, we don't regularly see undernourished widows begging in our streets. Our standard of living is so high that most widows are living well by the world's standards, and those who aren't have a host of social programs to assist them. But it was not that way in Jerusalem in A.D. 35. And it is not that way in much of the world today. For that reason, the ministry of *Heaven's Family* has a widows' fund that assists very poor Christian widows in developing nations. In my opinion, there should be thousands of such ministries in light of what Scripture teaches us. James wrote: "This is pure and undefiled religion in the sight of our God and Father, to visit orphans and widows in their distress" (Jas. 1:27). This is Christianity 101!

One problem always arises out of benevolence: More needy people start showing up for the handouts. Those who are overlooked start complaining, as if they have a right to free food. We see that phenomena in today's reading. Paul later addressed these kinds of problems in a few of his letters, telling the churches, "If anyone will not work, neither let him eat" (1 Thes. 3:10), and laying out detailed instructions regarding which widows should and should not be supported (see 1 Tim. 5:3-16).

There are always more opportunities to do good than any one of us have time for, and so we each should focus on those particular opportunities that, for us, have the most potential for fruitfulness. The apostles recognized that, although it was good to serve widows, it was not right to serve widows at the neglect of their higher calling of the ministry of the Word of God. By releasing what was a lesser opportunity for them, they opened a greater opportunity for some others, and the Kingdom advanced. Had the apostles not delegated their responsibility in order to focus on prayer and preaching, Luke may never have penned Acts 6:7: "And the word of God kept on spreading; and the number of the disciples continued to increase greatly in Jerusalem, and a great many of the priests were becoming obedient to the faith."

One of those men who was given a greater opportunity to serve Christ by being selected to oversee the widows' food distribution was named Stephen. It wasn't long, however, before he, too, had to walk away from serving tables, as God anointed him to be a powerful evangelist. Take note that Stephen was faithful to serve in whatever way he could, and God promoted him. That is just how God works. He tests us in small responsibilities to see if we can be trusted with larger responsibilities. When we are only willing to do "great things" for God that earn us money or make us famous, then we disqualify ourselves. We must be willing to serve God in any capacity, and for no reward. Only then are we qualified to do anything in His kingdom. God only promotes those whom He can trust. If we are unfaithful in small things, God knows He can't trust us with more.

Incidentally, those seven men who were selected to serve widows are often considered to be the church's first deacons, a word that in the original Greek simply means "servant," not "one who sits on a deacon board to run the church and make the pastor's life miserable!" (Couldn't resist!)

The signs and wonders performed by Stephen are today's mention of miracles in the book of Acts! Every chapter we've read so far has contained a record of the manifestation of God's supernatural power. We pray again today, *"Lord, less of us, and more of You!"*

Day 35, Acts 7

Why did Stephen make such a lengthy defense and recount so much of Israel's history? According to his accusers, he had been speaking against the Temple and the Law of Moses (Acts 6:13-14) and thus needed to prove he was not anti-temple or anti-Law. His long discourse revealed his great knowledge and respect for his Jewish heritage, Moses, and the Law.

But Stephen's defense was much more than a history lesson. It was a convicting sermon centered around two stories of God-sent men who were rejected by their own, namely Joseph and Moses. The lesson was obvious.

Stephen also recited a messianic prophecy that God gave through Moses, attempting to point the Sanhedrin to Jesus (7:37). And he challenged their religious traditions and unscriptural view of God and His Temple (7:48-50). In his closing statement, Stephen nailed them to the wall: "You men who are stiff-necked and uncircumcised in heart and ears are always resisting the Holy Spirit; you are doing just as your fathers did. Which one of the prophets did your fathers not persecute? And they killed those who had previously announced the coming of the Righteous One, whose betrayers and murderers you have now become" (7:51-53). No beating around the bush there!

Keep in mind that Stephen was anointed by the Holy Spirit as he made his defense (7:55). It was God speaking through him, and God wanted the Sanhedrin to be fully accountable for what they had done and for what they were about to do. When Stephen finished, they would be without any excuse. This was no blaspheming heretic they were about to stone; this was a devoted Jew who was very knowledgeable of Scripture and who had believed in the Messiah God had sent.

Stephen's Spirit-inspired speech also revealed insights into Old Testament stories that we would not have otherwise known. For example, we discovered that Moses knew forty years prior to the exodus that God had called him to deliver Israel, but he acted prematurely and in his own wisdom (7:25). God's work should be done God's way and in God's time. We need more than just God's calling. We need His plan.

We also learned that before Moses was forty years old he "was educated in all the learning of the Egyptians, and he was a man of power in words and deeds" (7:22). As an adopted son of Pharaoh's daughter, Moses would have enjoyed a high political position in Egypt. He could have looked forward to a future of wealth, power, and prestige. But he identified with God's chosen people who were suffering oppression and injustice. Moses stands as an example to us, as the author of Hebrews wrote:

> By faith Moses, when he had grown up, refused to be called the son of Pharaoh's daughter; choosing rather to endure ill-treatment with the people of God, than to enjoy the passing pleasures of sin; considering the reproach of Christ greater riches than the treasures of Egypt; for he was looking to the reward (Heb. 11:24-26).

Like Moses, Stephen also stands as a timeless example of a man who sought to please God rather than man. As he was being condemned by the men who would soon stone him, Jesus, whom Scripture tells us is seated at the right hand of God, stood to His feet, I suspect in admiration (7:56). Not only that, but Jesus opened Stephen's spiritual eyes to see Him standing. What a privilege, and what an honor!

With his final breath, Stephen prayed for his persecutors, "Lord, do not hold this sin against them!" (7:6). How that gracious prayer must have pierced the consciences of his murderers, testifying against them that they had just condemned another innocent man. Notice that, unlike Jesus' prayer for the Roman soldiers from the cross, Stephen apparently did not add the words, "for they do not know what they are doing" (Luke 23:24). The Sanhedrin knew exactly what they were doing, and for that reason, I have to doubt if God answered Stephen's prayer.

Day 36, Acts 8

Some suggest that God permitted the Jerusalem persecution so that the gospel might be spread outside of Jerusalem. Jesus did command His disciples to take the gospel to Jerusalem, Judea and Samaria and to the uttermost parts of the earth (Acts 1:8), and it was to Judea and Samaria that the Jerusalem believers were scattered (8:1). Wherever they went, they shared the gospel (8:4). How many saints have experienced God's redemptive purposes in what first appears to be their misfortune? I certainly have. When "all hell breaks loose," heaven has a plan.

Philip is the only person named in the New Testament as an evangelist. He was also a cross-cultural missionary, as he ministered to people of a different ethnicity. (Remember that Jews and Samaritans generally hated each other.)

Notice that Philip's ministry was anointed with gifts of healing and other miracles, as paralyzed and lame people were healed and the demonized were delivered. If Philip had not been so supernaturally equipped, his message may well have gone unheard, because Simon the magician had already captured the Samaritans' attention with his magic arts. Isn't it tragic that so much of the modern church is powerless, sometimes even denying God's supernatural power, while cults and false religions promote themselves by means of minor miracles of satanic origin? *Help us, Lord!*

We read today that the people of Samaria believed Philip's gospel and were being baptized, having "received the word of God" (8:12-14). They were thoroughly born again. Yet we also read that the Holy Spirit "had not yet fallen upon any" of those thoroughly born-again believers (8:16). The Holy Spirit was *inside* them through the new birth, but He had not yet come *upon* them. They still needed to be clothed with power, and that is precisely why Peter and John journeyed to Samaria—"that they might receive the Holy Spirit" (8:15). This is one more indication that there is a second experience with the Holy Spirit that is available to every believer.

These truths are so plain and simple that only theologians can deny them. Nothing is said in this passage that this incident was some kind of one time, special event orchestrated by God so that the Samaritan church would have a visible divine endorsement that would never be needed again. It was nothing more than what Scripture says it was: The Samaritans who believed in Jesus were born again but had not experienced the baptism in the Holy Spirit. So Peter and John traveled to Samaria to pray for them that they might receive the Spirit.

When Peter and John prayed for those new believers in Samaria, the Bible doesn't say that they spoke in tongues, yet we know something supernatural happened, because Simon saw something so spectacular that he tried to buy the ability to impart the Holy Spirit. He had already seen healings take place and demons being cast out (8:7), so whatever he witnessed must have been quite amazing. It seems safe to assume that they were speaking in tongues, just as Peter and John did along with 118 others on the day of Pentecost.

The story of the Ethiopian eunuch teaches us that God knows how receptive every person is, and that He will lead us to spiritually hungry people. This eunuch was ripe for salvation, reading from the most messianic chapter of the entire Old Testament, wondering what it meant! An evangelist's dream come true! We should ask God to guide us to receptive people.

Immediately after the eunuch made his confession of faith in Jesus, Philip baptized him in water. This was the first indication that the eunuch truly believed in Jesus. People who say they believe in Jesus but who are unwilling to obey His simple command to be baptized are fooling themselves.

Finally, notice that there was no way for Philip to "follow up" on his new convert, because he was immediately and supernaturally transported to another location. The modern urgent necessity of following up on new "converts" is an indictment against the impotence of the modern gospel. True disciples will abide in Christ's word, just as He said (see John 8:31). They won't need to be coerced to act like believers.

Day 37, Acts 9

It is no wonder why Paul described himself as the world's foremost sinner in 1 Timothy. He held the coats of those who stoned Stephen, being in "hearty agreement with putting him to death" (Acts 8:1). Soon after, he "began ravaging the church, entering house after house; and dragging off men and women, he would put them in prison" (Acts 8:3). Paul later wrote that he had previously "persecuted the church of God beyond measure, and tried to destroy it" (Gal. 1:13), and described himself as being a "blasphemer and a persecutor and a violent aggressor" (1 Tim. 1:13). During his testimony to King Agrippa he admitted: "I thought to myself that I had to do many things hostile to the name of Jesus of Nazareth....not only did I lock up many of the saints in prisons...but also when they were being put to death I cast my vote against them. And as I punished them often in all the synagogues, I tried to force them to blaspheme; and being furiously enraged at them, I kept pursuing them even to foreign cities" (Acts 26:9-11).

Yet God forgave him! Paul wrote in 1 Timothy 1:15-16: "It is a trustworthy statement, deserving full acceptance, that Christ Jesus came into the world to save sinners, among whom I am foremost of all. And yet for this reason I found mercy, in order that in me as the foremost, Jesus Christ might demonstrate His perfect patience, as an example for those who would believe in Him for eternal life." This should give hope to the world's second-greatest sinner (that would be me), and everyone down the line! Amazing grace!

Jesus said, "Saul, Saul, why are you persecuting Me?" (9:4). When someone persecutes the church, he persecutes Jesus, which is His body. Likewise, how you and I treat Christ's followers is how we treat Jesus. When we provide food, drink, clothing, shelter and comfort for "the least of these" among Christ's body, we're doing those things for Him, proving our love. When we ignore "the least of these," we're ignoring Jesus, and prove that we don't believe in Him. This is what He taught (see Matt. 25:31-46).

Surely Saul/Paul was born again on the road to Damascus. When he heard the Lord's voice, he said to Jesus, "Who art Thou, Lord?" (9:5). He was calling Jesus Lord before he even knew to whom he was speaking. (Wouldn't you have done the same?) He subsequently obeyed Jesus' instructions. And notice that Ananias, when he first met Saul, called him "brother Saul" (9:17). Yet Ananias told "brother Saul" that he had come so he would regain his sight and be filled with the Holy Spirit. Saul was born again, but had not been filled with the Holy Spirit. This is so obvious that only theologians will debate it.

The Bible doesn't record Paul's actual experience of receiving the Holy Spirit, but we know that sooner or later he spoke in other tongues, because he said so in his letter to the Corinthians (1 Cor. 14:18). We're seeing a pattern develop here.

Peter was involved in the beginnings of at least two major revivals, one in Lydda/Sharon and the other in Joppa. Both were precipitated by miracles.

Notice the differing receptivity between the people of Lydda/Sharon and the people of Joppa. As a result of the miracle of Aeneas' healing, "*all* who lived at Lydda and Sharon...turned to the Lord" (9:35). In Joppa, as a result of Tabitha's being raised from the dead, "*many* believed in the Lord" (9:42). These cities were near one another, yet the people in Lydda/Sharon were more receptive to God than the people of Joppa. This phenomena can be observed all over the world. Receptivity varies from nation to nation, state to state, city to city, and neighborhood to neighborhood. Receptivity also changes over time. There haven't been any revivals in Joppa lately.

God knows who is receptive and who is not, as He is constantly trying to reach every person through His creation and through their consciences. He will direct us to receptive people wherever they are, whether there be a receptive multitude or single individual. Let's stay in tune with the Spirit!

Acts 1:1 — 11:18

Day 38, Acts 10

Today's reading illustrates God's favor upon sincere seekers. He goes to great lengths to make sure they hear about Jesus. He still does today.

Cornelius, a Roman army commander in charge of 100 men, was stationed in Caesarea, a strategic Roman port on the Mediterranean Sea. His sincere faith was manifested by his "fear of God," his continual prayers, as well as his gifts to the poor, and none of these went unnoticed before the Lord. Cornelius and his household were chosen by God to be the first Gentiles in the body of Jesus Christ.

There was, however, an obstacle. The early church consisted entirely of Jews who did not mix with Gentiles, considering them unclean. Associating with Gentiles was unlawful (not according to God's Law, but according to their man-made traditions). Remember that Jesus had already commanded His disciples to make disciples of all the nations, or as the Greek says, all ethnic groups (Matt. 28:19). Jesus also told them that they would be His witnesses in Judea, Samaria, and the remotest parts of the earth (Acts. 1:8). But His message hadn't penetrated their minds very deeply! So God had to take drastic action to help the church overcome its prejudice carried over from Judaism.

Peter didn't immediately understand his God-given vision, but within time it became clear to him. Repentant Gentiles, just like repentant Jews, could be forgiven and cleansed by God and included in the church.

But here is a question I can't help but ask: If Cornelius had died before Peter's visit, would he have spent eternity in hell? It is hard for me to accept the idea that God would send a sincere, God-fearing, continually-praying, alms-giving Gentile to hell just because he had not believed a gospel that he had never heard, a gospel that had he heard, he would have immediately believed (as proven by the record)! Salvation has always been offered to anyone who would believe (see Romans 4:1-3), and this was true before, during, and after the old covenant. Cornelius was certainly a believer in the God of Israel before Peter ever arrived, and he was living out his faith.

All of this is to say that Cornelius and his believing household were not "saved" that day in the sense that they escaped a sentence of hell. That happened when they originally believed in God and repented. Cornelius and his household were saved that day in the sense that they came to believe in Jesus (whose life and ministry they already knew something about; see 10:37-38), were then born of the Spirit, incorporated into the body of Christ, and also baptized in the Holy Spirit.

Today's "gospel" often shares little resemblance with the one Peter preached. Note that Peter declared that Jesus is Lord of all and not just a Savior (10:36). Jesus had died on a cross and was resurrected on the third day (10:39-41). God had appointed Him as "Judge of the living and the dead," and He had ordered His disciples to solemnly testify of that fact (10:42). The prophets had foretold of Jesus (10:43) and God will welcome every person "who fears Him and does what is right" (10:35), which is another way of saying that repentance is required for salvation. The primary benefit for those who believe is "the forgiveness of sins" (10:43), which obviously implies the truths of humanity's guilt and God's wrath. Give me that old time religion!

It goes without saying that Cornelius and those gathered believed everything Peter told them. They didn't need to pray a "sinner's prayer." The Lord immediately confirmed that they were full-fledged members of His family by pouring out His Spirit on them just as He had done on the day of Pentecost on 120 Jews. It was so convincing that Peter ordered them to be baptized in water.

How did Peter and the others know those gathered had received the Holy Spirit? They heard them speaking in other tongues (10:45-46). So we see a continuation of the pattern we have been observing in Acts. Speaking in other tongues is a biblical evidence for baptism in the Holy Spirit.

Day 39, Acts 11:1-18

Our reading today ends happily, but how sad is the beginning! Rather than rejoicing that the Gentiles had "received the word of God" (11:1), "those who were circumcised" in Jerusalem (which would have consisted of all the church's leadership) were upset at Peter for eating with Gentiles! Even more tragic is the fact that eating with Gentiles was not forbidden by the Law of Moses, but only by the tradition of the Jewish elders. This would not be the last time in church history when the love of tradition (or pet doctrines) would supersede love for people. May the Lord help us to be innocent of such pharisaism.

Peter corrected those who took issue with him very gently, and naturally so, knowing that he would have agreed with the nature of their complaint prior to his recent experiences in Joppa and Caesarea. What had happened, however, had clearly been the work of God. Thankfully, the Jerusalem elders had the humility to admit their misunderstanding, resulting in a landmark moment in church history: Gentiles could become God's children, heirs of eternal life, through Jesus! Still to come, however, was a related controversy concerning Gentile believers' obligation to keep the Law of Moses.

When Peter recounted his story before the Jerusalem council, he reported something that we did not read in the original story recorded in Acts 10, namely that the angel who appeared to Cornelius had said to him, "Send to Joppa and have Simon, who is also called Peter, brought here; and he will speak words to you by which you will be saved, you and all your household" (11:13-14). As I wrote yesterday, it is difficult for me to accept the idea that Cornelius needed to be saved from a sentence of hell, otherwise we would have to conclude that God might send a sincere, God-fearing, continually-praying, alms-giving, believing Gentile to hell just because he had not believed a gospel that he had never heard, a gospel that had he heard it, he would have immediately believed. So I still must maintain that when Peter visited Cornelius and his household, they became saved in the sense that they were then born of the Spirit and incorporated into the body of Christ, having become spiritual children of God.

In the end, the Jerusalem elders concluded that "God [had] granted to the Gentiles also the repentance that leads to life." Does this statement prove, as some claim, that God sovereignly grants the ability to repent to certain individuals whom He has predestined for salvation and that God does not sovereignly grant the ability to repent to those whom He has not predestined for salvation? It is tragic that such a question even needs to be asked. The conclusion of the Jerusalem elders was not, "God has granted to a limited number of pre-selected Gentiles the ability to repent" but, "God has granted to *the Gentiles also* the repentance that leads to life." That is, God has granted to *all* the Gentiles, just as He has granted to *all* the Jews, the opportunity to repent and gain eternal life. And of course, God does more than simply grant an opportunity to the human race to repent. He actively works to influence them to repent through creation, conscience and the proclamation of the gospel. No one can (or would) come to Jesus unless the Father draws them (John 6:44).

ced and lowest paying jobs available. So James' readers were generally poor.

Day 40, James 1

We break from our journey through the book of Acts knowing that James authored his only epistle sometime shortly after the Jerusalem believers were scattered following Stephen's martyrdom (see Acts 11:19). The church was about ten years old when James wrote to encourage and admonish the Christian diaspora, the "twelve tribes who are dispersed abroad" (1:1), mostly Jewish believers. James wrote to a suffering and questioning church.

It is interesting to think that until this point in church history, there was no reading of any New Testament scripture at any gathering of Christians. There were no sermons in which the apostle Paul was quoted. It is very likely that none of the four Gospels had been penned either. The early Christians had only the Old Testament revelation and the oral teachings of Jesus passed down via the apostles. As we read James' letter, we'll see that it draws heavily from the Old Testament and Jesus' Sermon on the Mount.

In American sermons, James' "various trials" (1:2) are often described as those days when the washing machine breaks down, the dog gets sick, and it rains at the golf course. But those little inconveniences suffered by the world's wealthy are not what James had in mind. Having been forced to leave behind their homes and livelihoods, the scattered believers of James' time were experiencing a genuine "testing of their faith" *in Jesus*. Their "various trials," however, were not something outside of God's control or plan. Thus there was reason to rejoice. Their perseverance validated the sincerity of their faith in Christ, which insured an eventual "crown of life" (1:22)—perhaps not a literal crown, but an expression signifying the glorious time when eternal life will be realized.

We should also "count it all joy" when we suffer persecution for our faith in Jesus! Then our faith is being proved genuine. That means eternal life awaits us!

The scattered Jerusalem believers also naturally experienced financial hardship as a result of being driven far from their homes. If any employment was available, it would have been the least desirable, such as labor in the fields of wealthy landowners. The scattered believers would have been tempted to be envious of those who had much more, and they would have been tempted to abandon their faith in Christ in order to return to their former prosperity. James admonishes them in this regard. The current inequity would one day be reversed, and so the humble brother "should glory in his high position" while the rich man should "glory in his humiliation" (1:9-10). James will return to this theme in tomorrow's reading.

James also reminds the scattered and suffering flock that, although God may certainly be testing them in the midst of their trials, He is not tempting them. God entices no one to do evil. It is interesting that James doesn't mention the devil, but blames temptation on the individual who allows himself to be "carried away and enticed by his *own desires*" (unfortunately translated "lust" in 1:14 and 15). Yielding to temptation results in sin, which James said results in *death* (1:15). Don't forget the historical context of James' words. He was talking about the temptation to abandon one's faith in Jesus and return to one's formerly non-persecuted life. This is a warning against apostasy that James will later repeat (see 5:19-20) and one of numerous biblical proofs that salvation can be forfeited through unbelief.

What is the most important thing? Obedience to God's commandments, or being "doers of the word" (1:22). Those who think themselves virtuous because they simply hear or know God's Word are deluded, which describes not a few pew-warming Christians. James will later elaborate more fully on the folly of faith that is void of works. Today, however, he focuses on works that demonstrate one's obedience to "the law of liberty," which tomorrow's reading will reveal is the commandment to love our neighbors as ourselves. Works of love validate one's faith. Paul would later write of "faith working through love" (Gal. 5:6). James specifically cites caring for distressed widows and orphans as what characterizes "pure and undefiled religion" (1:27). So glad *Heaven's Family* does those things!

Day 41, James 2

Faith in Jesus is incompatible with partiality, because God is impartial. He certainly doesn't show partiality to the rich—something that is often done in human societies—and unfortunately by some in the early church as well. Keep in mind that the believers to whom James wrote had been driven from Jerusalem, and thus were financially disadvantaged refugees. If a rich man visited one of their gatherings, they would be tempted to favor him over a poor person, hoping to gain some benefit, and revealing "evil motives" (2:4). There should be, however, no distinctions made. The poor should be treated with the same consideration as the wealthy, following Jesus' example, who died for all. Moreover, as James points out, generally speaking, it is usually the rich who oppress people and blaspheme Christ's name. Why should such people be shown favor over the poor, whom God has chosen "to be rich in faith and heirs of the kingdom" (2:5), by Christ's people?

Two other items are worth noting in this first passage. First, to be classed among the rich, one only needed to have a set of fine clothing and a gold ring. One was classed among the poor if he had one set of dirty clothing. It is likely most everyone reading these words is in the rich category.

Second, the early church had no church buildings or meeting halls. For the most part, they gathered in homes. Note that the poor man was told by the host, "Sit down by my footstool" (2:3).

James was certainly not shy about quoting old covenant commandments—namely two of the Ten Commandments and one that Jesus said was the second greatest commandment—quoting them as if they were binding upon new covenant believers. James clearly believed that Jesus "did not come to abolish, but to fulfill" the Law and the Prophets, just as He had declared in His Sermon on the Mount (Matt. 5:17). Notice that James refers to the commandment to love your neighbor as yourself as the "royal law" and the "law of liberty," saying that the believer who fulfills it is "doing well" (2:8). According to James, we should live as people who will be judged by that law, a law that, incidentally, is mentioned once in the Old Testament and quoted seven times in the New Testament. With such endorsements, I wonder why it is not more often mentioned in Christian circles?

According to James, keeping that royal law involves showing mercy (2:12-13). If we fail to show mercy, we will receive no mercy at our judgment (2:13). This, again, is just what Jesus taught in His Sermon on the Mount: "Blessed are the merciful, for they shall receive mercy" (Matt. 5:7). Jesus also said that we will not be forgiven unless we forgive others (Matt. 6:14-15).

James has more to say about the poor beyond being impartial on their behalf. It is interesting that in his example of useless faith, he cites the person who does nothing to help a brother or sister who is without clothing or in need of daily food (2:14-17). This is certainly reminiscent of what Jesus taught about the future judgment of the sheep and goats (Matt. 25:31-46). James is quite dogmatic about it. Faith without works is dead, useless, and cannot save. Faith is always accompanied by works, as proven even by demons, who, believing in God, shudder.

It is amazing that a mantra of evangelical Christianity is, "We are justified by faith alone," when the only place in the entire Bible where the words *faith* and *alone* are found in the same verse is James 2:24: "You see that a man is justified by works and not by faith alone." Perhaps the mantra should be changed? Better to say, "We are justified by a living faith that works."

In regard to faith, works, and salvation, we are *not* saved by faith alone, because genuine faith is *never* alone, that is, void of works. If you have faith, you also have works. If you don't have works, you have no faith. Many pew-warmers are so inebriated with a false understanding of faith that their "assurance of salvation" is really just a "deception of salvation."

Day 42, James 3

As I read through James, I like to remind myself that it was the complete New Testament at the time it was written. There were no other New Testament books or letters then, so what we are reading was the spiritual diet of the early church when it was *at least* already 10 years old. Clearly, foremost in James' mind was the necessity of holiness, and in today's reading he elaborates on a subject introduced in chapter 1, where he wrote, "If anyone thinks himself to be religious, and yet does not bridle his tongue but deceives his own heart, this man's religion is worthless" (James 1:26). This theme resurfaces often in James' letter.

Note that, according to James, Christians possess tongues that need to be restrained. That means we will be tempted to say things that we shouldn't. That is normal.

Second, if we don't restrain ourselves from saying what we should not say, it is evidence that our faith is bogus. True believers restrain themselves from wrong speaking.

This is not say, however, that true Christians never speak wrongly. No, we who bless God sometimes curse men who are made in God's image (3:9). James writes that if we don't stumble in what we speak, we are perfect, and that "we all stumble in many ways" (3:2). That makes me feel better! Keep in mind that "stumbling" is a non-intentional thing. When one stumbles, it is not something that was premeditated or planned.

I love James' vivid analogies. The tongue is like a wild animal that is seemingly impossible to tame. It is like a small fire that sets a forest in flames. As I look back at my life, my tongue was the source of every regrettable conflict. How I wish I had just kept my mouth shut! James also compares the tongue to a rudder, comparatively small to the ship, but able to set its course. So our tongue has set the course of our lives, an amazing claim for such a small part of our bodies! Our tongue is setting the *future* course of our lives. This is not because our words "activate spiritual laws" or "have creative power," as some teach. It is because the course of our lives is determined by our relationships with others, and our relationships are by and large determined by what we say.

For all these reasons, James admonishes us earlier in his letter to be "slow to speak" (1:19). Great advice! Two verses in the book of Proverbs come to mind:

> The heart of the righteous ponders how to answer, but the mouth of the wicked pours out evil things (Prov. 15:28).

> When there are many words, transgression is unavoidable, but he who restrains his lips is wise (Prov. 10:19).

Jesus taught that "the tree is known by its fruit" and "the mouth speaks out of that which fills the heart" (Matt. 12:33). Hearts full of evil can't speak good words. Thus the first key to taming the tongue is purifying the heart. It is quite obvious from reading James' entire letter that there were false believers in the early church—those whose "faith" had no works—whom he was trying to rescue from their self-deception. They were those who were following a wisdom that was "earthly, natural, [and] demonic," and who had "bitter jealousy and selfish ambition in [their] hearts," the fruit of which was "disorder and every evil thing" (3:13-14). James was not describing true believers!

In contrast, those who are following God's wisdom demonstrate "good behavior," "deeds of gentleness," as well as purity, peace, reasonableness, mercy, steadfastness and sincerity (3:13, 17). They are true believers.

The final verse in today's reading gives us some insight into Jesus' beatitude about peacemakers. James wrote, "And the seed whose fruit is righteousness is sown in peace by those who make peace" (3:18). That "seed" could be nothing other than the word of the gospel, because only that seed produces righteousness. Sharing the gospel is the ultimate peace-making act, because when it is received, the result is peace with God and others (see Rom. 5:1; Eph. 2:14). If the end result is peace, naturally it should be shared peacefully.

Day 43, James 4

Was James writing to heaven-bound Christians in the first half of this chapter? Keep in mind that he previously addressed some who professed to be saved, but whose faith was void of works, proving them to be unsaved (2:14-17). I tend to think that same theme has surfaced once more in 4:1-10, and James was again addressing false or backslidden believers. Notice he said that they were guilty of murder (4:2). If he meant that literally, that proves they were unsaved. The New Testament declares that no murderer possesses eternal life (1 John 3:15). Borrowing an Old Testament metaphor, James also called them "adulteresses" because their friendship with the world made them enemies of the Lord (4:4), a sobering warning to modern worldly "Christians." It seems quite possible that at some point in the past those whom James was addressing were obedient followers, but if so, it is clear they had grossly backslidden. How can "enemies of God" be heaven-bound believers?

Obviously they can't, which is why James called them to repentance. His words in 4:7-10 are appropriate for an evangelist calling sinners to Christ: "Submit therefore to God. Resist the devil and he will flee from you. Draw near to God and He will draw near to you. Cleanse your hands, you sinners; and purify your hearts, you double-minded. Be miserable and mourn and weep; let your laughter be turned into mourning, and your joy to gloom. Humble yourselves in the presence of the Lord, and He will exalt you."

But what about James' words in this passage about God jealously desiring "the Spirit which He has made to dwell in us" (4:5)? This could well be a warning to those who return to loving the world—spiritual adulterers—of the possibility of losing the Spirit within them whom God "jealously desires." Still, grace was available to those who would repent.

Beginning in 4:11, James turns his attention to the "brethren." And he again borrows a theme found in Jesus' Sermon on the Mount, that of passing judgment. Like Jesus, James was referring to the sin of speaking evil of a fellow believer, a sin that is especially grievous when it is committed by someone with a "log in his own eye." As we learned when we studied Jesus' words on the same subject, we are not forbidden from making moral appraisals of other people (and clearly, James was doing that very thing throughout his letter). We absolutely must appraise other people morally if we are going to obey Jesus' commandments not to "give what is holy to dogs" and not "throw our pearls before swine" (Matt. 7:6). And we must appraise people if we are going to identify and avoid false prophets (Matt. 7:15). This passage in James must also be balanced with other scriptures such as 3 John 9-10 and Galatians 2:11-14, which teach that sometimes it is proper to expose a person's sins publicly in order that hypocrisy might be exposed or that others might be protected.

In any case, we need to be extremely cautious that we don't put ourselves in God's place of Judge, speaking evil of a genuine believer. If you've ever been a victim of evil speaking, you know how it hurts, especially when there is more to the story than what is being told.

Is it wrong to make future plans according to James 4:13-17? No, but it is presumptuous and boastful to talk about what we are intending to do without acknowledging the Lord's rule. We can do only what God permits, and since we are "just a vapor that appears for a little while and then vanishes away" (4:14), we may not be around tomorrow. Yesterday, more than 150,000 people died on planet Earth. How many thought they would be alive today? They would have benefitted from James' words. How wise it is to pray like David:

> Who understands the power of Thine anger, and
> Thy fury, according to the fear that is due Thee?
> Teach us to number our days, that we may present
> to Thee a heart of wisdom (Ps. 90:11-12).

Day 44, James 5

I think it is important to note that James condemns, not the rich in general, but the unrighteous rich. They gained their riches by not paying laborers who mowed their fields, and they "condemned and put to death the righteous man" (5:6).

The unrighteous rich, however, are not only condemned by how they gained their wealth, but also because of what they did with the wealth they gained. One might gain his wealth without sin (like Job and Abraham of old), but if one does not steward his wealth according to the will of God, he is still in the category of the unrighteous rich. Those whom James condemned did exactly what Jesus, in His Sermon on the Mount, forbade His followers to do, namely, they laid up their treasure on the earth (5:3). They "lived luxuriously on the earth and led [lives] of wanton pleasure" (5:5), typical of many modern professing Christians who ignore Jesus' stewardship commands. If you are reading these words, there is a very good chance that you are very rich. If you make $50,000 annually, you are in the top 1% of the world's wage earners (see www.globalrichlist.com). You should be laying up lots of treasures in heaven!

It seems likely that some of those unpaid laborers who mowed the fields of the rich were among James' readers. They would have taken comfort in his condemnation of those who exploited them. Their circumstances were so dire that Jesus' return was a source of great hope of deliverance (5:7-8). James wrote that the Lord's coming "is at hand" (5:8). No one in the early church dreamed that Jesus would not return for at least 2,000 years.

Another theme from Jesus' Sermon on the Mount surfaces in today's reading, that of the sin of swearing with an oath. Just as Jesus taught, a simple "yes" or "no" is sufficient when we give our word. There is nothing wrong with making promises. But swearing by an oath is an admission that one's simple promise is not trustworthy.

Clearly, the early church believed that the Lord was still in the healing business. Notice that it was not the elders or their oil that effected healing, but the "prayer offered in faith" (5:14). Jesus often credited people's faith as the reason for their healing, and nothing has changed. If we believe, however, that it may not be God's will for us to be healed, then it is virtually impossible to pray in faith for healing.

This healing promise in James 5:14-15 ought to be enough to convince any sick believer of God's will in the matter! The only qualifications for healing, according to James, are faith and righteousness, qualifications that can be obtained by any and all Christians. And if one is lacking in righteousness, forgiveness is available to those who repent, a forgiveness that places one in the righteous category! And don't be among the deceived dunderheads who try to claim that they are "righteous in Christ" while living unrighteously! That kind of alleged righteousness is not an asset in getting prayers answered. John wrote, "Whatever we ask we receive from Him, because we keep His commandments and do the things that are pleasing in His sight" (1 John 3:22).

There is little doubt that Scripture teaches that sin can open the door to God's discipline in the form of sickness (Ex. 15:26; Num. 12:1-15; Deut. 7:15; 28:22, 27-28, 35, 58-61; 1 Sam. 5:1-12; 1 Kings 8:35-39; 2 Kings 5:21-27; 2 Chron. 16:10-13; 21:12-20; 26:16-21; Ps. 38:3; 106:13-15; 107:17-18; Is. 10:15-16; Jn. 5:5-14; Acts 5:1-11; 1 Cor. 5:1-5; 11:27-34; Rev. 2:20-23). James also makes this clear, pointing out that the sick may need to confess their sins committed against other believers. If our relationships with other believers aren't right, our relationship with God is not right, just as Jesus taught in His Sermon on the Mount (Matt. 5:23-24). Verse 16 does not say we ought to confess all our sins to other believers as a regular practice. It must be read in context. Don't forget that James was writing to Christians who had been complaining against each other (see 4:11; 5:9).

Day 45, Acts 11:19-30 & ch. 12

An interesting point to ponder is that, at this point in church history (about 15 years after the church's birth on the day of Pentecost), the book of James comprised the entire New Testament. The book of Galatians wouldn't be written for at least another three years. Conservative biblical scholars estimate that the synoptic Gospels—Matthew, Mark and Luke—were not written for at least another 15 years! Yet the church thrived during its first 30 years. Of course, they had the apostolic oral accounts of Jesus' life that were passed along. It makes me wonder if the modern church is not guilty of over-emphasizing the New Testament epistles at the expense of Jesus' teaching that we now find in the four Gospels. Remember, Jesus did tell His disciples to go and make disciples, teaching them to obey all that He commanded (Matt. 28:18-20). That is the important thing!

I'm wondering if you caught the interesting phrase in 11:21: "A large number who believed turned to the Lord." It seems to say that not all who believe necessarily *turn* to the Lord, that is, repent. If so, such unrepentant believers could be called "unsaved believers."

It was in the Gentile church in Antioch where the disciples were first called Christians. It was probably unsaved Gentiles who bestowed that title upon the disciples, as they observed that their conversations and lifestyles all revolved around Christ. Thus a title that was meant to be derogatory became regarded by the early disciples as one of honor. True disciples can say with Paul, "To live is Christ" (Phil. 1:21).

I like today's story about the prophets, one of whom was named Agabus, who came down to Antioch from Jerusalem. His prophecy was not some vague, mystical forecast that we so often hear from the many alleged prophets who roam from church to church today. I so pity the gullible people who, when they find just a few words in one of their many nebulous prophecies that seemingly come to pass, are convinced these self-proclaimed prophets are from God. Agabus spoke specifically. His word of the coming famine *was* his message, it was not vaguely contained within a prophecy that included scores of other vague "messages."

I also like how the church responded to Agabus' prophecy. They obeyed Jesus, who will one day say to everyone one of two things, either "I was hungry, and you gave me something to eat," or "I was hungry, and you gave me nothing to eat" (Matt. 25:35, 42). So many modern "prophecies" cater to the selfish desires of those listening.

How could Peter sleep so soundly on the eve of his execution? Jesus had promised him years before that he wouldn't die until he grew old (John 21:18-19), so Peter had no worries. Moreover, God obviously has a tremendous prison ministry!

Why did God deliver Peter from death but allow James to be martyred? That we don't know. But perhaps we should ask a different question: "Why did God let James go to heaven so soon but kept Peter on this lousy earth?" Death is a great blessing to those in Christ (Phil. 1:21-23).

Take note that the prayer meeting for Peter was held in a house, as were most gatherings of the early church. There is no record in Acts of any special church buildings during the first 30 years of the church's history. The early disciples didn't need special buildings then to make disciples, and church buildings really aren't needed today. In fact, church buildings often work against the making of disciples. They rob money from missionaries and the poor.

The Jewish historian, Josephus, recorded the same story about Herod Agrippa that we read today, writing that shortly after Herod gave his speech in Caesarea that won him undue praise, he was struck with a violent stomach illness. He died after five days of agony at the age of 54. Those were five days of mercy.

John Stott wrote a fitting summary of Acts 12: "The chapter opens with James dead, Peter in prison, and Herod triumphing. It closes with Herod dead, Peter free, and the word of God triumphing." Amen.

Day 46, Acts 13

It is now around 48 A.D., 18 years from the church's birth on Pentecost. The church in Antioch was not fragmented into scores of denominations separated by doctrine and traditions. Rather, the believers, who regularly gathered in houses in many locations, considered themselves to be members of *one* church. The leaders, knowing Jesus' commandment to love one another, did just that, regularly gathering themselves. They included more than just elders/pastors/overseers (all the same New Testament ministry), but also prophets and teachers (13:1).

Those leadership gatherings apparently included times of "ministering to the Lord and fasting." Keep in mind that one may fast by skipping just one meal. It was during one of those times that the Holy Spirit spoke, likely through prophecy: "Set apart for Me Barnabas and Saul for the work to which I have called them."

First, notice that the prophetic word was not telling anyone that she would be married within two years, or that he would soon be landing a better job (as so many alleged prophecies do in some modern church circles). Rather, the prophetic word was focused on God's plan to expand His kingdom.

Second, notice the Holy Spirit did not tell Barnabas and Saul (Paul) precisely what their "work" was. They already knew it in their hearts, where the Holy Spirit speaks to all true believers, and the prophetic word was simply a confirmation. The lesson? Don't be led by prophecy! Follow the inward guidance of the Spirit. If you receive a prophecy that doesn't confirm what you already know, forget it.

So Barnabas and Saul (Paul) were "sent out by the Holy Spirit" (13:4), and from then on were classified as apostles, or "sent ones" (see 14:14). God sent them first to the island of Cyprus in the Mediterranean Sea (see map on page 534). Upon arrival, they began preaching in synagogues, hoping that the Jews and God-fearing and proselyte Gentiles would be receptive to hearing their message. Not all were, and Luke highlights one named Bar-Jesus, a Jewish false prophet and magician. Don't you just love God's gentle tact as He spoke to Bar-Jesus through Paul's lips, "You who are full of all deceit and fraud, you son of the devil, you enemy of all righteousness, will you not cease to make crooked the straight ways of the Lord?" (13:10). Bar-Jesus soon found his physical eyes as darkened as his spiritual eyes.

From Cyprus the missionaries sailed to Perga and Pisidian Antioch, in the ancient region of Galatia, on the western coast of modern Turkey. Much of Paul's ministry would be focused on this part of the world during his missionary journeys, and he experienced great success. Today, however, among modern Turkey's 70 million people, the majority are nominal Muslims, while Christians number only in the thousands.

Paul's first sermon in the Jewish synagogue in Pisidian Antioch was a simple telling of the story of Jesus' death and resurrection, how it fulfilled Old Testament prophecy, how it could benefit those who would believe, and how it spelled the doom of those who would not believe. God was offering forgiveness and freedom from sin through His Son.

Note that Paul did not give an altar call at the conclusion of his preaching or lead anyone in a "sinner's prayer." Those who believed were born again and naturally wanted to learn more about Jesus, so they followed Paul and Barnabas to seek more understanding. The preachers didn't have to chase down the new "converts." Rather, the new disciples followed the preachers. That is biblical "follow up!"

Tragically, many of the Jews in Pisidian Antioch did not believe, but the Gentiles were *amazingly* receptive, "rejoicing and glorifying the word of the Lord" (13:48).

Does the phrase "as many as had been appointed to eternal life believed" indicate that God has predestined some to be saved and others to be damned? No. The New Testament teaches that, before the foundation of the world, God chose to save all who would believe in Jesus. He foreknew who would believe and appointed them to eternal life, recording their names in His book. Peter wrote that we are "chosen according to the foreknowledge of God" (1 Pet. 1-2). If you believe, you were also "appointed to eternal life!"

Day 47, Acts 14

This incident of the healing of the crippled man in Lystra raises some interesting questions. According to what we read, Paul was preaching "the gospel" (14:7) in Lystra. Listening to Paul's gospel, a man who had been lame from birth was inspired with faith that healed him completely (14:9). How is that? He must have heard something more than just a message about a God who was offering forgiveness of sins.

Perhaps he heard from Paul that Jesus never turned away anyone who came to Him requesting healing, including crippled people, and that He was alive and still doing the same miracles. Perhaps Paul quoted Isaiah's prophecy that the Messiah would not only be "pierced through for our transgressions and crushed for our iniquities," but that He also "took our infirmities, and carried away our diseases" and that "by His scourging we are healed" (Is. 53:4-5; Matt. 8:17). Surely an evangelist whose ministry is accompanied by genuine miracles will be much more effective than one whose ministry is not. How effective would Paul have been in Iconium without healings and miracles (14:3)?

Something else worth considering about this particular story: Luke wrote that the crippled man had "faith to be made well" (14:9), even while he was still crippled. It wasn't until Paul told him, "Stand upright on your feet," and he obeyed Paul's words, that he was actually healed. What an illustration of the truth that faith without works is dead. The crippled man had to act upon his faith before it was effectual, a principle the Bible teaches over and over again. *If you want to walk on the water, you have to get out of the boat.* Get going!

And what an illustration of the power of encouragement! Paul told the crippled man to get up, while so many preachers would have told him not even to get his hopes up! Encouragers are the mothers of miracles. I wonder where I would be today without the past encouragement of family and friends. Now is a good time to ask yourself, "Am I an encourager?"

After being stoned and left for dead, Paul was either revived or supernaturally resurrected. Then the "stonee" walked back into the city of his "stoners." Paul was no wimp, and what God had said years earlier was becoming a reality: "He [Paul] is a chosen instrument of Mine....for I will show him how much he must suffer for My name's sake" (Acts 9:15-16).

In the city of Derbe, Paul and Barnabas "made many disciples" (14:21). According to the Bible, a disciple is not just someone who professes to believe in Jesus, but someone who is a whole-hearted follower of Christ, one who is learning to obey all of His commandments (see John 8:31-32; Matt. 28:19-20; Luke 14:25-33). This exposes the fundamental error of much of the modern evangelical church, which proclaims a false gospel founded on a false grace that results in false converts. Today we are told that one can be a believer in Christ without being a disciple of Christ, and that one can gain heaven without holiness! This faulty doctrine is often derived, at least in part, from isolated verses extracted from Paul's Galatian letter, which we are about to begin reading, *in context*, tomorrow.

Returning to the cities where they had recently preached, Paul and Barnabas appointed elders in every church (14:23). Churches need leaders, and generally speaking, with age comes wisdom, thus *elders* were appointed. Older Jewish converts, in particular, would have been the most qualified to serve because of their familiarity with Scripture. But none had spent any time in Bible School or seminary. In the New Testament, the words *elders*, *pastors*, *overseers*, and *bishops* all describe the same ministry. They disciple little flocks.

Keep in mind that almost everything we read yesterday, and everything we read today, occurred in the ancient region of Galatia, in modern western Turkey. In particular, take note that Paul's primary antagonists in Galatia were unbelieving Jews (13:50; 14:2,4-5,19). Also remember that Paul was stoned and left for dead in the Galatian city of Lystra. This is all important to know as we read Galatians.

Day 48, Galatians 1

There is little doubt that Paul penned his letter to the Galatian churches not too long after his first missionary journey to their region (see 1:6), which we've been reading in the books of Acts over the past two days. So the year was around 48 A.D., 18 years from the church's birth in Jerusalem. That means the early church did quite well for 18 years without the book of Galatians. Or it could be said this way: God did not feel that the book of Galatians was needed by the church until then.

Why the need in 48 A.D.? Simply because a unique problem had surfaced. The gospel was being distorted (1:7). Paul wrote to fix that problem. Tragically, however, some have ripped verses from this letter—a letter that was meant to correct a distorted gospel—and used those verses to distort the gospel once again. We will consider the evidence for that over the next six days.

Having already read Matthew, James, and the first 14 chapters of the book of Acts, a foundation has been laid for us concerning the gospel. We've read Jesus' major teachings. We know He consistently taught that heaven is only for the holy. We've read James' words that faith without works cannot save anyone. We've studied the sermons of the apostles during the first 18 years of the church, and heard them call their audiences to repentance. So when someone tries to tell us that Paul, in his Galatian letter, was correcting a false doctrine that was misleading people into thinking that holiness is necessary for heaven, warning lights should start flashing in our minds! In fact, if we've ever read the entire book of Galatians, we're immediately going to think of passages such as Galatians 5:19-21:

> Now the deeds of the flesh are evident, which are: immorality, impurity, sensuality, idolatry, sorcery, enmities, strife, jealousy, outbursts of anger, disputes, dissensions, factions, envying, drunkenness, carousing, and things like these, of which I forewarn you just as I have forewarned you that those who practice such things shall not inherit the kingdom of God (Gal. 5:19-21, emphasis added).

Clearly, Paul was not trying to correct the "misconception" that holiness is required for heaven!

So how had the gospel been distorted? Some Jewish believers were teaching that Gentiles could not be saved unless they were circumcised. Circumcision was clearly the main issue. This is why we find circumcision mentioned at least thirteen times in the six chapters of Galatians. It was also being taught by some that Gentiles could not be saved unless they started keeping all the Law of Moses, particularly its feast days and more ritualistic, rather than moral, aspects. Consequently, in the minds of some Galatians, salvation had become something that one earned through circumcision and keeping some rituals, not something that was purchased by Christ and granted by God's grace to believers. It was indeed, "a different gospel" (1:6).

One of the final and concluding verses of Paul's letter says:

> For neither is circumcision anything, nor uncircumcision, but a new creation (Gal. 6:15).

That sentence sums up the entire letter. If we understand nothing else in Galatians, we can understand that. Clearly, Paul was declaring that circumcision has no bearing on salvation. The important thing is that one be a new creation in Christ. It was not the removal of a little piece of flesh that saves, but the removal of the old fleshly nature of sin, a circumcision of the heart (see Deut. 10:16; 30:6; Jer. 4:4). And it was all by grace through faith! But not a dead faith!

In this first chapter, Paul focuses on proving the divine origin of the gospel he preached. By recounting the story of his former life as a devoted Pharisee and persecutor of the church, his supernatural conversion, and his scant contact with the early Christian leaders in Jerusalem, Paul attempts to persuade his Galatian readers that his message of salvation by grace through faith was given to him by God, not man. This was necessary, because the false teachers no doubt had their list of Old Testament scriptures in which God commanded circumcision.

Day 49, Galatians 2

As Paul recounts his second trip to Jerusalem, once again we see that the primary issue was that of circumcision. Paul took Titus, a Greek Gentile, with him on that second trip, and Titus remained uncircumcised, before and after (2:3). The point? It proves that back in those early days, no Christian in Jerusalem, including Peter, James and John (2:9), thought that Gentiles needed to be circumcised to be saved. Paul had, in fact, traveled to Jerusalem for the very purpose of submitting the gospel that he had been preaching to the Gentiles to the scrutiny of the highest Christian leaders there. They gave it their full endorsement. Neither Peter, James or John said to Paul, "You must tell the Gentiles that they need to be circumcised to be saved."

At a later point in time, however, Peter succumbed to pressure from Jews who believed otherwise. Paul thus recounts the incident so his readers will know the facts, lest anyone try to dispute Paul's gospel on the basis of Peter's temporary fall from the truth.

Peter had traveled to the thriving Gentile church in Antioch, initially enjoying full fellowship with uncircumcised Gentile believers. He ate with them, something forbidden by Jewish tradition. But when some others, whom Paul refers to as "the party of the circumcision," arrived from Jerusalem, Peter began to "hold himself aloof" from the Gentile believers, and his example was ultimately followed by other Jewish believers in Antioch, including even Barnabas.

Paul could not keep silent about their hypocrisy. They professed to believe that salvation was available to anyone who would believe in Jesus, circumcised or uncircumcised, yet were living in contradiction to their profession. So Paul rebuked Peter publicly, saying (and I paraphrase 2:14): "If you, as a Jew, have been eating with uncircumcised men, indicating by your example that circumcision is not necessary for acceptance by God, why are you now acting in such a way to make Gentiles think that they must be circumcised to be accepted by God?" Again, it is clear that circumcision was the primary issue.

The final six verses of today's reading are not as clear as I wish they were. But this much is clear: the fundamental problem of salvation through circumcision is that it nullifies God's grace and the need for Jesus' death. No Jew has ever been saved by keeping the Law of Moses, because no Jew has yet *kept* the Law of Moses. Jews, although perhaps not as sinful as the average Gentile (2:15), are still sinners who need grace to be saved, and so salvation is granted to Jews who believe in Jesus. If circumcision doesn't save Jews, why would it be required of Gentiles for salvation?

Paul's testimony, as a Jew, was that "through the Law I died to the Law" (2:19). That is, the Law only condemned him, and so he gave up all hope of being saved by it. Losing hope in the Law, however, is what paved the way for him to ultimately "live to God," that is, live in obedience. Now spiritually reborn, Paul's righteousness stemmed not from his own feeble efforts, but from Christ who lived within him. Everyone who has been genuinely born again can say with Paul, "It is no longer I who live, but Christ lives in me" (2:20). Praise God!

So you can see that Paul's gospel of grace was anything but a license to sin. Rather, it was a message of Christ-empowered holiness. And what an insult it is to Jesus to say to a Gentile for whom He died and within whom He now lives, "If you want to be saved, you must be circumcised and start keeping all the laws given to the Jews." That is tantamount to saying that one is saved by being circumcised and keeping the Law of Moses, and it makes Christ's death needless.

One final point. When Paul submitted to Peter, James and John the gospel he had been preaching to Gentiles, they had nothing to add to it (2:6). They only requested that he "remember the poor" (2:10). We can't rightfully claim to be a "New Testament church" unless we are caring for the poor.

Day 50, Galatians 3

The controversy Paul addressed in his letter to the Galatians was not a debate over whether or not true Christians obey God's commandments. Rather, it was a debate over whether or not Gentiles must be circumcised and keep the Law of Moses in order to be saved. The clear answer is that they don't, and for a number of good reasons, many of which Paul mentions in this chapter.

Keep in mind that God has given three major "sets of rules" in human history. The first is the "law of the conscience," given to every person since Adam. That set of rules existed thousands of years before the Law of Moses, and God has *always* expected *everyone* to obey those laws, which is why He has wired every human in history with a conscience (see Rom. 2:14-16).

Second, God gave the Law of Moses to the descendants of Israel. It was given only to them, and it included many laws that, unlike the law of conscience, were not moral in nature, such as laws about feast days, a priesthood, animal sacrifices and so on. The Law of Moses was only intended to be temporary, lasting until the time of the new covenant (see Jer. 31:31-34; Heb. 7:12; 8:6-13). It included many moral laws that were also part of the "law of conscience."

Third, God gave the Church the "law of Christ," which includes everything Christ commanded. The law of Christ includes all the moral laws that were also part of the "law of conscience." All Jewish and Gentile believers in Jesus are obligated to follow the law of Christ, and they do strive to follow it, by virtue of the fact that they are born again. None, including Jewish believers, are obligated to follow the Law of Moses any longer (see 1 Cor. 9:19-21). It took quite a while, however, for early Jewish Christians to accept this fact. As we've seen, some even thought that Gentiles should be obeying the Law of Moses.

In today's reading, Paul succinctly lists many reasons why Gentiles don't need to be circumcised and keep the Law of Moses to be saved. The foremost is, of course, that God forgives and regenerates them when they believe in Jesus. God gives His Spirit to those who believe, not first requiring their circumcision and Mosaic law-keeping (3:2-5).

Salvation has always been received through faith, as proven in the Old Testament (see 3:11), and by Scripture's testimony regarding Abraham, who "believed God, and it was reckoned to him as righteousness" (3:6). Abraham's true descendants follow his example of faith (3:7), and they include believing Gentiles, as God had originally promised Abraham (3:8-9).

In fact, when God promised Abraham that all the nations would be blessed through his seed, that is, through Christ, it was a promise made 430 years before the Law of Moses was given. Paul argues that, even in a covenant made between men, the conditions can't be altered after the agreement is made. Surely when God gave the Law of Moses, He wasn't adding conditions to the covenant He made with Abraham 430 years earlier to bless Gentiles through his seed! So the Law of Moses has absolutely *nothing* to do with Gentiles receiving the blessing that God promised them through Jesus, Abraham's singular seed.

Another reason salvation can't be gained by keeping the Law of Moses is because that Law promises a curse on any who don't keep it perfectly, something no one has ever done (with the exception of Jesus).

So what purpose did the Law of Moses ultimately serve? It helped Jews, who because of God's great dealings with them might have been tempted to think they had salvation "in the bag," to realize their need to be saved, and saved by some means other than the Law. So the Law became, for Jews, a tutor to lead them to Christ (3:24). Paul clearly states that believing Jews are no longer under that tutor (3:26).

So Jews and Gentiles are in the same boat. All can be saved only through faith. When they do believe, they are born again to be sons of God, "clothed in Christ" (3:27), now acting like Him!

Day 51, Galatians 4

Paul's son/slave analogy (4:1-7) does not illustrate how obedience to God is optional for Christians, as some say. Rather, it illustrates how a Jew's relationship with the Law of Moses changes when he believes.

Prior to believing in Jesus, a Jew under the old covenant is comparable to a child of a wealthy Roman family in ancient times. He is under "guardians and managers" at first, and his life bears little difference to that of a household slave (4:2). He is, however, destined for better things as he grows older, and at the date set by his father, is adopted into his family to enjoy the full privileges of sonship. Similarly, God the Father set a time when the Jews, in slavery under the Mosaic Law, would be freed through Jesus' sacrifice to become His full-fledged children, born of His Spirit. Clearly, Paul believed that no Jew (or Gentile) was obligated to obey the Law of Moses.

However, under the influence of the false teachers who had infiltrated the church, not only were Gentile believers being circumcised and embracing the Law of Moses, but Jewish believers were apparently reverting to their former slavery to the Law's ritualistic aspects (4:9). Notice it was *not* the Galatians' holiness or morality that caused Paul such great concern. Rather, he wrote, "You observe days and months and seasons and years. I fear for you..." (Gal. 4:10-11). Paul was concerned that the Galatian Christians were trying to merit salvation by means of circumcision and following ritualistic aspects of the Law of Moses.

Finding himself now in competition with the false teachers for the hearts and minds of the Galatian believers, Paul asks them to remember their special relationship with him. He reminds them that, even though he had "bodily illness" (or better translated, "bodily weakness") that "was a trial" to them when he was with them, they did not despise him (4:13-14). Paul must have been referring to his appearance after he had been stoned and left for dead in Lystra (Acts 14:19). Imagine how he looked until his swelling subsided and his bruises slowly healed. His appearance, however, only served to endear him even more to the Galatian believers, as they knew he had suffered for their sakes.

Some commentators try to convince us that because Paul told the Galatians, "If possible, you would have plucked out your eyes and given them to me" (4:15), Paul must have had a terrible eye disease! If I say to someone, "You loved me so much you would have cut off your right hand for me," does that prove my right hand is diseased? Hardly. We would wonder how Paul would have been able to inspire people in Galatia with faith to be healed if he himself had been suffering a terrible eye disease.

Paul's second analogy in today's reading, constructed using Old Testament imagery, also serves to help Jewish believers understand their new relationship with God apart from the Mosaic Law.

Abraham's son Ishmael was born because of Abraham's own efforts, while his son Isaac was born supernaturally because of his faith. Additionally, Ishmael's mother was a slave, whereas Isaac's mother was free. Clearly, Ishmael represents unbelieving Jews who are in slavery to the Mosaic Law as they attempt to obtain salvation by their own efforts, whereas Isaac represents believing Jews who are free from slavery to the Mosaic law, having received salvation through faith.

Paul draws a few additional parallels in his allegory. Hagar the slave, and the Law of Moses, correspond with "the present Jerusalem," a city in which most of the residents in Paul's day were still in bondage to the Law. Believers in Christ, however, look to the Jerusalem above, the New Jerusalem, as their true home or "mother." And just as Isaac was persecuted by Ishmael, so those who are "born of the Spirit" (believing Jews) are persecuted by those who are "born of the flesh" (unbelieving Jews).

What will be the final outcome? The children of the "bondwoman" (those still in slavery under the Law of Moses) will be "cast out," while the children of the "freewoman" will inherit salvation (see 4:30-31). Interesting shadowy parallels from the Old Testament!

Day 52, Galatians 5

Once again we see that the main issue in Galatia was circumcision for Gentiles, mentioned four times in this short chapter. The teaching that circumcision was essential for salvation made Paul quite angry! He wrote, (and I paraphrase 5:12): "If these fellows think that the removal of a little skin is so beneficial, why don't they just go ahead and castrate themselves?"

Paul writes that those Gentiles who do receive circumcision are "under obligation to keep the *whole* Law" (5:3), the emphasis being on the word *whole,* meaning not just the moral aspects—but every ritualistic aspect of the Mosaic Law as well. If one adopts the Mosaic Law as his means of salvation, he must keep it all perfectly, or be cursed. That is why Paul refers to it as "a yoke of slavery" (5:1).

Tragically, by twisting Paul's words and ignoring context, some make him say that those who are striving to be holy, or who think that holiness is essential, have "severed themselves from Christ" and "fallen from grace" (5:4). Remember, however, that Paul was addressing those who had believed in Jesus and were reborn, but who were now being circumcised and keeping Jewish rituals, trusting that by doing those things they were earning their salvation. Those, and only those kinds of people, are severing themselves from Christ and falling from grace. They are vastly different from the people who, having believed in Jesus, and knowing that they have been saved by the grace made available through His substitutionary death, are now striving to follow Him obediently by the power of the indwelling Spirit. The former attempts to save himself by his own efforts apart from God's grace, whereas the latter is saved by God's grace, which not only provides forgiveness, but also the ability to be holy.

All of this is further substantiated by Paul's words in 5:6: "For in Christ Jesus neither circumcision nor uncircumcision means anything, but faith working through love." A living faith, *characterized by works*, particularly of loving one's neighbor, is what is essential.

Moreover, Paul wrote in this same chapter that those who practice the deeds of the flesh will not inherit God's kingdom (5:19-21). Holiness, true holiness, is the fruit of saving faith and the new birth.

Clearly, freedom from the Law of Moses is not to be confused with freedom from holiness: "For you were called to freedom, brethren; only do not turn your freedom into an opportunity for the flesh, but through love serve one another" (5:13). Paul also wrote that those who are led by the Spirit are not under the Law of Moses (5:18), but obviously, the *Holy* Spirit leads people to be *holy*.

Incidentally, isn't it amazing that so many modern teachers tell us that it is impossible to forfeit salvation or "fall from grace," when Paul writes so plainly in this chapter of the danger of both?

We learn today that born again people are two-natured, and experience an inward battle between evil desires, what Paul refers to as "the flesh," and the inward-dwelling Spirit. Clearly, we decide who wins that battle. There is no magic formula or deep spiritual secret to walking in holiness. We must simply "walk by the Spirit," and when we do, the result is that we "will not carry out the desire of the flesh" (5:16).

Your flesh, or "old nature" as it is sometimes called, left unrestrained, would pull you into immorality, drunkenness, and continual strife. But true believers, "those who belong to Christ...have crucified the flesh with its passions and desires" (5:24). What is crucified is not yet dead, but is definitely restrained. When someone truly believes in Jesus, he makes an inward commitment to obey Him and resist sin. Although he is still tempted by the old nature, he resists it. Even if he yields, he feels an inward resistance the entire time, and afterwards, a huge sense of condemnation that pulls him towards confession and repentance. All of that is part of the process of sanctification as the Spirit works in us to make us more holy. More evidence of God's amazing grace!

Day 53, Galatians 6

If it hasn't been clear before, it couldn't be clearer today. When Paul wrote of our freedom from the Law in this letter, he was speaking about the *Law of Moses*. He certainly wasn't speaking about the law of Christ, because we read in 6:2: "Bear one another's burdens, and thereby *fulfill the law of Christ.*" We are expected to keep Christ's law!

Yet many commentaries on the book of Galatians will tell you that the theme of the letter is "salvation by faith alone, apart from works." This is only true if by "works," it is meant "works of the *Law of Moses, particularly circumcision.*" So often, however, the phrase "salvation by faith alone" is construed to imply that holiness has nothing to do with salvation, so you can live like hell and go to heaven as long as you say you believe in Jesus. That, however, is heresy. Don't forget, just three years before Paul wrote this letter to the Galatians, a letter from James was circulated among all the churches that included the statement, "You see that a man is justified by works and not by faith alone" (Jas. 2:24).

Moreover, in this final chapter, Paul warns his readers that everyone will reap what he has sown. Only holy people, those who are "sowing to the Spirit" as opposed to "sowing to the flesh," will reap eternal life (6:7-8). "Sowing to the Spirit" simply means to do good continually (6:9-10). A sower plants lots of seeds. Remember, Paul warned yesterday that those who practice the works of the flesh will not inherit God's kingdom (5:21). Today he repeats that warning using slightly different words (6:8).

Again, we see that circumcision was the primary issue, as Paul mentions it five times today. In fact, Paul summarizes the point of his entire letter in 6:15: "For neither is circumcision anything, nor uncircumcision, but a new creation." It makes no difference if one is circumcised or uncircumcised. What is important is if one is born again and living like a new creation. Such people are the only people who are truly holy, as they are being transformed by God's Spirit.

Paul points out that the false teachers who are so focused on circumcision do not keep the rest of the Law of Moses. They boasted in their circumcision, as if that is what made them righteous in God's eyes, effectively denigrating Jesus' death on the cross and nullifying salvation by grace through faith. We can say along with Paul, however, that we boast only in the cross of Christ, because it was there that our salvation was purchased through the work of God, and from there His grace flowed to save us. Our old self was crucified with Christ, and we have become dead to the world and the world has become dead to us. It no longer has the attraction for us that it once had, as we see it now in its darkness and rebellion. We long for a better place.

True Christians are radically different from the world. We feel like aliens living on this planet. We can't understand why everyone doesn't repent and receive the forgiveness and transformation that God so graciously offers to all. We love to do good, and we live to please God.

Finally, a side thought. Today we read, "The one who is taught the word is to share all good things with the one who teaches him" (6:6). This is an admonition for Christians to support their pastors/elders/overseers materially, as well as any apostles, prophets, evangelists or teachers from whom they've benefitted spiritually. It is heart-breaking to observe today how many wolves in sheep's clothing are profiting from the sheep whom they regularly fleece. I admonish you, dear reader, don't give any of God's money to alleged "apostles" and "prophets" who flaunt their wealth and proclaim their gospel of greed, or to false teachers and evangelists who turn God's grace into a license to sin. Don't attend or support an apostate church overseen by a hireling pastor. Support those who unashamedly proclaim the truth! Help spread the truth!

Day 54, Acts 15

You should have felt right at home reading Acts 15 today, having just read Paul's letter to the Galatians. Both focus on the same problem and both reveal the same remedy. It stands to reason that Paul wrote his Galatian letter before the Jerusalem council of Acts 15, otherwise he would have surely mentioned it in his letter.

Sadly, what we read today is often twisted by false grace teachers to promote their strange gospel. Notice, however, that the issue was not whether Gentiles should obey the law of Christ. Rather, the issue was circumcision and the Law of Moses (15:1, 5), and more specifically, the ceremonial and ritualistic aspects of the Law of Moses, since the Gentile believers would have been keeping the moral aspects of the Mosaic Law by virtue of the fact that they were following Christ's commandments. Thus, their deficiencies in the eyes of the false teachers were only regarding circumcision and rituals, which allegedly disqualified them from being saved (15:1).

Luke highlighted the most persuasive arguments presented at the gathering of the Jerusalem elders and apostles. Peter recounted how God dramatically poured out His Spirit on the first Gentiles who believed the gospel, and without requiring their circumcision. Echoing Paul's words that we read yesterday (Gal. 6:13), Peter also questioned why his theological opponents would expect Gentile believers to keep laws that none of them had ever kept. The Mosaic Law was an impossible *yoke*—unlike Jesus' "easy yoke" (Matt. 11:30). Peter maintained that we are saved by grace.

It was out of consideration for Jews that James recommended to the council that they request believing Gentiles to "abstain from things contaminated by idols and from fornication and from what is strangled and from blood" (15:20). Notice that the basis for his recommendation was not "because God requires these things of them to be saved," but because "Moses from ancient generations has in every city those who preach him, since he is read in the synagogues every Sabbath" (15:21). That is, if the Gentile believers ate what was sacrificed to idols, or meat from animals that had been strangled rather than butchered so that the blood was drained—practices that were particularly abhorrent to scrupulous Jews—it could well be a stumbling block to their salvation. Additionally, those practices could also offend believing Jews within the church who did not yet fully understand their freedom from the Mosaic Law.

Paul would later address these same issues in two of his letters, stating that it was not a sin to eat meat sacrificed to idols, but that one should abstain from doing so if it would cause a brother to stumble (Rom. 14:1-23, Cor. 10:19-33).

What about the council's recommendation that believing Gentiles abstain from "fornication"? Would not fornication be forbidden in the law of Christ? So why was it emphasized here?

Because the other three recommendations focused on eating offenses, it is likely that "fornication" here is a reference to eating meat that was purchased at a pagan temple where sex with a temple prostitute was a regular religious practice. Believing Gentiles who maintained any connection with their former pagan practices—even if it was nothing more than purchasing meat from a pagan temple which had been strangled, sacrificed to idols, or connected to some sexual perversion—may well have discredited their testimonies in the eyes of observing, unbelieving Jews.

Four respected representatives delivered the council's decision to the Antioch believers, and it is no wonder they rejoiced when they heard it, having faced the prospect of lining up to be circumcised without anesthesia, not to mention the prospect of having to keep the entire Law of Moses! But don't make the error of thinking that the sum total of everything God expected of them was found in those four recommendations. The law of Christ and the law of conscience were never called into question.

Paul and Barnabas' disagreement and split over Mark finds a happier ending many years later, when Paul wrote to Timothy, "Pick up Mark and bring him with you, for he is useful to me for service" (2 Tim. 4:11). Paul softened, or Mark improved! Or both!

Day 55, Acts 16

As I'm sure you realized, Paul had Timothy circumcised, not because he believed Timothy couldn't be saved otherwise. Rather, it was because Paul knew that Jews would not be receptive to an uncircumcised man who was bringing a message about the Jewish Messiah. This shows us how amazingly important circumcision was to the Jews of Paul's day. It was *the* litmus test, and I hate to think that any Jews actually required Timothy to drop his drawers to verify his credentials, but yet such a thing seems possible in light of what we've just read!

We're reading today of Paul's second missionary journey. You can see on the map on page 534 that he visited some of the places where he planted churches during his first missionary journey, but that he traveled far beyond Galatia (in modern Eastern Turkey) to the eastern coast of modern Greece on his second missionary journey. Notice also on the map that Paul and Silas initially made no preaching stops in "Asia" (modern western Turkey) because they had been "forbidden by the Holy Spirit to speak the word" there (16:6). Obviously it was a matter of strategy and timing, because Paul eventually made a brief stop in the Asian city of Ephesus on his way home, and he eventually settled in Ephesus for two years during his third missionary journey. As a result, "all who lived in Asia heard the word of the Lord" (19:9). How important it is to be sensitive to God's will *and* His timing.

Luke wrote that "the Lord opened the heart" (16:14) of Lydia, the first disciple in Europe. This does not prove, as some say, that God zapped her with some "irresistible grace" due to the fact that she was specially chosen to be saved. Luke's words simply emphasize God's influence on her heart, an influence to which she yielded. If I said, "Your speech tonight melted my heart," does that prove that you exercised some kind of irresistible power over me that affected me apart from my own receptivity to your words? Obviously not.

Note that the spectacular guidance Paul and Silas received via a night vision to preach the gospel in Macedonia was soon followed by a beating and imprisonment. When God guides us through such spectacular means (beyond the gentle inward leading of the Spirit), it serves to warn us that difficulties lie ahead. The Lord knows we'll need the extra assurance of being in His will that only spectacular guidance provides. Beware of those who claim to have visions and see angels on a daily or weekly basis, especially those who do nothing else to build God's kingdom but have visions and see angels.

Certain that they were in the center of God's will, Paul and Silas were able to sing praises to God, even while their feet were fastened in chains to a prison wall. The Lord's very effective prison ministry resulted in a jailhouse shaking and revival!

The Philippian jailer, however, got more than "jailhouse religion." When he asked what he needed to do to be saved, Paul did not tell him to invite Jesus into his heart or accept Jesus as his personal Savior. Neither did Paul tell him to believe in Jesus. Rather, Paul told him to believe in the *Lord* Jesus (16:31). He did, and his faith went right to work. He washed Paul and Silas' wounds, fixed them a meal, was baptized, and "rejoiced greatly" (16:34). He demonstrated four fruits of the Spirit: love, joy, kindness and goodness (see Gal. 5:22).

Paul was not saying in 16:31 that if the jailer believed, it guaranteed that his whole family would be saved. That would contradict many other scriptures (see, for example, 1 Cor. 7:16). Paul was simply saying that if the jailer *and his family* believed in Jesus, they would all be saved. Notice that Paul preached the gospel to everyone in the jailer's household (16:32), and they all individually believed (16:33-34). We cannot "claim" Acts 16:31 for our families to guarantee their salvation. We should tell them the gospel and live godly lives before them.

Day 56, Acts 17

How interesting it is to read of the varying receptivity of those to whom Paul preached as he journeyed in Madedonia and Achaia, what is now modern Greece. In Thessalonica, after initial success, the persecution from unbelieving Jews grew so intense that Paul and Silas had to flee for their lives under the cover of darkness. At their next stop, however, in Berea, they found "more noble-minded" Jews who "received the word with great eagerness, examining the Scriptures daily" (17:11). Because of their open hearts, "many believed, along with a number of prominent Greek women and men" (17:12). Note that Luke was no Calvinist. He did not pin the responsibility on God, but on free-willed human beings, for their salvation.

Fleeing persecution in Berea that was instigated by Thessalonican Jews, Paul boarded a boat for Athens, a seat of idolatry. Luke highlights Paul's interaction with Epicurean and Stoic philosophers there, and knowing something about their different philosophies helps us to appreciate Paul's message to them on the Areopagus.

Epicureans denied any divine activity by the gods, believing that everything occurred by chance, and asserting that man's chief aim is pleasure. Life's goal was to live without any physical pain or mental anxiety, fully enjoying material things, as well as sex, companionship, acceptance and love. In their minds, there was no such thing as life after death.

Stoics were pantheists who believed that everything was governed by an irresistible fate, and that virtue was its own reward, while vice was its own sufficient punishment. Rather than making pleasure their highest goal, they focused more on the virtues of wisdom, bravery, justice and moderation. The perfect person yielded himself without passion to fate, and it is from this philosophical school that we derive our English adjective, *stoic*, which means "forbearing."

Paul began his sermon to the philosophers by complimenting them for being religious (17:22). We often see people's false religion as a barrier to the gospel, but we should use it, as Paul did, as a bridge to their hearts. Paul didn't castigate the Athenian philosophers for their idolatry, but used their altar "to an unknown god" as a launching point for the gospel (17:23).

Notice that Paul didn't quote any Old Testament scriptures as was his custom when preaching the gospel to Jews. They would have been all but meaningless to his Gentile audience. Rather, he briefly explained some fundamental truths about God's nature and even quoted a Greek poet who wrote that all people are God's offspring (17:28). Paul could have pointed out the technical error of their poet's thinking, as he (Paul) knew that only those who are born again are truly God's offspring. Yet he no doubt agreed that all people have been created by God, and he used the poet's line to help persuade his audience of the folly of idolatry. How could we, as God's offspring, have been created by idols of gold or stone? Why would the superior worship the inferior?

Not only did Paul strive to find points of agreement with his audience, but he displayed respect, humility and tact as he spoke. It was not a condescending sermon. Notice how he identified with his listeners as he used the editorial, "We" instead of "You" in his sentence, "We ought not to think that the Divine Nature is like gold or silver" (17:29).

Paul did not, however, compromise the gospel or make it more appealing in hopes of gaining more converts. He proclaimed Jesus' resurrection, the necessity of repentance and the coming day of judgment (17:30-31). Recognizing the mixed reactions of his audience, Paul did not press for immediate decisions or even share what could be considered a complete gospel. Rather, he gave them just enough information to motivate those whose hearts were receptive to question him later, which they did, and some ultimately believed.

According to what Paul said, God expects all people to seek Him and find Him, because He has revealed Himself to everyone (17:27). If any person, anywhere on the face of the earth sincerely seeks to know God, God will see to it that the person finds Him. Jesus promised, "Seek, and you will find" (Matt. 7:7).

Day 57, Acts 18:1-17

Corinth was the capital of the region of Achaia, today part of southern Greece. It was a strategic location, a commercial center through which people from many places in the ancient world passed. Once Jesus' church was established there, the gospel would spread to many other places.

By the time Paul brought the gospel to Corinth, 20 years had passed since the church was born in Jerusalem. After two decades, the New Testament consisted of only two letters, namely James and Galatians, and both were intended to have a limited circulation. It was from Corinth, however, that Paul wrote his two letters to the believers in Thessalonica, bringing the number of New Testament books to four. Again, however, those two letters were written for Christians in just one region.

These facts help us put the epistles in a proper perspective. Obviously, they were not the centerpiece of the early Christian Church. Nor were they dissected and debated so that they divided the early church. Rather, the early believers were simply focused on following Jesus by obeying His commandments.

Corinth had a reputation as being one of the most licentious cities in the ancient world, a seaman's paradise. As many as 1,000 temple prostitutes worked as an integral part of the Corinthian religious experience at the temple of Aphrodite, goddess of love. It was paganism at its worst, but the Lord knew there were hearts that would open to the gospel. So He sent Paul.

Before Paul ever arrived, however, God had already been working on hearts, and some had opened. We read today of a Gentile named Titius Justus who lived right next door to the synagogue in Corinth and whom Luke calls "a worshiper of God" (18:7). It would seem probable that Titius' living next to the synagogue was indicative of his spiritual hunger. He was a Gentile who had responded to his conscience, and he was drawn to the truth he found in Judaism. He is the second Gentile in the book of Acts whom Luke refers to as a "worshiper of God" (see 16:14). Moreover, on four other occasions, Luke refers to certain Gentiles as "God-fearing" (10:22; 13:43; 17:4, 17).

Keep in mind that fear of God is a prerequisite to salvation, as Scripture says that "the fear of God is the beginning of wisdom" (Prov. 9:10). People who truly fear God are open to the gospel, and people who don't fear God are not, because they don't see themselves in need of being saved from God's wrath.

God, of course, knows who does and doesn't fear Him. He does not want His servants to waste their time on hardened hearts that have no fear of God. Rather, He will direct them to invest their time reaching out to those who are open. The Lord said to Paul when he was in Corinth, "Go on speaking and do not be silent... for I have many people in this city" (18:9-10). So Paul settled there for 18 months, reaching people whom God foreknew would turn to Him.

I'm sure Paul was relieved to know in advance, by the Lord's promise, that he would not be attacked or harmed while he remained in Corinth (18:10). Remember that not long before, he had been beaten with rods and imprisoned in Philipi (16:22-24), and had run for his life both in Thessalonica (17:10) and Berea (17:14). He had perfect peace, however, when he was brought before the judgment seat of Gallio, proconsul of Achaia.

Ancient writers such as the famous Seneca tell of Gallio's easy-going and careless personality. Too bad for him! He missed the chance of the lifetime to hear the gospel through the lips of Paul. Incidentally, an inscription found at Delphi, Greece dates Gallio's proconsulship from 51 to 52 A.D. So we easily date Acts 18 and the writing of 1 and 2 Thessalonians.

Take note that Paul was the original "tent-making missionary," a modern phrase that refers to missionaries who live, not from offerings, but from their own labor. All true disciples, however, who earn their living by their labor are tent-making missionaries. They see their jobs as the means to support their ministries. We're all called!

Day 58, 1 Thessalonians 1

As I previously pointed out, Paul penned his letters to the Thessalonian believers while he was settled in Corinth for 18 months. He had established a church in Thessalonica some months before, but because of Jewish persecution (17:1-10), he didn't stay as long as he would have liked. So he wrote to encourage a young and persecuted church that consisted mostly of formerly-pagan Gentiles along with a spattering of Jews.

What is a Christian? Most fundamentally, it is someone who, as Paul wrote, is "in God the Father and the Lord Jesus Christ" (1:1). This is exactly what Jesus taught His disciples, saying, "I am in My Father, and you in Me, and I in you" (John 14:20). Obviously, we are in Christ in a spiritual, not a physical, sense. How so?

Being creatures who are spirit, soul and body (1 Thes. 5:23), having had our spirits reborn by the Spirit, and now indwelled by His Spirit, we become one spirit with God. Amazing! That, of course, is what empowers us to live in conformity to His will. Jesus said, "I am the vine, you are the branches; he who abides in Me and I in him, he bears much fruit, for apart from Me you can do nothing" (John 15:5). The Thessalonian believers, although young in Christ, were already budding with good fruit, and Paul specifically mentioned their "work of faith" (faith always goes to work) as well as their love, hope, joy and service (1:3, 6, 9).

Take note how often, just in this short chapter, the concept of discipleship surfaces. Paul wrote of the *example* that he and Silvanus and Timothy had set before the Thessalonian believers, their subsequent *imitation* of that example, and finally their *example* to "all the believers in Macedonia and in Achaia" (1:5-7). The goal is to become like Christ, and that is learned best, not by listening to lectures, but by observing and imitating those who are like Him. Paul and his traveling companions did not just preach sermons to those who would listen in Thessalonica. They lived in close fellowship with them so their lifestyles could be observed.

Contrast that with the modern idea that pastors should remain a "professional distance" from their congregational members in order to "maintain respect" and "effectively influence them." Most parishioners have no idea how their pastor lives. They only see him behind the pulpit once a week, and perhaps share a few sentences with him as they shake his hand on the way out of the sanctuary. For true discipleship to occur, that must change, which is one reason the early churches consisted of small groups that met in homes, and discipleship was everyone's responsibility, not just the pastor's.

One final thought: Paul stated that the Thessalonians were "God's choice" (1:4). Does this prove that they were "unconditionally elected" before time began to be saved? No, nothing is said about an "unconditional choice," which is actually an oxymoron, since all choices are based on conditions. If God has "unconditionally elected" some to be saved, then there is no reason why He chose those whom He did, and people's salvation was determined purely by chance. Moreover, they aren't saved so much by grace as they are saved by luck!

The truth is, the Thessalonian Christians were *conditionally* chosen by God, as are all Christians, based on their faith which God foreknew (see 1 Pet. 1:1-2). However, Paul was not even talking in this chapter about any *individuals* being chosen by God, because what proved the Thessalonians were chosen by God, according to Paul, was the fact that his gospel came to them "in power and in the Holy Spirit and with full conviction" (1:5). That is, it was supernaturally confirmed as being true by God Himself.

The Thessalonian Gentiles could be sure God had chosen *even them* for salvation, and not just Jews, because God confirmed His gospel to them. If Paul meant in 1:4 that God had unconditionally pre-selected only *certain* Thessalonians to be saved, we would have to wonder how God's supernatural confirmation that was performed in front of *all* the Thessalonians added credence to that fact.

Day 59, 1 Thessalonians 2

You may recall from what we've previously read in Acts and Galatians that Paul did not begin his apostolic ministry the day he was born again. He did, however, begin to preach the gospel, first in the synagogues of Damascus, then in Jerusalem, and later in Syria and Cilicia (Acts 9:20-30, 11:25-26; Gal 1:21). It wasn't until at least 12 years after his conversion that he was called as an apostle and departed on his first missionary journey. The office of apostle is the highest office to which one can be called (see 1 Cor. 12:28). All of this is to say that Paul was promoted as he was found faithful.

Paul wrote in our reading today that he, Timothy and Silvanus had been "approved by God to be entrusted with the gospel" and that God had "examined" their hearts (2:4). In the original Greek, the words *approved* and *examined* are the same words and could well be translated "tested." In other words, Paul was saying that God had tested him, along with Timothy and Silvanus, before He entrusted them with their current ministry.

More specifically, Paul indicates that God had tested their motives, because the Lord wants ministers who are motivated by love—for Him and humanity. It is likely that Paul's antagonists in Thessalonica were accusing him and his apostolic band of being motivated by something else, and so it seems Paul was intent on proving the purity of their motives. It was obvious to any who closely observed them in Thessalonica that they weren't preaching to gain money, because they supported themselves with their own hands (2:9). It was also obvious that they weren't preaching to gain glory from people, as they came to Thessalonica running from those who hated them, and they found more of the same when they arrived. Nor could anyone rightly accuse them of any other evil motivation, as they behaved "devoutly and uprightly and blamelessly" (2:10).

Clearly, Paul and his companions were motivated by love, as they treated the new believers in Thessalonica with gentle care, like "a nursing mother tenderly cares for her own children" (2:7), and "were exhorting and imploring each one...as a father would his own children" (2:11). That sounds like love expressed in genuine discipleship!

And just in case any of the Thessalonian believers might be tempted to think Paul and his companions' affections were just a temporary act, Paul reminded them that they were not absent by choice, but by circumstances beyond their control, and they were longing to be reunited. In fact, Paul had attempted to return more than once to Thessalonica, but was thwarted by Satan (2:18). To him, the Thessalonian believers were his "hope...joy...crown of exaltation" and "glory" (2:19-20). This is definitely the "love chapter" of 1 Thessalonians. How blessed are young believers who are under the loving care of those who understand that the word *minister* means "servant" and not "sovereign."

Paul also mentions that the Thessalonians were suffering at the hands of their countrymen just as he and his apostolic companions had suffered at the hands of the Jews in Judea. This was par for the course and was not reason to doubt. Years later, Paul would write, "Indeed, all who desire to live godly in Christ Jesus will be persecuted" (2 Tim. 3:12).

Finally, Paul declared that wrath had come upon the Jews in Judea "to the utmost" (2:16). We don't know exactly how that wrath fell. We do know, however, that about nineteen years later, Jerusalem would be besieged by Titus and the Roman Legions, and as many as one million Jews would perish in the holocaust. Jesus had forewarned of that day, saying, "But when you see Jerusalem surrounded by armies, then recognize that her desolation is near. Then those who are in Judea must flee to the mountains, and those who are in the midst of the city must leave, and those who are in the country must not enter the city; because these are days of vengeance, so that all things which are written will be fulfilled" (Luke 21:20-22). Because of that warning, no Christians perished then. Praise God!

Day 60, 1 Thessalonians 3

I'm reminded again how helpful it is to read the epistles within the chronological context of the book of Acts. In today's chapter, Paul recounts a time period that we just read about in Acts a few days ago.

Remember that Paul and Silas may have spent no more than a month in Thessalonica before they were run out of town by jealous Jews (17:1-10). So naturally they were concerned about the young believers whom they had left behind after their premature departure. Paul had attempted to return to Thessalonica several times, but was "thwarted" by Satan (2:18). Worried that the young believers may have abandoned their faith under the fires of persecution, Paul eventually sent Timothy from Athens to Thessalonica, an event not recorded in the book of Acts. His hope was that Timothy would find believers who were holding fast, and a church not needing to be salvaged, but only strengthened and encouraged.

To Paul's great relief, Timothy returned to Athens with a good report. The young Christians in Thessalonica were holding firm in their trials, and their faith was evident by their love.

Paul obviously believed what Jesus plainly taught, that those who initially receive the gospel with joy may end up falling away when they face the "affliction and persecution [that] arises because of the word" (see Matt. 13:5-6, 20-21). Paul was concerned that his labor in Thessalonica may have been "in vain" (3:5). Clearly, he would not make such a statement if he believed in the modern doctrine of "unconditional eternal security," often referred to as "once saved always saved." There is no way that Paul's work could have been in vain if people in Thessalonica ultimately escaped hell because of his preaching. If, however, it is possible for believers to stop believing, and if continuing in faith is a requirement to gain entrance into heaven, then the possibility existed that all of Paul's labor could be for nothing.

Paul would later promise the Christians at Colossae that Jesus would present them before God "holy and blameless and beyond reproach," but only *if* they would "*continue* in the faith firmly established and steadfast, and *not moved away from the hope of the gospel*" (Col. 1:23, emphasis added). Obviously, if people are saved through faith, then those who don't have faith are not saved, even if they possessed it previously. This is why Paul wrote to the Thessalonian believers, "For now we really live, *if* you stand firm in the Lord" (3:8, emphasis added). Paul would not have made such a statement had he believed there were no adverse consequences for those who did not stand firm in the Lord.

I remember once hearing one of America's most famous preachers quote Jesus' promise, "He who has believed and has been baptized shall be saved" (Mark 16:16). Based on that promise he declared that, if one believed for any moment of time, that person was saved and eternally secure, even if he never believed again. His conclusion was based on the fact that "Jesus said, 'He who *has* believed' (past tense)." I wondered why he didn't keep reading Jesus' very next words in Mark 16:16: "But he who has disbelieved shall be condemned," and apply the same logic. If he had, he would have had to conclude that if anyone disbelieved for any moment of time, that person was condemned and eternally damned, even if he never disbelieved again.

Paul's prayer for the Thessalonians at the end of today's reading reveals what truly is the most important thing: "May the Lord cause you to increase and abound in love for one another, and for all people...so that He may establish your hearts without blame in holiness before our God and Father at the coming of our Lord Jesus" (3:12-13). Loving others—by the ability that God gives—is the preeminent thing. That is the essence of true holiness. It will be the only thing any of us are concerned about when Jesus returns.

Incidentally, Paul's "night and day" prayers to be reunited with the Thessalonians—for their spiritual benefit—were answered, as he was able to return to Thessalonica during his third missionary journey.

Day 61, 1 Thessalonians 4

Two decades after Jesus commissioned His disciples to make disciples, teaching them to obey all that He commanded, Paul was not developing "Pauline theology" that could be scrutinized in seminaries. Rather, he was making disciples, teaching them to obey all of Jesus' commandments. During his few weeks in Thessalonica, Paul instructed the believers how "to walk and please God," teaching them "commandments...by the authority of the Lord Jesus" (4:1-2). Those words are nothing less than a reference to Jesus' Great Commission, which the Head of the Church has never rescinded. As Paul wrote, the will of God is our *sanctification*, that is, our ever-increasing holiness. To be sanctified means to be set apart for holy use. It is for that reason that God gives His children the *Holy* Spirit (4:8).

In today's reading, Paul first turns his attention to one area of holiness that was apparently needful for the Gentile Thessalonians, namely, sexual purity. Focusing on the sin of adultery, he specifically addresses men, warning that God is the avenger against one who "defrauds his brother in the matter" (4:6). The adulterer steals what belongs to another. Take note that Paul was teaching the commandments of Christ, who, as you know, warned that adultery, either in flesh or mind, is a damning sin (see Matt. 5:27-30).

Technically, the man who commits fornication (having a sexual relationship as an unmarried person), is also potentially "defrauding his brother in the matter" by virtue that he is having sex with someone else's future wife. God wants His people to be sexually pure in every regard, and Paul warns in his letters that immoral people will not inherit God's kingdom (1 Cor. 6:9-10; Gal. 5:19-21; Eph. 5:5).

Next, Paul turns his attention to "love of the brethren," something that God Himself teaches all true believers by the indwelling Spirit (4:9), but not something that happens without their cooperation (4:10). That love is expressed, of course, by meeting pressing needs, but it is also expressed by working hard so as not to burden others with our pressing needs (4:11-12)! This was apparently something that was also needful for Paul to say to the Thessalonians, as we'll read in his second letter to them, "If anyone will not work, neither let him eat" (2 Thes. 3:10). Generous Christians should be careful not to foster laziness.

Apparently, since Paul's departure from Thessalonica, some believers had died, and the surviving Christians, many of whom were previously ignorant pagans, were grieving without hope. Paul explains basic Christian doctrine regarding life after death and the return of Jesus. Those who have died in Christ are better spoken of as having "fallen asleep" (4:13-14) because their physical bodies will awaken at the return of Jesus, being resurrected then.

This does not mean, however, that those who have died in Christ are in a state of unconsciousness or suspended animation. Their spirits are very much alive and with Christ. In fact, when He returns, they will return with Him (4:14). At that same time, their bodies will be resurrected from the earth and will rise to "the clouds to meet the Lord in the air" (4:17). Their resurrected bodies will then be rejoined with their spirits.

Those who are alive when Jesus returns will rise to meet Him in the clouds, and they will also receive new, imperishable bodies. Paul obviously believed that he, as well as the Thessalonians, could be alive for that event. He would later write to the Corinthians:

> We shall not all sleep, but we shall all be changed, in a moment, in the twinkling of an eye, at the last trumpet; for the trumpet will sound, and the dead will be raised imperishable, and we shall be changed. For this perishable must put on the imperishable, and this mortal must put on immortality (1 Cor. 15:51-53).

As Christians, we naturally grieve when a brother or sister in Christ dies. But we don't grieve for them; we grieve for ourselves. Moreover, we don't grieve as the world does, that is, without hope. Rather, we know that our absence from those who have fallen asleep in Christ is only temporary (4:18). Comforting truths indeed!

Day 62, 1 Thessalonians 5

In today's chapter, Paul writes of "the day of the Lord," a phrase that is found four other times in the New Testament and fourteen times in the Old. It always refers to a final day, one of cataclysmic wrath and terrible judgment, when God will punish the world for its evil (see Zeph. 1:14-18; 2 Pet. 3:10). On that day, Scripture repeatedly tells us that the sun and moon will turn dark and stars will fall from the sky (see Is. 13:6-11; Joel 2:1-11, 31; 3:14-16; Acts 2:20; Rev. 6:12-17). That is the day Jesus will return, as He told His disciples during His Olivet Discourse:

> But immediately after the tribulation of those days the sun will be darkened, and the moon will not give its light, and the stars will fall from the sky.... And then the sign of the Son of Man will appear in the sky, and then all the tribes of the earth will mourn, and they will see the Son of Man coming on the clouds of the sky with power and great glory. And He will send forth His angels with a great trumpet and they will gather together His elect from the four winds, from one end of the sky to the other (Matt. 24:29-31).

As you will recall when we originally read the Olivet Discourse, Jesus left His disciples with the clear impression that they could be alive to see that monumental day. They, however, would not suffer God's wrath, but could expect to be gathered in the sky (as we just read).

Although it is popular today to believe that Jesus will return twice, first to rapture believers, and then, seven years later, to pour His wrath out on the earth, it isn't easy to find support for such a view in Scripture. Keep in mind that there were no chapter divisions in Paul's original letter to the Thessalonians. At the end of chapter four and the beginning of chapter five, Paul was clearly writing of Jesus' return, the resurrection of deceased believers, the rapture of the saints who are alive at His coming, and God's great judgment on the world (4:14 - 5:3), referring to that time as "the day of the Lord"(5:2). It is so obvious only a theologian could miss it! Jesus is not returning twice in the course of seven years! Just as He taught and Paul affirmed, He's coming back once.

From the Olivet Discourse, Paul borrowed Jesus' "thief in the night" analogy (Matt. 24:32-44). Paul similarly assured his readers that Jesus' coming would be a surprise only to those in darkness. Destruction "will come upon *them*" (5:3), but "God has not destined us for wrath" (5:9). This is not to say, however, that Christ's followers are not destined for persecution, which, according to Jesus, will grow quite severe just prior to His return.

Note that the Thessalonian church, although just a few months old, had leaders who were in charge and gave instruction (5:12-13). Obviously, none possessed years of seminary or Bible College training. I suspect they were born-again Jews who naturally would have had more biblical knowledge than Gentile believers. In any case, the biblical role of a pastor/overseer/elder is not nearly as complex as it has become in the modern church. In the New Testament, such men were responsible for discipling a few people who could all fit into one house, and obedience to Christ's commandments was the simple goal. Note, also, that the burden of discipling was not solely the leaders'. Rather, it was everyone's responsibility to "admonish the unruly, encourage the fainthearted, [and] help the weak" (5:14).

How easy it is to "despise prophetic utterances" (5:20) when so many modern prophecies are products of the flesh rather than the Spirit. Nevertheless, we would do well to "examine everything carefully" and then "hold fast to that which is good" (5:21). I would encourage suspicion of any prophecy that doesn't sound like Scripture, that caters to selfishness, or that leads one segment of Christ's followers to think they are special.

What should be the church's goal? Everyone's entire sanctification through God's help, so we're all ready for Jesus' return (5:23).

Day 63, 2 Thessalonians 1

It is assumed that Paul's second letter to the Thessalonians was also written when he was settled in Corinth for 18 months. Paul elaborates on some of the same issues as he did in his first letter, so this second letter may well have followed the first by just a few months.

Persecution had not abated in Thessalonica (1:4). Interestingly, Paul wrote that the "persecutions and afflictions" the believers were enduring were "a plain indication of God's righteous judgment" (1:5). He was not saying that the persecution itself was a manifestation of God's righteous judgment. Rather, the current persecution against God's people vindicated His righteous and ultimate plan to punish persecutors and reward the persecuted. Such a plan is "only just" according to Paul (1:6), and those who scoff at the idea of future punishment and reward need to think again. A God who delays judgment upon sinners and pardons those who repent is merciful. A God who does not, however, ultimately punish unrepentant evildoers or reward the righteous is unjust. To claim that there is no such thing as ultimate future punishment and reward is to accuse God of injustice.

In light of these simple truths, it is astounding that so many professing Christians think that they can continue sinning with impunity once they have prayed a prayer to accept Jesus, and that holiness is unimportant since they are allegedly "covered in the blood of Jesus." The New Testament solemnly warns against such "conversions":

> For if we go on sinning willfully after receiving the knowledge of the truth, there no longer remains a sacrifice for sins, but a certain terrifying expectation of judgment, and the fury of a fire which will consume the adversaries (Heb. 10:26-27).

In this same regard, notice that Paul wrote that the gospel was not just something to *believe*, but something to *obey* (1:8). It is the gospel of "our *Lord* Jesus" (1:8), and we must not overlook that word, *Lord*. The gospel calls everyone to turn from sin and bow their knee to the King of kings and Lord of lords.

It is those who patiently endure their persecutions who prove themselves "worthy of the kingdom of God" (1:5). If our faith does not cost us something, it is worthless.

The idea that everyone ultimately will be saved, even those who are cast into hell (known as *Universalism)*, is debunked by Paul's warning in 1:9: "And these will pay the penalty of eternal destruction, away from the presence of the Lord and from the glory of His power." The destruction of the wicked is *eternal*. Incidentally, Paul's words, "eternal destruction," have been interpreted in at least two ways. Some see a never-ending cycle of destruction and reconstruction that will be suffered by the unrepentant in hell. Others, who consider eternal conscious punishment to be unjust, see a one-time annihilation of the wicked—with no hope of resurrection. Thus, it is a destruction that is eternal. Personally, I would prefer to believe that second interpretation of the phrase "eternal destruction," but there are some scriptures that stand in my way.

Did Paul believe that Jesus would return twice, first to rapture His church, and then, seven years later, return once again to pour out His wrath on the world? If the answer to that question has not been clear before, it is today. Paul wrote that Jesus would "give relief" to the afflicted Thessalonian believers *when* He would be "revealed from heaven with His mighty angels in flaming fire, dealing out retribution to those who do not know God" (1:7-8). This, of course, harmonizes perfectly with what Jesus taught in His Olivet Discourse. Jesus will rapture His surviving remnant when He returns to pour out His wrath on "the day of the Lord" (see Matt. 24:29-31). This means that there will be a generation of believers who will face the persecution of the antichrist, as foretold by the prophets Daniel (see Dan. 7:21-25) and John (see Rev. 13:7).

Still not convinced? Wait until tomorrow's reading!

Day 64, 2 Thessalonians 2

If you've always heard that believers will be raptured well before the antichrist is revealed, you now know that what you've always heard has been wrong. Just as we learned in 1 Thessalonians 4-5 and in Matthew 24:29-31, today's reading again affirms that the rapture of the church will occur during "the day of the Lord" (2:1-2). Moreover, Paul explicitly states that Jesus will not come, and we will not be "gathered together to Him," until the "apostasy" takes place and the antichrist is revealed (2:3-4). It couldn't be more clear.

What is the "apostasy" of which Paul wrote? To apostatize is to renounce one's belief. Remember that Jesus foretold of an apostasy prior to His return:

> Then they will deliver you to tribulation, and will kill you, and you will be hated by all nations on account of My name. And at that time many will fall away and will deliver up one another and hate one another (Matt. 24:9-10).

Under intense global persecution and the threat of death, many professing Christians will apostatize. Worse, those who do apostatize will betray those who don't. Apostates will be handing over church membership directories to the authorities. Sheep who attended goat churches will surely regret it then!

Paul wrote that the antichrist would take "his seat in the temple of God, displaying Himself as being God" (2:4). When Paul penned those words, the temple in Jerusalem was still standing. It was destroyed in 70 A.D. by the Romans, however, and has never been rebuilt. Yet, because many Jews in modern Israel hope to see the temple rebuilt, and because of what Paul wrote about the antichrist taking his seat in the temple of God, many Christians believe that the Jerusalem temple will be rebuilt.

Others, however, take a more figurative interpretation of Paul's words, thinking that the temple of which Paul wrote is the church, as he did in other places (see 1 Cor. 3:16-17; 2 Cor. 6:16). They maintain that the antichrist will "take his seat in the temple of God" by becoming a central figure in the apostate church, and that he will lead the global persecution against true believers, and thus we should not anticipate the rebuilding of the temple in Jerusalem. However, if the temple of which Paul wrote in 2:4 is the *true* church and the antichrist is a central figure in the *apostate* church, it can hardly be said that he "takes his seat in the temple of God" (2:4). So I still think the temple will be rebuilt in Jerusalem.

There are other debates as well. Some say that the "restrainer" of 2:6-7—who restrains the antichrist "so that in his time he may be revealed"—is also the church, interpreting 2:7b to say, "The church that now restrains the antichrist from being revealed will continue to restrain the antichrist until the church is taken away at the rapture." That interpretation, however, flatly contradicts Paul's previous words about the rapture not occurring until after the antichrist is revealed (2:1-3). Also, I wonder how the church has restrained the antichrist for 2,000 years, especially since the antichrist obviously was not even alive for at least 1,950 of those years!

All of that being so, I think the one who restrains the antichrist must be God, and I suspect that the first "he" of 2:7 refers to Him, and the second "he" of 2:7 refers to the antichrist, whom God will "take out of the way" when Jesus returns, just as Paul describes in the very next verse (see 2:8).

The antichrist will be empowered by Satan to perform signs and false wonders, but he will not be outside the control of God. In fact, Paul tells us that the antichrist will help to fulfill God's plan to delude those who have already rejected the truth (2:11). Note that they are not people whom God sovereignly willed from eternity past to be deceived. Rather, they are people whom God gave opportunity to be saved yet who "did not believe the truth, but took pleasure in wickedness" (2:12). God has, however, "chosen...from the beginning" to save those who would have "faith in the truth" (2:13).

Day 65, 2 Thessalonians 3

If you've ever wondered what is a good way to pray for evangelists, apostles, and missionaries, today's reading offers some insight. Paul requested prayer "that the word of the Lord may spread rapidly and be glorified...and that we may be delivered from perverse and evil men" (3:1-2). Similarly, from a prison cell in Rome, Paul would later write, "For I know that this will turn out for my deliverance through your prayers and the provision of the Spirit of Jesus Christ" (Phil. 1:19). Paul believed that the prayers of God's people could make a difference in his circumstances.

Although he certainly had his share of persecution, prison time, and death plots, the Lord faithfully delivered Paul every time—at least until his martyrdom. Near the end of his life he would write to Timothy:

> But you followed my...perseverance, persecutions, and sufferings, such as happened to me at Antioch, at Iconium and at Lystra; what persecutions I endured, and out of them all the Lord delivered me! (2 Tim. 3:10-11).

In a sense, even martyrdom is not a failure on God's part to provide deliverance. It is the *ultimate* deliverance, as Paul would confess in that same letter to Timothy:

> The Lord will deliver me from every evil deed, and will bring me safely to His heavenly kingdom; to Him be the glory forever and ever (2 Tim. 4:18).

The worst thing anyone can do to us is send us to heaven sooner than we expected! So never forget that if God wants you alive, no person can kill you. And if He wants you dead, no person can keep you alive. We're in His hands!

Apparently, a problem that Paul addressed in his first letter still persisted among the Thessalonian believers. Some in the church were sponging off of others, a phenomenon that soon surfaces whenever charity is available. To love our neighbors as ourselves certainly includes meeting the pressing needs of fellow believers; in fact, our very salvation is authenticated by such acts of mercy (see Matt 25:31-46). On the other hand, to love our neighbors as ourselves also includes not being a burden to others, expecting them to meet our needs from their labor. Laziness and sponging off of others is a sign of selfishness. Thus, "If anyone will not work, neither let him eat" (3:10)

For this reason, we must be careful that our kindness doesn't enable laziness or empower irresponsibility. Rather, we should focus on meeting the needs of those who cannot provide for themselves, such as widows and orphans.

I am not, however, speaking of wealthy widows or well-off orphans in Western nations, but of those in poorer places who have no one to care for them. Yet even compassion for poor widows can result in fostering laziness in widows who can work or serve. Paul would later write guidelines for charity towards widows that clearly addressed that very issue. No widow who "gives herself to wanton pleasure" should be supported by the church (1 Tim. 5:6). Only those widows who "continue in entreaties and prayers night and day" and who are "devoted...to every good work" are worthy of assistance (1 Tim. 5:5, 10).

Finally, notice how often the principle of discipleship is subtly mentioned today. Paul and his companions had set a good example before the Thessalonians of leading disciplined lives, working hard to provide for their own needs so as not to be a burden to anyone (3:7-9). Paul's life was his greatest sermon.

One final thought: Pastors who must work "secular" jobs to support themselves because they serve small flocks are often looked upon as lesser pastors, but as we have just read, they have a biblical precedent. Similarly, Paul told the pastors/elders in Ephesus, "You yourselves know that these hands ministered to my own needs and to the men who were with me. In everything I showed you that by working hard in this manner you must help the weak and remember the words of the Lord Jesus, that He Himself said, 'It is more blessed to give than to receive'" (Acts 20:34-35). God

Day 66, Mark 1

Our unique reading plan is designed so that we journey through the New Testament chronologically, with the exception that we are reading one of the four Gospels every quarter. Hopefully, it has been helpful to know that after two decades of the church's existence, the New Testament consisted of only four epistles—James, Galatians, and 1 & 2 Thessalonians, the latter three being written for a limited readership. So it was not the epistles that were the central focus of teaching within the early church, but the teachings of Christ, orally passed along. The goal was to make disciples who obeyed all of His commandments.

Moreover, according to early church historian Eusebius, the Gospel of Matthew may well have been penned and begun its circulation among the churches as early as A.D. 42, about 12 years after Pentecost. Ultimately, of course, there were *four* Gospels. If each Gospel author was inspired to write his Gospel—and I believe each was—then that says something about what God feels is most important. And the redundancy of Matthew and Mark should serve to remind us of that fact. Taking a cue from God, I might be a little redundant myself as we work our way through Mark's Gospel, the shortest of the four!

There was revival down at the Jordan River, but it wasn't characterized by people acting drunk and testifying of strange visions, nor was it led by a slick evangelist in a silk suit telling stories and taking up offerings. Rather, it was characterized by the tears of people who were confessing their sins, and it was led by a man who was the epitome of simplicity, who wore rough clothing and ate locusts and honey. (I suspect he roasted the locusts and dipped them in honey sauce to make them go down a little easier!)

Take note that John was "preaching a baptism of repentance for the forgiveness of sins" (1:4). That was God's offer, and that has always been God's offer. *God forgives those who repent.* That is why Jesus proclaimed, "Repent and believe in the gospel" (1:15). That is why Jesus told His disciples after His resurrection that "repentance for forgiveness of sins would be proclaimed...to all the nations" (Luke 24:47).

God forgives those who repent. Those five words sum up the true gospel and the true grace of God. God isn't offering grace for people to continue sinning. He has never offered that kind of grace. He isn't offering forgiveness for those who simply "accept Jesus," or who "invite Jesus into their hearts," or who tell God they are sorry for their sins. He forgives those who turn away from sinning. The call to holiness is part and parcel of the gospel, yet it has been all but lost from the modern American gospel.

How I would have loved to sit outside Peter's home in Capernaum with a video camera the evening that "the whole city had gathered at the door" as Jesus healed the sick and cast out demons (1:33)! To see the miracles and the expressions on people's faces would be pure ecstasy! And we could have made a movie and shown it to everyone in the world! So why didn't Jesus wait to come to earth until after the invention of the video camera? Perhaps it was because He had something even better in mind— namely continued healing miracles and deliverances through His servants, just as we have read about in the book of Acts. Again our hearts cry today, *Lord, restore Your power to Your true church! May true miracles be wrought through your true servants so that Your name is magnified!*

After Jesus cleansed the leper whom we read about today, He told him to show himself to the priest as a testimony to them (1:44). I suspect the priest to whom he showed himself had to search through his scrolls to find out what to do, as this was most likely the first time any Israelite leper had been healed since the Law was given. The tradition of elders, held by the rabbis, stated that if any such miracle ever occurred, it would reveal the Messiah. Yet they still rejected Jesus.

Day 67, Mark 2

Let us imagine what must have occurred as we consider Mark's short rendition of the story of the paralytic in Capernaum.

First, the paralyzed man's four friends must have discussed among themselves what to do when they heard that Jesus was back in town. Somebody came up with the idea to take him to Jesus, and it may well have been the paralyzed man himself. If not, he certainly had to at least agree with the plan of his four friends. So they picked him up on a pallet and headed towards the house where Jesus was teaching. All five had faith.

When they arrived, however, every door and window was blocked with people. I wonder why they didn't just wait for Jesus to exit at the conclusion of the meeting. Perhaps they were afraid that Jesus, who was definitely in an elusive mode, might elude them! I also wonder why they didn't attempt to persuade people to move out from the doorway to let them through. Perhaps they did, but no one was willing to give up his spot. If so, it may have just fueled their determination. I suspect that one of the four was the owner of the house, since only he would have had the right to destroy the roof of the house.

So they carried their paralyzed friend up on the roof—which would have been flat—probably by means of an outside stairway. The exterior roof of the house would have been the same as the interior ceiling, constructed of hardened clay and supported by timber rafters. Thus, Mark wrote that the four men had to "dig" an opening (2:4).

Digging an opening was not something that would have gone unnoticed inside. There would have been pounding and digging sounds reverberating through the house and pieces of clay falling from the ceiling. Dust would have begun to fill the air. Eventually the men would have broken through, and a shaft of light would have pierced the room. And how long might it have taken them to dig an opening large enough to accommodate a full-grown man lying horizontally?

I can't imagine that some folks on the inside didn't vocalize their disapproval, particularly as the interior atmosphere filled with dust. And since the opening that the four men dug was directly over Jesus, I can't help but wonder if Jesus was able to continue His sermon in light of the distraction above Him. There is no record, of course, of Him shouting up through the ever-widening whole, "Hey, can't you see you are disrupting our meeting and filling our lungs with dust?" Personally, I just imagine Him stepping back, folding His arms, and leaning up against a wall with a big smile on His face, as He enjoyed observing faith in action.

Eventually, there was a large opening in the ceiling above Him, and four faith-filled faces were peering over the edges. They were right on target! After more commotion on the roof, the opening suddenly darkened, and slowly, by means of four ropes, a paralyzed man on a pallet was lowered into the room—not an easy feat to accomplish without dumping the man off the pallet. One mistake, and he may have ended up even more paralyzed!

But finally, after what must have been at least a half-hour distraction, there was a man lying in front of Jesus. His faith was evident. Jesus assured him that his sins were forgiven (perfectly playing the part of God), and then told the man to get up. He could have responded, "I'd love to, but I'm paralyzed," but he acted on his faith and found that he was able to do the impossible.

Wow, what a story! What can we learn? Primarily this: *Believers aren't quitters.* So don't quit!

Mark, like Matthew, also highlights the scribes' and Pharisees' growing animosity towards Jesus, who was not the least bit enthusiastic about their traditions which had no basis in God's Word. They were like old, inflexible leather wineskins—unfit for the truth that bubbles like fermenting new wine inside those of us who believe! It makes us feel good on the inside and happy on the outside!

Day 68, Mark 3

It would seem that Jesus' healing of the man with the withered hand should be classified, not as a healing, but as a creative miracle. The man's hand was not diseased, but disfigured. Bones and flesh were created as he obeyed Jesus and stretched out his hand, perhaps what was impossible for him to do from a natural standpoint. Meditate on that and let it build your faith in Jesus!

Almost equally amazing as the restoration of that man's hand is the hardness of the hearts of the Pharisees, who, upon seeing that incredible miracle, immediately began conspiring how they might kill Jesus (3:6). The scribes, of equal hard-heartedness, declared that Jesus cast out demons by the power of Satan, an imbecilic statement to be sure, and one that Jesus exposed for its stupidity (3:22-27). It was in the context of those callous religious leaders that Jesus warned of the sin of blasphemy against the Holy Spirit, and no wonder. Anyone who could witness such miracles, done by the power of the Holy Spirit, and call it the work of Satan, has a heart beyond redemption. More specifically, as Mark points out, the scribes were saying that Jesus was possessed by an unclean spirit (3:30). That is tantamount to calling the Holy Spirit a demon.

You may have heard that there is a website called "The Blasphemy Challenge," where people can receive a free DVD that promotes atheism if they will upload a video to YouTube of themselves blaspheming the Holy Spirit. It is certainly interesting for a group that doesn't believe in God to be quoting on their website Jesus' warning in Mark 3:29 against blaspheming the Holy Spirit, and challenging people, as their website says, to "damn themselves to hell." Why waste your time recording a video of yourself blaspheming the Holy Spirit if there is no God and no hell?

It reminds me of a story I heard years ago of a young Christian girl who lived in communist Russia. Her school teacher demanded that she stand in front of her class and curse God. Her response was full of simple wisdom: "Teacher, if there is a God, then I dare not curse Him. And if there is no God, there is no reason to curse Him, as there is no one to curse."

Mark certainly conveys to us how overwhelmed Jesus was with people who wanted healing and deliverance (3:7-10, 20). At one point along the Sea of Galilee, the crowd was pressing in to such a degree that Jesus had His disciples make a boat ready. This indicates, as do other scriptures, that Jesus operated in His earthly ministry as a man anointed by the Holy Spirit with gifts of the Holy Spirit. Thus, He could not do a miracle, such as walk on water, any time He desired. Gifts of the Spirit operate as the Spirit wills (1 Cor. 12:11; Heb. 2:4). Jesus Himself testified of His limitations, saying "the Son can do nothing of Himself, unless it is something He sees the Father doing" (John 5:19). That is why He did no miracles until after He was anointed by the Holy Spirit when baptized by John. Unless the Holy Spirit imparted a gift that made walking on the water possible, Jesus was limited like any other person. He had to use a boat.

I have never understood why the demons would shout through people in Jesus' presence, "You are the Son of God!" (3:11). It would seem that they were defeating their own purpose. Mark says that the demons would fall down before Jesus at such times (3:11). It was almost as if they were compelled, in terror, to do it. Whatever their motivation, to me it is one more revelation of Jesus' greatness. In His presence, demons are compelled to fall before Him and confess who He is. How amazing it is that while demons are so compelled, God has given human beings free wills whereby they can ignore Him or even spit on Him. In this regard, we might advise human beings that they could learn something from demons! Fear God!

Day 69, Mark 4

We, of course, read Jesus' Parable of the Sower and the Soils in Matthew's Gospel three months ago. Let's consider it a little more closely today. It is not a parable about heaven-bound Christians who are more or less receptive to their pastor's sermons. It is a parable that explains why some people are saved and some are not. Describing the first soil, Jesus said, "the devil comes and takes away the word from their heart, *so that they will not believe and be saved*" (Luke 8:12).

Notice that it was not the sower who determined which seeds germinated, grew, and bore fruit. The sower simply scattered the seed. Rather, it was each soil that determined if the sower's seeds germinated, grew and bore fruit. I can almost hear a stampede of Calvinists running for the doors! Sorry my beloved Calvinist friends, I didn't write the Bible! God wants everyone to be saved (1 Tim. 2:4; 2 Pet. 3:9), which is why Jesus died for everyone (1 John 2:2) and why He told us to preach the gospel to everyone (Mark 16:15). Yet some hearts are receptive, and some aren't. That is why some are saved and others are not.

In the first scenario, some seed fell beside the road where the soil would have been hardened by foot and animal traffic. It was easy pickings for the birds. Similarly, hardened hearts make it easy for Satan to "take away the word which has been sown" (4:15).

God is grieved by people's hardness of hearts (3:5; 16:14), which would make it quite odd if He was the one who was hardening their hearts. Calvinists are quick to point out a few verses that speak of God hardening Pharaoh's heart. Indeed, as an act of righteous judgment, God may further harden the heart of someone who has already hardened his own heart to the degree of sending away his day of grace. God is not, however, in the business of hardening the hearts of people who otherwise would have been receptive. That would make God worse than Satan and worthy to be spit upon, and Calvinists will not find a scriptural example of Him ever doing such a wicked, unrighteous thing.

In the second scenario, the seed fell on rocky soil. It germinated and sprouted, but because the soil was thin, when the sun rose the soil dried up and the plant withered, having no deep roots. Jesus said this represents those who initially receive the word with joy, but who fall away when affliction or persecution arises. According to Luke's version of this parable, Jesus said that these are people who "believe for a while" (Luke 8:13). They are temporary *believers*. So these plants represent people who hear the gospel, happily believe it, experience new life (germination) and even begin to grow spiritually. Under persecution, however, they abandon their faith. Surely I've now started a stampede of "once-saved-always-saved" advocates who are running for the doors!

In the third scenario, the seed fell among the thorns. Those seeds also germinated, sprouted and began to grow, indicating that Jesus was describing new believers. Thorn bushes, however, choked the young plants. The thorns represent "the worries of the world, and the deceitfulness of riches, and the desires for other things" (4:19) which, taking priority, prevent believers from bearing fruit, which is not a good condition to be found in at harvest time. So beware of worries, riches, desires, and anything that might take priority over serving God!

The fourth soil is the only good soil, representing, according to Luke's account, "an honest and good heart" (Luke 8:15). It is the only soil that produces fruitful plants, which means it is the only soil that produces people who will ultimately be saved, since faith without works cannot save (Jas. 2:14). In spite of soothing sermons that assure us that God's grace is sufficient to overpower the warnings of God's word, Jesus *never* lies.

For this reason it is all the more important that we obey Jesus' admonition to "take care what you listen to" (4:24). Satan is extremely generous when it comes to sharing his lies. Beware!

Day 70, Mark 5

We also read about the Gerasene demoniac in Matthew's Gospel, but I didn't comment then knowing that Mark's Gospel contains the most detailed report. Matthew reported *two* demon-possessed men (Matt. 8:28), whereas Mark and Luke reported only one. Keep in mind that Matthew was an eyewitness (Mark 3:18). If Mark and Luke knew there were two demoniacs, they may have simply focused on one of them. Some folks spotlight little discrepancies like these to prove the Bible can't be trusted, but that seems quite foolish to me in light of the fact that 99% of what Matthew, Mark and Luke report harmonize perfectly. What real difference does it make if Jesus delivered one or two men that day?

Again we read of a demon who, animating himself through a man, bowed before Jesus, fearful of being tormented "before the time," according to Matthew (Matt. 8:29). Demons have no hope of salvation, and apparently anticipate with terror the day when they will be cast into the lake of fire with Satan, whom Scripture tells us will be tormented there "day and night forever and ever" (Rev. 20:10). How tragic it is that humans, who, unlike demons, have an opportunity to find forgiveness, choose instead to waltz through life, never once bowing before the only One who can save them from the lake of fire.

The legion of demons in this man made him supernaturally strong—enough to break chains. No doubt everyone in his region was terrified of him. The demon in him, however, was terrified of *Jesus*, begging not to be tormented! In light of this, what a dishonor it is to Jesus when Christians are fearful of demons. It is like elephants being afraid of mice! The truth is, demons are terrified of Christ who lives in us!

We can only speculate how this man became so possessed. I think it is safe to say, however, that he was not simply walking along one day, perfectly in his right mind, when suddenly a demon jumped inside of him and instantly turned him into a raving lunatic. Rather, it seems much more likely that the man began to entertain demonic thoughts, and he slowly became obsessed. Gradually, as he continually yielded, his condition grew worse, until his downward spiral took him beyond obsession to oppression and then possession. Satan gains entrance through people's thoughts, and thus he can be kept at bay by simply following Paul's admonition to dwell upon whatever is true, honorable, right, pure and so on (Phil. 4:8).

Apparently, at least 2,000 demons dwelled in that man, as that is how many pigs rushed into the Sea of Galilee. What a sight that would have been to see—2,000 pigs suddenly going berserk and committing suicide! It may seem rather unkind of Jesus to allow those demons to enter the pigs—unkind not only to the pigs, but also to the owners of those pigs, who lost a lot of money that day. Why didn't Jesus forbid the demons to enter the pigs, especially in light of the fact that once those pigs were possessed, they were soon dead?

Some have speculated that, because pigs were considered unclean under the old covenant and Jews were forbidden to eat pork, Jesus was sending a strong message in that regard to the pig's owners and everyone else. Personally, I don't know. I do know, however, that the Son of God, maker of all things, not only owns "the cattle on a thousand hills" (Ps. 50:10), but all the pigs as well. He can do what He wants with them. I've noticed that the frequent natural disasters in the world, obviously permitted by God, regularly result in millions of dollars of losses. The Lord gives and the Lord takes away (Job 1:21). I do hope that stunning display of God's power along the Sea of Galilee was enough to wake some sinners from their slumber! Better to lose your pigs and gain salvation than vice versa.

Although those demons had the sense to bow before Jesus, the people of the Gerasene region were not so wise, asking Jesus to leave them. He graciously complied, but left behind an evangelist with an amazing testimony.

Day 71, Mark 6

From Capernaum, Jesus walked about 25 miles to the town where He grew up and where His family still lived, Nazareth. We learn that He had at least four younger brothers and two younger sisters, and He was known in Nazareth as a carpenter (6:3). According to Luke's Gospel, during an earlier visit, Jesus had offended the people of Nazareth during His sermon, and they attempted to murder Him then (Luke 4:16-30). Quite mercifully, Jesus made this second visit some months later, perhaps hoping that the reports of His many miracles throughout Galilee would have softened the hearts of the people in His hometown. Nothing, however, had changed.

As a consequence of their unbelief, we read that Jesus "could [not *would*] do no miracle there" (6:5). Jesus' ability to do miracles in His hometown—certainly a place where He wanted to do miracles—was limited by the unbelief of the residents there. Once again we see that God's sovereignty cannot be blamed for lack of miracles. God is searching for faith.

Not being enlightened to the truths of Calvinism, Jesus "wondered at their unbelief" (6:6). Had Jesus known what so many Calvinists understand today, He would not have wondered, knowing that God sovereignly grants faith to those whom He has preselected. Their unbelief was simply a consequence of their not being sovereignly chosen by God. Too bad Jesus didn't understand that!

Obviously, I speak in jest. God has sovereignly wired human hearts to be free-willed. This is why in Scripture He so frequently bemoans people's resistance to Him, why He holds them accountable for their choices, and why He ultimately judges them for their choices, three things that would make no sense at all if the doctrines of Calvinism were actually true.

This chapter in Mark's Gospel contains additional lessons about faith. Jesus sent the twelve out in pairs to preach to the villages of Galilee, but He did not allow them to take along any provisions for their journeys (6:8-9). God would meet their needs as they obeyed

Him. I have never known the Lord to work any other way. He calls people to a task, they take steps of faith, and He then meets their needs to accomplish their God-given task. So many, however, are "waiting on God" to give them provision before they take their first step. Tragically, some wait all their lives. The truth is, God is waiting on them.

It takes faith to obey God's calling, and the first step is always the scariest! But as God proves His faithfulness, our faith grows, enabling us to trust Him for greater things.

Faith was also necessary for the apostles to heal people successfully or cast out demons. Before anyone was healed, the apostles *first* had to anoint sick people with oil, and before anyone was delivered from a demon, the apostles *first* had to command it verbally to come out (6:13).

Like the early apostles, church elders/overseers/pastors have been given a ministry of healing by means of anointing with oil and prayer, but faith is required of them:

> Is anyone among you sick? Then he must call for the elders of the church and they are to pray over him, anointing him with oil in the name of the Lord; and the prayer offered in faith will restore the one who is sick, and the Lord will raise him up (Jas. 5:14-15).

Elders/overseers/pastors who never anoint the sick with oil and pray for them are motivated by their lack of faith. Sick people who never ask the elders/overseers/pastors to anoint and pray for them are similarly motivated.

Feeding the 5,000 was an act of faith, as the crowd was arranged in groups of hundreds and fifties so that all could be efficiently served, and that was done when there were only five loaves and two fish!

Finally, did you notice that Jesus "intended to pass by" the struggling disciples as He walked across the Sea of Galilee (6:48)? What a lesson for us! Jesus will let us struggle against the wind if we fail to invite Him into our boat! I wonder how many times He's walked right by me?

Day 72, Mark 7

Mark mentions how the Pharisees observed "the traditions of the elders" (7:3, 5), one of which was the requirement to wash their hands carefully before eating, and another of which was cleansing themselves after returning from the marketplace. Those traditions were originally based on God's commandments and were designed to put a hedge around them, so that by following the "fence laws," there was no possibility of breaking God's laws.

For example, the Mosaic law declared, "You shall not boil a young goat in its mother's milk" (Ex. 34:26). This related to an occult fertility rite practiced by the Canaanites—whom the Israelites dispossessed after their deliverance from Egypt. God didn't want His people practicing pagan superstitions. The Jews, however, ignored the spirit of that particular law and created fence laws to prevent anyone from getting anywhere close to breaking the letter of it.

For example, a person might, at the same meal, drink goat's milk and eat goat meat. There was some chance—albeit a slim one—that the milk might be from the mother of the goat that was being eaten. Once mixed in the stomach and heated there, a "boiling" of sorts would occur, and one would be guilty of boiling a goat in its mother's milk! So a fence law was established to prevent such a "transgression" from ever occurring. That law forbade the eating of *any* meat and dairy product together, because you never know if some goat's meat may have mixed with some beef at the slaughter house, or if some goat's milk may have been mixed with some cow's milk at the dairy!

If one ate any meat product, he must wait a specified time for it to be fully digested before consuming any dairy product, and vice versa, lest they mix in one's stomach. And all meat and dairy products should be kept in separate kitchens, lest there be any accidental mixing of the two. Moreover, completely separate dishes must be kept for eating meat and dairy products, because there was a chance that a small particle of cheese might remain on your plate from a previous meal. If that cheese was made from goat's milk, and if you happen to eat some goat's meat on that same plate, that goat's meat might be from a goat whose mother's milk was used to make the cheese, and thus when combined in your stomach, you'd be guilty of boiling a young goat in its mother's milk! (It was because of these fence laws that I found it impossible to order a cheese pizza with pepperoni the last time I visited in Israel!)

There were at least 1,500 fence laws surrounding the single commandment that forbade working on the Sabbath. Walking across a field on the Sabbath was forbidden, because you might inadvertently cause a grain of wheat to separate from its stalk, thus making you guilty of reaping on the Sabbath. Your foot might also step on a grain that had fallen on the ground, and by stepping on it, you might cause the wheat to be separated from the chaff, making you guilty of threshing on the Sabbath. It was also possible that your garment could create a breeze that would cause the chaff to blow away, making you guilty of winnowing on the Sabbath. And if a bird saw that grain and swooped down to eat it, you would be guilty of storing grain on the Sabbath!

Eventually, all those fence laws came to be considered as binding as the Mosaic Law, and they were compiled into what is called the *Mishna*. If there was disagreement between the two, the Mishna, by its own testimony, actually superseded the Mosaic Law. This Jesus condemned, citing an example of how the scribes and Pharisees invalidated the fifth commandment, and by their tradition released people from responsibility of caring for their elderly parents. Their doctrines were "precepts of men," which proved that their hearts were far from God.

The lesson for us? Beware of man-made doctrines. And if we understand the reasons behind God's commandments, we're less likely to be misled by those who want to saddle us with heavy burdens.

Day 73, Mark 8

According to John's account of the feeding of the 5,000, Jesus first asked Philip, "Where are we to buy bread, that these may eat?" (John 6:5). John then comments on Jesus' question, saying, "This He was saying to test him; for He Himself knew what He was intending to do" (John 6:6). In our reading today, we can't help but wonder if Jesus was similarly testing all of His disciples when He expressed His concern for the hungry multitude. I wonder if He was hoping they would respond by saying, "Lord, there are a thousand fewer men here than when you multiplied food just a few days ago, and we have two more loaves of bread than we did last time! This should be an easy miracle for you!" Regrettably they said, "Where will anyone be able to find enough to satisfy these men with bread here in a desolate place?" (8:4). I imagine a big sigh from Jesus. Why do we always consider the difficulty of a situation rather than the power of God to overcome anything?

If Jesus wasn't disappointed with His disciples' lack of faith as He was about to feed the 4,000, He certainly was disappointed a short time later as they crossed the sea of Galilee. He warned them then to beware of the leaven of the Pharisees, the word *leaven* being a metaphor for "teaching" (Matt. 16:12). Rather than interpreting the word *leaven* in light of its surrounding context, however, they ignored all the context and focused only on the literal meaning of leaven. Since they had forgotten to take sufficient bread with them for their crossing, they assumed Jesus was rebuking them for that. This was a small foreshadowing of how Jesus' words would often be misunderstood for the next 2,000 years!

Jesus' exhortation in the boat was not the only time that He warned of false teachers or false teaching. And having already read James, Galatians, and 1 and 2 Thessalonians, we have some idea how frequently James and Paul made efforts to do the same. Almost all of the book of Galatians, for example, is a warning against and an expose' of false teaching. Today it is often considered uncharitable to preach a sermon that addresses false teaching. Pastors often feel pressured to "keep it positive." To warn the sheep, however, is to imitate Christ and the apostles. As we continue reading through the New Testament epistles, you may be surprised to learn how often the apostolic writers dealt with false teaching and false teachers. If we only feed the sheep but never warn them, we only fatten them for slaughter.

Compounding the apostles' misinterpretation of Jesus' warning was their lack of faith regarding God's ability to supply their needs. Seeing how Jesus had recently fed 5,000 and 4,000 men with only a few loaves and fish, it would seem unlikely for Him to be worried or upset that the twelve brought only one loaf of bread with them as they ferried across the Sea of Galilee. And here is good lesson for us all: God is never worried! If our Father isn't worried, why should we worry?

Jesus' words about the necessity of denying oneself and taking up one's cross were not a call for heaven-bound believers to make a deeper commitment, as they are often construed. They were a call to *anyone* who wanted to "come after" Jesus (8:34). Jesus went on to declare that only those who lose their lives for His sake and the gospel's sake will ultimately save their lives. All others, though they may gain the whole world, will forfeit their souls (8:35-36). These are obviously words about salvation. Thus we can safely say that only those who deny themselves, take up their crosses (an expression for accepting inevitable hardship), and lose their lives for Jesus' and the gospel's sake (give up their personal agendas and dedicate themselves to Jesus' agenda) will be saved. All others will "forfeit their souls" (8:36). Such people are, in reality, ashamed of Jesus and His words. Jesus will be ashamed of them when He returns (8:38). If only this simple truth could be understood and applied by every professing Christian!

Day 74, Mark 9

Peter, James and John, Jesus' inner-most circle, were quite privileged to see Him gloriously transfigured as He will appear in His kingdom. If they had any doubts about who He was before then, all doubts were erased, especially as they heard God say, "This is My beloved Son, listen to Him!" (9:7). They would never forget it, and decades later, a short time before his martyrdom, Peter would write:

> For we did not follow cleverly devised tales when we made known to you the power and coming of our Lord Jesus Christ, but we were eyewitnesses of His majesty. For when He received honor and glory from God the Father, such an utterance as this was made to Him by the Majestic Glory, "This is My beloved Son with whom I am well-pleased"—and we ourselves heard this utterance made from heaven when we were with Him on the holy mountain (2 Pet. 1:16-18).

Peter sealed the truthfulness of his testimony with his own blood, as he was crucified for his faith. According to church father Origen, Peter requested to be crucified upside down, considering himself unworthy to die in the same manner as his Master. Peter's faith strengthens ours, as we know that he would not have been willing to suffer martyrdom to promote a lie.

It would be difficult to imagine how Jesus could have said these words, "O unbelieving generation, how long shall I be with you? How long shall I put up with you?"(9:19) without a tone of exasperation or anger in His voice! He was upset with the lack of faith of the nine apostles who were not with Him on the Mount of Transfiguration, and who had failed to cast a demon out of a young boy. They had apparently made an attempt, commanding the demon to come out as they had done many times before (Mark 6:13), but this time were unsuccessful. According to Jesus, their faith was too little (Matt. 17:20), and prayer (perhaps accompanied with fasting) was the remedy (Matt. 17:21; Mark 9:29).

Jesus had no lack of faith, however, and even though the demon put on quite a show in His presence, He was not intimidated. When the boy's father requested His help by saying, "If you can do anything, take pity on us and help us," Jesus replied as if insulted (and I paraphrase): "'If you can?' Of course I can! All things are possible to him who believes" (9:23). Jesus believed and delivered the boy.

We might as well face up to it—Jesus is understandably insulted when we don't trust Him. So instead of becoming angry with preachers who simply state what is obvious to anyone who reads the Bible honestly, why don't we become angry at ourselves for our lack of faith? And instead of blaming God for our failures, why don't we humble ourselves and admit our part? Faith pleases God (Heb. 11:6). Doubt displeases Him. So let's trust Him! Knowing that Jesus is justifiably angered by doubt, we know it must be possible for doubters to believe.

I sat in a large church last weekend and heard the pastor tell his congregation that they can never forfeit their salvation, because their holiness has nothing to do with whether or not they would gain entrance into heaven. But today I read Jesus' words to His closest disciples:

> If your hand causes you to stumble, cut it off; it is better for you to enter life crippled, than, having your two hands, to go into hell, into the unquenchable fire, where their worm does not die, and the fire is not quenched" (9:43-44).

Jesus repeated this same statement twice more, warning about feet and eyes that might cause one to stumble. So whom shall I believe, that mega-church pastor, or Jesus? I think I'll stick with Jesus!

At least 15 different interpretations for Jesus' metaphorical words in 9:49-50 about salt (and fire) have been suggested. None really satisfy me. But I'm not going to let that bother me. As Mark Twain quipped, "It ain't the parts of the Bible that I can't understand that bother me, it is the parts that I do understand."

Day 75, Mark 10

The issues of divorce and remarriage are ones that have been hotly debated within Christian circles. As you seek for a true understanding, let me encourage you, first of all, to consider all that Scripture teaches on the subject. If our interpretation of Jesus' words that we read today, for example, makes Him contradict other scriptures, then we need to re-think our interpretation. The Bible has one author, and He is not confused!

Second, let me encourage you to use that good brain that God has given you! If every person on the planet who is divorced and remarried is regularly committing adultery, then those people are all doomed to hell, because Scripture says that no adulterer will inherit God's kingdom (1 Cor. 6:9-10). Thus there could be only two possible remedies. Those "adulterers" could get divorced, which of course is a sin Jesus condemned and one that God hates (Mal. 2:16). Or those "adulterers" could remain married, live together for the rest of their lives, love one another, hug and kiss one another, perhaps enjoy sex together to some degree (if adultery is defined as intercourse), but avoid "going all the way," thus avoiding "adultery." But does that make a bit of sense? What would be gained? Is the only thing that grieves God about divorce and remarriage the sexual intercourse in the remarriage? Or is there a greater reason why God hates divorce?

All of this is to say that it is obvious that Jesus was addressing an alleged loophole that Israel's corrupt religious leaders had found in the Mosaic Law. Their very liberal interpretation of what constituted an "indecency" in Deuteronomy 24:1-3, along with some twisting of the words found there, permitted them to divorce with impunity (in their own minds) and quickly remarry another whom they were lusting after, all while maintaining that adultery was wrong. Anyone who is honest, however, knows that the person who divorces his or her spouse *in order to marry another* is doing what is no different than adultery. But that is not the same as the person who tries to save his or her marriage but fails, whose heart is torn apart in the process, and who slowly recovers so that years later succeeds in having a happy second marriage.

It goes without saying, of course, that there is no excuse for two genuine Christians to divorce. Those who do should be reconciled or remain unmarried (see 1 Cor. 7:11). If you care to read more, I have written much more extensively on this topic at: www.heavensfamily.org/ss/pdf/dmm/dmm_13.pdf.

Isn't it wonderful that Jesus took time to bless children? God could have populated the earth instantly with adults, but He gave us children to remind us continually of innocence and purity of heart—what is needed to enter heaven. The most wicked adults in the world at one time were innocent little children! Yet the hope remains for them to recover their lost purity through Jesus if they will repent and believe! Amazing grace!

This necessity of holiness to gain heaven is underscored by Jesus' clear words to the rich, young ruler. Jesus unmistakably declared that inheriting eternal life is for those who obey the commandments, and if one is rich, that includes liberal giving to the poor (10:17-21). It is quite amazing how such clear truths are obscured by modern ministers who have no higher motive other than to keep goats coming back each week to their churches.

Jesus said, "It is easier for a camel to go through the eye of a needle than for a rich man to enter the kingdom of God" (10:25). If you earn more than $125 each month, you are among the top 25% of the world's richest people. If you earn more than $2,100 each month, you are among the top 10% of the world's richest people (see GlobalRichList.com). Thus it is easier for a camel to go through a needle's eye than for most of us to enter God's kingdom. Thankfully, it *is* possible with God, but not because He will overlook our greed, but because He can transform us into generous people who care for the poor. Obviously, that transformation requires our cooperation!

Day 76, Mark 11

It wasn't just Jesus' closest disciples who believed that He was about to set up His kingdom in Jerusalem (Luke 19:11). The crowds who lined His way from the Mount of Olives also believed it, and they gave Jesus a king's welcome. But His triumphal entry was anticlimactic. Jesus didn't overthrow the Jewish rulers or the Romans. He did, however, according to Matthew's account, overthrow the tables of the money changers. But He was soon on His way back to Bethany to lodge for the night. It must have been a major disappointment for many of Jesus' enthusiastic followers. I wonder how they would have reacted if they had been told that it would be at least 2,000 years before the messianic kingdom would begin?

The next morning, Jesus and the twelve walked back from Bethany to Jerusalem, which would have been crowded with Passover pilgrims. On the way there, Jesus cursed a fig tree, "finding nothing but leaves" (11:12). Mark informs us that "it was not the season for figs" (11:13).

Jesus wasn't expecting to find figs; nor does Mark say that He was. Rather, He "went to see if perhaps He would find *anything* on it" (11:13). Fully-formed figs would not appear on fig trees for another six weeks in Jerusalem. When fig leaves appear in late March, however, they are accompanied by small knobs known as *taqsh*, that drop off before the real figs are formed. Those taqsh are eaten by the poor and hungry. If leaves appear on a fig tree unaccompanied by taqsh, there will be no figs that year either. So Mark's report makes sense. Jesus was looking for taqsh, not figs.

Surely there was something more to this story than Jesus' anger at a fruitless fig tree! I suspect that His curse was symbolic of the divine curse that would come upon Jerusalem for its fruitlessness. Jesus later told a parable about a landowner who only wanted to receive his rightful fruit from those who tended his vineyard. The vine-growers would not give him what he was due, even killing his messengers and his son, and in the end, they were brought to an end (Mark 12:1-11). It was a foreshadowing of the doom that awaited fruitless Jerusalem, and according to Luke's account, Jesus wept as He anticipated the future holocaust of 70 A.D.:

> When He approached Jerusalem, He saw the city and wept over it, saying, "If you had known in this day, even you, the things which make for peace!.... For the days will come upon you when your enemies will throw up a barricade against you, and surround you and hem you in on every side, and they will level you to the ground and your children within you, and they will not leave in you one stone upon another, because you did not recognize the time of your visitation" (Luke 19:41-44).

Jesus summed up the message of the parable of the landowner by saying, "The kingdom of God will be taken away from you and given to a people, producing the fruit of it" (Matt. 21:43). God is looking for fruit in our lives as well (John 15:1-8).

The other message in this incident of the cursing of the fig tree is one about faith in God. Jesus said that whoever believes can move a mountain into the sea by his command. As I mentioned when we considered this same incident in Matthew's gospel, we can only have faith for what God has promised. Unless God reveals to you that it is His will for a certain mountain to be cast into the sea, your commanding it to do so would be ineffectual. (If you don't believe me, then I suggest that you try to command a dirty plate to fly from your table into your kitchen sink!) Nevertheless, there is no greater power available to us than that of faith in God. So Jesus promised, "All things for which you pray and ask, believe that you have received them, and they will be granted you" (11:24). Notice that He said, "Believe that you have received them," not, "Believe that you are going to receive them." There is a difference.

Day 77, Mark 12

Since I mentioned some of today's reading in my last commentary, I think I'll mention some of our last reading in today's commentary! Specifically, I would like to consider Jesus' words about forgiveness in Mark 11:

> Whenever you stand praying, forgive, if you have anything against anyone, so that your Father who is in heaven will also forgive you your transgressions. But if you do not forgive, neither will your Father who is in heaven forgive your transgressions (Mk. 11:25-26).

It is obviously a very serious thing not to have your transgressions forgiven by God. If He does not forgive us, then He is still holding our sins against us. If He is holding our sins against us, then we will have to be repaid for them. That should motivate us to forgive others!

What does it mean to forgive? When God forgives us, He no longer holds our sin against us. Our "debt" is erased and our relationship with Him is restored. We are reconciled. So when we forgive another person, it should also result in reconciliation. When we see that person, we should no longer be angry with them. Yet so often, folks claim they've forgiven someone who has sinned against them, but there has been no reconciliation. A little probing reveals that they are still angry with the person whom they've supposedly forgiven.

The reason for this is because they are trying to obey one of Jesus' commandments while disobeying another one of His commandments, namely, His commandment to confront those who have sinned against them. They attempt to "forgive" people whom they've not confronted and who have not admitted their sin or asked for forgiveness. True forgiveness and reconciliation only occurs after sin has been admitted and forgiveness has been requested.

For this reason, God doesn't forgive everyone, but only those who repent (Mark 1:4; Luke 3:3, 24:47; Acts 2:38). And that is why Jesus told us:

> If your brother sins, rebuke him; and if he repents,
> forgive him. And if he sins against you seven times
> a day, and returns to you seven times, saying, "I
> repent," forgive him (Luke 17:3-4).

Of course, confrontation and reconciliation is possible with fellow believers, but often not so possible with unbelievers. In those cases, we should obey Jesus' commandment to "love our enemies." It is certainly possible to love someone yet not forgive him, as God loves people yet He doesn't always forgive those whom He loves. If you care to study more, I've written more extensively on this topic at: www.heavensfamily.org/ss/pdf/dmm/dmm_24.pdf.

Mark highlights some questions posed to Jesus, first by some Pharisees and Herodians who wanted to trap Him, then by some Sadducees who were hung up on their pet doctrines, and finally by a scribe, whose heart was apparently pure. That scribe understood what many then and now have missed—that there are some commandments that are greater than others. Namely, that loving God and neighbor "is much more than all burnt offerings and sacrifices" (12:33). His understanding provoked Jesus to tell him that he wasn't "far from the kingdom of God" (12:34). Christians can easily find themselves side-tracked from what is most important, and in so doing, drift from what should be at the core. We should strive to obey all of Christ's commandments, but if we zealously obey the lesser ones while ignoring the greater ones, we can become like Pharisees who "strain out a gnat and swallow a camel" (Matt. 23:24).

It is interesting that contributions to the temple treasury could be made in full public view. It was likely designed that way by those who knew that people generally give more when they receive public praise, since so many give, motivated not by love, but by self-love. This is why Jesus told His followers to give in secret.

Jesus' comment on the size of the widow's gift is a window into the righteous judgment of God. He considers how much money we have before determining the praise-worthiness of our gifts, looking at percentages and sacrifices more than dollar amounts. "From everyone who has been given much, much will be required" (Luke 12:48). *Help us, Lord, to understand how much we have!*

Day 78, Mark 13

Jesus' foretelling of the destruction of the temple was fulfilled in 70 A.D. when the Roman Legions besieged Jerusalem. His disciples, upon hearing His prediction, naturally wanted to know when such an unthinkable demolition would occur. Jesus, however, never revealed to them that He was speaking of a time forty years away.

According to Matthew's account of Jesus' Olivet Discourse, Jesus' disciples not only asked about the future destruction of the temple, but also about the signs of His coming and the end of the age (Matt. 24:3). They may have assumed that the destruction of the temple, which He had just foretold, would occur at the end of the age. They may have been correct—if the rebuilt Jerusalem temple will also be destroyed. We read in Ezekiel 38:18-20 of a future earthquake in Israel that could certainly cause a rebuilt temple to be destroyed:

> On that day there will surely be a great earthquake in the land of Israel....and all the men who are on the face of the earth will shake at My presence; the mountains also will be thrown down, the steep pathways will collapse and every wall will fall to the ground (Ezek. 38:20).

The prophet Zechariah also foretold of a day when the Lord will stand on the Mount of Olives, and when He does it will "split in its middle from east to west by a very large valley, so that half of the mountain will move toward the north and the other half toward the south" (Zech. 14:4).

In light of just those two prophecies, it would seem quite possible that the future Jerusalem temple could be demolished so that "one stone is not left standing upon another."

Luke recorded a portion of Jesus' Olivet Discourse that was not included by Matthew and Mark, and it seems to have specific application to the temple's destruction that took place in 70 A.D.

(Luke 21:20-24). For that and other reasons, some think that everything Jesus predicted in His Olivet Discourse was fulfilled by 70 A.D., even including His coming, which they interpret as His "coming in judgment" by means of Titus and the Roman Legions. Personally, I can't accept that particular interpretation. Jesus spoke of cataclysmic events in the heavens, tribulation unlike any the world had seen before or after, false messiahs and prophets showing great signs and wonders, people seeing "the Son of Man coming in clouds with great power and glory," and Him sending forth the angels to gather His elect "from the farthest end of the earth to the farthest end of heaven" (13:26-27). Those things did not occur around 70 A.D.!

Jesus' frequent use of the personal pronoun *you* in His Olivet Discourse, as well as His promise, "Truly I say to you, this generation will not pass away until all these things take place" (13:30) are also presented as proof that everything Jesus predicted must have been fulfilled within forty years. But I would rather murder one scripture to save a hundred than murder a hundred scriptures to save one! Because all that Jesus foretold obviously did not come to pass within forty years of His Olivet Discourse, I can only conclude that He was not speaking of the generation that was alive then, but of the generation that would be alive when He returns. If that interpretation is correct, then we should expect that all that Jesus foretold will take place in the span of one generation, which I would peg at around seventy years.

In regard to the fact that Jesus frequently used the personal pronoun *you* as He foretold future events to Peter, James and John, and the claim that this proves Jesus' words were fulfilled in their lifetimes, the fact is that neither Peter or James lived to see the destruction of Jerusalem in 70 A.D. James was martyred 12 to 14 years after Jesus' Olivet Discourse (Acts 12:2). Peter was martyred between 64 and 68 A.D. Certainly none of them lived to see "the Son of Man coming in clouds with great power and glory," or the angels gathering His elect from the four winds (13:26-27)!

Day 79, Mark 14

It seems incredible to think that someone who lived with Jesus for three years, who heard Him teach and witnessed His miracles, could turn against Him. Yet in one sense Judas is not so uncommon, because God performs continual miracles before all of us every day, and He constantly speaks to us through our conscience, but most, like Judas, prefer 30 pieces of silver over a relationship with Him. I wonder if Judas witnessed so many miracles that they became to him as commonplace as the daily miracles that we ignore.

It also seems incredible that when Jesus announced to the twelve that one of them would betray Him, none of the disciples suspected Judas. Rather, each was concerned that the betrayer might be himself! Judas must have been an incredible actor, the ultimate wolf in sheep's clothing. On a side note, I can assure you that if you serve Jesus you will share in His sufferings, which means you, too, may well feel the kiss of a "Judas" sooner or later.

In a sense, the other eleven also betrayed Jesus, but to a lesser degree than Judas, as they all abandoned Him during His arrest, even after previously claiming that they would all stand with Him to the death (14:31). How easy it is to declare our loyalty! The test comes when we are tempted, and the truth is revealed by our actions. At least Peter, who seemed the most boastful about his loyalty, stayed in the proximity of Christ during His trials. Yet fearing for his own life, he denied any association with Jesus three times, and turned to cursing and swearing to convince his questioners. How incredible it is that he would be the primary leader of the early church just a few months later! Amazing grace!

Although it is appropriate to follow Jesus' example in the Garden of Gethsemane by ending some prayers with the words, "If it be Thy will," it is not appropriate to end all prayers that way, particularly when God has clearly revealed His will. For example, it wouldn't be appropriate to end a prayer to receive salvation and forgiveness with the words, "If it be Thy will," because God has made His will quite clear in that regard. To end a salvation prayer with the words, "If it be Thy will," would be the equivalent of saying to God, "I know that You said that it is Your will to forgive my sins, but just in case You lied about it, I only want You to forgive my sins if it is really Your will." That would be insulting to God, wouldn't it?

When God has *not* revealed His will, then it is appropriate to end one's prayer with the words, "If it be Thy will." A prayer of consecration often ends that way. We might say, "Lord, if it be Thy will, I will become a missionary to Africa." Such a prayer, like Jesus' Gethsemane prayer, can be prayed repeatedly. To repeatedly ask God to forgive the same sin, however, is inappropriate, as it reveals a lack of faith that God forgave the sin the first time forgiveness was requested.

Incidentally, in Jesus' Gethsamane prayer, not only was He not praying a prayer based on God's revealed will, He was praying a prayer that was against God's will! He knew it was His Father's will that He go to the cross. So He submitted. Had He not, there would be no gospel.

The high priest was undoubtedly relieved that there could be an end to the inconsistent testimonies once Jesus declared who He was at His mock trial. Also undoubtedly relieved were the esteemed members of the Sanhedrin who poured out their contempt for Him with their spittle and fists. Amazingly, had you asked any one of them, they would have told you that they loved God! I submit that there are many today just like them, who claim to love Jesus Himself, but they actually love *American Jesus* and hate *Bible Jesus*. For evidence, we need look no further than how they despise any minister who actually teaches what Jesus taught.

Day 80, Mark 15

Seven-hundred years before Christ, Isaiah wrote of Him:

> He was oppressed and He was afflicted, Yet He did not open His mouth; Like a lamb that is led to slaughter, And like a sheep that is silent before its shearers, So He did not open His mouth (Is. 53:7).

Fulfilling Isaiah's words, Jesus suffered silently as He was accused, mocked, spit upon, beaten, whipped and crucified. He must have been tempted to say, "You just wait, you wretches! One day you'll regret how you've treated Me!" His self-restraint was amazing. Peter, an eyewitness to much of Christ's sufferings, would later write, "And while being reviled, He did not revile in return; while suffering, He uttered no threats, but kept entrusting Himself to Him who judges righteously" (1 Pet. 2:23). This, Peter also wrote, serves as an example for us to imitate when we suffer unjustly for our faith (1 Pet. 2:21).

Jesus was, of course, motivated by more than just a desire to fulfill prophecy as He suffered silently. He was "wounded for our transgressions and bruised for our iniquities" (Is. 53:5). He desired that all men might be saved, even those who mocked Him, and the only way that would be possible was if He suffered, paying for their sins. God would see "the anguish of His soul" and "be satisfied" (Is. 53:11). Justice and love met on the cross.

And what a contrast of purity and wickedness! Jesus shines as a beacon in the darkness amongst those who hated Him. Their cruelty is nothing more than a demonstration of universal human nature, manifested every day in political prison camps and on the playgrounds of your local elementary school. But once a person is born again, the same Jesus who died for the world comes to live inside him by the Holy Spirit, resulting in a supernatural transformation. Thereafter, the new creation in Christ shudders as he remembers the former selfishness that ruled him and marvels at how others can be so cruel.

The Romans always crucified people along major roads so that as many people as possible would walk by the condemned, making them an object lesson to all. So try to erase those crucifixion scenes from religious movies out of your mind, which portray Jesus hanging from His cross on a distant hill, with a few mourners standing to watch along with the Roman guards. Jesus hung naked, bleeding and dying in agony, along a major road just outside one of Jerusalem's gates, as hundreds, perhaps thousands of people streamed by Him, going about their daily business. Many mocked Him in passing. Yet He made no reply.

Just before He expired, Jesus cried out with a loud voice, "My God, My God, why have You forsaken Me?" (15:34), quoting the first verse of Psalm 22. Had any of those present bothered to read that psalm, they would have been amazed that, a thousand years earlier—before crucifixion was even invented as a means of capital punishment—David penned prophetic words that expressed Jesus' anguish on the cross:

> My God, my God, why have You forsaken me? Far from my deliverance are the words of my groaning.... All who see me sneer at me; they separate with the lip, they wag the head, saying, "Commit yourself to the Lord; let Him deliver him; let Him rescue him, because He delights in him"....I am poured out like water, and all my bones are out of joint; My heart is like wax; it is melted within me. My strength is dried up like a potsherd, and my tongue cleaves to my jaws; and You lay me in the dust of death. For dogs have surrounded me; a band of evildoers has encompassed me; they pierced my hands and my feet. I can count all my bones. They look, they stare at me; they divide my garments among them, and for my clothing they cast lots (Ps. 22:1, 7-8, 14-18).

Psalm 22 by itself should be enough to convince anyone to repent and believe!

Day 81, Mark 16

Although Jesus repeatedly told His disciples that He would be killed and rise from the dead after three days (see Mark 8:31, 9:31, 10:34), they never got it. Even when Mary Magdalene reported to them on Sunday morning that Jesus was alive and that she had seen Him, they still didn't believe (16:11). And that evening, when two men, whom Jesus appeared to on the road to Emmaus, reported an encounter with Jesus, they still refused to believe (Luke 24:12-16). I always feel better about myself when I read about those future church leaders. With Jesus, there is hope even for me!

On Sunday evening, while they were still "mourning and weeping" (Mark 16:10) over Jesus' death and hiding "for fear of the Jews" (John 20:19), the eleven found that there was one Jew from whom they couldn't hide, namely Jesus. According to Luke's account, just as they were expressing their disbelief at the report of the two Emmaus road disciples, Jesus appeared in their midst. Excellent timing on His part, and I imagine they almost jumped out of their skins. The first thing He did was reproach them "for their unbelief and hardness of heart" (16:14). He didn't say, however, "That was the last straw, and I'm through with you!" Rather, after He rebuked them, He commissioned them to go into all the world and preach the gospel. Jesus gives jobs to bone-heads, which again makes me feel better.

Jesus also told them about some supernatural signs that would follow those who believe. In the book of Acts, we see that those signs were fairly common. On at least three occasions, we read in Acts of believers speaking in tongues, which was the most common of the five signs. We also read of demons being cast out and people being healed through the laying on of hands.

The only example of "picking up serpents" we have in the book of Acts is when Paul was bitten by a poisonous snake on the island of Malta (Acts 28:1-5). It should have killed him, but he shook it off and suffered no harm. A few folks have interpreted Jesus' words about picking up serpents to mean that God wants us to have snake-handling services in our churches. That, however, would fall into the category of tempting God. You won't find any snake-handling services in the book of Acts!

Similarly, there is no record of anyone drinking poison and not suffering any harm. Certainly we should not intentionally drink poison to prove our faith, thus tempting God. If someone intentionally poisons us, we then have the right to claim it won't hurt us.

Some have challenged the inspiration of Mark 16:9-20, claiming it was added later to Mark's original Gospel by an over-zealous scribe (a Pentecostal one, no doubt!). Although Mark 16:9-20 is not included in some early manuscripts, 16:9 was cited by Iranaeus, and 16:20 was referred to by Justin Martyr, both well-known second-century Christian apologists and church fathers.

You've probably heard the story of the mother who excitedly called her son, who was studying at a seminary, to tell him some good news. She had just visited a Pentecostal church, and the pastor's sermon had been on the various supernatural signs that would accompany believers found in Mark 16:17-18. At the end of the service, she had gone forward to receive prayer, and found herself speaking in a language she had never learned. She was ecstatic, and thought her son would be just as overjoyed.

He, however, explained to her that, according to some of his seminary professors, Mark 16:9-20 was not found in some ancient manuscripts, and was thus considered to be uninspired. She was, however, undaunted by his dousing, enthusiastically responding, "Wow! If God can do all that with uninspired verses, imagine what He can do with inspired ones!"

The fact is, even if we do away with Mark 16:9-20, we still have the entire book of Acts, not to mention Jesus' words, "He who believes in Me, the works that I do, he will do also; and greater works than these he will do" (John 14:12). So let them remove those "uninspired verses" if they want to!

Day 82, Acts 18:18-28 & ch. 19

It is nice to be back into the book of Acts, even if only for one day. I almost wish I had designed our chronological study so that we would not be interrupted by one of the Gospels each quarter, but I wanted to space them throughout the year rather than reading them one right after another.

After staying in Corinth for at least eighteen months (18:11), Paul headed back to Antioch, from where he originally began, concluding his second missionary journey in about two years (see map on page 534). He didn't stay long, however, heading out on his third missionary journey that would keep him traveling for five years until his imprisonment in Jerusalem.

In Ephesus, Paul found 12 baptized disciples. Take note of his initial question to them: "Did you receive the Holy Spirit when you believed?" Paul's question reveals two things: (1) He believed those 12 disciples had believed in Jesus. And (2) he believed there was a possibility that they had not received the Holy Spirit when they believed.

Paul also obviously suspected that those 12 disciples had not received the Holy Spirit, otherwise he would not have asked his question.

In response to Paul's question, those 12 baptized believers indicated that they didn't even know that there was a Holy Spirit (19:2). So Paul then asked, "Into what then were you baptized?" If they had been baptized "in the name of the Father and the Son and the Holy Spirit" as Jesus instructed in His Great Commission, they would have heard of the Holy Spirit (Matt. 28:19).

Finally the truth was revealed. They had been baptized into "John's baptism," perhaps by Apollos before he was more enlightened to the truth (18:24-28).

So Paul told them the good news that Jesus had come (25 years earlier). He then baptized them in the name of the Lord. I can't imagine anyone would claim that those 12 men were not thoroughly saved after that! By that time they were certainly all born again and thus indwelled by the Holy Spirit. Yet we next read that "Paul laid his hands upon them" and "the Holy Spirit came on them, and they began speaking with tongues and prophesying" (19:6).

So, once again, we see Scripture plainly teaches that one may have the Holy Spirit *within* him, but not yet *upon* him. Those 12 disciples were no different than the believers in Samaria whom we read about in Acts 8. You may recall that Peter and John were sent to Samaria to pray for the new believers there "that they might receive the Holy Spirit, for He had not yet fallen upon any of them" (Acts 8:15-16).

Once again the initial evidence of this Holy Spirit baptism was speaking with other tongues, and in the case of those 12 men, also prophecy. Millions of believers since then can testify of the same experience. If you have not yet been baptized in the Holy Spirit with the evidence of speaking in other tongues, you are just a prayer away!

Paul's daily teaching for two years in the school of Tyrannus in Ephesus resulted in everyone in Asia, or modern western Turkey, hearing the gospel (19:10). I can only think that was accomplished, not as a result of everyone in Asia traveling to the school of Tyrannus over a two-year period to listen to Paul, but as a result of Paul's students, whom he discipled at Tyrannus' school, traveling throughout Asia to proclaim the gospel. That is a beautiful picture of the power of discipleship. And with the many extraordinary miracles that God was doing, Paul enjoyed a very fruitful time in a region where the Holy Spirit once forbade him to preach (Acts 16:6). It was a true revival characterized by public repentance (19:18-19) and a public riot (19:23-41)!

Take note that in Ephesus, "Paul purposed in the spirit [not in his head] to go to Jerusalem after he had passed through Macedonia and Achaia, saying, 'After I have been there, I must also see Rome'" (19:21). That decision, made with the Spirit's leading, set the course of Paul's ministry for years, as we will see as we continue reading Acts.

Day 83, 1 Corinthians 1

We've started reading 1 Corinthians now because Paul wrote it during his three-year sojourn in Ephesus. Concerning his ministry there, Paul wrote to the Corinthians, "A wide door for effective service has opened to me" (16:8). Having just read about his very fruitful ministry in Ephesus, we know what Paul was talking about!

The date of this letter is around 55 A.D., 25 years after the day of Pentecost. Therefore, after 25 years of the church's existence, the New Testament epistles were five in all: James, Galatians, 1 and 2 Thessalonians, and 1 Corinthians. Four of those letters were written to specific churches for specific reasons. All of this is to say, once again, that the central focus of the early New Testament churches was obviously not the epistles, but the teaching of Christ. The epistles were supplementary, and were often corrective in nature, and that is certainly true of Paul's letters to the Corinthians.

About four years after he founded the church in Corinth, Paul learned that divisions had surfaced—divisions that foreshadowed splits that would characterize the Church for the next 2,000 years. The Corinthian believers were breaking into factions based on their favorite church leaders. The difference between then and now is this: Then, the teachers over whom they were dividing were in doctrinal agreement, and each would have been horrified to learn of the divisions that were occurring in Corinth over them; now, however, church leaders lead the divisions.

Claiming to be "of Christ" can be just as carnal as claiming to be "of Peter" or "of Paul" (1:12), if one's label is designed to distinguish himself from others in the body of Christ. As soon as one adopts a title other than *Christian*, one sets himself apart from other members of the body of Christ. How tragic it is that we continually advertise our lack of unity to the world by the labels permanently planted in front of our church buildings.

Those of us who want to please Christ should work to build unity in His body, even with those who have adopted distinctive denominational and doctrinal labels, lest we be guilty of being little one-church (or worse yet, one-person) denominations. Pray that the labels of all true believers will be discarded!

According to Paul (1:17), it is possible to void the cross of Christ by means of speech that is clever, or more literally, *wise* (Greek: *sophia*). How so? If the simple message of the gospel, what Paul calls "the word of the cross," is enhanced to make it more appealing, softened to make it more acceptable, or altered in any way, it is effectively voided. We should proclaim "Christ crucified" (1:23) even if it seems foolish to some.

Indeed, as Paul said, "The word of the cross is foolishness to those who are perishing" (1:18). This was especially true in ancient Greece, of which Corinth was a part, where the philosophies of Socrates, Plato, and Aristotle were held in high esteem. Yet human philosophy and its partner, pride, cannot hold a candle to God's truth, as Paul so eloquently stated. And God, who humbles the proud but exalts the humble is well-pleased to choose "the foolish things of the world to shame the wise" (1:27), "so that no man may boast before God" (1:29).

Those of us who have believed the gospel are not shamed by the world's condescension, because we have experienced transforming and saving power. To us, all the world's wisdom, religions and philosophies amount to nothing by comparison. We have found "the treasure hidden in a field" (Matt. 13:44)! Jesus has become our wisdom, righteousness, sanctification and redemption, and we boast in Him (1:30-31).

Tragically, the modern gospel has indeed voided the cross. The message of "Christ crucified" has become the message of "Christ falsified," altered to make it more appealing to those who would otherwise reject it.

Let us then, with Paul, not be ashamed of the gospel of Christ. It is "the power of God for salvation to everyone who believes" (Rom. 1:16). I believe it!

Day 84, 1 Corinthians 2

You may recall that when Paul first visited Corinth, he had just come from Athens where he'd spent time reasoning with Epicurean and Stoic philosophers, experiencing mixed results (Acts 17:16-34). I suspect Paul had endured his fill of human wisdom—of which Greeks were so fond—making him even more appreciative of the divine revelation of the gospel. Perhaps that is why, as he recounted his ministry in Corinth, he wrote:

> I did not come with superiority of speech or of wisdom, proclaiming to you the testimony of God. For I determined to know nothing among you except Jesus Christ, and Him crucified....and my message and my preaching were not in persuasive words of wisdom, but in demonstration of the Spirit and of power, so that your faith would not rest on the wisdom of men, but on the power of God (2:1-5).

The message of the cross has generally always been spurned by intellectuals, as they judge it to be below their brilliance. The truth is, however, that it is far above their brilliance, having its origin in heaven. Among believers there may not be "many wise according to the flesh" (1:26), yet they comprise the wisest group of people on earth, having partaken of God's wisdom. The wisdom of the world is foolishness, not only to God, but also to those of us who know God. Moreover, we are not intimidated, impressed or enamored by the intellectual, philosophical and religious elite of the world. Rather, we feel sorry for them, knowing they are groping in darkness, blind leaders of the blind.

Having received God's Spirit, we now possess a wisdom that is hidden from the world, a wisdom that "God predestined before the ages to our glory" (2:7). Obviously, that predestined wisdom revolves around God's plan to redeem us through the sacrifice of Christ. The Spirit has revealed to us "all that God has prepared for those who love Him" (2:9), which includes forgiveness of our sins, our spiritual rebirth as God's sons, and a home in heaven, to name a few.

But have we been sovereignly selected to possess this wonderful wisdom from the Spirit? No. Scripture tells us that "with the humble is wisdom" (Prov. 11:2). Those who humble themselves put themselves in the position to receive God's wisdom. Pride is always the enemy of true wisdom, and always the comrade of worldly wisdom.

Paul wrote that, had "the rulers of this age" understood that predestined wisdom, "they would not have crucified the Lord of glory" (2:8). Who are those "rulers" of whom he speaks? Some think it unlikely that Paul would refer to a few regional political leaders, namely, Pilate and Herod, along with a group of local religious leaders, the Jewish Sanhedrin, as being "rulers of this age" (2:6). For that reason, it is thought that Paul was referring to the demonic rulers who influenced everyone who had anything to do with Jesus' death, starting with Judas, whom Scripture says "Satan entered" (Luke 22:3). Paul wrote of demonic spiritual rulers in his letters to the Ephesians and Colossians (Eph. 3:10, 6:12; Col. 1:16, 2:15). Those evil spiritual rulers were indeed outwitted by God. As they influenced men to crucify Christ, they unwittingly helped redeem millions of people from Satan's dominion!

Some think that Paul's statement, "Which things we also speak, not in words taught by human wisdom, but in those taught by the Spirit" (2:13) is a reference to speaking in other tongues, something the Corinthians were doing a lot of, and a subject that surfaces later in Paul's letter. No one knows for sure, as Paul doesn't say. Certainly speaking with other tongues could be considered to be speaking words "taught by the Spirit." Yet proclaiming the gospel could also be considered speaking words "taught by the Spirit." Neither are accepted by "the natural man" (those who are not born again), as they are "foolishness to him" (2:14). So I'm unsure of what Paul was speaking about. When I see Paul in heaven I'm going to ask him why he didn't write more clearly!

Day 85, 1 Corinthians 3

It is from this chapter that the modern doctrine of the "carnal Christian" has been extracted, which promotes the idea that one can be a true Christian but be "carnal" (or "fleshly" as the NASB translates it), and thus be completely indistinguishable from unbelievers. This idea is taken largely from Paul's words in 3:3, where he asks, "Are you not walking [living] like mere men?"

As with most all false doctrine, this one has its basis in ignoring context. A quick survey of everything Paul wrote to the Corinthians reveals that they were not indistinguishable from the world. Describing some of them, Paul wrote that they had previously been fornicators, idolaters, adulterers, homosexuals, thieves, covetous, drunkards and swindlers, but were no longer (6:9-10). Paul also instructed the Corinthian Christians "not to associate with any so-called brother if he should be an immoral person, or covetous, or an idolater, or a reviler, or a drunkard, or a swindler—not even to eat with such a one" (5:11). Obviously, the Corinthian believers were not guilty of these things themselves, otherwise Paul would have been telling them not to associate with themselves.

This first Corinthian letter was, in part, Paul's response to a letter he had received from them concerning several issues. They had asked him questions regarding what was right and wrong, indicating their own desire to do what was right.

The Corinthian Christians regularly partook of the Lord's Supper and gathered together for Christian worship (1 Cor. 12, 14), something not done by unbelievers in their day. They were also zealous of spiritual gifts (14:12). They had been collecting money for poor believers in Jerusalem (16:1-4; 2 Cor. 8:10, 9:1-2), displaying their love for the brethren, exactly what Jesus said would mark His true disciples (John 13:35). Paul wrote in 11:2: "Now I praise you because you remember me in everything, and hold firmly to the traditions, just as I delivered them to you."

The conclusion? When Paul wrote that the Corinthian Christians were "walking like mere men," he obviously did not mean that they were completely indistinguishable from unbelievers in every respect. They were acting just like non-Christians do in one way, yielding to jealousy and strife, but in many other ways they were acting like devoted disciples of Christ.

Hoping to eliminate that strife among them over their favorite leaders, Paul painted those leaders as they really were—servants who were nothing in comparison to God. Paul had laid a spiritual foundation in Corinth that Apollos, a teacher, built upon. They were one, working for the same cause (3:8). Yet, each would receive his own reward "according to his own labor" (3:8). Paul then figuratively represented their labor with six different types of building materials, gold, silver and precious stones—which are costly and inflammable—and wood, hay and straw, which are relatively inexpensive and burn easily. One day the works of God's servants will be put through a fire to test their quality.

Obviously, those who built with wood, hay and straw will see their works consumed in the fire, and they will go unrewarded, yet still be saved (3:15). Ministers who are not wolves in sheep's clothing, yet who still compromise truth, water down or alter the gospel, or who mislead goats into thinking that they are sheep, will be blessed to suffer nothing more than to watch their works burn in the fire and lose their subsequent rewards. False teachers, on the other hand, will find themselves, not just their works, in God's fire.

Paul issues a solemn warning to those who engender strife. They actually destroy God's temple, the church, and God will destroy them (3:16-17). Wow. Paul then concludes with an admonition not to divide over their favorite leaders, but to recognize that every God-sent leader belongs to them all. Those leaders are just one small expression of God's great love for them, and are representative of His greatest blessing, namely, Christ Himself.

In a sense, the believers in Corinth were like little children of a rich king arguing over small coins. The small issues that divide us vanish when we focus on what is truly important.

Day 86, 1 Corinthians 4

What began as a relatively benign letter now grows somewhat passionate. Obviously, if there were factions in the Corinthian church, there were leaders of those factions. And those that were claiming to be "of Peter" or "of Apollos" rather than "of Paul" (1:12) were likely pitting themselves, not only against those who are "of Paul," but against Paul himself. So Paul had his work cut out to win back the affections of everyone in the Corinthian church, and to unify them once again. In this chapter, he goes right to work.

He first reminds the Corinthians that it is not their judgment of him that matters, or even his own judgment of himself. It is only the Lord's judgment of him that matters (4:3). This is something that is true for all of us, and it ought to help us when we are the victims of other people's judgments.

Paul slips in the fact that he does, in fact, judge himself, and by his own judgment he is not conscious of anything wrong that he is doing. (How many of us could make the same claim?) That was a subtle way of telling the Corinthian believers that if they have found a flaw in him, they were likely mistaken. And in regard to their judgment of his hidden motives, that is something that should be left to God alone. They can rest assured that He will one day reveal what is hidden in people's hearts, and then "each man's praise will come to him from God" (4:5).

Keep in mind that some people's hidden motives are not so hidden, and thus we are safe to judge them. In Paul's case, however, there was no evidence against him, and thus no rightful basis for forming judgments about his motives.

Pride is the root of most strife, so Paul attacks the root. He again reminds the Corinthians that he and Apollos are only Christ's servants and their servants, and nothing more. How foolish it was for any of the Corinthian believers to become arrogant over their favorite nobodies!

Moreover, the Corinthian believers had no right to be arrogant about anything or anybody, possessing only what God had given them (4:7). They had been blessed by God to a degree that far superseded what Paul and the other apostles, by virtue of their calling, had enjoyed. They were kings by comparison. To make his point, Paul elaborated on his lifestyle as it compared with theirs. He and his fellow apostles were a spectacle to the world, looked upon as fools. Even as he wrote his letter to the Corinthians, he and his band were hungry, thirsty, poorly clothed, roughly treated, and homeless. Being reviled, persecuted and slandered was their regular fare. And they were the men who originally brought to the Corinthians all the blessings they now enjoyed in Christ. Yet some in the Corinthian church were speaking against them!

I'm sure Paul's Corinthian readers were ashamed as they read. Paul obviously realized that, writing, "I do not write these things to shame you" and then affectionately adding, "but to admonish you as my beloved children" (4:14). He then reminded them of their special relationship with him. Others might be their tutors, but he was their "father through the gospel" (4:15). Such words should have melted their hearts and vanquished any suspicion of his having wrong motives.

Finally, notice Paul's admonition, "Be imitators of me" (4:16). Every minister's goal should be to be able to honestly say that to his or her disciples. Yet such a statement is meaningless if a minister gives people nothing more to imitate than how he acts when he is in the pulpit. Paul was able to say that Timothy would remind the Corinthians, not of his sermons, but of His ways "which are in Christ" (4:17). Paul discipled Timothy, and so Timothy was very familiar, not just with Paul's sermons, but his lifestyle. That is what true discipleship is all about. Keep in mind that making disciples is not just the task of ministers, but a commandment that is given to us all.

Day 87, 1 Corinthians 5

Why didn't Paul instruct the Corinthian believers to follow Jesus' three steps of church discipline—which we read in Matthew 18—regarding the man in their midst who was living in a sexual relationship with his stepmother? The reason is because those are three steps that are to be taken with *believers*, but Paul rightfully judged that this perverted man was not a true believer. Paul had previously instructed the Corinthians "not to associate with any *so-called brother* if he is an immoral person, or covetous, or an idolater, or a reviler, or a drunkard, or a swindler—not even to eat with such a one" (5:11). Those who claim to be believers in Christ who are sexually immoral are not believers at all. This is also true for professing believers who are covetous, idolatrous, drunks and cheats. We will read in the very next chapter of Corinthians:

> Do not be deceived; neither fornicators, nor idolaters, nor adulterers, nor effeminate, nor homosexuals, nor thieves, nor the covetous, nor drunkards, nor revilers, nor swindlers, will inherit the kingdom of God (1 Cor. 6:9-10).

Paul warned, "Do not be deceived." How tragic it is that so many within evangelical Christianity have believed the lie that such people can be classed as "carnal Christians," fully saved but walking after the flesh, indistinguishable from unbelievers. The Corinthians had adopted a similar attitude, accepting the immoral man's profession of faith as being genuine, proud of their tolerance, when they should have been mourning that they had permitted such a blight in Christ's body (5:2). It is obvious that this immoral man was not a true Christian. Paul referred to him as being guilty of immorality "of such a kind as does not exist even among the Gentiles" (5:1), as "a so-called brother" (5:11), as one who was worthy to be excommunicated and delivered to Satan for the destruction of his flesh, as a man who was not currently saved (5:5), and as a "wicked man" (5:13).

Without apology, Paul stated that he had already "judged" the immoral man (5:3). Obviously, there is nothing wrong with making such judgments. In fact, there is everything right about them. Paul unequivocally stated that those within the church have an *obligation* to judge those within the church (5:12). What a refreshing balance this brings to the common misunderstanding regarding passing judgment on others. Jesus' prohibition against passing judgment revolved around finding faults with others by those who possess greater faults (Matt. 7:1-5). But moral people in the church have every right to judge immoral people within their midst.

Clearly, the church of Jesus Christ is supposed to be a holy, self-cleansing body. And the responsibility for that self-cleansing does not just fall on the shoulders of pastors. Paul wasn't writing just to pastors. He was writing to the entire body in Corinth. We should all be devoted to keeping Christ's church a light that shines in the world's darkness, pure and holy, obedient to our Lord. This most basic quality of the church is virtually impossible to attain within common modern church structure, where the church is a group of people who know very little about each other and who gather for a weekly production under the leadership of a pastor who knows very little about them. The body of Christ cannot remain pure before the world apart from biblical churches that are small, where people actually know each other.

By excommunicating the immoral man in Corinth, the Corinthian believers sent a message to the watching world: "If you want to be one of us, you must be sexually pure." They additionally sent a message to the immoral man: "We do not accept your profession of faith in the Lord Jesus as genuine. However, we do not excommunicate out of hatred, but rather out of love, hoping our actions will wake you from your self-deception so that you may repent, be truly born again, and be 'saved in the day of the Lord Jesus'" (5:5). Apparently, the Corinthian believers formally delivered the immoral man "to Satan for the destruction of his flesh" (5:5). Finding himself ill and perhaps even dying, hopefully he would be saved. Serious stuff indeed!

Day 88, 1 Corinthians 6

Many of us have thought that it wrong to make a moral appraisal of anyone since Jesus told His followers not to judge. Yet we're learning that we've been quite unbalanced in that regard. Jesus once told a crowd, "Do not judge according to appearance, but judge with righteous judgment" (John 7:24). Why doesn't anyone ever quote *that* commandment? In the previous chapter of 1 Corinthians, we learned that it is entirely appropriate for devoted followers of Jesus to judge unrighteous people within the church in order that the church might remain pure.

Granted, this idea has been pushed to extremes by some Pharisaical pastors, who set human standards, such as hair lengths and tithing quotas, in order to keep their trembling little flocks "pure" or submissive to them. That is not, however, what Scripture advocates. Paul wrote about judging people who claim to be Christ's followers, yet who are guilty of obvious sins that are clearly very grievous to God according to Scripture, such as sexual immorality, idolatry, greed, drunkenness, thievery, and so on.

Today the theme of judgment within the church continues, and we learn that "the saints will judge the world" as well as angels (6:2-3). I wish we had other scriptures to give us more insight on that, but what Paul wrote certainly ought to motivate us to sharpen our judgment skills. We'll be participating in some very significant judgments in the future, and our appraisals of men and angels will of course be based on God's standards of right and wrong. Thus it would be tragic for us to abdicate our responsibility to judge during the present time in smaller matters within the church.

In the Corinthian church, some believers were taking each other to court in order to let unbelievers judge between them. Paul questions why there isn't at least one wise person in the church who could arbitrate disputes, just as Jesus prescribed (Matt. 18:15-17). One might win his lawsuit against a brother in Christ, but the loss of reputation suffered by the church before the watching world would more than offset the gains.

The appropriate thing to do if one is defrauded by another in the church is to follow Jesus' instructions in Matthew 18:15-17, which keeps all judgment between believers in the church. If the person who defrauded another does not ultimately repent, he should be excommunicated, as Paul warns that not only will no idolaters, adulterers, homosexuals, thieves, and so on inherit God's kingdom, but neither will any swindlers. Such people, when unrepentant, are not true believers in the Lord Jesus.

Do Paul's words, "All things are lawful for me, but not all things are profitable" (6:12), mean that Christians have no laws to obey since we are "under grace," as some teach? Clearly not, as just three verses earlier Paul solemnly warned that the unrighteous will not inherit God's kingdom (6:9-10). So what did He mean when he said that all things were lawful? Paul could have been referring only to the believer's relationship to the Law of Moses, and that will become more clear later in this letter as he elaborates on this theme. In fact, in the tenth chapter, he repeats that same phrase about all things being lawful. For now, let it suffice to say that Paul knew he was free from all the distinctive requirements of the Mosaic Law, such as the dietary laws and so on, yet he still found it wise to obey some of them, primarily out of love for Jewish believers.

Paul next turns his attention to the subject of sexual immorality, of which Corinth reeked. Residents and visitors indulged in sex with temple prostitutes as part of the "religious" experience. Paul lists a number of reasons why such immorality is wrong for Christians, the foremost being that our bodies are temples of the Holy Spirit. As we keep that fact in mind it motivates us to avoid many other things that grieve the Holy Spirit. The Holy Spirit wants no part in anything unholy. That includes not only acts of immorality, but images and thoughts of the same. Flee every form of immorality! All immoral acts begin as immoral thoughts.

Day 89, 1 Corinthians 7

Obviously referring to males and females who were not married to each other, the Corinthians had written to ask Paul, "Is it good for a man not to touch a woman?" Paul answered in the affirmative. That is the safe standard to prevent any sexual immorality, at least from a physical standpoint. One touch might lead to another. When magnets get too close, the attraction becomes unstoppable.

Sexual desire is God-given, thus it is not something that is evil in itself. Because it is God-given, we should follow the instructions of its inventor—who understands it best. He knows how it is stimulated, and He knows how strong a desire it becomes if stimulated. It is a desire, however, meant to be stimulated and fulfilled only in marriage. Additionally, a healthy sexual relationship in marriage is also a preventative against immorality. Thus Paul admonishes husbands and wives not to neglect their "duties" to each other in this regard (which seems to be an odd way to describe something so pleasurable). One is less tempted to steal the Ford parked across the street when one has a Mercedes parked in the garage.

Often overlooked in this chapter is the insight we gain into what is supposed to be normal Christian devotion. Husbands and wives may agree to abstain from sex temporarily in order to devote themselves more fully to prayer. Single people are advised to remain single so that they will not be distracted from devotion to the Lord due to trying to please a marriage partner. These are not far-fetched concepts for those who love God supremely, with all their heart, mind and strength, and who understand that anyone who loves father, mother, son or daughter more than Jesus is not worthy of Him (Matt. 10:37).

Although Paul recommended singleness, he fully understood that celibacy is a gift from God which not many have. He also understood the power of sexual desire, thus recommending marriage for those who would otherwise "burn with passion" (7:9). Paul told it like it is.

His instructions concerning marriage, divorce and remarriage are straightforward, logical, and harmonize well with the rest of Scripture. Christian married couples are not to divorce. In the event that they do, however, they should remain single or reconcile (7:10-11). Christians married to unbelievers should not divorce their unbelieving spouses due to the negative effects it would have on spouse and children (7:14). Although Paul's words in this regard are not as clear as we'd like, it is easy to understand how a divorce initiated by a Christian could well ensure that the spouse and children would permanently harden their hearts towards Christ.

On the other hand, it is amazing to me how some pastors and Christian counselors, "sticklers for the Word," yet lacking much sense, will counsel a woman in an abusive relationship to "obey the Bible" and not divorce her ruthless husband. It seems to me that Paul covers all those kinds of unusual cases in his final statement, "Only, as the Lord has assigned to each one, as God has called each, in this manner let him walk" (7:17). That leaves room for evaluating every case by its own merit. Remember, "The Lord Thy God hath given thee a brain!"

Although Paul recommended singleness for Christians who had been previously divorced, he plainly stated that they would not sin if they remarried (7:27-28). The only way to reconcile this with Jesus' words that "everyone who divorces his wife and marries another commits adultery," is if Jesus was speaking about those who divorce in order to remarry someone they've already targeted, and Paul was speaking about those who divorce because they cannot get along. If that is the case, it is easy to understand why Jesus condemned divorce and remarriage as being equivalent to the sin of adultery, and why Paul did not.

"Circumcision is nothing, and uncircumcision is nothing, but what matters is the keeping of the commandments of God" (1 Cor. 7:9). The first half of that verse would have been considered heresy by Jews. Sadly, the second half of that verse is heresy for many modern false-grace preachers who downplay obedience.

Day 90, 1 Corinthians 8

Paul turns his attention to a second question from the Corinthians—about the lawfulness of eating meat that had previously been sacrificed to idols. Before he tackles that issue, however, he first warns of a venom that often poisons those who possess knowledge, namely, pride. "Knowledge puffs up," he says (8:1). The antidote for knowledge-born pride is not ignorance, but love, consisting of humility, forbearance and concern for those who lack the same knowledge. Those who are growing in the true knowledge of the Lord are also growing in their realization of how little they know, and thus humility should proportionately increase with knowledge. Daily Bible readers, take note!

Paul plants himself squarely on the side of those believers in Corinth who believed that it was not sinful to eat meat that had been previously sacrificed to idols. Certainly God is offended by people's devotion to idols, a devotion that rightfully belongs to Him. The one who eats meat that was sacrificed to an idol by someone else, however, does not participate in his sin. Yet it is quite easy to see how some, who love God with all their hearts, might think otherwise. This is just what had happened at Corinth.

Paul was concerned that some, who like himself, knew that eating meat sacrificed to idols was not wrong, might cause those who believed otherwise to stumble into doing what they considered sinful. He offered an example:

> For if someone sees you, who have knowledge, dining in an idol's temple, will not his conscience, if he is weak, be strengthened to eat things sacrificed to idols? (8:10)

That is, if a believer (who thinks that eating meat sacrificed to idols is wrong) might see a fellow believer (who knows otherwise) eating at a restaurant connected to an idol's temple, he might be tempted to join his brother, and in so doing, violate his conscience. Although he isn't actually sinning by his act of eating meat sacrificed to idols, because he *thinks* he is sinning, he *is* sinning, because he is making a decision in his heart to do what he thinks is sin. So his heart rightfully condemns him as he eats.

Paul addressed this same issue in his letter to the Romans, writing:

> But he who doubts is condemned if he eats, because his eating is not from faith; and whatever is not from faith is sin (Rom. 14:23).

Because of this, not only is the believer with the weak conscience guilty of sin for doing what he thinks is sin, the one who caused him to stumble into violating his conscience is also guilty of sin against his brother and Christ (8:12). For this reason, we should be sensitive towards fellow believers with "weak consciences," being careful to do nothing to lead them into doing what they might think is sin. There is nothing wrong, however, with trying to help a believer with a weak conscience overcome his doubts by enlightening him with truth, as proven by Paul's declarations in this very chapter of the lawfulness of eating meat sacrificed to idols.

Sadly, some have twisted what Paul wrote about "Christian liberty," promoting liberty from God's commandments. But standards have been set in God's Word. Although Paul did not condemn Christians eating meats that were sacrificed to idols, he condemned idolatry as an eternally damning sin, according to what he wrote two chapters earlier (6:9-10). Similarly, when professing believers disagree over the lawfulness of viewing sexually-explicit movies, for example, there is no application found in what we read today. Scripture condemns all forms of immorality, including immorality of the mind.

From this chapter we again see how important it was to the early church to obey the Lord and keep a clear conscience, as well as help others in Christ's body to keep a clear conscience. If we are unsure about the lawfulness of something, we ought to avoid it until we are sure. According to what we read today, one whose weak conscience is "wounded" might end up "ruined" (8:11-12), or alternately interpreted, "destroyed," another difficult scripture to reconcile with the idea of unconditional eternal security.

Day 91, 1 Corinthians 9

This chapter continues the theme of the previous one, that of making sacrifices for the sake of others, which is the essence of love. Paul uses himself as an example.

Paul possessed the God-given right to make his living from the gospel, that is, to be paid by the people to whom he preached. Motivated by love, however, he denied himself that right in Corinth in order to "cause no hindrance to the gospel" (9:12). Remember that we already read in the book of Acts that Paul first earned his living in Corinth by making tents (Acts 18:1-3). When evangelists receive money from those to whom they preach, onlookers are apt to question their motives, using their suspicion as an excuse to reject the gospel.

So is Paul's example the pattern that every minister of the gospel should follow?

First, any minister who serves at his or her own expense so as not to cause hindrance to the gospel deserves our admiration. Sadly, ministers who also work "secular" jobs are often considered lesser ministers, but Paul set that very example before the elders in Ephesus (Acts 20:34-35).

Second, although Paul did make tents when he first came to Corinth, as soon as Silas and Timothy arrived, he "began devoting himself completely to the word" (Acts 18:5). So it seems that from then on, Silas and Timothy provided for Paul's needs by their labor (and praise God for folks like them in Christ's body). Obviously, it was better that Paul devote his full time to the gospel, and when he could do so without having to receive an offering in Corinth, he did. Generally, it is always best if ministers can devote their full time to their ministry, as they will naturally be more fruitful then.

Also keep in mind that Paul was an apostle, and much of his ministry was directed toward the unsaved. By publicly receiving offerings, it may have hindered his ministry. Those whose ministries are directed toward the saved, however, don't have the same concern. Remember that we read Paul's words to the Galatians,

"The one who is taught the word is to share all good things with the one who teaches him" (Gal. 6:6).

All of this is to say that any evangelist or apostle who can find a way to keep from asking for money from his audiences will find a less suspicious reception, and he will likely enjoy more fruit. Along those same lines, every evangelist and apostle should avoid any hint of extravagance or the love of money. Otherwise, he will ensure the damnation of many of his listeners who rightfully doubt his sincerity and thus disbelieve his message, which is obviously not powerful enough to deliver him from his own sin. Pity the many modern televangelists who will soon stand before God, after having flaunted their wealth for years while continually manipulating their audiences to send them more money. For every soul that is saved by their efforts, one hundred are damned.

Several verses that we read today leave us with no doubt regarding Paul's view of his obligation to keep the Mosaic Law. Even though he was Jewish, he did not consider himself to be under the Law of Moses, but rather, only under the law of Christ (9:20-21). Modern Christians err who put themselves under the Mosaic Law.

That being said, there is moral overlap between the Law of Moses and the law of Christ, so one who keeps the law of Christ will automatically keep part of the Mosaic Law. Moreover, Paul kept some of the distinctive regulations of the Mosaic Law whenever not keeping them would cause hindrance to the gospel, namely, when he was ministering to Jews. We will yet read examples of that very thing as we continue our journey through the book of Acts. Once again, Paul was setting the example of sensitivity that he also prescribed for the Corinthians.

I'm sure you noticed that Paul also prescribed disciplined effort, not unlike that of athletes, in our spiritual race and fight. There is no hope of spiritual progress or ultimate reward without it. Self-denial is the essence of following Christ. Let's not forget that!

Day 92, 1 Corinthians 10

It is sometimes debated what Paul meant in the last verses of chapter nine regarding his fear of being "disqualified" if he failed to "discipline his body and make it his slave" (9:27). Reading those words within their context of the first part of chapter 10, however, makes it obvious that Paul was fearful, not just of forfeiting some heavenly rewards, as some say. Rather, he was fearful of forfeiting heaven. Citing the Israelites as an example, Paul reminds us that, although they were delivered from Egypt, were "baptized" when they crossed the Red Sea, ate God-given food and drank God-given water that was representative of Christ, in the end, "God was not well-pleased with most of them," and "they were laid low in the wilderness" (10:5). They never entered the promised land.

This serves as a warning to us that greed, idolatry and immorality—three sins that Paul already warned of in this letter that will exclude one from inheriting God's kingdom (6:9-10)—as well as grumbling and rebellion, could result in our forfeiting our relationship with God. Paul reminds us that immorality, for example, resulted in the deaths of 23,000 Israelites on a single day! We are not to suppose that those immoral people inherited eternal life!

So we must "take heed" that we don't similarly fall, disciplining our bodies, lest we be "disqualified." Clearly, the temptation to commit sexually immoral acts exists for believers, and we are capable of yielding. Thankfully, however, God will not allow us to be tempted beyond what we are able to resist, and He always provides a way of escape (10:13). None of us are forced to sin. Moreover, there is grace offered after sin to those who repent.

Obviously, even though Paul listed idolatry as a sin that angers God, will exclude one from heaven, and is a form of demon-worship, he did not believe that eating meat that had been sacrificed to idols was idolatrous. There is, however, sometimes a valid reason to avoid eating such meat. That reason is love for a fellow believer who is persuaded that doing so is wrong. Although eating meat that is sacrificed to idols is not an issue that most of us face, we can certainly apply the concepts that Paul advocates, being sensitive to the peculiarities that exist within the body of Christ. Love is the important thing.

Again we read very similar words that Paul had written earlier in this same letter: "All things are lawful, but not all things are profitable. All things are lawful, but not all things edify" (10:23). It goes without saying that Paul did not mean that greed, idolatry and immorality, for example, are lawful in God's eyes, but to be avoided only because they are not profitable or edifying. That would make Paul contradict himself within this very chapter. Considering the context, we note that Paul was speaking of eating meats sacrificed to idols. It was lawful, but not always profitable or edifying to do so. That makes sense.

Therefore, even if we know that something is not wrong, we should strive not to offend those who are persuaded otherwise, lest we hinder them from inheriting eternal life. Paul specifically lists Jews, Greeks and the church, all of whom possess their various scruples. I suspect that it was the Jews in the Corinthian church, because of their previous devotion to the Mosaic Law and the many fence laws surrounding it, who objected to eating meat sacrificed to idols. So Paul's words, "All things are lawful," were a reference to our freedom from the law of Moses. (But we are all under the law of Christ.)

Finally, notice that Paul admonished those who thought it was wrong to eat meat sacrificed to idols to also walk in love towards those who were persuaded otherwise. He wrote, "For why is my freedom judged by another's conscience? If I partake with thankfulness, why am I slandered concerning that for which I give thanks?" (10:29-30). Those who pointed their fingers at Paul for eating meat sacrificed to idols should think again about holding him to their personal convictions, especially in the light that he ate with thankfulness to God!

Day 93, 1 Corinthians 11

Unlike most other days, today I'm glad I'm limited to 700 words, which will be my excuse for not engaging in a lengthy commentary on women's head coverings! Paul's words are not as clear as I wish they were on this subject. So I will limit myself to a few observations.

First, there are no unique Greek words for *husband* and *wife*, and so clearly the words translated *man* and *woman* in parts of this passage would be better translated *husband* and *wife*. Otherwise we might conclude that *every* man is the head of *every* woman. The truth is, only husbands are heads of their wives (Eph. 5:23).

Second, it seems to me that the underlying spiritual principles of which Paul wrote are more important than the "symbols" of those principles. A wife can wear a head covering, "a symbol" of her husband's authority over her (11:10), yet continually "disgrace her head" (11:5), her husband, in many other ways. So the important thing is that she always honors her husband, and this is contained in Scripture (Eph. 5:33).

Third, I chuckle when someone says that Paul's words about head coverings have nothing to do with cultural practices in the ancient world, and thus they should be implicitly obeyed by all generations of Christians in all cultures. Paul wrote, for example, that the woman who prays with her head uncovered is "one and the same as the woman whose head is shaved" (11:5). How many women in your culture shave their heads? In how many cultures of the world, old and more recent, would Paul's example have any relevance?

If head coverings were a *God-ordained* "symbol" (11:10), one required by God to be worn by all wives during prayer, you would think that would have been mentioned a few other places in Scripture.

Finally, if you are a woman who is persuaded that God wants you to cover your head when you pray, then do it. But don't throw a little napkin on top of your head or wear a fancy little hat to church! Cover your entire head! And remember that wearing a head covering does not exempt one from the obligation to obey the second greatest commandment.

Selfishness was surfacing in Corinth even when the believers partook of the Lord's Supper. Keep in mind that the Lord's Supper was intended to be a *supper* and not a snack, which is why it is called the Lord's *Supper*. It was a full meal in Corinth, and that is very obvious from what Paul wrote. Moreover, the Corinthians didn't meet in specially-built church buildings, and so most likely, they ate the Lord's Supper where they ate most of their meals, in their homes. Members came together and shared food.

Some, however, who arrived first, arrived hungry. Not waiting for the others, they started eating and drinking, with the result that some who arrived late and who were too poor to bring food to share found everything consumed! Worse, they found some who were drunk from the wine! This is not what Jesus envisioned for the sacred meal that He gave to His followers!

Paul admonished the Corinthian believers not only to wait for one another, but also to examine themselves before they partook of the bread and cup, lest they partake in an "unworthy manner" (11:27). Otherwise they endangered themselves of being disciplined by the Lord in the form of sickness and even premature death. Such discipline from God ensures that we "will not be condemned along with the world" (11:32). That is, if God didn't discipline wayward children, the result is that they would be cast into hell with the unsaved. This is not proof of the doctrine of "once-saved-always-saved," however, as Scripture teaches that we can reject God's discipline (Prov. 3:11). Rather, it is one more proof that holiness is required for heaven and not just "faith."

Is it wrong for Christians to drink wine? Since Paul didn't condemn the Corinthians for drinking wine (with alcoholic content) during the Lord's Supper, then the answer must be "no." Drunkenness, however, is a sin that will exclude one from God's kingdom (6:9-10). Avoiding all alcohol is always a sure way to stay sober.

Day 94, 1 Corinthians 12

This really isn't a chapter about spiritual gifts and various ministries. It is a chapter about preserving unity among all the diversity in the church, a chapter about love! The manifold work of the Spirit should not divide us, but be appreciated as being from one source, unifying us. Similarly, even though the church consists of many ethnicities and cultures, one Spirit has baptized us into one body, and one Spirit indwells us all. Paul emphasizes this truth to the point of redundancy in this chapter, hoping we don't miss it!

Paul lists nine spiritual gifts that the Spirit distributes, but notice that his emphasis is not on the gifts, but on the one Spirit who gives all the gifts. Also take note that the spiritual gifts are given *as the Spirit wills* (12:11), so no one possesses them or can turn them on or off at will.

The names Paul gives to each gift help us, to some degree, to define them. Three are gifts of revelation. When God reveals to one of us information about the future, that is a "word of wisdom," whereas a "word of knowledge" would be a supernatural revelation of current or past facts. "Discerning of spirits" is God-given insight into the spiritual world, so that one might see an angel, Jesus, or a demon. People who claim to know everyone's motives through the "gift of discernment" actually have the "gift of suspicion," a gift not given by the Holy Spirit!

Three are gifts that display God's power. If God gives you a "gift of healing" for someone else, you can heal them, even if they have no faith. The "gift of faith" is a supernatural impartation of faith to receive a miracle, whereas the "effecting of miracles" is simply an ability to do something miraculous.

Three are gifts of utterance, and they were quite prevalent in the Corinthian church. Prophecy is Spirit-inspired utterance in a known language, whereas "various kinds of tongues" is Spirit-inspired utterance in an unknown language. The "interpretation of tongues" is self-explanatory!

Speaking of speaking in other tongues, the obvious answer to Paul's rhetorical question in 12:30, "All do not speak with tongues, do they?" is "no." We will see clearly, however, when we read chapter 14, that the ability to pray in tongues, given when one is baptized in the Spirit, is somewhat different than the spontaneous "gift of tongues" that is only granted to some. That spontaneous gift is what Paul must have been referring to in 12:30.

The problem in today's church with trying to apply Paul's words about preserving unity among the many diverse members of Christ's body is that so much of today's church is not part of Christ's body! Pastors whose congregations consist of sheep mixed with goats who think they are sheep can find little application from this chapter for their churches. God doesn't give spiritual gifts to goats. Goats don't have the Spirit in them. When another member of the body suffers, goats don't care. Goats only care about themselves. Goats are inclined towards division. In reality, they hate Bible Jesus, and so they also hate anyone who truly loves Bible Jesus. A recipe for division!

Paul's words in this chapter only have application among true followers of Christ. They consider their relationships with each other to be sacred. They genuinely care for one another.

In the church, God has appointed "first apostles, second prophets, [and] third teachers"(12:28). There is no biblical evidence that has ever changed. Apostles plant churches by the power of the Holy Spirit. Prophets are frequently granted the gifts of revelation and prophecy. Teachers instruct the church to obey Christ's commandments.

Scripture, of course, also warns against false apostles, prophets and teachers, of which there is no shortage today. False apostles aren't planting churches; they are elevating themselves over existing churches to gain wealth and power. False prophets are prophesying to people what they want to hear in order to enrich themselves. And false teachers also tickle people's ears, downplaying or ignoring any teaching on holiness, again, in order to make money. Money is indeed the driving force behind every wolf in sheep's clothing. Beware!

Day 95, 1 Corinthians 13

It is fun to read this famous chapter, so often recited in sermons about love, within its context of the entire Corinthian letter. It appears that everything that Paul wrote to define love has some direct application to a situation in Corinth, where love was definitely lacking.

For example, when we read the very next chapter in 1 Corinthians, we'll learn that speaking in tongues had superseded love in the Corinthian church. Some were speaking with other tongues in a selfish manner. Paul's lovely and poetic words that are often read at wedding ceremonies—"If I speak with the tongues of men and of angels, but do not have love, I have become a noisy gong or a clanging cymbal"—were a stinging rebuke to the Corinthians. Truly, there is little that is more obnoxious than a Pentecostal gong or Charismatic clanger! All noise, no love!

Similarly, Paul puts spiritual gifts, with which the Corinthian believers were so enamored, into their proper perspective. One might possess the gift of prophecy, amazing revelation, and even mountain-moving faith, but without love, he amounts to absolutely nothing (13:2). Such words no doubt deflated many Corinthian egos as they were first read. Love is the important thing.

Paul also points out the fact that not all that *appears* to be loving *is* love. One can do "unselfish" things for selfish reasons, including giving to the poor and making great personal sacrifices, if such things are done for the praise of others. Paul reiterates what Jesus taught; there will be no reward for such "good deeds." The selfish "lover" profits nothing (13:3).

Let's imagine we are Corinthians as we read Paul's definition of love. Here is more of what we might hear:

> "Love is patient, so it waits for everyone to show up at the Lord's Supper before eating. Love does not brag, and it is not arrogant about favorite Christian leaders, saying, 'I am of Paul' and, 'I am of Peter.' Love does not seek its own, and so it is

willing to forgo eating meats sacrificed to idols if a fellow saint with a weak conscience might be caused to stumble. Love does not rejoice in unrighteousness, such as when it knows that a man in the church is living in an immoral relationship with his stepmother. Rather, love rejoices in the truth. Love also bears all things, believes all things, hopes all things, and endures all things, so those of you who are always complaining about each other need to stop grumbling!"

Some say that Paul's foretelling that tongues would cease, along with the other spiritual gifts that he mentions such as the word of knowledge and prophecy, was fulfilled when the last book of the Bible was written, because Paul wrote, "we know in part and we prophesy in part; but when the perfect comes, the partial will be done away" (13:8-10). Supposedly, we no longer need spiritual gifts since we have the complete Bible.

The truth is, however, that even with the complete Bible, we still "know in part," and we continue to "see in a mirror dimly" (13:9, 12). Only when Jesus is reigning on this earth will that no longer be true. And that is comforting to those of us, like me, who are perplexed about so many things now. Think of how different your understanding was when you were a child compared to how it is now as an adult. Similarly, when you are in the future kingdom, you will look back at your earthly life and say to yourself, "How very little I understood!" Now it is as if we are looking at everything in a mirror's reflection, and under dim light! Everything is backwards and indistinct, and we're only seeing a small fragment of the entire picture. We know so very little that there is no room for pride, as Paul wrote a few chapters earlier, "If anyone supposes that he knows anything, he has not yet known as he ought to know" (1 Cor. 8:3).

I know so little. I am D—U—M dum! But don't laugh at me! You're a dummy reading a commentary written by another dummy!

Day 96, 1 Corinthians 14

The early church gatherings were not characterized by the majority passively listening to a trained clergyman. Rather, there was participation among everyone who shared what the Holy Spirit gave him. Thus it could be said, as Paul did, "When you assemble, each one has a psalm, has a teaching, has a revelation, has a tongue, has an interpretation" (14:26).

There was, however, some disorder at believers' gatherings in Corinth. Specifically, there were three groups that were speaking when they should not have been. Some, for example, were publicly speaking in tongues without any interpretation, which provided no benefit to the gathering. Paul instructed such folks to "keep silent in the church" (14:28). They should speak to themselves and God.

Why would God give someone the ability to speak in tongues without the accompanying gift of "the interpretation of tongues" that Paul listed in 12:10, especially since one who spoke publicly in tongues without an interpretation was out of order?

The only possible answer, and one that harmonizes with the experience of millions of Christians, is that the ability to pray in tongues is different than the spontaneous "gift of tongues." The former is something that the Lord grants believers when they are first baptized in the Spirit. That supernatural ability operates any time they will it from then on, just as Paul indicated in 14:15, while the genuine "gifts of tongues" operates only as the Spirit wills (12:11). The former is for private use by believers in their personal devotions for self-edification, and they do not know what they are praying (14:14), whereas the latter is for the public benefit of the church, and is always accompanied by the "gift of the interpretation of tongues" (otherwise God would be the source of disorder).

All of this is to say that there must be two kinds of speaking in tongues. In Corinth, Spirit-baptized believers were speaking out in tongues, but not because they were suddenly anointed by the Spirit to do so, which would be a manifestation of the "gift of tongues." Rather, they were publicly speaking out in tongues using their ability to pray in tongues, given to them from the time they were baptized in the Holy Spirit.

In this light, Paul's rhetorical question that we read in chapter 12, "All do not speak with tongues, do they?" (12:30), is easy to harmonize with other scriptures that lead us to believe that speaking in tongues can be experienced and enjoyed by every believer once he or she is baptized in the Spirit. Paul's question referred to the spontaneous "gift of tongues," not to the ability to pray in tongues.

Paul really encouraged the practice of prophecy and then he corrected two other groups who were speaking out of order—certain prophets and certain wives. I don't believe that Paul's instruction to women to "keep silent in the churches" (14:34) was intended to keep them completely and continually silent any time the churches gathered. He had already written in this very letter about women publicly praying and prophesying (11:5). Paul was specifically addressing wives who were interrupting the flow of the gathering by conversing with their husbands.

Keep in mind that in this same chapter, Paul also told two other groups to be "silent"—out-of—order tongues speakers (14:28) and certain prophets (14:30). In neither case did he mean that they were to remain completely and continually silent any time the churches gathered.

Granted, this chapter in Corinthians raises as many questions as it answers. Some statements within it seem so contradictory from one verse to the next that some commentators think Paul was quoting from the letter that the Corinthians had written to him, and then immediately correcting what they wrote. For example, they believe that the words about women in 14:34-35 are a quote from the Corinthians' letter, and the verse immediately following is Paul's rebuttal: "Was it from you that the word of God first went forth? Or has it come to you only?" (14:36). That is, "Who are you to be making up such regulations about women not speaking? Are you the final authority from God on the matter?" Many women approve of that interpretation!

Day 97, 1 Corinthians 15

Note that Paul's gospel was something by which one could be saved if one "held fast" to it (15:2). Paul did not believe in an unconditional eternal security.

Notice also that the part of Paul's gospel that was "of first importance" was that "Christ died for our sins" (15:3). Unless humanity is sinful and God is wrathful, then there was no need for Christ to die for our sins. These twin truths are the foundation of the gospel.

Not only is Christ's death for our sins an essential part of the gospel, but so is His resurrection from the dead. If this chapter teaches us anything, it teaches us that the concept of resurrection is a major tenet of Christian doctrine. Some in Corinth, however, like the Sadducees who once challenged Jesus (Matt. 22:23), denied it. Yet to deny the possibility of resurrection is to deny Christ's resurrection and to make false witnesses out of hundreds of Jesus' contemporaries, including the eleven apostles. If Jesus didn't come back to life, we would have to wonder why at least 10 of 11 were willing to die for something they knew was a lie.

If Jesus was not resurrected, then He was a liar, because He promised He would rise from the dead; He was not the Son of God; our sins have not been forgiven; and the Holy Spirit does not live in us. "If we have hoped in Christ in this life only, we are of all men most to be pitied" (1 Cor. 15:19). You might as well throw your Bible and *HeavenWord Daily* in the trash.

According to Paul, if Christ has not been raised, we might as well go on sinning, because holiness is unimportant. This indicates that if one believes that Christ has been raised, *it is vital that he or she lives obediently*. Note that among all Paul's words about the doctrine of the resurrection that he plugs holiness: "Become sober-minded as you ought, and stop sinning" (15:34). His concluding statement at the end of this long chapter about the resurrection is also an admonition to obedience: "Therefore, my beloved brethren, be steadfast, immovable, always abounding in the work of the Lord, knowing that your toil is not in vain in the Lord" (15:58).

Thank God Jesus has been raised from the dead! And the risen one promised a resurrection for the righteous and the wicked.

> Do not marvel at this; for an hour is coming, in which all who are in the tombs will hear His voice, and will come forth; those who did the good deeds to a resurrection of life, those who committed the evil deeds to a resurrection of judgment (John 5:28-29).

The resurrection of the righteous will take place when Jesus returns, but the resurrection of the unrighteous will not take place until 1,000 years later (Rev. 20:4-5, 13).

Believers who are alive when Jesus returns will also receive new bodies "in a twinkling of an eye" (15:52). What will those new, resurrected bodies be like? They will not be "flesh and blood," but will be "spiritual," "heavenly," "glorious," "powerful," "imperishable" and "immortal." Those bodies will never grow old or die. Eternal youth! Great news for the over-thirty crowd!

The only verse in the entire Bible that speaks of people being "baptized for the dead" is the one we just read today in 15:29, so it is difficult to interpret what Paul meant. I've never read a satisfying explanation. But surely the practice of Mormons, who search genealogical records in order to be baptized on behalf of their deceased ancestors to gain them some spiritual status is not what Paul had in mind. Such a doctrine denigrates Jesus' sacrifice, superseding it by a relatives' quick dip, which becomes one's ticket to heaven. Can you imagine someone suffering in hell who one day is tapped on the shoulder by a demon who says, "Lucky for you that your grand nephew just took a little dip under the water and repeated your name...now you can get out of here and go to heaven with the saints and angels!" Seems somewhat unlikely, doesn't it?

Day 98, 1 Corinthians 16

It is going to be difficult to restrain myself from writing the truth today, so I think I will just throw caution to the wind. If you've stayed with me four-and-a-half months, there is probably little danger of losing you now! So here goes!

I can't tell you the number of times I've seen 1 Corinthians 16:2 quoted on church offering envelopes: "On the first day of every week each one of you is to put aside and save, as he may prosper..." This verse is used to motivate churchgoers to give to the church on a weekly basis, and it is a classic example of ripping a verse from its context.

Notice that Paul was not referring to receiving collections for churches. He was writing about a "collection for the saints," namely the very poor among the believers in Jerusalem (16:1-3). Why there were so many poor Christians in Jerusalem we are not told, but I suspect it was due to the high degree of persecution leveled against them by the Jews.

There are no biblical records of any offerings "for the church." The reason is because churches had no expenses. They had no special buildings to pay for because small flocks met in homes, just as we read today of a church that met in the house of Aquila and Prisca (16:19). There were no mortgages or utility bills. There were no "building fund drives" to add a "fellowship hall" or "Sunday school annex." Moreover, there were no staff salaries to pay. There were no "senior pastors," "associate pastors," "administrative pastors," "youth pastors," "music ministers" and so on, all creations of modern church structure. There were only pastors/elders/overseers, and most of them did not need remuneration due to the part-time nature of their responsibilities to care for and disciple a small group. We will soon be reading, in Acts, Paul's address to the elders of the church of Ephesus, in which he said:

> I have coveted no one's silver or gold or clothes.
> You yourselves know that these hands ministered
> to my own needs and to the men who were with

me. In everything I showed you that by working hard in this manner you must help the weak and remember the words of the Lord Jesus, that He Himself said, "It is more blessed to give than to receive" (Acts 20:33-35).

At the most, pastors/elders/overseers who devoted part of their time to shepherd their flocks needed only part-time wages. But many, like Paul, worked to support themselves, thus having something to share with "the weak," and by so doing, set a good example before their flocks. Paul, typical of traveling ministers in his time, normally relied on free-will offerings from those he served, as well as the shared earnings of his traveling band.

As I survey the great mass of frustrated pastors around the world, I can't help but think they would all be much happier and more fulfilled if they simply adopted a biblical pattern for their ministry, so I write this out of love for them!

Most churches receive offerings every Sunday, often using envelopes on which 1 Corinthians 16:2 is written. Yet very little, if any, of what is collected is used to support poor Christians who are lacking basic necessities such as food and covering. This is an astonishing fact, and it shows how far we have drifted from the biblical pattern. Think of the millions upon millions of dollars that are collected in wealthy Western churches every Sunday, dollars that are used for things that are never mentioned or recommended in Scripture, while more than half of the Christians in the world live on less than two dollars a day!

Were there any administrative costs related to meeting the pressing needs of the Jerusalem believers? Certainly a small percentage of what was collected in Corinth had to be used to pay for delivering the collected funds to Jerusalem. But no one, I can assure you, was taking $400,000 per year for their administrative work in serving the poor, as are some today who head large Christian humanitarian organizations. May God have mercy on their souls!

Day 99, Acts 20:1-6 & 2 Corinthians 1

It is helpful to know something of the occasion of this letter in order to understand the letter itself. Everything, however, is not so clear. I suspect that Paul had no idea that his letters would be studied for hundreds of years by future Christians, otherwise he would have worked harder at making them easier to understand by those of us who were not part of his intended readership.

After his three-year sojourn in Ephesus, where he penned 1 Corinthians, Paul traveled along the coast of the Aegean Sea back to Macedonia and Greece. At some point he briefly visited the Corinthian believers. That visit didn't go as well as he had hoped, and after his departure, he wrote a letter to the Corinthians that was quite severe, penned "with many tears" (2:3-4). Fearing that his severe letter may have done more damage than good, Paul headed back towards Corinth. On the way there, he eventually met up with Titus who informed him that his letter had, for the most part, accomplished the intended result. Paul wrote 2 Corinthians after receiving Titus' encouraging report (2:12-13; 7:6, 13). This means, of course, that 2 Corinthians is actually 3 Corinthians! (Actually, 2 Corinthians is at least 4 Corinthians, because Paul wrote a letter to the Corinthians that predated 1 Corinthians; see 1 Cor. 5:9).

Paul began this letter by focusing on God's mercy and comfort. Because of Titus' good report, he had been comforted, and he wanted to comfort the Corinthians who were no doubt troubled about their relationship with him. In keeping with that theme, Paul related his experience with God's comfort when he was recently in Asia, where he and his band "despaired even of life" (1:8). Paul must have been referring to the uproar and riot in Ephesus, of which his ministry was the cause, that we read about in Acts 19:23-40. Apparently there was more danger that surrounded that incident than Luke's account in Acts reveals. Regardless, Paul enjoyed "the peace that surpasses all understanding" (Phil. 4:7) in the midst of a very stressful situation. That comfort is available to you, but faith is what activates it.

Paul credited the Lord with his deliverance from those who would have killed him, but he also credited the prayers of the Corinthian believers (1:9-11). It is encouraging to know that our prayers help keep God's front-line servants safe from harm.

There was apparently some misunderstanding on the part of the Corinthians regarding Paul's intended traveling schedule as it related to his coming to visit them. We don't know all the details so it isn't easy for us to sort out. We do know that when Paul was in Ephesus, he "purposed in the spirit" to journey to Macedonia and Achaia and then on to Jerusalem and Rome (Acts 19:21). That is the exact course he ultimately followed. According to what we read today, he intended to go through Corinth twice, but the second visit never occurred, and so Paul explained why.

He did not want the Corinthian believers to think that he was charting his own course or vacillating in his intentions, an indication that he was "purposing according the flesh" (1:17). It seems Paul was even more concerned that his loss of credibility regarding his traveling intentions might cause the Corinthian believers to doubt his message about Christ. So he first addressed that issue, affirming that the message preached by himself, Silvanus and Timothy was fully trustworthy. And then—without resorting to swearing with an oath, but calling on God as a "witness to his soul" (1:23)—Paul explained why he didn't visit Corinth the second time as he had intended. It was to spare them. Rather than visit, he decided to send a letter instead.

Perhaps you've found yourself in a similar situation, when writing a letter to someone seemed like a better thing to do than speaking to them face-to-face. A letter gives them time to think about their reaction before they respond. A letter rather than a face-to-face encounter can be an act of wisdom and love. But not always! Every situation requires its own evaluation.

Day 100, 2 Corinthians 2

Not wanting to visit Corinth a third time to face the same unresolved problems, Paul determined to wait. Remember that when we read 1 Corinthians, we learned that there were factions in Corinth over favorite teachers and leaders. Although one group was loyal to Paul, others were declaring their allegiance to Peter or Apollos (1 Cor. 1:12). Thus, there was a group that was opposed to Paul. You can be sure that if there was a group that was opposed to Paul, there was a leader of that group. It seems that during Paul's second brief visit to Corinth he dealt with that opposition leader rather harshly, excommunicating him with the support of the majority, which proved to be devastating to that unnamed man. Paul now urged the Corinthian believers to forgive and comfort him, reaffirming their love.

Some have surmised that the unnamed man whom Paul encouraged the Corinthians to forgive and reinstate was the incestuous man whom Paul instructed the Corinthians to excommunicate in 1 Corinthians 5. You may recall that he was living with his stepmother in an immoral relationship, clearly marking him as a "so-called brother," that is, not a brother at all, and one that would not inherit God's kingdom (1 Cor. 5:11; 6:9-10). It is, of course, possible that the immoral man had repented, and if so, receiving him back into fellowship would have been appropriate.

Regardless of who the offender was who had been disciplined and then reinstated, take note that Paul was not recommending "universal forgiveness," something that is advocated today in some Christian circles. God's forgiveness of people is predicated upon their repentance. If it wasn't, then He would be unrighteous, approving of sin. God *never* approves of sin. When Christians "forgive" those who are unrepentant, they likewise show themselves to be unrighteous, approving of sin. This is the flaw in the message of "universal forgiveness" that is being propagated. The truth is, "universal forgiveness" is ungodly. Paul instructed the Corinthians to forgive the unnamed man because he was on the verge of being "overwhelmed by excessive sorrow" (2:7). He was repentant. Keep in mind that Jesus advocated excommunication for unrepentant offenders in the church (Matt. 18:15-17). He also declared: "Be on your guard! If your brother sins, rebuke him; *and if he repents, forgive him*" (Luke 17:3).

As Paul journeyed back towards Macedonia and Achaia, he had hoped to meet Titus in Troas, which was on the opposite side of the Aegean Sea, to learn from him how the Corinthians had received his severe letter. Titus didn't show up in Troas as he had hoped, and so Paul left for Macedonia himself, in spite of the fact that a door for the gospel had been opened in Troas (2:12-13). The health of the Corinthian church was prioritized over starting a new church in Troas. It's always a good idea to prioritize preserving what has been gained before trying to gain more.

What are we to make of Paul's words that "we are a fragrance of Christ to God among those who are being saved and among those who are perishing; to the one an aroma from death to death, to the other an aroma from life to life" (2:25-26)?

In ancient Rome, when a general returned from winning a battle, he would lead a victory procession through the streets of his capital city. Behind the incense bearers came the enemy captives bound in chains. To the conquerors, the incense was the smell of victory. To the defeated captives, the incense signified defeat and death. Applying Paul's analogy, Jesus is our conquering general who is leading us in His triumphant procession. We are like incense-bearers from whom wafts an aroma that testifies of life to believers and death to unbelievers. To God's enemies, we are giving off an aroma of death. When they reject our message, they seal their doom.

Even in Paul's day there were those who, to borrow his words, "peddled the word of God" (2:17), using it for personal profit. Not much has changed since then, has it?

Congratulations, by the way. You've just completed 100 out of 260 days of reading through the entire New Testament!

Day 101, 2 Corinthians 3

Paul's critical comment at the end of chapter 2, "We are not like many, peddling the word of God," is our first indication in this letter that there may have been false teachers who had gained some influence in Corinth. Paul's comment could have been considered prideful by his readers, so he quickly reminded them that he needed no self-commendation (as the false teachers likely did). Moreover, Paul and his band needed no letters of reference to gain the Corinthians' trust, and for that matter, needed no letters of reference from the Corinthians to gain the trust of others. The transformed lives of the Corinthians themselves were, metaphorically speaking, Paul's letter of reference, as he was the human instrument whom God used in their transformation. (How many modern pastors would want their flocks to serve as their letter of reference?) Paul made sure his readers knew that he was not boasting in himself, but in the Lord, who made him "an adequate servant of the new covenant" (3:6).

Paul's comparison of the old and new covenants gives us some idea what the false teachers were promoting in Corinth, and it should come as no surprise to us at this point in our study. It was the same old issue of Jewish teachers trying to put Gentile believers under the Law of Moses. Paul was quite bold, saying that the difference between the old and new covenants is death versus life, the letter that kills versus the Spirit that gives life. The only thing that the Law of Moses has ever done for anyone was curse them, since it promised a curse upon transgressors, and no one ever kept it. Thinking one was saved by circumcision, one small requirement of the Mosaic Law, while ignoring the majority of the rest of the Law, was especially ludicrous.

Certainly the Jewish teachers could expound on the glories of how God gave the Law to Moses—recounting how it was written by His finger in stone tablets—as they attempted to convince their audiences of uncircumcised men to line up for some very painful minor surgery. Remember that when Moses carried those stone tablets down from Mt. Sinai, he did not realize that his face was literally glowing with God's glory. Upon seeing him, the people of Israel were afraid to come near him. Consequently, Moses covered his face with a veil to hide the glory that shown from his skin (Ex. 34:27-35). You can imagine Jewish teachers wowing young Gentile men with that story.

Perhaps seizing the Jewish teachers' strongest argument, Paul pointed out that the glory on Moses' face faded, symbolic of the temporary nature of the old covenant, whereas the promised new covenant was never-ending. And there was a second analogy. Moses' veil that hid the glory from Israel symbolized their alienation from God and spiritual darkness, as revealed by their continual rebellion and hardness of heart, even until Paul's day. How tragic it was that people who heard the Law read every Sabbath remained spiritually blind, separated from the glory of God, because they sought salvation in what could only condemn them. When any of them turned to Christ, however, that veil was lifted, revealing the glory that had previously been hidden from them.

So, although the old covenant revealed God's glory, the greater glory was largely hidden and waiting to be fully revealed in Christ and the new covenant. Consequently, the glory of the old was of no comparison to the new, and how foolish it would be for any Gentile believer to listen to those still veiled in darkness who were trying to take them backwards from new life to old death!

I've heard Paul's phrase, "Where the Spirit of the Lord is, there is liberty" (3:17), used to encourage people in church services to abandon their reservations and enjoy the freedom of the Spirit, often an invitation to imitate some bizarre charismatic behavior, an incredible contextual misapplication of Paul's words! Paul was not talking about acting like idiots in church services. The indwelling Spirit, given in the new covenant, grants Jews freedom from the Mosaic Law. Where the Spirit is, there is liberty!

Day 102, 2 Corinthians 4

This chapter offers a glimpse into the heart and ministry of the apostle Paul that should have touched the hearts of the Corinthian believers as they considered the price he paid for their sakes. Paul's intent, I suspect, was to subtly contrast himself with the false teachers who had infiltrated Corinth, men whose motives were selfish.

Every minister, and every Christian for that matter, who reads this chapter should be inspired to imitate Paul's servanthood and steadfastness in the midst of suffering. Because of his calling to ministry, Paul recognized that he must be holy, and so he "renounced the things hidden because of shame" (4:2). Every minister needs to understand that his calling to ministry is, first of all, a calling to holiness, because the goal of every minister is to make disciples who obey all of Christ's commandments.

Along these same lines, a second characteristic of Paul's that is worthy of every minister's imitation was his conviction to "preach...Christ Jesus as Lord" (4:5). That should be the heart of all preaching, but not just as a worn-out and meaningless cliche', but as the most fundamental and vital doctrine of true Christianity, so that listeners understand that Christ should be ruling every aspect of their lives.

Not only did Paul live and preach Christ's lordship, but he consequently considered himself to be a servant of all, which would only be right for one whose Lord is Christ, since Christ taught us to be servants. The word "minister" does not mean "little king" as you might think from observing some modern ministers, but is actually a synonym for "servant." Paul's willingness to serve motivated him to endure continual physical hardship and persecution, which he described as "always carrying about in the body the dying of Jesus, so that the life of Jesus may also be manifested in our body" (4:10). The wider context seems to indicate that he was referring to the inseparable correlation between his sufferings and the fruitfulness of his ministry. Just as Christ's death resulted in new life for others, so Paul's sufferings (even to the point of being stoned and left for dead) contributed to the new life that the Corinthians enjoyed. "So death works in us, but life in you" (4:12), he wrote.

That knowledge helped to keep Paul from losing heart in his sufferings. Not only that, but he knew there was a reward waiting for him one day. "Momentary, light affliction is producing for us an eternal weight of glory for beyond all comparison" (4:18). So Paul kept his eyes, not on the temporary and visible, but on the eternal and invisible. So should we. Contemporary "Christianity," however, sadly lacks this perspective, and books with titles such as, *Your Best Life Now*, become best-sellers. When you follow Christ, there is a price. At the very least, you will find yourself misunderstood and alienated. We should not be surprised, however, since we are aliens on this earth (1 Pet. 1:1; 2:11)!

So be encouraged today. Chances are, your sufferings for Christ are minimal compared to Paul's. That should also be an encouragement to be willing to suffer more and make greater sacrifices, as we know that those who suffer more will be rewarded more in the end.

Today's reading includes a short passage that is sometimes extracted from its greater context in order to encourage unscriptural practices under the banner of "spiritual warfare." Paul wrote that his gospel was veiled to "those who are perishing, in whose case the god of this world has blinded the minds of the unbelieving so that they might not see the light of the gospel" (4:4). Notice Paul did not go on to recommend "binding demons in the atmosphere in order to release people from Satan's blinding them." From reading the rest of Scripture, we know that Satan's blinding is a secondary cause for people's rejection of the gospel. The primary reason is the hardness of their hearts. Satan simply supplies the lies that hard-hearted people love to believe, giving them excuse to continue in their sin and violate their consciences. Satan can't stop anyone from humbling himself and believing.

Day 103, 2 Corinthians 5

Paul, never short of metaphors, today offers two relating to Christian death. For believers, death is like a day when we will change our residence, and it is definitely a move to a nicer neighborhood, from a temporary tent to an eternal house (5:1). Death is also like going from a state of nakedness to putting on clothes. Being clothed is, generally speaking, a much more secure feeling than being naked. So in both metaphors, death is presented as something positive. For believers, death is actually our preference! "We are of good courage...and *prefer* to be absent from the body and to be at home with the Lord" (5:8). And there is a third metaphor! Death is like going home.

Of course, only those who look at death by faith rather than by sight possess such an attitude about it. To the eye, death seems to be anything but favorable. The world recoils at the thought of dying (and so they should), but we face it courageously knowing it promises better things for us. Twice Paul refers to our current "groanings," alternately translated as "deep sighs." Our hearts are longing for the place for which we've been prepared, longings which are birthed by the indwelling Holy Spirit who has been given to us by God as a "pledge," or "down payment," of our future inheritance. The best is yet to come! This life is the only hell believers will ever know, while this life is the only heaven unbelievers will ever experience.

Knowing what is to come motivates us to strive to please God now, because we also know that our first stop on the other side of death is repayment at the judgment seat of Christ. Everyone, believers and unbelievers alike, will stand before Christ to give an account (and this is certainly illustrated in the judgment of the sheep and goats of which Jesus spoke in Matthew 25). Everyone will be repaid, reaping what they have sown. That is a very fearful thing for those who have never repented (5:11). Believers will be rewarded for the good they have done, but obviously, they will also suffer loss for the good that they *could* have done, but didn't. So judgment won't necessarily be all joy for every believer. For pseudo-believers, like the goats Jesus spoke of in Matthew 25, there will be great shock, followed by weeping and gnashing of teeth.

Take note of Paul's words, "Having concluded this, that one died for all, therefore all died" (5:14). That is, because of the fact that Jesus died for everyone, we know that everyone was spiritually dead. This one verse exposes the error found in the Calvinistic concept known as "Limited Atonement," the idea that Jesus only died for those who were allegedly pre-selected by God. Paul clearly states that Jesus died for all, and not "all" in the sense that Calvinists twist it to mean "all who were preselected to be saved." No, Paul states that because Jesus died for all, we can therefore be sure that "all died." Calvinists universally agree that all unregenerate people are spiritually dead, and not just those who are allegedly pre-selected to be saved. So if the "all" in the second part of that verse means "all human beings" (which it must) then the "all" found just two words earlier also refers to all human beings. There is no way to escape this fact.

Why did Jesus die for all? "So that they who live might no longer live for themselves, but for Him who died and rose again" (5:15). There's the gospel in a nutshell. Jesus died, not just to forgive us, but to make us holy, or as Paul said, "so that we might become the righteousness of God in Him" (5:21). One must ignore the context of 5:21 to claim, as so many do, that Paul was speaking only of our being made "legally righteous" without being made practically righteous. True Christians have been made "new creatures" (5:17), people who have been spiritually reborn and indwelled by the Holy Spirit, all so they might live righteously. As John would later write, "Make sure no one deceives you; the one who practices righteousness is righteous (1 John 3:7).

Day 104, 2 Corinthians 6

In the previous chapter, Paul made mention of certain antagonists in Corinth who "took pride in appearance and not in heart" (5:12). This theme surfaces more frequently as Paul's letter progresses, and it becomes quite clear that he had found himself competing with Jewish legalists for the affection and loyalty of the Corinthian believers.

It was a delicate matter that required great wisdom on his part, and rather than launch an all-out attack on his adversaries, Paul reminded the Corinthians of the sacrifices he had made on their behalf. It was a subtle strategy that provided an obvious contrast with the Jewish legalists. They could not say that they had endured afflictions, hardships, beatings, imprisonments, sleeplessness, hunger, dishonor, slander and punishments for the gospel's sake, as Paul could! Additionally, the Jewish legalists could not hold a candle to Paul's Christ-like purity, patience, kindness, love and joy (6:6, 10). He had the indwelling Holy Spirit; they did not! They were still dead in their sins, trying to save themselves apart from Christ; he was alive in Christ, saved by grace through faith.

Paul then makes his appeal for the Corinthian believers, whom he says were "restrained in [their] own affections" (6:12), to open wide their hearts to him. How could they resist? Later in this same letter, Paul will take a greater risk, openly and dramatically comparing himself to his antagonists. How delicate are human relationships! And how difficult it sometimes is to maintain harmony, especially when there are selfishly-motivated slanderers trying to cause division.

It is sometimes difficult to follow the flow of thought in Paul's epistles, understanding how one paragraph might have any logical relationship to the paragraph that precedes it. But it is safe to assume that Paul was no dummy, and knowing that, also to assume that there might well be some relationship between paragraphs that seem to bear no relationship. An example of what I'm speaking about is found in today's reading. Paul seems to jump from appealing for the Corinthians to open their hearts to admonishing them not to be bound together with unbelievers. Is he introducing an entirely new subject, or is there some connection to what he had just written?

I think it is quite possible (and logical) that Paul was subtly referring to the Corinthian's relationship to the false teachers who had infiltrated the church. There is little doubt that the Jewish legalists—Paul's frequent adversaries—were not saved. Thus, Paul was reminding the Corinthian believers that they really had nothing in common with them.

Some have gone to extremes in practicing separation from the world, keeping themselves safely cloistered away, consequently having no impact upon the world. We are supposed to be "*in* the world but not *of* the world." Our lights should be shining in the world's darkness so that they see our good deeds (Matt. 5:16), but we should avoid any partnerships with the world that make us participants in their evil.

While 2 Corinthians 6:14 is so often applied to marriage partnerships, it has much greater application than that. I am persuaded, for example, that holding shares in mutual funds that own shares in companies that manufacture or promote what God hates is an example of being "bound together with unbelievers." When a production company profits from producing an immoral movie, so do all the shareholders. Should Christians be profiting from a film that glorifies what God hates? Other examples could be cited. The point is that our holy Father expects us, His children, also to be holy. For that reason, we should have no partnership with those who do evil.

What do modern prosperity preachers do with Paul's declaration that he was poor, yet made many rich (6:10)? They avoid it! Paul could have meant nothing else than that he was materially poor, yet through his ministry, he made many spiritually rich. He certainly was not claiming to be *spiritually* poor yet making many *materially* rich! If he made many materially rich through "teaching the secrets of divine prosperity" (as some claim), we would have to wonder why he couldn't get those secrets to work for himself.

Day 105, 2 Corinthians 7

Our sanctification—our growing in holiness—is not something that is done by the Lord as we "let go" and "stop trying to be holy by our own efforts" as is sometimes taught. Believers must "strive against sin" (Heb. 12:4), "resist the devil" (Jas. 4:7), and "crucify the flesh with its passions and desires" (Gal. 5:24), to mention just a few biblical phrases that emphasize our part in the sanctification process. Today we read of our duty to "cleanse ourselves from all defilement of flesh and spirit, perfecting holiness in the fear of God" (7:1). Clearly, that is something *we* must do.

This is not to say, however, that the Holy Spirit doesn't help us to be holy. Sanctification occurs as we cooperate with the Spirit inside us. Maintain this balanced perspective!

From this same scripture passage, we also see the error in the idea that sin cannot originate from a Christian's spirit, or heart, but only from his flesh. Paul wrote of the need to cleanse ourselves from every defilement of flesh *and spirit*. Christians may possess wrong motives, which is why, for example, Jesus warned His followers about praying in public to be seen by others and why Paul cautioned about giving to the poor without love (Matt. 6:5-6; 1 Cor. 13:3).

Paul's words about "perfecting holiness in the fear of God" reveal to us that Christians aren't perfect, otherwise they would not need perfecting! On the other hand, his words also reveal that Christians are somewhat holy, otherwise they couldn't perfect their holiness.

Notice also that being motivated by fear of God is not a bad thing (as so many say today), but a very good thing that Paul recommends (7:1). I'm sure that God, like most parents, would prefer that His children obey Him out of love. But for most children, fear of discipline is a major motivation to obey their parents. Our Bibles tell us that God disciplines those whom He loves, and "He scourges every son whom He receives" (Heb. 12:6). Christians who ignore or don't believe in God's discipline are likely to be rebuking

Satan when they are disciplined rather than examining themselves and repenting. Big mistake!

Themes from previous chapters resurface in today's reading. Paul continues to appeal to the Corinthian believers to open their hearts to him by reminding them of his love for them. He recounts how troubled he was after sending his severe letter to them (of which we have no copy), and how relieved he was when Titus returned to him from Corinth with a good report of their repentance (7:5-7).

How strange it is that so many professing Christian leaders speak negatively of guilt, as if it is something no Christian should accept since we've been declared righteous in Christ, and something that, when experienced, should be considered an attack from Satan. Paul wrote of "the sorrow that is according to the will of God [that] produces a repentance without regret" (7:10), and he was quite glad that the Corinthian believers had experienced that sorrow. Is there any relationship between guilt and sorrow for sin? If they are not the same thing, they are certainly quite similar. And it is very clear that the godly sorrow of the Corinthians resulted in a wonderful turn-around in their spiritual lives. Without guilt, no one would repent, and without repentance, no one can be saved. Thank God for guilt!

Where is there a single scripture that says anything about Satan making someone feel guilty? There isn't one in the Bible! About the closest thing is a scripture that speaks of Satan as being "the accuser of the brethren" in Revelation 12:10. But there it says that Satan accuses the brethren *before God*, not that he makes the brethren feel guilty. Why would Satan make anyone feel guilty? He would run the risk of motivating them to repent! If they are unsaved, it might lead to their salvation! Imagine that—Satan helping someone escape hell. Food for thought!

Day 106, 2 Corinthians 8

This and the next chapter of 2 Corinthians beautifully reveal a full and balanced picture of Christian stewardship. Note that the occasion was not the receiving of an offering by Paul for his ministry, or for a church building program, but rather, for poor believers in Jerusalem.

Paul began by informing the Corinthians of what had recently happened among the churches of Macedonia. Even though they were suffering "an ordeal of affliction" as well as "deep poverty" (8:2), they had given liberally. In fact, by God's grace, and without being pressured, they had given even "beyond their ability" (8:3), "begging...with much entreaty for the favor of participation in the support of the saints" (8:4). The Macedonian Christians were the ultimate cheerful givers. Paul expected that the Corinthian believers would follow their example.

Paul then stressed that one's giving is *limited* by his resources, but that one's responsibility is also *determined* by his resources, twice using a word that is almost anathema in materialistic culture, the word *equality* (8:12-15). If one Christian has abundance, he should use it to supply another Christian's need. And if that formerly-poor Christian prospers while the formerly-prosperous one becomes needy, their roles should then be reversed (8:14). It amounts to nothing more than "loving our neighbors as ourselves" and "doing unto others as we would have them do unto us" (Mark 12:31; Luke 6:31).

In 8:9 we read, "For you know the grace of our Lord Jesus Christ, that though He was rich, yet for your sake He became poor, that you through His poverty might become rich."

Prosperity preachers often claim that it is *material* poverty and *material* wealth that Paul had in mind throughout this entire verse. That is, they say that Jesus was *materially* rich in heaven, but He became *materially* poor during His incarnation, so that we can now become *materially* rich. Bigger houses and more expensive cars are now ours to be claimed by faith because Jesus became poor that we might become rich.

There is little doubt that Paul was speaking of material wealth when he wrote that Jesus was rich but became poor. There is good reason to doubt, however, that earthly, material wealth was the benefit Paul had in mind when he wrote of our becoming rich because of Christ's poverty. Such an interpretation stands in contradiction to the immediate biblical context. If Jesus became poor so that Christians might become materially rich on earth, why were there any poor Christians in Jerusalem who needed an offering? Why did Paul, in this same chapter, say that the Macedonian Christians were suffering "deep poverty" (8:2)? Why did Paul describe himself as being poor in 6:10? Why didn't he just claim his rightful, earthly, material wealth that Jesus made possible?

In spite of what prosperity preachers claim, just because Paul was writing about *material* wealth in one part of a sentence, that doesn't prove that he was talking about *material* wealth in another part of the same sentence. For example, Jesus Himself said to the poor believers in Smyrna, "I know your tribulation and your poverty (but you are rich)" (Rev. 2:9). Who could intelligently claim that Jesus was saying that the Christians in Smyrna were *material* poor but also *materially* rich? No, Jesus was obviously saying that they were materially poor but *spiritually* rich, and He said it all in one sentence.

Jesus, because of His incarnation and death on the cross (during which He lost even His clothing, the ultimate poverty), has provided spiritual and eternal riches for us beyond our dreams. Praise God that He has also promised to supply all our material needs (not "greeds") as well!

Paul understood the need for accountability in the administration of benevolence projects, and he was careful to ensure that the offering he received would be used for the purpose for which it was collected. A number of men who had proven their trustworthiness would be involved in the project (8:16-23). Financial accountability is of utmost importance in corporate offerings to the poor, otherwise people are given an excuse to cling to their treasures, claiming that their potential gifts might be mishandled. And who can blame them?

Day 107, 2 Corinthians 9

According to Paul, the Corinthian believers had previously promised a "bountiful gift" (9:5), which would, of course, be made possible only by bountiful giving. Thus Paul cautioned against covetousness (or better translated "greed") that might affect the Corinthians' giving. Clearly, covetousness and greed are not just attitudes of the heart as so many claim. Rather, they are attitudes that are always revealed by actions. If the Corinthians yielded to greed, they would give less. Their selfish attitude would affect their actions.

Paul continued with a warning to those who might yield to greed and a promise to those who would be generous: "Now this I say, he who sows sparingly shall also reap sparingly; and he who sows bountifully shall also reap bountifully" (9:6).

Paul was not revealing "divine secrets for prosperity," encouraging his readers to "sow a big financial seed and reap abundant riches" so that they could then enjoy a lavish lifestyle, as some prosperity preachers want us to believe. If he was, then he was promoting the very thing he was warning against in 9:5, that is, greed. If people give just so they can grow rich and have many possessions, that is nothing more than selfishness disguised as love.

Thus, the reason one should want to "sow bountifully" and thus "reap bountifully" is so one can "sow even more bountifully," blessing more people. This truth Paul plainly repeats three times in 9:8-11. You may want to read those verses again to see for yourself.

Once a sower reaps, he then must decide what to do with his harvest. If he still has more than he needs, and there are still others with pressing needs, then there is no doubt what he should do. His former self-denial certainly wouldn't give him the right to be greedy then. The whole reason to reap is not so one may lay up earthly treasures in disobedience to Christ, but so that one may sow some more and lay up more treasures in heaven.

What constitutes sowing that is "sparing" or "bountiful?" That, of course, is different for each person. The widow who put her two copper coins into the treasury gave more than all the rich people who put in large gifts, according to Jesus (Mark 12:41-44). She "sowed bountifully" while they "sowed sparingly," even though their gifts were much larger. What impresses God is self-denial. Bountiful and sparing sowing are determined by what one keeps.

Finally, Paul also instructed each of the Corinthians to "do just as he has purposed in his heart; not grudgingly or under compulsion; for God loves a cheerful giver" (9:7). This verse has often been twisted to relieve the consciences of selfish people. They are told, "God wants only what you can give cheerfully, so let that be your gauge. Only give what you can give without grudging." Consequently, greedy people give little or nothing, demonstrating no self-denial or love, and think God approves since He doesn't want what they can't give cheerfully.

Paul, however, was not trying to make greedy people think that God is comfortable with their greed, as the context so clearly reveals. He was trying to help each person consider what is in his heart. If one is giving under compulsion or grudgingly, he is not giving because he loves needy brethren.

By the same token, the reason God "loves a cheerful giver" is because a cheerful giver is motivated by love for God and neighbor. He finds joy in sacrificing on behalf of those with pressing needs because he loves them. The one who gives grudgingly or under compulsion, however, reveals a greedy heart, and thus gives hypocritically, because he is doing what his heart would prefer not to do. Thus, it would be better for him not to give at all. But let him not think that God approves of him in either case. God wants him to repent of his selfishness, be transformed by His grace, and become a cheerful giver who denies himself with joy. God, and only God, can turn greedy people into cheerful givers. They then become imitators of Him, who gave sacrificially from a heart of grace and love (9:15). Praise God!

Day 108, 2 Corinthians 10

Paul once more turns his attention to defending himself against his antagonists in Corinth, whom he refers to as false apostles in the next chapter (11:13). It is apparent that they were not only boasting of their "credentials"—in order to boost their status in the eyes of the Corinthian believers—but they were also quite critical of Paul, for the same reason.

How frequently are criticism and pride related. People often put down others for the purpose of exalting themselves, especially when they want something that the object of their criticism possesses. Such was the case with Paul's antagonists. They wanted the allegiance of his disciples in Corinth. Paul consequently found himself in the very difficult position of trying to win back the Corinthians' allegiance—not for his sake, but for theirs—without stooping to the same tactics as his opponents.

One of their criticisms of Paul was that he was bold in his letters but meek when face-to-face (10:1). They said, "His letters are weighty and strong, but his personal presence is unimpressive, and his speech contemptible" (10:10). Paul brushes off that attack, confidently asserting that his character—in words and deeds—was consistent. It is certainly true, however, that words written on a page are in some ways inherently inferior to face-to-face communication, with its facial and body expressions, its tone of voice, and its back-and-forth spontaneity. How many letters have been misunderstood that required a face-to-face meeting to mend? On the other hand, one who writes can give more thought to his words before they are released to discharge their premeditated duty. Wisdom must dictate between written and spoken communication, and sometimes a combination of both is necessary to seal understanding between two parties.

Paul offered his own subtle criticism of his Corinthian opponents, who "measured themselves by themselves" (10:12). It is easy to feel good about yourself when you compare yourself with those who are substandard. Dry pigs who compare themselves with pigs who are lying in the mud might be tempted to feel superior, but the fact is, they're still dirty pigs. In truth, the false teachers who had infiltrated Corinth were of no comparison to Paul, but that was not easy for him to say without sounding as if he were commending himself, something for which he condemned the false apostles.

Paul also gently pointed out that he, unlike the false apostles, had no need to "boast beyond his measure" (10:15). He was the apostolic pioneer in Corinth, and the false apostles had settled later in his territory, yet acting as if they had founder's rights (10:14-15).

Notice also that Paul was hoping, and depending, on the Corinthians to help him reach even further with the gospel (10:15-16). We are so apt to credit God's ministers for their accomplishments in building the kingdom, but their supporters are just as important in God's plan. "How will they preach unless they are sent?" Paul would later ask (Rom. 10:15). Those who support God's apostles will share in their reward in the end. Every apostle needs those who support his ministry.

I'm sure you noticed the "spiritual warfare" passage in today's reading. It is another one of Paul's metaphorical masterpieces that has been abused to promote some strange practices. Paul's weapons of warfare were "divinely powerful for destruction of fortresses" (10:4). Was he referring to demonic strongholds over cities that, if bound in Jesus' name, will then release people from spiritual darkness, precipitating a revival? No mention of that in this passage or its context! Rather, Paul was speaking of "destroying speculations and every lofty thing raised up against the knowledge of God, and...taking every thought captive to the obedience of Christ" (10:5). This is just a figurative way of describing the preaching of the gospel and the making of disciples. It is like a war, but a battle between truth and lies. Truth destroys speculations and takes lies captive.

Our greatest weapon is God's Word, because with it, we expose the lies that so many people believe. Then it rests on them, of course, to believe the truth or a lie. That is the essence of biblical spiritual warfare.

Day 109, 2 Corinthians 11

The identity of the false apostles in Corinth becomes more clear in today's reading. They were preaching "another Jesus" and a "different gospel" (11:4). That second phrase, in particular, Paul also used in his letter to the Galatians, where he fought the influence of Jewish legalists who were telling Gentile believers that they needed to be circumcised and keep the Mosaic Law (Gal. 1:6). The false apostles in Corinth were definitely Jews (11:22). So it seems that perhaps the same problem that had followed Paul elsewhere had tracked him to Corinth.

Paul considered himself "not in the least inferior to the most eminent apostles" (11:5), but he found it so difficult to boast about his own apostolic credentials. He felt that he had no choice, however, since the false apostles in Corinth were boasting of their credentials and influencing the impressionable believers. Paul's motives for his boasting were obviously entirely different than theirs. He was motivated by love for the Corinthian believers, while the false apostles were motivated by love for themselves.

Note Paul's expression, "I am jealous for you with a godly jealousy" (11:2). We generally equate jealousy with selfishness, and for that reason, some have stumbled over God's claim to be "a jealous God" in the Old Testament (Ex. 20:5; Deut. 5:9). God's jealousy is unselfish. He was opposed to Israel's idolatry, not for His sake, but for theirs. It is akin to a parent's jealousy for his child's affection if he sees his child being drawn to those who might lead him astray.

When Paul spoke of his godly jealousy, he may well have meant, "I am motivated to say these things because I understand *God's* jealousy over you," because he went on to say, "for I betrothed you to one husband, so that to Christ I might present you as a pure virgin" (11:2). That is, because the Corinthian believers had submitted to Jesus, marrying Him as it were and becoming part of His bride, He would naturally be jealous over them if they were giving their affections to someone else. Paul was fearful that their misguided affections might result in their being led astray from what is of paramount importance, that is "the simplicity and purity of devotion to Christ" (11:3).

I mention this because it is not only possible for believers to wrongly give their affections to false teachers (as did the Corinthians), arousing God's jealousy, but they may do the same for *legitimate* teachers and Christian leaders, similarly arousing God's jealousy. This is one reason why Jesus forbade His followers from addressing anyone but God as *Teacher*, *Father* or *Leader*. He said that we only have One who is our Teacher, Father, and Leader (Matt. 23:8-10). How tragic it is when Christians become caught up in pet doctrines or spiritual fads, following the leading of the latest popular TV preacher, and are thus sidetracked from the "simplicity and purity of devotion to Christ." Their conversations may be about spiritual things, but they talk about everything other than Jesus. Let's be careful not to make Jesus jealous. And if we are entrusted with a position of leadership in Christ's body, let's be careful, as was Paul, to keep exalting Jesus, and not ourselves, before those whom we serve.

As we read through Paul's list of his sufferings for Christ's sake, it helps us to put our little sufferings in perspective. Paul was not a quitter, that is for sure. His perseverance ought to inspire us to greater devotion and willingness to sacrifice for the gospel's sake.

Paul's list of his sufferings also helps us to realize what an incomplete record we have of his ministry in the book of Acts. Keep in mind that we've read of Paul's ministry from Acts 9 to 20, covering a period of about 20 years, but we've not read of a single instance of him receiving 39 lashes from the Jews. Yet during that time, Paul suffered that punishment five times according to what we just read. That's a total of almost 200 lashes! Every stripe was a testimony of his love for Christ. No wonder Paul could write, "I bear on my body the brand-marks of Jesus" (Gal. 6:17).

Day 110, 2 Corinthians 12

What a struggle Paul had as he worked to win back the hearts of the Corinthian believers who had been duped by false apostles. He was loathe to boast about himself—knowing that he was a "nobody" yet also "in no respect inferior to the most eminent apostles"—but he felt that he had no other option. So we find him writing of a man whom he knew—surely speaking of himself—who "was caught up into Paradise and heard inexpressible words" and received "surpassing revelations" (12:4, 7). It was such a sacred event to Paul that it was not something he readily shared.

The potential for Paul to be lifted up in pride because of his heavenly journey and wonderful revelations was apparently so great that God took significant measures to make sure that he would not exalt himself. Paul was given a "thorn in the flesh" (12:7), clearly a figurative expression.

This passage has unfortunately been used to rob sick Christians of faith to be healed. May I point out that Paul never said that he was ill, he never said that he asked God to heal him, and he never said that God would not heal him. Paul clearly revealed what his "thorn in the flesh" was, calling it "a messenger of Satan." The word translated "messenger" in 12:7 is the Greek word *aggelos*, which is translated 168 times in the New Testament as "angel" and only 7 times as "messenger." Paul's thorn in the flesh was an angel of Satan sent to torment him. Paul asked the Lord three times that "it" might leave him, but the Lord denied his request, which would make sense if it was the Lord who originally permitted the angel to torment Paul in order to prevent him from exalting himself.

How exactly that angel of Satan tormented Paul we are not told, but the result was that Paul found himself weak and needing to depend on the Lord, so that the "power of Christ" was manifested in him. I suspect that tormenting angel was responsible for much of the persecution that was stirred up against Paul, as he referred in this same passage to the weaknesses, insults, distresses, persecutions, and difficulties that he experienced, problems that made him weak, but that ultimately resulted in his being strong, since God's "power is perfected in weakness" (12:9-10). Notice that there is no mention of sickness in Paul's list of difficulties here; nor was sickness mentioned in Paul's earlier list of his various sufferings listed in 11:23-33.

I have two final questions for those who still cling to the idea that Paul's thorn in the flesh was some sickness or disease, using it as their reason to remain sick: "How many journeys to heaven have you experienced that make it necessary for God to keep you from exalting yourself by means of your sickness?" And, "If God wants you to remain sick, why are you going to a doctor or taking medication to thwart God's will?" (I rest my case!)

It is good to always remember that what God said to Paul is true for us all. Our weakness is an opportunity for God to show His strength. When our own resources are inadequate, God's resources are unlimited! We can thus say with Paul, "When I am weak, then I am strong" (12:10). When you feel lousy, God feels great! So trust in Him!

Note Paul's contrast of himself and the false apostles: "The signs of a *true* apostle were performed among you...by signs and wonders and miracles" (12:12). That would seem to indicate that not a few of the modern "apostles," whose greatest sign or wonder is pushing someone over in a prayer line, are not apostles at all.

In spite of Titus' good report, it is obvious that Paul remained apprehensive that his upcoming visit to Corinth might uncover "strife, jealousy, angry tempers, disputes...impurity, immorality and sensuality" (12:20-21), sins that, according to Paul himself, will prevent people from inheriting God's kingdom (Gal. 5:19-21). This reveals the real root of the problem in Corinth. Goats, by nature, don't act like sheep. And goats don't belong with sheep. A showdown was on the horizon.

Day 111, 2 Corinthians 13

The somewhat foreboding and even threatening tone of this final section of Paul's letter set the stage for his eminent return to Corinth. Imagine if your church received a letter that ended this way from the apostle Paul. I bet there would be some serious self-examination!

Indeed, self-examination was precisely what Paul prescribed for Corinth: "Test yourselves to see if you are in the faith; examine yourselves! Or do you not recognize this about yourselves, that Jesus Christ is in you—unless indeed you fail the test?" (13:5). Obviously Paul had some doubts that all in the Corinthian church were "in the faith," that is, true believers. He had good reason to doubt, as he wrote in the previous chapter about his fear of finding "strife, jealousy, angry tempers, disputes...impurity, immorality and sensuality" (12:20-21) on the occasion of his next visit.

Sadly, it could be said that those sins are found in a majority of churches today, and it seems few are concerned. The bumper sticker that says, "Christians aren't perfect, they're just forgiven," summarizes our theology and at the same time advertises our excuse for acting no different than the world.

Yet Paul believed that the sins of "strife, jealousy, angry tempers, disputes...impurity, immorality and sensuality" (12:20-21) were sure indications that those who practiced them were not truly born again. Read what he wrote to the Galatians and see if you notice any similarities in his list of "exclusionary sins" there and those sins which he feared he would find in the Corinthian church:

> Now the deeds of the flesh are evident, which are: immorality, impurity, sensuality, idolatry, sorcery, enmities, strife, jealousy, outbursts of anger, disputes, dissensions, factions...and things like these, of which I forewarn you, just as I have forewarned you, that those who practice such things will not inherit the kingdom of God (Gal. 5:19-21, emphasis added).

Paul wrote to the Corinthians that Christ lived in them—unless they "failed the test" (13:5). The test of whether or not Christ lives in someone is if he acts like Christ. It is just that simple. Christ was holy and when He comes to live in people by His Holy Spirit, He transforms them. Immoral people become moral. Hot-tempered, factious people become gentle and kind. This is not to say that Christians attain instant perfection, but there is no escaping the repeated teaching of Scripture. Christians are not "*just* forgiven." They are new creations in Christ, filled with His Spirit. Their lives are characterized by a sincere desire to please God, a desire that is lived out through daily obedience and holiness.

One of the most frequent criticisms that is leveled at those of us who hold to a biblical gospel is that we are preaching salvation by works. If we mention anything about the necessity of righteous conduct, or if we encourage people to examine themselves, we are branded as legalists. We are told, "When you tell people that they can determine if they are saved by examining fruit in their lives, you are encouraging them to trust in their works, rather than in Christ, for their salvation."

Yet 2 Corinthians 13:5 is still in the Bible! Paul admonished unholy people to examine themselves for proof that Christ lived in them. And there is a vast difference between trusting your works to merit your salvation and gaining assurance that Christ lives in you because of the outward evidence of His indwelling.

What did the unrepentant in the Corinthian church have to fear from Paul's eminent visit? They faced the prospect of excommunication, the very same treatment Paul called for regarding the immoral and unrepentant man whom we read about in 1 Corinthians 5. Paul had instructed the Corinthian believers "not to associate with any so-called brother if he is an immoral person, or covetous, or an idolater, or a reviler, or a drunkard, or a swindler—not even to eat with such a one" (1 Cor. 5:11). You can be sure that any who followed Paul's instructions were branded as "holier than thous." And they were, as are all true Christians! "Holier than thou," but hopefully humble, because our holiness stems from Christ in us!

Day 112, Romans 1

From considering the internal evidence, it is assumed that Paul wrote his letter to the Romans from Corinth during his third visit there, sometime between AD 55 and 57. Paul had never been to Rome himself, but it is clear that he was well acquainted with the Roman churches and the challenges they were facing.

It is thought that initially, the church in Rome was comprised of Jews who continued to keep the Mosaic Law, who then influenced believing Gentiles to adopt the same pattern. So we are going to be wading once more into the now very familiar debate over the Mosaic Law, its relationship to salvation, and the obligation of believing Jews and Gentiles to obey it.

About six years before Paul wrote this letter, all Jews, believing and non-believing, had been expelled from Rome by the Edict of Claudius, due to their vigorous disagreements over Jesus' messiahship, leaving behind a predominantly Gentile church. Claudius died around AD 54, and his successor, Nero, permitted all Jews to return to Rome. Likely there were tensions then, not only between believing and non-believing Jews, but between believing Jews and Gentiles.

Not surprisingly, Paul's letter to the Romans has been twisted in modern times to promote a false gospel that removes the necessity of holiness under a banner of grace that is not grace at all, but a license to sin. As we read Paul's defense of the gospel of salvation by grace through faith, keep in mind that it was an answer to unsaved Jews who believed that salvation was obtained by keeping the Mosaic Law, to believing Jews who supposed that keeping the Mosaic Law was also essential for salvation, and to believing Gentiles caught in the midst of all the confusion. Also keep in mind that the validity of the law of conscience and the law of Christ were never questioned. They were, in fact, repeatedly affirmed in this letter.

Right from the outset, Paul declared that Jesus was raised by the "Spirit of *holiness*" (1:4), that his calling was to "bring about the *obedience* of faith among all the Gentiles" (1:5), the believers in Rome were "called as saints" or literally "*holy ones*" (1:7), and that his gospel revealed "the *righteousness* of God" (1:17). These declarations and others like it within this epistle were likely an answer to those who accused Paul of preaching a message that nullified both God's righteousness and the importance of righteous living. But nothing could have been further from the truth. Paul's message magnified God's righteousness and resulted in unrighteous people repenting and living righteously.

Paul will later thoroughly establish that salvation by faith is not his unique revelation, but one that is grounded in Old Testament revelation, but in this chapter he briefly introduces that fact, quoting from Habakkuk 2:4: "The righteous man shall live by faith." He then begins to lay down two foundational truths of the gospel, namely, the sinfulness of humanity and God's wrath against that sin. Apart from those twin truths, Christ's death is all but meaningless.

People are without excuse before God for their sin, because God has revealed Himself through His creation, and His disapproval of and wrath against sin is also revealed to them in their consciences and by their experience. Even their bondage to sin and perverse behavior is an indication of His wrath, an object lesson to all. God in essence says to rebels, "Since you prefer to worship the work of your own hands and violate the instinctive code of conduct I have placed in your hearts, I will give you over to your desires so that they will hold you in slavery, pulling you towards ever-perverse behavior, to the point of unnatural sexual desires that are not even found among the basest of creatures."

Yet people "suppress the truth in unrighteousness" (1:18). "Professing to be wise, they became fools" (1:22). The world is full of depraved fools today, who know within themselves that their behavior is wrong in God's eyes, yet who continue in their rebellion as their consciences continually call them to repentance. Yet, obviously, the call to repentance is also an offer of forgiveness. Amazing grace!

Day 113, Romans 2

Paul's logic is indisputable. When we condemn others for wrongdoing, we testify before the court of heaven that we know what is right and wrong. Moreover, we desire that wrongdoers be justly punished for their selfish deeds, don't we? So when we do what we have condemned in others, we stand self-condemned, bearing witness that we deserve to be punished for our own selfishness. Yet most people continue in their sin, "storing up wrath for themselves" (2:5), completely unprepared for the day when God, the righteous Judge, will "render to each person according to his deeds" (2:6). This is the foundation upon which the gospel is built: All of us, Jew and Gentile, are all self-condemned sinners who deserve God's wrath.

Anyone who may have accused Paul of proclaiming a gospel that nullified either God's righteousness or the necessity of righteous living to gain eternal life would have been silenced by today's reading. Paul declared that God will give eternal life to "those who by perseverance in doing good seek for glory and honor and immortality," and that He will give "glory and honor and peace to everyone who does good" (2:7, 10). In contrast, "wrath and indignation" awaits those who "are selfishly ambitious and do not obey the truth, but obey unrighteousness" (2:9). Moreover, "there will be tribulation and distress for every soul of man who does evil" whether they are Jew or Gentile (2:10).

These same statements also contradict the modern message of "grace" that is being proffered and that gives license to sin. Only the holy will inherit eternal life, and since all are sinners, the only way to gain holiness is through repentance, forgiveness and empowerment by the Holy Spirit. But I'm getting ahead of Paul!

Just as so many in our day assume that they are saved by virtue of being baptized church members, so Jews in Paul's day were convinced that, as God's chosen people, they had salvation "in the bag" by virtue of the fact that they were circumcised and had been given the Law of Moses. Paul exposes the fallacy of those assumptions. How absurd it would be to think that God would accept and eternally reward law-ignoring but circumcised Jews while rejecting and punishing a Gentile who, although uncircumcised, kept the moral aspects of the Mosaic Law as he followed his God-given conscience. To say otherwise would be to make God unjust and elevate circumcision above morality.

So Paul puts circumcision in its proper perspective: "For indeed circumcision is of value if you practice the Law; but if you are a transgressor of the Law, your circumcision has become uncircumcision" (2:25). That is, your circumcision is useless, because it will not save you. A true Jew, Paul says, is one who is not just circumcised outwardly, but circumcised inwardly in his heart by the Spirit, that is, one who is born again.

With this first subject matter, Paul is preparing to demolish the grand Jewish objection to his message—that Gentiles can be justified, or made righteous, through faith apart from the Law of Moses. The plain truth was that the Jews were not obeying the Mosaic Law and were sinners every bit as much as Gentiles. They themselves could not hope to be saved through the Mosaic Law which they didn't keep, and so they needed some other way of salvation--one that would obviously require grace from God. That way of salvation, as you know and as Paul will soon reveal, is through the sacrificial death of Jesus. *Jews can only be saved through faith in Him.* That being so, it seems reasonable to conclude that Gentiles, as well, cannot be saved through the Law of Moses, but like the Jews, only through faith in Christ. Paul's logic is quite compelling.

One final note. Paul wrote, "the kindness of God leads you to repentance" (2:4). Based on this verse, some say that we should never mention God's wrath or humanity's guilt when we preach the gospel, since God's kindness is what leads people to repentance. Might that be taking Paul's words out of their context? (Hint: The answer begins with the letter Y!)

Day 114, Romans 3

As we read through Romans, it helps to imagine Paul debating with an imaginary Jew who objected to his gospel of salvation by grace through faith, a salvation offered to both Jews and Gentiles. In today's reading, Paul answers several objections that he must have frequently encountered during his two decades of preaching. Some of his answers may not be as clear as we'd like, but we've become used to that.

Paul's downplaying of circumcision certainly would have met with Jewish criticism. If circumcision didn't guarantee salvation, of what benefit was it, and why would God require it? Paul lists one significant benefit: "They [the Jews] were entrusted with the oracles of God" (3:2). That is, above all peoples on the earth, the people of Israel, whose males were marked by circumcision, were blessed because God revealed Himself to them through His written Word.

Some Jews apparently argued that Paul's gospel nullified God's faithfulness to the Jews, because it excluded all unbelieving Jews from salvation. This objection was based on the very false assumption that salvation was the guaranteed right of all Jews. It wasn't, and so Paul's gospel did not nullify God's faithfulness to them.

Some had slanderously reported that Paul was preaching, "Let us do evil that good may come," simply because Paul affirmed that people's unrighteousness revealed God's righteousness, perhaps simply by contrast, but certainly by His righteous wrath poured out at times upon unrighteous people. "So Paul," they reported, "is encouraging people to sin so that God's righteousness will be magnified." Such slander hardly deserved a response. God will, of course, righteously judge the world, and He is certainly not going to reward those who made Him look good by their evil.

Using many quotes from the Old Testament, Paul proves that Jews are every bit as much sinners as Gentiles (3:9-19). Until people understand their sinfulness, they see no need for salvation. In the case of the Jews, until they realized their sinfulness, they would continue to cling to their circumcision, their lineage, or their limited law-keeping as their means to salvation, and they would certainly see no reason for a Messiah to come and die for their sins. So it was essential that they perceive themselves as being just as dirty as the Gentiles whom they so disdained. Far from saving them, the Mosaic Law only exposed their unrighteousness even more, and condemned them.

Finally, Paul reaches the goal he has been working towards since the beginning of his letter. Contrary to what his critics claimed, his gospel did not nullify God's righteousness, but rather revealed it. His gospel was founded in God's righteous law that righteously condemns sinners. It revealed God's righteousness in everyone who believed it, as they turned from unrighteousness to righteousness. It revealed how God maintains His righteousness and yet forgives sinners, because He offers forgiveness through Christ, the one who bore His wrath in payment for our sins. Paul uses the word *propitiation* to describe Christ's accomplishment (3:25), which means "an appeasing of wrath." Jesus' suffering and death appeased God's wrath against us.

Paul's gospel even provided an answer to those who thought God to be unrighteousness as He "passed over the sins previously committed" (3:25). That is, God has not seemed to be righteous when He has not punished sinners. In fact, He has not seemed to be righteous in forgiving even someone who sacrificed an animal. How can an *animal's* dying atone for a *man's* sin? The fact is, it can't, as the writer of Hebrews would later pen, "It is impossible for the blood of bulls and goats to take away sins" (Heb. 10:4). But by the sufferings and death of a God-man, one of infinite worth, God can righteously forgive sinners, because the penalty has been sufficiently paid.

So Paul has effectively answered three grand Jewish objections to his gospel. First, he has shown that Jews cannot be saved by circumcision or Mosaic law-keeping, but only through faith in Jesus. Second, he has shown that Gentiles can be saved by faith as well. Third, his gospel did not nullify the Mosaic Law, but rather established it (3:31). Only through the gospel is the Law correctly understood.

Day 115, Romans 4

Although we wish that today's reading were clearer and that Paul's reasoning made better sense, his general points are not beyond the grasp of our understanding.

Clearly, Paul continues to expose the error of Jews who believed that being right before God was something that was merited by circumcision and keeping the Law of Moses. Of course, had any Jew perfectly kept the Mosaic Law from birth until death, he would have been right before God, needing no grace or forgiveness. But like so many church-goers today, most Jews' obedience to God's commandments was very nominal, yet they assumed that they were OK.

Most Jews in Paul's day were also quite proud of their heritage and God's dealings with their ancestors, which further bolstered their assurance of God's approval. So Paul was very wise to use Abraham as an example of someone who was made right before God, not as a result of being circumcised and keeping God's laws (as we know from the biblical account that Abraham was not a perfect man), but by faith. Scripture says, "Abraham believed God, and it was credited to him as righteousness" (4:3; Gen. 15:6). That verse was written for the benefit of all who would read it, that they might understand how sinners can become right before God (4:23).

Genesis 15:5 tells us that God told Abraham to look up at the stars in the night sky and then promised him that his descendants would be as numerous. The very next verse says that Abraham "believed in the Lord, and [God] reckoned it to him as righteousness" (Gen. 15:6). Note that Abraham "believed *in the Lord*." That is, he didn't just believe a promise from the Lord, but believed in the Lord Himself. So we could say that Abraham was justified by faith in Jesus, even though he didn't know the Lord by that name! So, too, we must believe, not just some historical or theological facts about Jesus, but we must believe *in Him* (John 3:16). And since He is the Lord, if we believe in Him, we will begin to obey

Him. Our faith will be evident by our actions, just as Abraham's faith was evident by his actions.

Paul also points out that Scripture says the esteemed Abraham was made righteous *before* he was circumcised (4:10-11). That should have helped circumcised Jews understand that circumcision was obviously not the ticket to being right before God. It should have also helped them believe that Gentiles could be saved without being circumcised, just like Abraham was. Paul, in fact, sees God's promise to Abraham that he would become the "father of many nations" as a foretelling of him becoming a "father" as it were, of Gentiles who, like him, would be made right before God by faith, and without being circumcised.

Note that Abraham was made right before God hundreds of years before the Law of Moses was given. So we learn that, before the Mosaic Law, sinners could become right before God by faith. Paul also points out that highly-esteemed David, who lived *under* the Mosaic Law and who obviously did not keep it perfectly, was also made righteous by faith, experiencing the great blessing of having his sins forgiven (4:6-8). So we learn that being made right with God has always been through faith, before the old covenant, during the old covenant, and of course under the new covenant as well.

No one can intelligently argue against the plain fact that if sinners are going to be right before God, it will require God's grace. God has chosen, however, to give His grace only to those who have faith in Him, which requires humility and results in repentance. But being saved by grace through faith in no way mitigates the necessity of holiness. Rather, genuine faith results in holiness.

Jesus "was delivered over because of our transgressions, and was raised because of our justification" (4:25). There's the good news! Our salvation was made possible because Jesus suffered to pay our penalty, and after He had paid it in full by His death, He came back to life!

Day 116, Romans 5

We *do not* have peace with God through Jesus Christ. Rather, "We have peace with God through our *Lord* Jesus Christ" (5:1). Let us not overlook that important distinction. Formerly, we were enemies of God (5:10), destined for His wrath. But by virtue of Jesus' paying the penalty for our sins, along with our hoisting the surrender flag of faith and repentance, we've been reconciled to God. How silly it would be to think that we have peace with God had we done nothing more than "accept Jesus as our personal Savior" while continuing in sin!

Now reconciled, we "exult in hope of the glory of God" (5:2). That is, we rejoice knowing that we will one day be in the presence of God's glory. We also rejoice when we suffer persecution, because we know that our perseverance validates the sincerity of our character, which also fills us with hope for a glorious future. That hope is one that will not be disappointed. We already have a taste of its fulfillment through the indwelling Holy Spirit (5:3-5). The Spirit is, as Paul referred to Him in another place, a "down payment of our future inheritance" (Eph. 1:14).

For whom did Jesus die? Paul wrote that "Christ died for us" (5:8). Some say that proves that Jesus only died for the church, which they then define as those who were sovereignly pre-selected by God to be saved. But just two verses earlier Paul wrote, "Christ died for the ungodly." That includes everyone. So did Christ die for the church or the ungodly? Obviously, for both. The greater always includes the lesser. Jesus' atonement was not limited in its intention, but only in its effect by those who resist God (1 Jn. 2:2).

From what are we saved? Paul wrote, "...from the wrath of God" (5:9). Not only that, but we are also *justified* (5:9), which could be translated, "made righteous." To be justified is more than being forgiven. It means to be found not guilty.

The latter half of Romans 5 is not as easy to understand as the first half. Some commentators suggest that Paul is answering critics who questioned how one man's act could possibly result in salvation for so many people. So Paul goes back to Adam to show how one man's act negatively affected the entire human race, and then he draws an analogy with Jesus. It is an imperfect analogy, as are all analogies.

To those who believe that the Mosaic Law was a means to salvation we might ask, "If the Mosaic Law was given to save people, then how could people be saved before it was given?" Is it perhaps possible that God wasn't holding anyone accountable for their sin before the Mosaic Law, since no one knew God's laws? Paul shows how God was holding everyone accountable for their sin long before the Law of Moses. He writes, "For until the Law sin was in the world, but sin is not imputed when there is no law. Nevertheless death reigned from Adam until Moses" (5:13-14.). That is, people were sinning before the Mosaic Law was given. God, however, does not hold people accountable for their sin if they don't know His will. It is obvious, then, that He was holding them accountable for their sin before the Mosaic Law, because everyone between Adam and Moses died.

From this it is also obvious that God must have given laws to everyone before the Law of Moses. Clearly, they would be the laws that He wrote on everyone's consciences. God expected everyone to obey those laws, but they didn't. Paul wrote, "The Law [of Moses] came in so that the transgression would increase" (5:20). That is, the Mosaic Law was given to help Israelites to better realize their sinfulness, to lead them to repentance and faith. They were already fully condemned by the law written in their consciences, but I suspect they may have been tempted to ignore that inner condemnation by virtue of God's delivering them from Egypt, thinking that they automatically had His favor. So by means of the Mosaic Law, they stood doubly condemned, primed for repentance and saving faith.

Day 117, Romans 6

Some commentators say that Paul was writing of his personal Christian experience in the very next chapter of Romans—where he refers to "practicing what I would not like to do" and "doing the very thing I hate" (Rom. 7:15). The error of that interpretation, however, is exposed in today's reading of chapter 6, and it will be further exposed when we read chapter 8. The man of chapters 6 and 8 is a man free from sin, while the man of chapter 7 is in bondage to sin. Note how often in today's reading Paul mentions the believer's freedom from sin.

Because Paul affirmed that humanity's unrighteousness demonstrates God's righteousness (3:5), some were slanderously reporting that he was telling people, "Let us do evil that good may come" (3:8). Today Paul asks a rhetorical question that may well have been based on a similar slander, "Are we to continue in sin so that grace may increase?" (6:1). Such an idea was revolting to Paul, and he responded in kind: "May it never be!" (6:2). Continuing in sin is an impossibility for those who had died to sin, which Paul goes on to say includes all who have been "baptized into Christ Jesus" (6:2-3).

Our baptism as new believers was symbolic of what happened to us when we believed. We became one spirit with Christ (1 Cor. 6:17), united to Him in His death, burial and resurrection. To begin to understand this, you have to remove the element of time. Just as Christ in some sense joined Himself to you by bearing your sin in His body before you were born, so you, as a believer, are identified with Christ in what He did 2,000 years ago. When He was crucified, "our old self was crucified with Him" (6:6). When He died, so did we. And when He was resurrected, we were also resurrected to "walk in the newness of life" (6:4).

The purpose of this union with Christ is "that we would no longer be slaves of sin" (6:6) because we are "freed from sin" (6:7). But our freedom from sin does not automatically prevent us from sinning. Our free will still comes into play, which is why Paul admonishes his readers to consider themselves "to be dead to sin, but alive to God" (6:11), and not allow "sin to reign in your mortal bodies" (6:12). A drug addict may be set free from his addiction, but his freedom doesn't automatically prevent him from once again injecting drugs into his body. He must resist temptation to take drugs. Believers in Christ are similarly released from bondage to sin, but they must still resist temptation to sin.

Paul's words, "You are not under law but under grace" (6:14) have been ripped from their context and construed to mean, "You don't need to be concerned with keeping God's laws because grace releases you from accountability." But the immediate context shows that Paul would have been horrified by such a twisting of his words: "Shall we sin because we are not under law but under grace? May it never be!" (6:15).

Paul then reminds his readers of what takes place from the first moment of belief in Jesus. When we come to Christ, we present ourselves as "slaves for obedience," turning away from sin, our former master (6:16). Having been "freed from sin" we've become "slaves of righteousness" (6:18).

Is eternal life, what Paul calls a "free gift of God" (6:23), ultimately granted to the unholy? Paul writes, "Now having been freed from sin and enslaved to God, you derive your benefit, resulting in sanctification, and the outcome, eternal life" (6:22). That sentence describes a sequence. We are first freed from sin and enslaved to God, and the benefit is sanctification, or ever-growing holiness. The "outcome" of all this is eternal life, and there is obviously no outcome without the steps that lead to the outcome. That outcome is free because the steps to it are God's gracious work. But our cooperation is required. Like a free college scholarship, you've got to keep your grades up to continue to receive the benefits!

Day 118, Romans 7

Paul continues to address Jewish objections to his gospel. Imagine one of his Jewish opponents arguing, "It was God Himself who gave us the Mosaic Law! How can you claim that Jews who believe in Jesus need not keep it?" Paul replies with an analogy derived from the Law itself, which taught that a woman was free to remarry if her husband died. His death released her from the law that held her. So Jewish believers who are in Christ are released by His death from the Law that held them. But this is not a license to sin. Paul expands his analogy to say that, just as a widow might join herself to another husband, so Jewish believers are joined to Christ to "bear fruit for God" (7:4). Now they "serve in newness of the Spirit and not in oldness of the letter" (7:6). That is, Jewish believers are not absolved from obedience, but they now follow the indwelling Spirit who leads them in holiness, and have no real need for a written law. The same is true, of course, for believing Gentiles.

"But you are teaching that the Law, given to us by God, was an evil thing, because it only resulted in evil!" some apparently were saying. So Paul explained that it was sin against the Law, not the Law itself, that resulted in death. "The Law is...holy and righteous and good" (7:12).

It is quite obvious that in 7:4-13, Paul was writing about his (and his fellow Jewish believers') former experience under the Mosaic Law. When we then arrive at verse 14, should we conclude, as some do, that Paul began to write about his experience as a Christian simply because he started using the present tense, especially when the experience that he describes sounds no different than his experience prior to his being born again? I don't think so. All of us sometimes use the present tense to describe past events. I've been doing that in this day's teaching from the very first sentence: "Paul continues....Paul replies....Paul expands..." and so on. But I switched to the past tense in the second paragraph.

If Paul was describing his experience as a Christian in the last part of chapter 7, affirming that he was "sold into bondage to sin" so that he practiced the very evil that he hated (7:15, 19), why then in chapter 6 did he repeatedly affirm that Christians have "died to sin" (6:2), are no longer "slaves of sin" (6:6, 17, 20), are "freed from sin" (6:7, 18, 22), are "slaves of righteousness" (6:18), and are "enslaved to God" (6:22)? Can the man of chapter 6, set free from sin, be the same wretched man of chapter 7 who is a prisoner of sin? Can the man of chapter 6, whose old self was crucified with Christ that his "body of sin might be done away with" (6:6), be the same man of chapter 7 who longs for someone to set him "free from the body of this death" (7:24)?

If Paul was speaking in 7:14-25 of his present condition as a wretched prisoner of sin, practicing evil, it greatly surprises those of us who have read what he said about his personal holiness in other places (see 1 Cor. 4:4; 2 Cor. 1:12; 1 Thes. 2:10; 2 Tim. 1:3).

Some say that Paul must have been speaking of his current Christian experience because he said that he wanted to do right and "joyfully concurred with the law of God in the inner man" (7:21- 22). Surely, they say, no depraved unbelievers would say such a thing, being sinners to the core.

We must remember, however, that Paul was a very zealous Jewish Pharisee before his salvation. He, unlike the average unsaved person, was doing everything he could to obey God's laws, to the point of even persecuting the church. But he found that no matter how hard he tried, he remained a slave to sin. Truly, there is no more wretched person than the one who is trying to live by God's standards but who is not born again. Praise God for Jesus!

Day 119, Romans 8

You have just read what is, in my opinion, one of the Bible's best chapters! I wish I had more than 700 words today!

Jesus did what the Law couldn't do. He died in our place "as an offering for sin" (8:3), "so that the requirement of the Law," that is, death to sinners, "might be fulfilled in us" (8:4). He was our substitute. So we who are in Christ will not be condemned as we would have been otherwise (8:1). And what characterizes those who are "in Christ?" They "do not walk according to the flesh but according to the Spirit" (8:4). Those who walk according to the *Holy* Spirit are *holy*, obviously.

The decision to walk according to the flesh or the Spirit rests with each one of us. We are two-natured, and we can set our minds on the things of the flesh or on the things of the Spirit (8:6). The former results in death, the latter results in life and peace (8:6). Paul plainly warned, "If you are living according to the flesh, you must die; but if by the Spirit you are putting to death the deeds of the body, you will live" (8:13). This is hardly a promise of unconditional eternal security, and once again, we encounter biblical truth about the necessity of holiness for eternal life. Paul was of course speaking of eternal death and life in this solemn warning, as everyone will one day die physically, even those who are "by the Spirit putting to death the deeds of the body" (8:13).

How blessed are we who have believed in Christ! We've been adopted into God's family, having been born of Him. He is our Father, and that makes us heirs of His eternal glory with Christ our Lord. Paul says, however, that we must suffer with Christ if we hope to be glorified with Him (8:17), indicating that persecution is par for the course for true believers. Our temporal sufferings, however, are "not worthy to be compared with the glory that is to be revealed to us" (8:18). We long deep within our hearts for the coming day of our redemption. Paul says that all of creation, currently under God's curse of futility, also waits longingly for it.

Note that Paul did not write in 8:29-30 (or anywhere else in the New Testament) that God had predestined anyone to be saved or unsaved. Rather, Paul wrote that God predestined those whom He foreknew to be conformed to the image of His Son. God obviously foreknew those of us who would believe in Jesus, and He predestined us to be His sons, like Jesus. That is a far cry from being predestined to be saved by God's alleged sovereign "unconditional election" that eliminates our free will in believing in Christ.

Paul concludes this chapter by asking five wonderful questions. First, "If God is for us, who is against us?" (8:31). Obviously, there are many who are against us, but since God is for us, our opposition is ultimately meaningless.

Second, "He who did not spare His own Son, but delivered Him up for us all, how will He not also with Him freely give us all things?" The supreme proof of God's love for us was demonstrated on the cross. How can we doubt, in light of the giving of His Son, that He will freely give us every future blessing He has promised, as well as supply all our present needs?

Third, "Who will bring a charge against God's elect?" (8:34), and a related question, "God is the one who justifies; who is the one who condemns?" Others may judge you as guilty, but if God declares you not guilty, you're not guilty! The evidence for our justification is seated at the Judge's right hand!

Finally, "Who shall separate us from the love of Christ?" (Rom. 8:35). Paul then lists some specific adversaries and adversities that might tempt us to think God's love has diminished. None can nullify what Christ has done for us on the cross. Even if we are slaughtered like sheep, God's love for us ensures that ultimately we "overwhelmingly conquer" (8:37).

Out of allotted words!

Day 120, Romans 9

The greatest stumbling block to many Jews who heard Paul's message was that his gospel excluded from God's kingdom unbelieving, yet "law-keeping," circumcised Jews, while it welcomed believing Gentile sinners! To Jews who took pride in their heritage, lineage, law, or circumcision, considering themselves favored above Gentiles, Paul's message was an insult. So in this chapter, Paul helps Jews see that God can choose whomever He wants and reject whomever He wants, regardless of what anyone thinks! Moreover, God has historically demonstrated that He doesn't make His selections of people based on those things that most Jews were trusting in to make them right before God, such as physical lineage, birth privileges, or even personal holiness.

In regard to physical lineage, Paul reminds his readers of what they certainly already knew, that although God chose Abraham for a special blessing, He did not choose all of Abraham's descendants. Moreover, it was Isaac the second-born, not Ishmael the first-born, who was surprisingly chosen to inherit the blessing. (And Paul cannot resist pointing out that Ishmael was a product of Abraham's works, while Isaac was a product of Abraham's faith—an analogy that teaches about salvation.)

Moreover, God surprisingly chose Jacob, not Esau, to next inherit the blessing, and His choice was made before they were born, so Jacob's blessing was not based on his works. Knowing this, how can any Jew object to God choosing to save Gentiles without regard to their works? Their forefather and namesake, Israel, was chosen by God without regard to his works!

May I point out that this chapter doesn't teach that God chooses some individuals for salvation and (thus by default) chooses other individuals for damnation. Only those who rip verses from their context within this chapter and the entire book can come to such a conclusion. This chapter, from beginning to end, is about Jews and Gentiles as *groups* of people, and God's choice to offer mercy. Additionally, God's choices of Abraham, Isaac and Jacob were not choices regarding their salvation. That was not Paul's point.

In the strongest terms, Paul reminds his readers that God is never unjust (9:14). So when it appears to us that God is unjust, it shows we have the wrong perspective. For example, God's choices of Abraham, Isaac and Jacob may have appeared to be unjust favoritism, but it was actually an expression of God's mercy to the whole world, as they were chosen to carry the seed that would bring blessing to *everyone*.

I might add that had God chosen to save only descendants of Israel, that would make Him unjust without argument. And if He sovereignly grants salvation to some and not others, as Calvinists claim, that would also make Him unjust without argument. If He is going to remain fair and just and mercifully offer salvation to any, He must offer it to all. Moreover, it is perfectly just for Him to withhold His mercy from those who spurn it, and punish them, as He did Pharaoh. Clearly, from reading the story of the Exodus, God showed mercy to Pharaoh, but Pharaoh hardened his heart, and God's mercy decreased with each additional judgment, to the point when God actively hardened Pharaoh's heart as a just punishment. "God has mercy on whom He desires, and He hardens whom He desires" (9:18), but whichever He does, He does it justly, not arbitrarily!

Praise God that, as we will read in just two chapters, "God has shut up all in disobedience so that He may show mercy to all" (11:32). The first "all" in that sentence and the second "all" both mean "all"—all Jews and all Gentiles.

Yes, one can remove from its context Paul's potter and clay analogy and make it appear that Paul is saying that one's salvation is entirely up to God, the potter, and has nothing to do with us, the clay. But in context, Paul can only be teaching that God, the potter, can save believing Gentiles and not save unbelieving Jews, both from the clay of humanity.

If you care to read more, I have written much more extensively on Romans 9 at: www.heavensfamily.org/ss/calvinism/calvinism-unconditional-election.

Day 121, Romans 10

When Paul wrote his letter to the Romans, he did not, of course, write it in chapters and verses. He didn't intend that it would be read in short segments over 16 days, as we are doing. Rather, it was meant to be read in its entirety in one sitting. The danger we face by reading one chapter each day is that we might overlook the context of each chapter within its surrounding chapters. Surely that danger exists when we read these later chapters in Romans.

Calvinists, in particular, often lift verses from their context in these latter chapters of Romans to make them mean something that they don't actually mean. Notice, however, that the obvious theme of chapter 10, just like chapter 9, is God's acceptance of Gentile believers and His rejection of Jewish unbelievers. Keeping that context in mind is essential. Calvinists who claim that Paul teaches in Romans that salvation is limited to those whom God has sovereignly preselected need to read everything Paul wrote in Romans, not just isolated verses. Salvation is offered to all:

> For there is no distinction between Jew and Greek; for the same Lord is Lord of all, abounding in riches for all who call on Him; for "Whoever will call on the name of the Lord will be saved" (10:12-13).

Although I didn't mention it when we read chapter 9 (having run out of my allotted words), Paul concluded that chapter by explaining why it was not God's fault that Jews were a minority in the church by AD 55. Quoting Hosea and Isaiah, he showed that God had predicted centuries before that there would be a great influx of Gentiles into His kingdom combined with only a small remnant of Jews. And the reason? It was because so many Gentiles believed God's Word, receiving the gift of righteousness by faith, while the majority of Jews pursued righteousness by their works (9:30-32). Even this God had foretold through Isaiah—The One whom He sent to be the Chief Cornerstone became a stone of stumbling to those who would not believe in Him. Those who would believe in Him, however, would not be disappointed (9:33).

This same theme continues in chapter 10 as Paul contrasts the "righteousness which is based on the law" and the "righteousness based on faith" (10:5-6). He first refers to Moses' words found in Leviticus 18:5: "So you shall keep My statutes and My judgments, by which a man may live [be saved] if he does them." That was God's promise to the Israelites, but since none of them ever kept the Law, none received the promised benefit. Rather, they inherited the Law's promised curse. Thus, the "righteousness which is based on law" (10:5) was unattainable and out of reach.

The righteousness based on faith, however, is quite attainable and accessible. Once more borrowing Moses' words (this time from Deuteronomy), Paul applied them to Christ and the gospel. There is no need to scale the heights of heaven to bring Christ down to us nor descend deep into the earth to bring Christ up to us (10:6-7). Jesus has already come to us, bringing salvation and righteousness as near as it can be. To obtain it, we need only to hear and believe "the word [or message] of faith" (10:8), that is, the gospel of righteousness through faith. That message offers righteousness to everyone who believes, Jew or Gentile (10:11-13). That righteousness is much more than just forgiveness and a righteous legal standing before God. It includes practical righteousness, the fruit of the indwelling Spirit.

Of course, if people are to believe the gospel, they must hear it from someone, and so this explains why God had sent so many preachers, something also foretold by Isaiah (10:15). By the time Paul wrote Romans, the gospel had spread far and wide, and multitudes of Gentiles had believed while most Jews had rejected it. God had foretold through Isaiah and Moses of the Gentile inclusion and the Jewish exclusion (10:19-21). But the Jewish rejection was not God's fault. Through His outstretched hands, he had continually extended his grace to Israel, but they rejected it.

Day 122, Romans 11

Today we once again read verses about certain Jews whom God chose for salvation and certain ones whom He hardened. Ripped from their context, these verses are sometimes used to promote the idea that God has sovereignly preselected certain individuals for salvation. But we don't have to search very far within the context to see the error of that interpretation. Paul cites God's response to Elijah, who once thought himself to be the only surviving Israelite who was not an idolater. God told Elijah, however, that there were 7,000 others like him who had not "bowed the knee to Baal" (11:4). Paul then comments, "*In the same way then*, there has also come to be at the present time a remnant according to God's gracious choice" (11:5). In Elijah's day, God chose a remnant of Israelites who met His conditions—they made a choice not to bow to Baal. Likewise there was a remnant of Jews whom God chose in Paul's day. He chose them because they met His conditions—they believed in the Lord Jesus Christ.

Those Jews who had rejected Christ God hardened as He did to Pharaoh of old. But those Jews whom God chose to harden could have been among those whom He had chosen to save had they not rejected Christ. If Paul was saying that God hardened certain Jews whom He had not arbitrarily preselected for salvation, then Paul was an idiot, because he contradicted himself so many times within this very chapter and the rest of his letter to the Romans. For example, we read today of the possibility of Jews being grafted back in to the olive tree from which they were severed "if they do not continue in their unbelief" (11:23). So is it possible that God might change His mind regarding His alleged sovereign preselection of certain persons?

We also read Paul's words, "For God has shut up all in disobedience so that He may show mercy to all" (11:32). The "all" to whom God showed mercy are the same "all" whom He "shut up in disobedience." God is offering salvation to every sinner.

Referring to the prophecy of Moses that he had mentioned in chapter 10 (10:19), Paul states that God has shown mercy to Gentiles in order to provoke Israel to jealousy, attempting to motivate them to repent. Clearly, God desires that they would all repent. As Scripture teaches consistently, He desires that all people be saved and come to the knowledge of the truth, Jew and Gentile (1 Tim. 2:3-4). God's hardening of Christ-rejectors is apparently not a hardening that makes it impossible for them to repent. "God has not rejected His people whom He foreknew" (11:1).

Based on promises God made through His prophets, Paul knew that eventually there would be an awakening among the descendants of Israel. They will one day, en masse, embrace their Messiah whom they previously rejected. Their current hardening will end after "the fullness of the Gentiles has come in" (11:26). Won't that be a wonderful time, to see multitudes of Jews believing in Jesus?

Another modern doctrine that is debunked in today's reading is the idea that if one is saved, one is guaranteed to always be saved. Paul clearly warns Gentile believers that they face the danger of being severed from God's tree of salvation—just as Jews have been severed—if they abandon their faith:

> If God did not spare the natural branches, He will not spare you, either. Behold then the kindness and severity of God; to those who fell, severity, but to you, God's kindness, if you continue in His kindness; otherwise you also will be cut off (11:21-22).

How much more clear could it be?

From these same verses we also gain a picture of God that brings some balance to the over-emphasis that is placed on His love. Indeed, Scripture teaches us that "God is love" (1 John 4:8), but the same Bible also tells us that "God is a consuming fire" (Heb. 12:29) and, "It is a terrifying thing to fall into the hands of the living God" (Heb. 10:31). I think I'll "continue in His kindness" (11:22)!

Day 123, Romans 12

It has been said, "Anytime you see the word *therefore* in the Bible, stop and consider what it is there for." The word *therefore* always indicates that what is about to be said is based on what was just said.

The first word of today's reading is *therefore*. So the first verse could be read, "Because of what I just wrote, I urge you to present your bodies a living and holy sacrifice..." What had Paul previously written? A good portion of the previous chapter was a warning to Gentile believers that they could be severed from God's tree of salvation if they abandoned their faith (11:17-24). If they did not "continue in His kindness" they would experience God's "severity" (11:22). Israel was an object lesson of this very thing. Thus Paul urges his readers to be obedient to God, as obedience is the fruit of faith.

All true believers are committed to holiness, but their transformation takes time as their minds are renewed (which is what you are doing every day with me!). Not all learning produces spiritual growth, but you can be sure that no spiritual growth takes place without learning. Don't focus on the latest teaching fads or the "deeper truths" that side-track Christians and fill them with pride. Rather concentrate on learning what is God's will, so that you can demonstrate it in your own life.

Paul seems to indicate that every member of the body of Christ has a specific function, and each person's function is a result of a gift given to him or her by God's grace (12:4-6). Do you know what your gift is yet? Paul lists several possibilities, including prophecy, serving, teaching, exhortation (my wife has this one), giving, leading and showing mercy (my wife also has this one). Of course any of us might do any or all of those things at various times. But those who are gifted in one of those are bent towards it and everyone knows it. They are flowing in their gift often.

I don't think that Paul's list is exhaustive by any means. Whatever your gift is, you love functioning in it. In many churches only a minority of people know what their gifts are. That is because the majority don't have gifts because they aren't in Christ' body. Goats don't have gifts. Their pastors need to stop giving sermons on "How to Discover Your Gift," and start giving sermons on "How to Repent and be Born Again."

Christians are "love people," but they are also "hate people." They "abhor what is evil" (12:9).

Do you "associate with the lowly" (12:16), or do you associate only with those in your class or status?

Have you noticed how frequently Paul quotes from the Old Testament in this and other epistles? He obviously believed that there were truths and principles in the Old Testament that are relevant to new covenant believers. Sometimes he even quotes Old Testament commandments as if they are binding upon Christians.

But have you noticed that Paul never encouraged believers to keep any of the ritualistic aspects of the old covenant? This is because Paul practiced exactly what he and the other apostles preached, that Christ's followers are not obligated to follow the Law of Moses, but rather the law of Christ only. Of course, every moral aspect of the Mosaic Law was included in the law of Christ. That is why Paul sometimes quotes moral commandments from the Old Testament in his letters as being binding upon believers.

In the Law of Moses God said, "Vengeance is Mine, I will repay" (12:19). Since God never changes, that is still true of God, and that is why Paul could instruct his readers never to take their own vengeance.

Loving one's enemies is not a uniquely New Testament concept either, as it was prescribed in the Old Testament. Long before Christ, God was instructing people, "If your enemy is hungry, feed him, and if he is thirsty, give him a drink" (12:20; Prov. 25:21-22). This is the way to win our enemies, by overcoming evil with good. As the Chinese proverb so aptly says, "He who seeks revenge should dig two graves."

Day 124, Romans 13

Paul states that we are "to be in subjection to the governing authorities" because all authority stems from God, and thus any authorities that exist "are established by God" (13:1). This was not Paul's original idea. You may recall that when Pilate said to Jesus, "Do You not know that I have authority to release You, and I have authority to crucify You?" Jesus replied, "You would have no authority over Me, unless it had been given you from above" (John 19:10-11).

From this incident it is affirmed that even evil leaders have their authority only because it has been granted to them by God. If He is the one who grants them their authority, He obviously can take away their authority any time He desires. You might recall the story we read in the book of Acts when Herod accepted praise that belonged only to God. Scripture recorded, "Immediately an angel of the Lord struck him because he did not give God the glory, and he was eaten by worms and died" (Acts 12:23). Similarly, when Nebuchadnezzar, king of Babylon, was lifted up in pride, God removed him from his position until the time when he would "recognize that the Most High is ruler over the realm of mankind and bestows it on whomever He wishes" (Dan. 4:25).

But must we always submit to every earthly authority in everything? What if an earthly authority requires that we disobey God?

Certainly scripture teaches us that there is a place for civil disobedience. The Hebrew midwives, who refused to obey Pharaoh's command to kill every Hebrew male baby at birth, are a good example of this. "Because the midwives feared God, He established households for them" (Ex. 1:21). The apostles collectively refused to submit to the Sanhedrin's orders that they no longer speak or teach in the name of Jesus (Acts 4:18-20). And I hope that you have already made up your mind that, should you find yourself living during the time of the antichrist (who will certainly receive his authority only because of God's permission), that you will refuse to take his mark!

As long as earthly authorities do not require that we disobey God, then we are obligated to obey them. This makes even paying taxes an act of obedience to God, as we obey our Lord who told us: "Render to Caesar the things that are Caesar's" (Matt. 22:21).

We can praise God that He has established earthly authorities, as lawlessness, anarchy and chaos are the alternative. Can you imagine what would happen, for example, if there were no governing authorities in the United States, where one out of every 31 adults is in prison, or on parole or probation?

Notice Paul quotes four of the Ten Commandments in today's reading, clearly endorsing them as being valid for Christians, and saying that they are summed up in another old covenant commandment which he also endorses for new covenant believers, namely, "You shall love your neighbor as yourself" (13:9). Notice, however, that neither here nor anywhere else did Paul endorse any old covenant commandments that fall under the category of "ritualistic." Those particular laws from the Law of Moses have not been carried over into the law of Christ. However, everything that falls under the category of "moralistic" from the Law of Moses has been included in the law of Christ. Those laws, of course, pre-date the Mosaic Law, having been written in everyone's consciences from the dawn of human history.

"Make no provision for the flesh in regard to its desires" (13:14). From reading the verses that precede this one, it is clear that our "flesh," or "old nature" as it is sometimes called, if left unchecked, would draw us into "carousing and drunkenness...sexual promiscuity and sensuality" and "strife and jealousy" (13:13), sins that, according to Paul, exclude one from God's kingdom (Gal. 5:19-21; 1 Cor. 6:9-10). Thus we see once more the undeniable fact that just because one is born again, eternal life is not guaranteed. Heaven is only for the holy, which is why Paul reminds his readers that eternity is closer now than ever before (13:11-12).

Day 125, Romans 14

This chapter is about scruples. We all have them to a greater or lesser degree. We often refer to them as our "personal convictions." We have them because we love God and don't want to do anything that would offend Him. The problem is, we don't always agree on our convictions. Then we fight, forgetting that we should all have a personal conviction about loving one another!

In Rome, just as in Corinth, there were believers who had misgivings about eating meat that had been sacrificed to an idol. Some apparently had decided not to eat any meat at all, lest they run the risk of eating some that may have been sacrificed to idols. So they were vegetarians for Jesus! They loved Him, and wanted no association with idolatry. Like anyone whose convictions are motivated by love for the Lord, they deserved to be admired.

Then there were those who felt otherwise about eating meat, and among them was Paul. They knew that the Lord was not offended by eating meat that had been sacrificed to an idol. But the differences of believers' convictions resulted in problems. Imagine two believers sitting down at a restaurant to eat a meal together. One orders a steak and the other is shocked. He wonders out loud how his brother in Christ can profess to love God yet risk eating meat that has been dedicated to an idol! An argument begins and both stand up and walk out.

Or, perhaps a worse scenario is this: One orders a steak and the other, who thinks such a thing is wrong, goes ahead and orders a steak himself, succumbing to temptation because he was strengthened by the example of his friend. As he eats, however, his conscience condemns him. Thus, even though he is not technically sinning by eating meat, he *is* sinning because he is doing what he believes is wrong.

The remedy for all this is not forcing one person's convictions upon another, an impossible task. Rather it is love between differing parties. "The one who eats is not to regard with contempt the one who does not eat, and the one who does not eat is not to judge the one who eats, for God has accepted him" (14:3). And none should consciously do anything that might cause his brother to stumble. Both should respect those whose convictions differ.

Paul mentions an example that is contemporary to our day: "One person regards one day above another, another regards every day alike. Each person must be fully convinced in his own mind" (14:5). He must be speaking of keeping the Sabbath. Sabbath-keepers do indeed have some very good arguments. Yet there are no admonitions in the New Testament epistles for Christians to keep the Sabbath. Undoubtedly, there will never be universal agreement on this issue, at least until Jesus returns (and after that, most Sabbath-keepers say, all of His followers will keep the Sabbath according to Isaiah 66:23!). In the meantime, Sabbath-keepers and non-Sabbath-keepers should love and respect each other for their convictions.

Paul puts these things in their proper perspective when he writes, "The kingdom of God is not eating and drinking, but righteousness and peace and joy in the Holy Spirit" (14:17). When the entire focus of one's Christian life revolves around what he eats and drinks, one is way off balance. Our life in Christ is all about righteousness (that which is founded in God's Word), and peace and joy, all which stem from the indwelling Holy Spirit. How we are apt to be side-tracked by non-essentials that overshadow the essentials!

The lawfulness of drinking alcohol is one of those issues that divides sincere Christians. Everyone should be convinced in his or her own mind. (Drunkenness is, of course, a sin.) Opinions often differ about the celebration of certain holidays, such as Easter and Christmas, as well as our Lord's proper name (Yeshua? Jesus?). For all these, we need to apply the wisdom found in Romans 14.

Finally, it is outrageous to claim, as some do, that Paul's words have application to "strong" Christians whose consciences allow them to do what God clearly forbids in His Word.

Day 126, Romans 15

Today's reading brings us to the conclusion of the previous chapter's theme of the need for mutual respect between the "weak" (the "Vegetarians for Jesus") and the "strong" (those whose consciences did not condemn them for eating meat). Love was the answer, as it always is. Paul admonished both groups to accept one other, following Christ's example of accepting us. An old creed says it well: "In essentials unity; in non-essentials liberty; in all things charity."

The recurring theme of God's inclusion of the Gentiles surfaces one final time in this chapter. Paul quotes four Old Testament references that prove God is the God of the Gentiles. This ought to be obvious, as He is their creator. Descendants of Israel don't hold exclusive rights to Him! Christians who are caught up in things Jewish should remember that in Christ "there is neither Jew nor Greek" (Gal. 3:28).

Paul's words in 15:14 offer us some insight into what modern churches often lack that was apparently more common in the early church. He wrote, "I myself also am convinced that you yourselves are full of goodness, filled with all knowledge and *able also to admonish one another*." These words were not written to pastors only, but to all the believers in Rome, as was the entire letter. It is not just a pastor's responsibility to admonish the saints; it is the responsibility of every member of the body of Christ (Col. 3:16; 1 Thes. 5:14). We are all supposed to be dedicated to our collective spiritual progress.

Note that Paul did not measure his success by how many people "made decisions to trust Christ as personal savior." The fruit of his ministry was not short-lived converts who "walked the aisle" but who walked with Christ no further. Paul's ministry resulted in "the obedience of the Gentiles" (15:18). He made disciples.

Paul had not yet preached in Rome, primarily because of his calling to preach where Christ had not been named. When he wrote this particular letter, he was in Corinth, and in today's reading we learn of his next travel plans. He intended to soon depart for Jerusalem to deliver an offering to the poor Jewish believers there. Once that was accomplished he planned to visit his readers in Rome "in passing" (15:24) as he traveled onward to Spain. From studying Paul's journeys in the book of Acts, we know that the Holy Spirit was leading him on that route (Acts 19:21; 20:22-23; 21:11; 23:11). In fact, Jesus would even appear to him in a vision while he was in Jerusalem, telling him, "Take courage; for as you have solemnly witnessed to My cause at Jerusalem, so you must witness at Rome also" (Acts 23:11).

Even as he penned his letter to the Romans, however, Paul was aware of the danger that awaited him in Jerusalem due to his stand on the Mosaic Law. So he requested prayer from the Roman believers that he would "be rescued from those who are disobedient in Judea" (15:31). As Paul made his way towards Jerusalem, he was foretold via prophecy that he would be bound by the Jews in Jerusalem (Acts 21:11). The prayers of the Roman Christians were answered, however, as Paul was delivered three times from being lynched (Acts 21:30-31; 22:22-23; 23:10), once from a flogging (Acts 22:25) and once from a plot to ambush and kill him (Acts 23:12). He eventually did reach Rome, but not until at least three years later and as a prisoner, and after an almost fatal shipwreck and snake bite!

Paul undoubtedly hoped the offering received from Gentile believers in Greece given to assist poor Jewish believers in Jerusalem would have a greater impact than just supplying temporal needs. He was hoping it would solidify the unity between Jewish and Gentile believers and perhaps even soften some of Paul's Jewish enemies there to consider his message. We'll be reading about these things shortly in the book of Acts, which is the advantage of reading chronologically through the New Testament!

Day 127, Romans 16

Although Paul had never traveled to Rome, he knew quite a few saints who were serving there. You may remember Prisca (also named Priscilla) and Aquila, a wife and husband whom Paul mentions today (16:3). We first read about them in Acts when Paul first visited Corinth. They were Jews who had been forced to leave Rome under the edict of Claudius (Acts 18:2-3). As Paul temporarily worked with them making tents, he led them to the Lord, and they hosted a church in their house (1 Cor. 16:19). When Paul departed from Corinth many months later, they went with him (Acts 18:18). They were the ones who in Ephesus led Apollos to a more accurate understanding of the Messiah (Acts 18:24-26).

After Claudius died, his successor, Nero, permitted all Jews to return to Rome, which is what Prisca and Aquila apparently did, and there is little doubt that they were building God's kingdom there.

I've mentioned all of this history about Prisca and Aquila for a reason. I suspect that, as they were forced into exile from Rome, they were not happy campers. But years later, looking back at how God had used their circumstances to bring them in contact with Paul, and more importantly, with the gospel that he preached, I'm sure they thanked God for their previous "misfortune." How true it is that what we cry about today is often what we rejoice about tomorrow! If you are facing trials, keep your eyes open for the silver lining. And start rejoicing even before you see it!

Note that Paul sends his greetings to "Prisca and Aquila," not "Aquila and Prisca" (16:3), putting wife before husband. This is the same order in which they are twice mentioned by Luke (Acts 18:18, 26), and in another letter by Paul (2 Tim. 4:19). Such an order was not necessarily the cultural custom, as the reverse order is also used by Luke and Paul elsewhere (Acts 18:2; 1 Cor. 16:19). Husbands, how would you feel if someone addressed you and your wife by using your wife's name first?

Since I'm broaching this delicate subject, I might as well not conceal the fact that Paul lists at least ten women within these Roman greetings, five of whom he declares are workers for the Lord. One is an apostle named Junias (or Junia), and scholars debate if it is a masculine or feminine name, although the feminine is preferred. Imagine that!

Those who want to keep women in their "proper" place in the church prefer that we not read this chapter at all, especially in light of the fact that Paul begins it by commending to the Roman believers a *woman* from across the Aegean Sea. He calls her "our sister Phoebe...a servant of the church," and he instructs them to "receive her...in a manner worthy of the saints, and that you help her in whatever matter she may have need of you; for she herself has also been a helper of many, and of myself as well" (16:1-2). She may well have carried Paul's letter to the Romans. Thank God for all the female servants in Christ's body!

Incidentally, Andronicus and Junias are two apostles who are named among about 24 people who are listed as apostles in the New Testament. God called more than 12 to the office of "sent one." The world needs them more than ever.

Take note of Paul's admonition to turn away from those "who cause dissensions and hindrances contrary to the teaching" which they had learned (16:17). These false teachers cannot only be identified by their spurious doctrine, but by their unholy lifestyles. They are not, Paul says, "slaves of the Lord Jesus Christ," as are all true believers. Rather, they are slaves "of their own appetites" and are characterized by "smooth and flattering speech" by which they "deceive the hearts of the unsuspecting" (16:18).

Run from any "minister" whose life is not characterized by obedience to Christ's commandments! The true gospel results in the "obedience of faith" (16:26).

Day 128, Acts 20:7-38

Our reading today comforts me somewhat when people fall asleep during my preaching. I say "somewhat" because it was after midnight when Eutychus fell asleep. I've put them to sleep on Sunday mornings, just a few hours after they awoke from eight hours of sleep! At least none of those sermon sleepers died during my sermons, as Eutychus apparently did, although some might have testified, as they drove home after church, that they were bored to death as I droned on.

It does appear that something supernatural occurred as Paul embraced the fallen boy, and it reminds us of the time when the prophet Elijah similarly embraced a dead boy who subsequently came back to life (2 Kings 4:17-37).

When we read about Paul gathering the elders of the church of Ephesus, do not assume that this somehow proves that the Christians in Ephesus always met as one big group that was overseen by many co-equal elders (a theory sometimes proposed). Luke uses the word "church" to describe the entire body of Christ in Ephesus, which consisted of many small groups, each of which would have been overseen by at least one, and perhaps several, elders.

Paul's words to those Ephesian elders could change the face of Christianity today if they were taken to heart by Christian leaders. Paul reminded them twice of the tears he often shed when he was with them (20:19, 31). How we need more weeping elders today! Where is the passion?

Paul preached "repentance toward God and faith in our Lord Jesus Christ" (20:21). Why has repentance been removed from today's gospel? And why is Jesus so rarely mentioned as being *Lord*, or treated as Lord, the one whose commandments should be obeyed, the one who gives an inheritance only to "those who are sanctified" (20:32), that is, those who have become holy?

Also take note that Paul did not entertain the idea that preaching repentance and faith was somehow contrary to "the gospel of the grace of God" (20:24). In fact, those two were one and the same to him (compare 20:21 and 24). He knew that God was not offering anyone a license to sin, but was rather offering everyone a temporary opportunity to repent of sin and be forgiven.

Paul was not so big that he couldn't minister to small crowds. He taught "publicly and from house to house" (20:2). Moreover, he never once taught in a building specially built for Christian meetings; nor did he encourage anyone to construct one.

Paul was not afraid to suffer for Christ's sake, and wasn't looking for a more comfortable position as he worked his way up the church career ladder. Rather, he followed the Spirit's leading to Jerusalem, knowing full well that bonds and afflictions awaited him there. His goal was to fulfill the ministry that God had entrusted to him, and he was willing to die for that cause (20:22-24).

Paul did not cater to his crowds, telling them only what they wanted to hear, but rather declared what was truly "profitable," God's "whole purpose," warning people to repent (20:20, 25). He knew that it was the responsibility of the pastors/elders/overseers not just to feed God's flock, but to protect them from wolves that would arise from among them and teach destructive heresies.

Paul was no flashy prosperity preacher and was not motivated by money. Rather, he was willing to work with his hands to provide for his own needs and the needs of others. He practiced what he preached, knowing that greed and covetousness are damning sins. He lived simply, and in doing, set an example for the Ephesian elders. No pastor of a little flock, who earns his living in "secular" work, need be ashamed. He has a biblical precedent.

Finally today, I cannot help but point out that we read words from Jesus' lips that are found nowhere else in Scripture: "It is more blessed to give than to receive" (20:35). We should keep that in mind when theologians try to persuade us not to derive any doctrine from the book of Acts because it allegedly was given to us only for historical record. Perish the thought!

Day 129, Acts 21

As he journeyed towards Jerusalem, Paul and his companions landed in the Mediterranean port city of Tyre (see map on page 534). There the disciples "kept telling Paul through the Spirit not to set foot in Jerusalem" (21:4). So why did he continue his journey to Jerusalem?

You may recall that, many months before, Paul had "purposed in the spirit" (19:21) to journey to Jerusalem, and he also knew then that he would ultimately see Rome. Moreover, as he made his way toward Jerusalem, Paul testified before the Ephesian elders that he was "bound in spirit" (20:22), even knowing that "bonds and afflictions" awaited him (20:23).

In light of these and other verses, we can only conclude that the Spirit was leading Paul to Jerusalem. The Spirit had also revealed to the disciples in Tyre that trouble awaited Paul there, and because of that, they urged him not to go. But that was their own desire, not God's.

Along these lines, notice also that the Holy Spirit, through the prophet Agabus, only told Paul what would happen to him in Jerusalem, but did not tell him not to go there. He was indeed following the plan of God, even though it would result in his imprisonment. Still, everyone who heard Agabus' prophecy begged Paul not to go to Jerusalem. They, just like the disciples in Tyre, were motivated by their concern for Paul's welfare.

James and the Jerusalem elders were overjoyed to hear Paul's testimony of how God had used him to establish the kingdom among the Gentiles, but they had a problem. Many Jews who had believed in Jesus were zealous to keep the Mosaic Law, and Paul's reputation had preceded him to Jerusalem. Everyone knew his stand on the Law of Moses. Hoping to quell any trouble, they encouraged Paul to "become all things to all men" and make himself appear to be a good Law-keeping Jew. He submitted to their plan, and although it may have helped to calm the minds of Jewish believers who were still zealous for the Mosaic Law, it obviously proved ineffective in calming unbelieving Jews. Those Jews would have killed him if not for the providential intervention of some sword-carrying Gentiles.

It was not as though Paul was unprepared for what happened. In every city where he stopped on his way to Jerusalem, the Holy Spirit testified to him that "bonds and afflictions" awaited him. And just weeks earlier, Agabus had told him what would happen (21:11). These many incidents help us to see that God is well able to forewarn us of trouble that is coming. It also helps us to see that spectacular guidance, that is, guidance beyond the "still, small voice" of the indwelling Spirit, such as prophecy, is granted when it is needed for the extra assurance that it provides in difficult times. Don't wish for a prophecy! If you receive one that is really from the Lord, it may well mean that hardship is in your future and that you will need to cling to that prophecy in the face of trouble.

It is interesting that we discover that Philip, one of the original seven men who were chosen to serve widows in Jerusalem, was living now in Caesarea, a large port on the Mediterranean northwest of Jerusalem. You may recall that God had used him about 25 years earlier to bring the gospel to Samaria with the power of signs and wonders. Philip is also the one whom God used to lead an Ethiopian eunuch who had been reading Isaiah 53 (8:5-40) to the Lord. After Philip baptized the eunuch somewhere along the road that connected Jerusalem to Gaza, he was "snatched away" by the Spirit, and he found himself in Azotus, a city about 18 miles north of Gaza, not far from the Mediterranean coast. Luke tells us that he then "kept preaching the gospel to all the cities until he came to Caesarea" (8:40). Apparently, he settled there, and during the next 25 years he and his wife raised four very spiritual daughters whom the Lord used to prophesy frequently (21:9). Raising children is no insignificant ministry either, and worthy of mention in Scripture!

Day 130, Acts 22

It seems quite amazing that the violent mob, who had just attempted to brutally murder Paul, were willing to listen to him speak as he stood, bound with two chains, on the stairs to the Roman barracks. With a wave of his hand "there was a great hush" (21:40), and when they heard him speaking in Hebrew, "they became even more quiet" (22:2). Temporary sanity had been restored to the mindless mob. Obviously interested, they listened.

Even though Paul had just been unmercifully beaten at their hands, he addressed them graciously as "brethren and fathers" (22:1) and then complimented them for their zeal for God (22:3)—a lesson in diplomacy!

The mob was temporarily held by the amazing story of his conversion. Before them was a very educated Jew, a former Pharisee, who had been commissioned by the high priest and Sanhedrin to persecute Christians. His zeal was legendary, and Christians forfeited their lives because of it. But now he was promoting the very thing he formerly persecuted. It was because of his dramatic encounter with Jesus, who appeared in such brightness that he was blinded by the experience. Paul may have thought he was "in the light" before that divine encounter. But his "light" was darkness in comparison to the light of Christ. Such was the case for all of us who know Him now.

The divine origin of Paul's encounter was further validated when Ananias, a devout and well-respected man in Damascus, was used to restore his sight supernaturally. Ananias also prophesied to him that he would be a witness for God "to all men" of what he had seen and heard (22:15). As Paul related Ananias' words, I suspect he was measuring the crowd's response, especially when they heard his commission to be a witness "to all men." Had they caught that "all men" included Gentiles?

Notice also Paul's mention of Ananias' instructions for him to be baptized to "wash away his sins" (22:16). A zealous Pharisee needed to have his sins washed! Surely this was a subtle message to the self-righteous mob of their true spiritual state.

Finally, Paul related his third supernatural experience, when the Lord appeared to him while he was praying in the temple. Jesus specifically told him that the Jerusalem Jews would not accept his testimony. Obviously, their rejection was not what God intended. But their rejection explained why the Lord then commissioned Paul to go to the Gentiles. Tragically, that is when the mob refused to listen any further to his testimony. Blinded by religious pride and self-righteousness, the thought of God reaching out to Gentiles repulsed them. They did not realize that they were just as filthy as the Gentiles whom they despised, and were just as needy for a Savior. The riot began again, and Paul was brought safely into the Roman barracks. How ironic it was that his life was saved by Gentiles.

Paul was no stranger to scourging, having previously received thirty-nine lashes on five separate occasions at the hands of the Jews (2 Cor. 11:24). This time, however, his Roman citizenship saved him from the whip. Citizens had rights, and Paul took advantage of the law of Rome. God is not calling us to suffer injustice if it can be avoided.

Paul was no stranger to prison either, and he knew full well that the Lord could easily release him—if it was His will—just as He had done in Philippi (16:25-26). This time, it was God's will that Paul remain in Jerusalem for a while in order that some people in high places might have a chance to hear the gospel.

Day 131, Acts 23

Paul's opening line before the Sanhedrin certainly didn't win him any favor. It was interpreted by the high priest, Ananias, as prideful, while I suspect that Paul was simply expressing the sincerity of his faith, before and after he believed in Jesus. He wasn't claiming to be perfect or to have always obeyed his conscience, but that he had tried to be sensitive to his God-given conscience all his life. And might the consciences of the Sanhedrin have been pricked by what he said?

Paul's pointed response to the high priest's order that he be struck on the mouth similarly did not win him any favor. But it was so pointed that I suspect that it was inspired, not by his anger, but by the Holy Spirit (compare Paul's Spirit-inspired words in 13:10 for example). Remember that Jesus told his disciples not to worry about or plan what they should say when put on trial, because the Spirit would give them wise utterance at such times (Matt. 10:19-20). Thus, I believe that Paul's words were prophetic. Interestingly, about eight years later, the "whitewashed wall" was assassinated by Jewish revolutionaries. Ananias the high priest was demoted.

But did Paul, as he claimed, actually not realize that it was the high priest whom he had reviled? I don't know. I suspect, however, that his apology was a subtle way of saying, "Surely no true high priest of God would act like Ananias." It was an apology with a barb.

Paul's fourth statement before the Sanhedrin, "I am a Pharisee, a son of Pharisees; I am on trial for the hope and resurrection of the dead!" was another statement that carried a secondary subtle message. Paul used a figure of speech known as a "double entendre," a phrase that is intended to be understood in either of two ways. The first meaning is generally straightforward, while the second meaning is more subtle and is the truer meaning. For example, when the cannibal says to the missionary, "I'd like to have you for dinner tonight," that is a double entendre.

The real issue of Paul's trial was Christ's resurrection, and that was the more subtle meaning of his claim to be on trial "for the hope and resurrection of the dead." The Sanhedrin, however, missed that meaning, and just as Paul knew they would, interpreted his words as being his stance on a controversial doctrinal issue that divided them. Pandemonium was the result, and it seems as if that was Paul's Spirit-inspired intention, as he knew a fair trial was an impossibility. The entire episode was somewhat comical, yet the blindness of the Sanhedrin was tragic.

In light of the circumstances that were mounting against him, certainly Paul would have been tempted to think that he might soon forfeit his life. It was a time that he needed out-of-the-ordinary assurance, and the Lord granted it by personally appearing to him and assuring him he would be going to Rome (23:11). From that point on, Paul had no reason to fear, even as he learned of the plot of forty Jews to ambush and murder him.

Once again, Paul's life was providentially spared by Gentiles, in this case 200 of them carrying spears! An escort of honor indeed.

And there was more honor to come from the Gentiles. Upon his arrival in Caesarea, Roman governor Felix ordered that Paul be kept in Herod's Praetorium, an elaborate castle complex right on the Mediterranean Sea. A lovely spot! Paul would reside there for two years with considerable liberty, letting his light shine and quite possibly writing at least one letter that we have yet to read, his epistle to the Philippians. In that letter Paul wrote:

> Now I want you to know, brethren, that my circumstances have turned out for the greater progress of the gospel, so that my imprisonment in the cause of Christ has become well known throughout the whole *praetorian guard* and to everyone else, and that most of the brethren, trusting in the Lord because of my imprisonment, have far more courage to speak the word of God without fear. (Phil. 1:12-14, emphasis added).

This is why I love reading the New Testament chronologically!

Day 132, Acts 24

Like most earthly rulers who don't realize that their authority is delegated to them by God, governor Felix was a combination of good and evil. He was good enough to grant Paul a fair trial by gathering all the pertinent witnesses, and he was good enough to listen to Paul's views about God, but he also unjustly exploited his authority, hoping for a bribe, and showing partiality to the Jews who so hated Paul. Perhaps this is why we read at the end of today's reading that Felix was succeeded by Porcius Festus (24:27). That is, perhaps God humbled Felix and exalted Porcius.

Knowing a little background about Felix reveals the extent of the flattery of the Sanhedrin's attorney, Tertullus, as he began his very exaggerated accusations against Paul. History informs us that Felix had a reputation for cruelty and immorality. His rule was marked by internal feuds and disturbances, and he dealt with them severely. He was eventually accused in Rome of using a dispute between the Jews and Syrians of Caesarea as a pretext to slay and plunder them. That resulted in his losing his governorship. Incidentally, Felix's second of three wives, Drusilla (whom we read about in 24:24), whom he had persuaded to divorce her first husband in order to marry him, suffered a terrifying death about 24 years after she heard the gospel from Paul's lips, at about age 46, when Mount Vesuvius erupted in Italy. Ten to twenty-five thousand people perished with her that day, August 24, A.D. 79.

Knowing his own innocence, Paul wasted very little time defending himself before Felix, and seized the opportunity to preach the gospel. I'm sure you noticed that his message was laced with convicting themes. He spoke of his certainty of the future resurrection of the righteous and the wicked, implying the fact that all will one day stand before God to reap what they have sown. It was for this reason, Paul said, that he always did his best to maintain a "blameless conscience both before God and before men" (24:16).

In subsequent private conversations with Felix and Drusilla, Paul spoke about "faith in Christ Jesus" as well as "righteousness, self-control and the judgment to come" (24:24-25). That is an interesting list, since Jesus promised that the Holy Spirit would "convict the world concerning sin and righteousness and judgment" (John 16:8). Paul's message doesn't sound very much like the modern message that "God loves you and has a wonderful plan for your life." Rather, Paul focused on biblical truth that motivated Felix to examine his life and think about eternity. And it worked to some degree, as we read that "Felix became frightened" (24:25). Yet he didn't repent, and Luke mentions that he continued to be motivated by his love of money (24:26).

I can't help but mention that this example of Paul's method of sharing the gospel debunks the modern idea that it is inappropriate to motivate people by fear to turn to God, and that is better that we win them by speaking of God's love. "The fear of the Lord is the beginning of wisdom" (Prov. 9:10), and there is not a single instance recorded in the book of Acts of anyone mentioning the love of God while preaching the gospel.

Paul remained in Caesarea for two years due to Felix's whims, but we read that he was granted "some freedom," and that Felix did not prevent "any of his friends from ministering to him" (24:23). As I previously mentioned, Herod's Praetorium, where Paul stayed, was a palace complex directly on the Mediterranean coast, the ruins of which I have had the privilege of visiting on several occasions. It is a lovely setting, but I suspect that Paul would have preferred to have the freedom to travel and preach. Yet he kept on rejoicing. It was either during this time or later during his imprisonment in Rome when he would write a letter in which he used the word *rejoice* eight times. Here is a well-known sample: "Rejoice in the Lord always; again I will say, rejoice!" (Phil. 4:4)—a good motto for anyone who is tempted to be discouraged or downcast!

Day 133, Acts 25

Do you remember what the Lord said to Ananias when he objected to being commissioned to find and minister to Saul of Tarsus? If not, allow me to refresh your memory. The Lord said to Ananias, "Go, for he is a chosen instrument of Mine, to bear My name before the Gentiles and kings and the sons of Israel" (9:15).

Twenty-three years later, we begin to see the fulfillment of God's word that Paul would bear His name before kings, as he testified before the governor of Judea, Marcus Antonius Felix, his successor, Porcius Festus, and also King Herod Agrippa II, king over northern Judea and the seventh and last king of the Herodian dynasty, whom we read about today. It was Agrippa II's father, Herod Agrippa I, who ordered the beheading of the apostle James (12:2) and who was struck by an angel and subsequently died from worms, having not given glory to God when an audience exalted him (12:23). Agrippa II's great-grandfather, Herod the Great, is remembered for his slaughter of the babies of Bethlehem recorded in Matthew 2. And Herod Agrippa II's great-uncle, Herod Antipas, was responsible for the beheading of John the Baptist. Quite a family heritage.

Agrippa II arrived in Caesarea with his sister, Bernice (25:13). The Jewish historian Josephus recorded some facts about Bernice's three short-lived marriages, the first two of which ended with her husbands' deaths. Her second marriage was to one of her uncles. She deserted her third husband. Josephus also recorded contemporary rumors of Bernice's incestuous relationship with her brother (Agrippa II), who never married during his lifetime. All of this should give you a better idea about the people before whom Paul was being tried. All folks who needed Jesus!

It seems incredible that after two years of being kept in custody at Herod's Praetorium in Caesarea, the Jewish Sanhedrin still wanted Paul to be executed. It suggests that he was still quite influential through his letters and personal ministry to those who visited him.

In any case, Paul had known for years that he was destined to go to Rome (19:21), and it had been confirmed to him two years earlier when Jesus appeared to him in Jerusalem (23:11). As a Roman citizen, he had a right to a fair trial to defend himself before his accusers, and he also had the right of appeal. So he appealed to Caesar (the title used by Roman Emperors), who in Paul's time was a twenty-year-old named Nero.

Nero is remembered for his execution of his mother, for kicking one of his pregnant wives to death, and for being the emperor "who fiddled while Rome burned." Because of rumors that Nero himself was the arsonist, he placed the blame on the Christians, persecuting them in horrible ways. Some were even used as human torches to illuminate Rome at night. This was described by the Roman senator and eye-witness historian, Tacitus:

> Consequently, to get rid of the report, Nero fastened the guilt and inflicted the most exquisite tortures on a class hated for their abominations, called Christians by the populace. Christus, from whom the name had its origin, suffered the extreme penalty during the reign of Tiberius at the hands of one of our procurators, Pontius Pilatus, and a most mischievous superstition, thus checked for the moment, again broke out not only in Judaea, the first source of the evil, but even in Rome, where all things hideous and shameful from every part of the world find their centre and become popular. Accordingly, an arrest was first made of all who pleaded guilty; then, upon their information, an immense multitude was convicted, not so much of the crime of firing the city, as of hatred against mankind. Mockery of every sort was added to their deaths. Covered with the skins of beasts, they were torn by dogs and perished, or were nailed to crosses, or were doomed to the flames and burnt, to serve as a nightly illumination, when daylight had expired.

Of course, these days it is Nero who is burning.
And that ends our history lesson for today!

Day 134, Acts 26

As he defended himself before Agrippa, Bernice and Festus, it is quite clear that Paul had a higher goal than just to prove his innocence of the charges that had been leveled against him by Jerusalem Jews. He seized the opportunity to proclaim the gospel, and his message was incredibly persuasive.

Paul began by recounting his own background, something which could be verified easily. He had previously been a very well-known Pharisee who was more devoted to destroying Christianity than any of his peers. This was an undeniable historic fact. Yet now the persecutor had become the persecuted. Christianity's greatest antagonist had become its greatest ally. And Paul's change was not gradual but almost instantaneous. Obviously, something had happened that moved him to promote what he had previously sought to crush. What could possibly have happened that effected such a dramatic change? The catalyst must have been equally dramatic. And of course, it was.

As Paul's audience heard him recount his experience on the road to Damascus, they had a choice. They could believe that he was lying or telling the truth. If Paul was lying, it would beg the question, "Why was he lying?" His lie had gained him nothing and cost him everything! It was the very reason he was in chains as he stood trial. So there was no logical reason to believe that he was lying. The only logical conclusion was that he had indeed had a divine encounter, and as a result, he was a changed man.

Festus' response, "Paul, you are out of your mind! Your great learning is driving you mad," reveals that it was Festus, not Paul, who was "out of his mind." Are people who are greatly educated, as was Paul, more likely to report being knocked down by God, blinded by a bright light, and hearing God's voice? Do people who are zealously opposed to others, believing they deserve death, generally join those whom they so passionately hate? So we see that in Festus, as is always the case with every unbeliever, that his unbelief was not the result of the lack of convincing proof, but the result of his resistance to the truth.

Agrippa was somewhat more honest than Festus, admitting that Paul's testimony was very compelling, saying, "In a short time you will persuade me to become a Christian" (26:28). Obviously, if he were open to being persuaded, he would have asked Paul to continue so that he might learn more. But he didn't want to hear anything more, because what he had already heard was pulling him in a direction he did not want to go. The apostle John described both Festus' and Agrippa's attitudes when he wrote, "Men loved the darkness rather than the Light, for their deeds were evil" (John 3:19).

Today we learn something that Jesus said to Paul during his Damascus Road experience that we did not previously know. Jesus told Paul that He was sending him to the Gentiles "to open their eyes so that they may turn from darkness to light and from the dominion of Satan to God, that they may receive forgiveness of sins and an inheritance among those who have been sanctified by faith in [Him]" (26:18). It is those who turn from darkness and from Satan, and who turn to light and God, and only those, who receive forgiveness of sins. They are sanctified, that is, made holy, by faith in Jesus. Notice it is not faith in a doctrine about Jesus that makes one holy, but faith in the person of Jesus.

The *devil* believes every doctrine *about* Jesus. Faith in Jesus implies submission to Him, because He is Lord.

Because of those very things that Jesus said to Paul, he began preaching that people "should repent and turn to God, performing deeds appropriate to repentance" (26:20). Poor Paul! Such a legalist! He didn't know any better than to tell unsaved people to start keeping God's commandments, when all they really needed to do was invite Jesus into their hearts or accept Him as their personal Savior!

Day 135, Acts 27

It was now A.D. 59, and Paul had been a Christian for 24 years. He was no stranger to travel by ship, having already endured three shipwrecks, one of which required him to stay afloat for "a night and a day in the deep" (2 Cor. 11:25). But his premonition that he was about to experience his fourth shipwreck was more than just a suspicion. The Lord was revealing it to him. Of course, Paul knew he would make it to Rome, because the Lord had already personally appeared to him and assured him of that (23:11). See a map of his journey on page 535.

Notice, however, how the Lord revealed to Paul that another shipwreck was on the horizon. Paul said, "Men, I perceive that the voyage will certainly be with damage and great loss, not only of the cargo and the ship, but also of our lives" (27:10). Jesus did not appear to him; nor did he hear an audible voice. Rather, Paul simply "perceived" what was going to occur. He had an impression in his spirit. Normally, that is how God leads us. When God chooses to lead us by more spectacular means, it is generally because He knows we will need the extra assurance that accompanies such spectacular guidance.

An example of that more spectacular guidance, given when it was very much needed, is found in today's reading. When everyone had given up hope of survival, an angel appeared to Paul and spoke to him saying, "Do not be afraid, Paul; you must stand before Caesar; and behold, God has granted you all those who are sailing with you." He also told Paul that, although the ship would be wrecked, there would be no loss of life, and that they would "run aground on a certain island" (27:26). I love Paul's words in 27:25: "Therefore, keep up your courage, men, for I believe God, that it will turn out exactly as I have been told." God's promises are fear extinguishers.

If God could send an angel to that storm-tossed ship to speak to Paul, and if He could preserve all 276 people on board during a shipwreck (and if He could, incidentally, *create* the universe), why didn't He simply stop the wind, or cause it to blow in a different direction? That is a question for which I have no answer. I do know, however, that God is obviously motivated to turn people to Himself. He was certainly trying to reach the people on that ship, and after all they had heard and seen, they had no excuse not to seek to know Paul's God.

God tried to prevent the loss of the ship and the cargo by warning everyone in advance, but they wouldn't listen. So He let them have their way to face the consequences, as He often does with stubborn people, in hopes that they will see the wisdom in following Him all the time and humble themselves. Surely at least some of those 276 people on the ship with Paul became believers.

We'll learn in the next chapter that the Lord was also interested in reaching the people of the island on which Paul and his shipwrecked companions landed. In the midst of what seemed to be purely circumstantial, God was working His plan of love to reach the unreached.

I love this entire story. Paul was taken aboard that ship as a prisoner, but in the end he was the captain! Everyone was following his orders (27:30-36). People who are filled with the Holy Spirit ought to rise to the top in every circumstance!

I always groan when I read some theologian who weighs the likelihood of whether or not Paul ever stood trial before Caesar, since the book of Acts closes without telling us. To those of us who believe the Bible, there isn't any doubt that Paul eventually proclaimed the gospel to Caesar, as the angel who appeared to him on that Alexandrian ship told Paul, "You must stand before Caesar" (27:24). That means, of course, that God would have forgiven Nero for executing his mother and kicking one of his pregnant wives to death (among his many other atrocities) if he would have repented. Amazing grace!

Day 136, Acts 28

Isn't it amazing that Luke, who was with Paul on this journey and authored the book of Acts, never mentioned himself a single time? A very humble guy indeed.

From my calculations using Google Earth, a ship being blown in a westward direction in the Mediterranean Sea has about a 1 in 17 chance of landing on Malta as it crosses the same longitude as Malta (see map on page 535). But it would seem that providence, rather than chance, was the determining factor in the Malta shipwreck we've just read about. God was working in the storm. God is always working in *your* storms as well.

In this same vein, note that the spiritual awakening on Malta started as a result of something else that was bad but which God turned to good. Paul was bitten by a poisonous snake that would have killed anyone else. In this case, however, Paul had not one, and not two, but three promises from God upon which to stand. First, Jesus had promised him he would testify in Rome (23:11). Second, an angel had promised that he would testify before Caesar (27:24). Third, Jesus promised that one of the signs that would follow believers is that they would "pick up serpents" (Mark 16:18). Paul had nothing to worry about.

May I also point out that Paul, the same one who had voluntarily served food on the ship the day before (27:35-36), was also the one who helped gather sticks to build a fire to warm everyone who just came out of the sea. Poor Paul! He didn't know, as do so many modern "apostles," that apostles are too high for such humble tasks. Paul didn't know any better but to believe that in God's eyes, the greatest people are the servants!

Like every other spiritual awakening that we read about in the book of Acts, the one on Malta was spawned by Spirit-given miracles. The healing of a well-known man really got the ball rolling (28:8-9). It would seem safe to conclude that Paul left behind a congregation of believers in Malta, and he took another congregation with him on the ship to Rome. May I also point out that Paul was only on Malta for three months. When he left, he must have left behind church leaders, that is, elders/pastors/overseers. Obviously, none had spent years in Bible School or seminary. It doesn't require years of training to make disciples and oversee *biblical* churches.

Paul finally made it to Rome and waited for his trial before Nero. He was not "languishing in a dark, damp, Roman prison cell," as some mistakenly say when they speak of the condition under which Paul penned some of his letters from Rome. Rather, he stayed in his own rented quarters, under house arrest, where he was given liberty to preach and teach. Apparently he did have a chain attached to his leg and a single guard at all times (28:16, 20, 30). It was indeed from Rome that Paul wrote a few letters that we are scheduled to soon read, namely, Ephesians, Colossians, Philippians and Philemon.

True to his practice, in Rome Paul first attempted to win Jews, but as was so often the case, they rejected their own Messiah. So he turned to the Gentiles, of which there was no shortage in Rome.

It is assumed that Paul was ultimately acquitted before Nero and released around A.D. 61, as he indicates from some of his letters written from Rome that he expected to be released soon. After that, his life and ministry is mostly mystery. I think there is little doubt that he continued his travels within some of the regions where he had planted churches, and he likely also reached Spain (Rom. 15:24, 28). Eusebius of Caesarea, who wrote in the fourth century, states that Paul was beheaded during the reign of Emperor Nero. This event has been dated either to the year 64, when Rome was devastated by a fire, or a few years later, to 67. Just before he died, Paul penned his final letter to Timothy and then made his final journey—to heaven. There he received his reward and is still enjoying it today!

Day 137, Luke 1

We now turn the clock back about 68 years on our chronological journey through the New Testament, to the events surrounding the birth of John the Baptist. Interestingly, however, we're not changing authors, as we've been reading Luke's other book for the past 21 days, the book of Acts.

Luke was writing to someone named Theophilus (1:3), whose name is derived from the words *Theo*, meaning "God," and *philo*, meaning "love." So Theopilus means "lover of God," which leads us to wonder if Luke was actually addressing his Gospel to everyone who truly loves God. Luke was not one of the twelve original apostles and probably was not born again until after Christ's resurrection. So he did not write from first-hand knowledge about Christ's life, but from his careful investigation (1:3) over three or more decades.

Luke is the only Gospel-writer who gives us details about the birth of John the Baptist. We learn that John was born of godly parents. Luke writes that they were "righteous," but their righteousness was much more than just a legal stamp of forgiveness that had nothing to do with how they lived. According to Luke, they were "walking blamelessly in all the commandments and requirements of the Lord" (1:6).

By Jesus' day, there were thousands of descendants of Aaron, and they took turns fulfilling the priestly duties in the temple. The occasion of Zacharias' going into the holy place to burn incense was a once-in-a-lifetime event. I suspect that he was nervous, but imagine how he felt when he met an angel whom no one had seen since Daniel's time, about 600 years earlier! Gabriel informed Zacharias that the Elijah promised by Malachi 400 years before (Mal. 4:5) was about to arrive on the scene, and he would be Zacharias' son! Of course, John the Baptist was not Elijah reincarnated, but he came in Elijah's spirit and power (1:17).

Zacharias' discipline was clearly the result of his unbelief. We should learn from his error. It's better to say nothing at all than to speak words of doubt!

I always get a zing in my heart when I read Gabriel's words to Mary regarding Jesus: "He will reign over the house of Jacob forever, and His kingdom will have no end" (1:33). In a world of growing uncertainty, there is something we know about the future that is certain. Jesus will one day be ruling the earth, and from then on through eternity, everything will be secure. No reason to worry then! Therefore, there's no reason to worry now!

Scoffers will also scoff at the idea of a virgin birth, saying such a thing is impossible. I wonder how they explain even a normal conception and birth. There must be at least 10,000 miracles associated with the conception and development of every baby, so how difficult was it for God to add one more miracle to have a baby conceived without the aid of an earthly father? The most amazing thing in all of this was not that the virgin Mary had a baby in her womb, but that the baby in her womb was God.

There are so many wonderful phrases contained within Mary's prophecy, commonly referred to as the "Magnificat," but I want to highlight just one phrase that the Holy Spirit spoke through Mary about the works of God: "He has filled the hungry with good things; and sent away the rich empty-handed" (1:53). If God "sent away the rich empty-handed," that means the rich came to Him at a time of great need, when their riches were gone, and when they found themselves lacking food. But because when they were rich they ignored the plight of the hungry, God then ignored their plight. They reaped what they had sown, just as God promised in Proverbs 21:13: "He who shuts his ear to the cry of the poor will also cry himself and not be answered." Oh if people believed that God is just and that He will indeed repay every person according to his deeds! They would repent! Rich people (like all of us) who repent start caring for the poor and feeding the hungry.

Day 138, Luke 2

The Greek word translated "inn" in 2:7 is the word *kataluma*, which really doesn't describe an inn or hotel as we know it. It refers to a temporary shelter where overflow crowds would sleep during times such as Passover when masses of people would come to Jerusalem. For this reason, many think Jesus was born in the Spring, near the time of the Passover, because Jerusalem and nearby Bethlehem would have had *katalumas* erected to accommodate all of the pilgrims. Also, we know that during Passover there would have been numerous shepherds keeping watch over their flocks on the nearby hills, since thousands of lambs would be needed for Passover sacrifices.

Mary probably gave birth out in the open, in a stable, or in a shepherd's cave near Bethlehem. The "manger" in which Jesus was laid was an animal feeding trough. It was not a pretty picture. Unlike the Christmas cards in which the wise men, shepherds and animals all smile serenely at the warm, golden glow from the cradle, the true scene would have been heart-rending to most of us. What a way for the King of kings to be born! Jesus suffered rejection from the start.

Joseph and Mary were not wealthy people, as indicated by their offering when they presented baby Jesus at the temple. The Mosaic Law stipulated that the mother of a newborn son should bring a one-year-old lamb for a burnt offering, plus a young pigeon or turtledove for a sin offering. But if she couldn't afford a lamb, then she could substitute a pigeon or a turtledove (Lev. 12). Jesus was born into a family that lived at a standard that we can find today only in undeveloped nations.

All of the supernatural events that surrounded His birth recorded by Luke should be enough to convince anyone that Jesus was the Messiah. The supernatural conception of His forerunner, the appearance of Gabriel to both Elizabeth and Mary, the prophetic utterances of both of them as well as Zacharias, the virgin birth, the appearance of angels to certain shepherds, the revelations about the Child by godly Simeon and Anna, and Jesus' remarkable spirituality as a young boy, all indicate that He was a unique person of history. Isn't it amazing that multitudes of people hear Luke's account read in churches during Christmas time and remain unaffected? If you believe just what we read today, your life will be radically redirected to serve Jesus with all your heart!

Contrary to Roman Catholic theology, Mary was not sinless. According to Simeon, as a result of Jesus' coming, "a sword" would pierce even her soul (2:35), indicating that she, too, would be confronted with Jesus' piercing words and be brought to a place of decision. And you may recall that within her "Magnificat" which we read yesterday, she said, "My spirit hath rejoiced in God my Saviour" (1:47). Mary needed a Savior. How special it was for her, though, to have Jesus living in her! Don't forget, if you believe in Him, He now lives in you, too (by the indwelling Holy Spirit). You are actually more privileged than Mary, because she had baby Jesus in her, but you have Him grown up in you!

I've often wondered what Jesus was like during His younger years. It is hard to imagine a sinless kid! Mary and Joseph obviously considered Him responsible enough at age twelve to watch out for Himself, because they didn't check to make sure He was with their relatives when they departed from Jerusalem. In fact, they didn't know He was missing until they had already traveled "a day's journey" (2:44). Jesus must have considered Himself responsible enough at age 12 to stay by Himself in Jerusalem for three days and then make the sixty-five-mile journey back to Nazareth alone.

No doubt Mary and Joseph never had any trouble with Jesus, except in this one case where He remained in Jerusalem after the Passover. He was not rebellious during His teenage years, didn't spend any time sowing wild oats as a young man, and was a model older brother to his younger siblings. Hard to imagine, I know!

Day 139, Luke 3

According to Luke, John the Baptist "preached the gospel to the people" (3:18). Yet how different was John's gospel compared to what is often called the gospel today. John not only told his audience that Jesus was coming, he warned them of God's wrath and the fires of hell (3:7, 9, 17). He preached the necessity of works, warning fruitless persons that they would be cast into hell (3:9). He called his listeners to repentance, a repentance that was much more than just remorse, but a change of lifestyle (3:8-14). He revealed a Messiah who was coming to judge them, one who would separate the wheat from the chaff and then burn the latter (3:17).

So what's the good news in all of that? Only a small portion of what John said could actually be considered purely good news, and that is that the Messiah will "gather the wheat into His barn" (3:17). That's it. Everything else John said could be considered very bad news, but bad news that makes the good news *so* good! Unless the bad news is understood, the good news makes no sense.

This is perhaps the greatest flaw in the modern gospel. "God loves you and has a wonderful plan for your life" caters to selfish, sinful people, who easily interpret "God loves you" to mean "God approves of you," which is simply not true for sinners. God so disapproves of those in rebellion against Him that He intends to cast them into hell. And God's intention to cast people into hell is not exactly "a wonderful plan" for their lives.

"But people will not receive our message if we preach the gospel that John preached!" is often an honest excuse that is proffered by modern preachers. Yet is it better to preach a false gospel that results in false, deceived converts who are all cast into hell in the end, or to preach a true gospel that results in just a few converts? At least it is better for the rejected preacher to walk away, shaking the dust off his feet, knowing that he has no one's blood on his hands.

How do we know when our gospel is producing true converts? We know when they repent, and when they "bring forth fruit in keeping with repentance" (3:8). What kind of fruit is God looking for? When John's convicted audience asked what they should do, did John say, "Go to church faithfully every Sunday?" No, the very first things John said was this: "The man who has two tunics is to share with him who has none; and he who has food is to do likewise" (3:11). John knew that the Lord is going to say to everyone when they stand before His judgment throne one of two things, either, "I was hungry and you gave Me something to eat" or, "I was hungry and you did not give Me anything to eat." He will say either, "I was naked and you clothed Me" or, "I was naked and you did not clothe Me" (Matt. 25:31-36, 41-43).

If we aren't caring for the poor in Jesus' spiritual family, we really have no basis to believe that we are truly born again and on the road to heaven. This is a basic fact of Christianity, but one that is being ignored by much of the modern church.

Notice that most of the other things that John told his convicted audience to do to show their repentance revolved around their stewardship of money. In fact, five of the six specific acts of repentance that John prescribed had something to do with money: (1) Share your food with the hungry, (2) Share your clothing with the naked, (3) Don't overcharge your customers, (4) Don't steal other people's money, and (5) Be content with your wages. If one's "conversion" doesn't affect his attitudes and actions regarding money, one is not truly converted.

Finally, Luke's genealogy of Jesus is actually through Mary. Heli, whom Luke lists as being the father of Joseph (3:23), was only his father by marriage to Mary. Matthew's listing was Jesus' genealogy through Joseph, who (of course) was not really Jesus' father.

Day 140, Luke 4

Before Jesus could begin His public ministry, two things had to take place. First, He needed to be baptized in the Holy Spirit. Up until that time, Jesus had no special anointing for ministry. If Jesus needed to be baptized in the Holy Spirit before He began His ministry, it would seem reasonable to think that we, too, would need to be baptized in the Holy Spirit before we begin in ministry.

Second, Jesus had to be tested. Notice that it was the Holy Spirit who led Him into the wilderness to be tempted by the devil (4:1). Similarly, every believer goes through times of testing. God only promotes those whom He can trust. If we prove ourselves faithful in small things, then He knows He can trust us with bigger things. Jesus, of course, passed His forty days of testing with flying colors. He never sinned.

In Mark's Gospel we read of the unbelief Jesus encountered during His second visit to His hometown of Nazareth—unbelief that prevented Him from doing any miracles there except healing a few people with minor ailments (Mark 6:5). Luke's Gospel gives us details of Jesus' first visit to His hometown. He began by reading a text from Isaiah that actually spoke of Himself and how He was anointed by the Holy Spirit for supernatural ministry. According to Isaiah, the Messiah (which means "anointed one") was anointed to preach, to bring deliverance, and to heal. He wanted the people of Nazareth to believe that He was God's anointed. If they had, they could have received the benefits. But they would not believe.

Jesus had already performed quite a few miracles in Capernaum, and the news had no doubt traveled to Nazareth, only about 25 miles away. They had been waiting to see their "hometown boy turned miracle-worker" perform some tricks for them—not with expectancy, but with skepticism. Jesus told them a prophet is not without honor except in His hometown, and then He proved His point with two biblical examples. God used Elijah to supernaturally provide for the needs of a non-Jewish widow of Sidon even when there were many widows in Israel then who also needed help. Additionally, Elisha was used by God to cleanse a heathen leper even though there were plenty of Israelite lepers in his time.

In both cases, God used His prophets in gifts of the Holy Spirit. Gifts of the Holy Spirit operate as the Spirit wills (1 Cor. 12:11). They did not operate as Elijah and Elisha willed. Both of those prophets obviously would have used their gifts, if they could have, to help their own Jewish countrymen rather than Gentiles. Jesus was apparently under the same limitations as they were. Although He was divine, in His ministry Jesus operated as a man anointed by the Holy Spirit. Thus Jesus faced two major limitations to His effectiveness. First, He was limited by the faith or lack of faith of the people to whom He ministered. Second, He was limited to the Holy Spirit's will in manifesting gifts of the Holy Spirit. For some reason the Holy Spirit didn't will to manifest any of His gifts when Jesus was in Nazareth. (Perhaps unbelief was the reason?)

Jesus' audience, who initially were so pleased with His message, wanted to murder Him by the end. (I know the feeling.) They didn't like hearing how God passed up Israelites to bless Gentiles. This incident gives us insight into what Paul was up against from Jews as He preached the gospel to Gentiles. Incidentally, Jesus' escape from the murderous crowd must have been supernatural.

I've been blessed to visit, on several trips to Israel, the ruins of Capernaum along the sea of Galilee, and the supposed foundation stones of Peter's house there. A Roman Catholic church has been built there that looks somewhat like a flying saucer, and it is suspended directly above where Peter's home was supposed to have been. Peter would be shocked to see it today, and even more shocked to see what goes on inside that church every Sunday! If you'd like to see a one-minute video of me at that very place, visit: www.heavensfamily.org/ss/video/peter.

Day 141, Luke 5

Just for your information, the Lake of Gennesaret (5:1), the Sea of Chinnereth and the Sea of Galilee are all the same body of water. It is rather small, about eight miles wide and thirteen miles long.

This story of Peter's catching so many fish illustrates that it always pays to trust the words of Jesus in spite of the circumstances. Peter and his companions had worked all night and hadn't caught a single fish. The reason they worked all night is because they knew from experience that night was the time to catch the fish they were after. Now it was morning. They were tired and ready to go home after an unprofitable night's work. Plus, they had already washed their nets. However, their obedience to Jesus paid off.

It is sometimes pointed out by prosperity preachers how Jesus blessed Peter's business with abundance after borrowing his boat. These same preachers, however, rarely point out that Peter left all those fish on the beach (along with everything else) to start following Jesus, which of course was Jesus' original intention. Jesus isn't blessing people so they can have lots of stuff for themselves.

May I also ask: As Peter and his companions frantically worked to get every fish they could into their boats to the point of sinking them, all under the calm and holy gaze of Jesus, what was going through their minds? Could Peter suddenly have realized that his actions revealed his heart? Could he have realized that his frantic attempt to fill the boats to the point of sinking was a revelation of his greed? That he was only thinking of profits while he was standing in the midst of a miracle, and that his excitement was wrongly directed at the fish instead of the Miracle Worker? Could that have been why he then fell at Jesus' feet saying, "Depart from me, for I am a sinful man, O Lord!"? (How do you suppose Jesus would have reacted if Peter had announced that he was seeking speaking engagements for his new sermon series, "Secrets for Divine Prosperity?")

When Jesus called Levi (Matthew) the tax-gatherer, he "left everything behind" and began following Him (5:28), just as Peter,

James and John left everything to follow Him (5:11). When Jesus calls us to follow Him, anything that hinders us should also be left behind.

Israel, as you know, was under Roman authority during the time of Jesus. Roman officials sold the right to collect taxes in certain areas to the highest bidder, and that person would then become the chief tax collector. He, in turn, would hire others to help him collect the required sum. Tax collectors, however, would assess taxes at a rate that greatly exceeded what Rome required, pocketing the difference. They were looked upon as cheats and traitors by the average Jew. So that puts Matthew's reception for Jesus in perspective. Only wicked people, Matthew's friends, would have attended. So we can sympathize with the Pharisees when they complained to Jesus' disciples about attending a reception hosted by Matthew.

It was, however, an evangelistic opportunity from Jesus and Matthew's standpoint. Jesus came to save sinners. The only way to do that is to talk with them. The only way to talk with them is to be with them. The only way to be with them is to go where they are. I always cringe when I see Christians protesting against some sinful group of people, and verbally battling with them as they clash on the streets. Jesus had a better method. But He didn't compromise the truth. You can be sure that there were some convicted tax collectors at Matthew's house, as Matthew held the reception in Jesus' honor. I think we can assume that Matthew told all his cronies about Christ that evening.

Jesus summed up His ministry with the words, "I have come... to call sinners to repentance" (5:32). Why has that simple truth been lost to so many in Christendom? True Christians are former sinners who repented, and who now live to please God.

Day 142, Luke 6

Why were Jesus and the disciples going through someone else's fields and eating his grain? Isn't that stealing? Under the Law of Moses, it was not. God said in Deuteronomy 23:25: "When you enter your neighbor's standing grain, then you may pluck the heads with your hand, but you shall not wield a sickle in your neighbor's standing grain." Notice that the Pharisees were only angry that Jesus was picking the heads of wheat on the Sabbath.

Like any itinerant preacher or teacher, Jesus repeated Himself from place to place. What we've read today is not the "Sermon on the Mount," but a sermon on a plain (6:17). I suspect that Jesus repeated these same concepts scores of times as He ministered in different places.

Surely Jesus' sermons were relevant to the people to whom He spoke. Thus it is safe to assume that Jesus' followers were suffering some persecution, just as He was. Because He told them that they were blessed when they were hated, ostracized and insulted, it seems logical to conclude that at least some of them were experiencing those very things. Note that Jesus also told them what to do when they were cursed, mistreated and hit on the cheek. He wasn't talking about "those persecuted Christians in other countries." He was talking to His contemporary followers.

His contrast between righteous believers and evil unbelievers, and their ends, seems to underscore this even more. On one side were the rich, well-fed, laughing (mocking?), and popular, while on the other side were the poor, hungry, weeping and despised. Is it possible that Jesus' followers had already found themselves facing economic hardships due to their decisions to follow Him? Certainly it was, as indicated by His instructions to them of what to do in the event that someone would forcibly take their possessions (6:29-30). According to the book of Hebrews, some of the early Christians "accepted joyfully the seizure of their property" (Heb. 10:34).

Although it costs us now to follow Christ, in the end it will be worth it. Those who take the easier path of not following Christ will in the end regret it. God will repay everyone according to his or her deeds. Everyone will ultimately reap what they have sown, positive or negative. Knowing this helps motivate us to love those who hate us during this age of temporary grace, when God is giving sinners an opportunity to repent and be forgiven. We hope that our love will shame them and influence them to turn from their sin, as we did, while they still have a chance. One day God's mercy towards them will cease, and His wrath will begin. As Paul wrote:

> For after all it is only just for God to repay with affliction those who afflict you, and to give relief to you who are afflicted and to us as well when the Lord Jesus will be revealed from heaven with His mighty angels in flaming fire, dealing out retribution to those who do not know God and to those who do not obey the gospel of our Lord Jesus. These will pay the penalty of eternal destruction, away from the presence of the Lord and from the glory of His power (2 Thes. 1:6-9).

Jesus expects His followers to be lenders who aren't concerned if they are paid back, which is more like being a giver than a lender (6:34-35)! Jesus' contemporary followers were not lending money to help people buy luxuries, but necessities, and the borrowers would not have been borrowing had they not been poor. This principle should guide us in our lending as well.

There have always been false believers, even when Jesus was physically on the earth, which is why He asked professing followers, "Why do you call Me, 'Lord, Lord,' and do not do what I say?" (6:46). Then, just as now, people called Him their Lord, but by their actions denied Him. Good trees bear good fruit (6:43). The only people who are truly building their lives on the rock are those who hear and *obey* Jesus' commandments. That is salvation through faith!

Day 143, Luke 7

You can't help but appreciate this centurion. He cared about his dying servant. He loved the nation of Israel. He paid for the construction of the synagogue in Capernaum. He didn't consider himself worthy to come to Jesus personally to make his request, so he sent some Jewish elders on his behalf. And it bothered him when he learned that Jesus was taking His valuable time to visit his house, and so he sent some friends to tell Jesus that it wasn't necessary; all he wanted Jesus to do was to speak the word so that his servant might be healed.

Jesus was certainly impressed with this Gentile's faith. He "marveled at him" (7:9), declaring that his faith was greater than any Israelite He had yet encountered. Quite a compliment. When I read such stories, I always wonder what we're missing out on because of our lack of faith. Why do some professing Christians bristle when it is suggested that lack of faith might be the reason they are failing to receive what God has promised?

I love this story of Jesus' raising the widow's dead son at Nain. It was a major miracle, and the news of it spread far and wide. Can you imagine seeing someone come back to life at his funeral? But Jesus was doing many other miracles besides this one. Everyone in Judea was talking about Him. God was testing hearts.

Have you ever heard my Latin song titled *Everything Changes* that includes a verse about this miracle of the widow's son? If not, why not? You owe it to yourself to download the MP3 at: www.heavensfamily.org/ss/songs/everything_changes. Please pardon the vocalist and enjoy the lyrics.

A few of my remaining Calvinist friends have told me that I've been too hard on Calvinists in this daily commentary. I do confess that picking on Calvinists is a weakness of mine. But today I've decided to lay down my arms. I will resist the temptation to point out the fact that Luke wrote that "the Pharisees and the lawyers rejected God's purpose for themselves, not having been baptized by John" (7:30). Out of sheer kindness, I will not mention how obvious it is that God's purpose for all of them was to repent and be saved, but they resisted God's grace in salvation, a grace that Calvinists claim is irresistible. (Oops! I guess the devil made me do it!)

How was a woman able to wet Jesus' feet with her tears, wipe them with her hair, kiss His feet and anoint them with perfume as He was eating a meal with others around a table? The answer is that in Jesus' day, people ate their meals lying down, propped up on one arm, and fed themselves from food at a center table with their free hand. Thus the expression: "They *reclined* at table" (7:36).

If Jesus was only a "good man" or "a great moral leader," as some say, He would not have allowed this woman, or anyone for that matter, to worship Him. Good people don't allow other people to worship them, as they know only God is worthy of worship. And that is precisely why Jesus didn't stop her from worshipping Him.

Contrasted with the worshipping woman, Simon the Pharisee did not believe Jesus was the divine Son of God, evidenced by how he treated the Lord. In fact, he treated Jesus as being undeserving of even the common courtesies that would have been extended to any invited guest, such as having His dusty feet washed. Again we see that inward beliefs are revealed by outward actions.

Simon judged that Jesus was not a prophet, and judged the worshipping woman to be "a sinner" (7:39), probably because he knew she was a harlot. But both his judgments were wrong. Jesus knew much more about the worshipping woman than he did. Jesus knew that she had repented, and He had already forgiven her. She was no longer a sinner, but saved (7:5). Beyond that, Jesus knew what Simon was thinking, which is why He told him the parable of the two debtors. In God's eyes, Simon was the sinner! The harlot was a saint! Amazing grace!

Day 144, Luke 8

Isn't it interesting that Jesus and the twelve were financially supported, at least in part, by women of some means (8:2-3)? It would certainly seem likely that Joanna, for example, the wife (or perhaps the widow) of a steward of Herod Antipas, was likely a woman of wealth and influence. Isn't it also interesting that one who multiplied food for thousands of others subsisted on the generosity of creatures He had created? Unfathomable humility!

Jesus' ministry is still supported by individual donations from people who follow and love Him. People who believe in Him naturally want to support His on-going work with their finances.

We've already read the parable of the sower in both Matthew and Mark's Gospels. Luke, however, includes one little significant phrase by Jesus. Speaking of the person who represents the "good ground," Jesus said that person has an "honest and good heart" (8:15). Isn't that true? The condition of the heart determines if people will repent and follow Jesus. We should never hesitate to share the gospel, however, just because it *appears* people have hard hearts. I've seen people with seemingly very hard shells who wept tears at hearing the gospel. And I've seen others, who initially appeared very soft and kind, vehemently resist the truth. The gospel reveals what is in a person's heart.

Tragically, but justly, those who shut their ears to the truth are judged by God, who is not one to cast His pearls before swine. In some manner "even what they think they have shall be taken from them" (8:18), which is just as ominous as it is vague. Yet to those who open their ears, He gives more understanding (8:18). That's you!

How can we tell when people have truly received God's Word? They "bear fruit" and keep on bearing fruit (8:15). Jesus' *true* family members are those "who hear the word of God and do it" (8:21).

Apparently, Jesus was the only one who fell asleep while He and His disciples were crossing the Sea of Galilee. This shows us that, although He was divine, He was also human. If He stayed up late at night praying, He had to take a nap the next day. And if Jesus took naps, then naps are scriptural! Every siesta isn't a sign of laziness. Rather, naps can be an indication of faith, especially when you sleep through a storm. Worry is definitely the enemy of sleep. Jesus was apparently free from anxiety, because He was sleeping through a "fierce gale" (8:23) until awakened by His disciples, whom He subsequently questioned, asking, "Where is your faith?" (8:25). He had told them, "Let us go over to the other side of the lake" (8:22). In His opinion, they had no reason to be afraid that they weren't going to make it. It is good to remember that "Fear not!" is a commandment found often in the Bible, not a suggestion!

The demons who possessed the madman of the Gerasenes knew they were completely at the mercy of Jesus, as illustrated by their plea not to be sent out of the country (Mark 5:10), their entreaty to be permitted to enter the nearby herd of pigs (8:32), their begging not to be cast into "the abyss" (8:31), and their imploring Christ not to torment them (8:28). God always has been and always will be sovereign over Satan. Don't be afraid of the devil or demons. They are terrified of Christ in you.

Today's reading certainly emphasizes the importance of faith. Not only did Jesus rebuke His disciples for their lack of faith as they crossed the Sea of Galilee, but faith is credited as the reason that Jairus' daughter and the woman with the issue of blood were healed.

Of those three instances that had something to do with faith, two ended in miracles because faith was exercised, and one ended in a rebuke because faith was not exercised (that is until Jesus exercised His faith and rebuked the wind and the waves). Might there be a hidden lesson here?

Day 145, Luke 9

Luke 8 begins with an account of Jesus expanding His outreach as He traveled from "one city and village to another, proclaiming the kingdom of God" (8:1). Today, at the beginning of chapter nine, we read of His sending out the twelve (9:1). They could obviously reach more villages than He could by Himself. And at the beginning of the next chapter, we'll read of Him sending out 70 others (10:1). All 82 were commissioned by Him to heal the sick and cast out demons, which they did (9:1-2, 6; 10:9, 17). It was an unprecedented divine visitation, and all Israel was stirred. Yet Jesus knew that those He sent would be rejected in some cities, and He told them to shake the dust off their feet as they departed from such places (9:5). Woe to those cities.

We read that Herod "kept trying to see" Jesus (9:9) because of all that was happening. You would think that Jesus would have taken special time to accommodate a great political figure, but He didn't bother. Jesus took time to minister to little children, but had no time for a king (the murderer of His relative, John, incidentally).

It is interesting that Jesus was curious to know who the multitudes thought He was. It is also interesting that the mostly-Jewish multitudes thought He was someone who had been reincarnated, either John the Baptist, Elijah, or some other prophet from the past! Their idea may have been derived from Scripture, however, as God said through the prophet Malachi that He would send Elijah "before the coming of the great and terrible day of the Lord" (Mal. 4:5). We've previously learned that Elijah did come in a sense, not literally reincarnated, but in the person of John the Baptist, who came "in the spirit and power of Elijah" (1:17).

What is most interesting, however, is that after Peter confessed that he believed Jesus was "the Christ of God," Jesus warned His disciples not to reveal it to anyone. Perhaps such a proclamation and the subsequent reaction of the believing multitudes may have prevented His crucifixion, as Jesus mentioned His imminent sufferings in conjunction with His instructions to His disciples that they not reveal His true identity. Those instructions were, of course, temporary. After He was resurrected, the apostles openly proclaimed that Jesus was the Messiah (Acts 2:31, 36; 3:18, 20).

To take up one's cross daily is an expression for denying one's own desires, subordinating them to Christ's will, regardless of the subsequent consequences. This is required of all who want to "come after" Jesus (9:23). The same concept is expressed by the phrase, "to lose one's life for Christ's sake," which Jesus said results in one's life being saved, which again indicates the necessity of submission for salvation. Those who pursue a different course, that which the world is following, in the end forfeit themselves (9:25). Their pursuits reveal that they are ashamed of Jesus and His words. He will respond by being ashamed of them when He returns to judge the world in righteousness (9:26). These are "salvation scriptures," not "deeper-commitment scriptures" for the already-saved. How different is the salvation offer of Christ compared to the no-cost salvation offered in so many modern Christian circles!

Jesus' high standards for true discipleship are highlighted more in the final part of today's reading. Those who literally followed Him in His day had to be willing to wander homeless, just as He did. They had to risk offending relatives who were more earthly-than kingdom-minded, knowing that the proclamation of the gospel is the supreme priority. And they must never look back, longing for the life they left behind.

Being wholly committed, however, doesn't necessarily mean one is wholly perfect. James and John were wholly committed to follow Jesus, but they also argued with the other disciples as to whom among them was the greatest (9:46), not to mention their desire to be exalted to Jesus' right and left hand in His kingdom, or their hope to gain His permission to call down fire from heaven to fry some Samaritans (9:54). Difficult to believe that these guys would be church leaders in just a few weeks!

Day 146, Luke 10

Jesus was doing a very significant amount of traveling, as He sent out the seventy "in pairs ahead of Him to every city and place where He Himself was going to come" (10:1). At a minimum, they announced His coming to 35 cities. Like the twelve sent out before them, they were expected to trust God to meet their needs *as* they went, and not *before* they went. Faith acts. Doubt waits.

Theirs was a mission of mercy, manifested by divine healing, and also a mission of condemnation upon those cities that rejected them. Some cities had already sealed their doom, such as Chorazin and Capernaum, not having repented after being visited by the Son of God.

According to Jesus, Satan was in heaven before he fell (10:18). Scripture doesn't tell us everything that happened, but passages in Isaiah 14 and Ezekiel 28 indicate that the devil was lifted up in pride because of his beauty. He attempted to exalt himself above God, and for that reason was cast down. There was no cosmic struggle or "spiritual warfare" between God and the devil. He fell like lightning. One second he was in heaven, and the next second he was on the earth. Satan's power compared to God's power is of no comparison.

Incidentally, if Jesus was able to give the seventy authority over "all the power of the enemy" (10:10), then He first must have had that authority Himself. This disproves the theory that Satan gained authority beyond God's control when Adam fell. God always has been and always will be sovereign over Satan.

Now it is time for our (almost) daily instruction in the errors of Calvinism. Calvinists sometimes point to Luke 10:22 as proof that God selects certain individuals for salvation: "No one knows who the Son is except the Father, and who the Father is except the Son, and anyone to whom the Son wills to reveal Him." Considering the verse just prior to this one, however, reveals that Jesus believed that God was hiding truth from the "wise and intelligent" and revealing it to "infants." This is just another way of saying that

God resists the proud and gives grace to the humble. God has not chosen *arbitrarily* to hide or reveal truth to certain pre-selected individuals. Rather, He has chosen to hide it from or reveal it to those who don't or do meet His conditions. So we see once again God's "conditional election" rather than the Calvinists' "unconditional election." God reveals Himself to those who seek Him. He saves those who repent and believe.

Jesus obviously believed that the way to eternal life could be found in the Old Testament, and He affirmed the lawyer's belief that the way was to love God with all one's heart, soul, strength and mind, and to love one's neighbor as oneself, that is, following the two greatest commandments (10:25-28). This is troublesome to those who do not understand the inseparable correlation between faith and works and to those who have a faulty grasp of God's grace. Clearly, the questioning lawyer was not obeying the second greatest commandment (10:29), being a typical Jew who would have walked right by the wounded man in Jesus' parable, just as the priest and Levite did. But Jesus was giving the lawyer an opportunity to repent and begin to love his neighbor as himself, as He told him to do what he had not been doing and imitate the example of the Good Samaritan (10:37).

So *there* was the grace God was offering Him, the same grace that God is offering everyone who is not obeying the two greatest commandments. God will graciously forgive those who repent. Repentance implies a striving to obey from the moment of repentance. And of course, it is those who believe who repent.

If you are interested in a more in-depth look, I've written more extensively on Jesus' encounter with the lawyer and His parable of the Good Samaritan at: www.heavensfamily.org/ss/e_teachings/2006_11.

I'm so glad you are spending time each day sitting at Jesus' feet and listening. Like Mary, "You have chosen the good part, which shall not be taken away from you" (10:42).

Day 147, Luke 11

The Lord's Prayer, as it is commonly called, already seemed quite short in Matthew's rendition. But Luke truncates it even more. Long prayers are not necessarily better prayers. When you think about it, it does seem a bit odd, in a relationship between one who knows everything and one who knows virtually nothing by comparison, that the latter would do all the talking! It seems that it would be more important that we hear from God than that He hear from us! In any case, the Lord's Prayer helps us to order our prayers, prioritizing what is most important. Our foremost desire should be that our Father's name be hallowed.

It is to be regretted that the *New American Standard Version*, as well as some other versions, translates Jesus as saying in the conclusion of the parable of the midnight visitor, "Because of his persistence he will get up and give him as much as he needs." The Greek word translated "persistence" (*anaideia*), is derived from two other Greek words. One of those words means "shame" and the other is a negative prefix. So *anaideia* is better translated "shamelessness."

Additionally, Jesus' story doesn't illustrate the idea of persistence, but rather of boldness. The primary character in the parable had great nerve, or faith, to disturb his friend at midnight to request three loaves of bread. Imagine doing such a thing yourself! What would restrain you from making such a request? Only fear, or lack of faith. And that is exactly why Jesus then encouraged His disciples to ask, seek and knock. The key to answered prayer is to make requests that are according to God's will, and to ask boldly. This is certainly repeatedly illustrated in Scripture. One request we can make, certain of God's will in the matter, is for the Holy Spirit, whom Jesus assures us our Father will give us (11:13).

Of course, the parable of the midnight visitor, like all parables, is an imperfect comparison, and so we should be cautious that we don't ascribe to God every detail that we find in the reluctant and sleepy friend. God never sleeps (Ps. 121:4)! He is much more like the father who grants his child his exact requests (11:11-12) than a just-awakened and disheartening neighbor.

Truly, those who accused Jesus of casting out demons by Satan's power, and those who demanded a sign from Him, revealed the hardness of their hearts. Jesus had performed plenty of "signs from heaven," and anyone who did more than listen to gossip about Him, but observed His ministry for even a short time, knew that. Only wicked people demand proof for what has already been proven repeatedly. They won't be persuaded. Yet Jesus patiently responded to them, provoking them to consider how foolish their accusations were.

Today we read of the world's very first person who gave undue prominence to Jesus' mother, Mary. Raising her voice in the crowd, she said to Jesus, "Blessed is the womb that bore You and the breasts at which You nursed" (11:27). His correction of her should be heeded by all today whose devotion to Mary unduly supersedes devotion to Christ: "On the contrary, blessed are those who hear the word of God and observe it" (11:28). *That* is the important thing.

Jesus' contrast of those with "clear eyes" and "bad (or evil) eyes" was not as cryptic to His contemporary followers as it is to His modern followers. In Jesus' day, to say that someone had an evil eye was synonymous with saying that he had a greedy heart (Prov. 28:22; Matt. 20:15). So the clear eye is just the opposite of that. Jesus pointed out that greedy hearts reveal that one is full of spiritual darkness, something that is also affirmed by Paul, who wrote that no greedy person will inherit God's kingdom (1 Cor. 6:9-10; Eph. 5:3-5). Although the modern definition of greed allows people to hoard massive amounts of wealth, the unchanging truth is that the damning sin of the goats in Matthew 25:31-46 was their greed, illustrated by the fact that they did not share their God-given abundance with the poor. May our eyes be clear!

Day 148, Luke 12

Jesus' solemn declaration, "But there is nothing covered up that will not be revealed, and hidden that will not be known" (12:2), should terrify every hypocrite. It should also motivate those of us who profess to be Christ's followers to purge our lives of all hypocrisy. What no one else knows about you right now will be known by everyone one day. Jesus promised His disciples (12:1), "What you have whispered in the inner rooms will be proclaimed upon the housetops" (12:3). How would you live your life differently if everyone could hear your every word? How would you live your life differently if Jesus was your constant companion? (He is, by the way.)

These kinds of questions have a tendency to put the fear of God in us, and for that reason, some object, claiming that no Christian should be afraid of God. Jesus, however, *commanded* His disciples to fear God, because God is the one who has authority to kill and cast into hell (12:4-5). This is a wake-up call to anyone who assumes that his salvation is forever guaranteed just because he currently possesses it. Notice Jesus was warning His own disciples of the danger of hell. He also solemnly warned them that those who denied Him before men He would deny before the angels (12:8-9). Thus the question, "Can a Christian forfeit his salvation?" can be answered with another question, "Can a Christian deny Christ?"

This point is underscored by Jesus' words to His disciples about the unfaithful slave who backslid because he assumed that his master would be a long time in coming. In the end, he was "cut in pieces" and assigned "a place with the unbelievers" (12:46). Those who are acting like unbelievers when Jesus returns will be treated like unbelievers, even if they acted like believers at a previous time. This is a fearful prospect that should motivate all of us to stay ready.

Lest any disciple become overly fearful in this regard, however, Jesus assures us that we are of great value in God's eyes; thus we certainly should not fear being cast into hell on a whim. The hairs on our heads are numbered. Remember that Peter publicly denied Christ three times, but He repented and was forgiven and restored. We need to maintain a healthy balance.

Jesus certainly didn't have time to arbitrate a dispute between two brothers over a family inheritance. But He observed that the brother who publicly spoke ill of his brother and perhaps interrupted His sermon to do so was overly concerned about getting his fair share. Jesus seized the opportunity to warn the crowd about greed.

Greedy people think that "life consists of possessions," and their lives revolve around acquiring more. Such people will not inherit God's kingdom (Eph. 5:3-5). The parable of the rich man was told to illustrate that point. He was rich, but not "rich toward God." When he prospered, it never occurred to him that God blessed Him, not so he could lay up treasures on earth, but so he could lay them up in heaven. He should have used his wealth to love his neighbor as himself and glorify God in the process. Yet he only loved himself, and was judged because of it. His life was cut short by the decree of God. Jesus certainly didn't leave us with the impression that he went to heaven. If you are interested, I've written much more extensively about the story of the rich fool at: www.heavensfamily.org/ss/ttne/ttne_01.

A lesser sign that one is too focused on material things and not as in tune with God as one should be is when one worries about having enough material things, including even worrying about food and covering (12:22-31). If we know and serve God, we know He will supply our needs. Since there is no reason to worry, there is no reason to hoard; thus we can show our trust in God by dispossession, something Jesus commanded all His followers to do (12:33), but something that is rarely mentioned or practiced in most professing Christian circles.

This life is a preparation for the next life, and like a journey to court (12:58-59). Stay ready!

Day 149, Luke 13

Apparently, two contemporary tragedies during the time of Jesus' ministry had people talking. For some reason unknown to us, Pilate had ordered the execution of certain Galileans who had come to Jerusalem to make sacrifices. Also, a tower in Siloam had collapsed and killed 18 men. Believing that God is sovereign, people assumed that those who had perished deserved their fates, and they were correct. Yet they wrongly assumed that those who hadn't perished were undeserving of such a fate. Although God's passive wrath upon sinners may have been demonstrated in those two tragic events, God's mercy was demonstrated to an even greater degree, in that there were so many who were still alive. They were, quite mercifully, being given time to repent, as are all unrepentant humans who are still breathing.

This same concept is well illustrated by Jesus' parable of the unfruitful fig tree. There is always tension between justice and mercy, and with God, mercy overcomes justice for a time. God works to influence sinners to repent, and He patiently waits for them to change. Eventually, however, His patience wears out, and then judgment falls. So everyone should be cautious that they don't mistake God's mercy for His approval. Jesus warned His audience of that very thing, calling them to repent or ultimately perish (13:3, 5).

All this being so, the oft-asked question, "Why do bad things happen to good people?" reveals a flawed understanding about people. Since, as Jesus once said, "No one is good except God alone" (Mark 10:18), a better question to ask would be, "Why does anything good happen to anyone, since all people deserve God's immediate wrath?"

Take note that the sickness of the woman who was "bent double" was "caused by a spirit" (13:11). Moreover, Jesus said that *Satan* had bound her for 18 years (13:16). Then He, whom according Peter "went about doing good and healing all who were oppressed by the *devil*" (Acts 10:38), laid His hands on her and healed her. So Satan is the one who causes sickness; God is the healer! Let's not forget that. Certainly Scripture teaches us that God may permit Satan to afflict someone with sickness as a means of His punishment or discipline. But if any of us is sick for those reasons, then it stands to reason that our repentance would open the door to healing, and that sickness is not God's perfect will for us.

The parable of the mustard seed and the parable of the leaven both illustrate the same concept. Although God's kingdom on earth during Christ's day was quite small (as those who had submitted to God's kingship were a tiny minority), one day God's kingdom will rule the earth, as the redeemed from all the ages will live in peace together there, and all unrepentant rebels will be forever banished. So rejoice! We're still a minority, but not forever.

Did Jesus believe that holiness is required to gain entrance into heaven? Apparently so, as He said that the door to salvation is narrow (13:24), and warned that He would one day say to some who would attempt to gain entrance, "Depart from Me, all you *evildoers*" (13:27). That will include church-going evildoers, Bible-quoting evildoers and born-again evildoers. Of course, as we've already discussed, all are evildoers before they turn from their sins. Yet the greatest deception is that of people who have "become Christians," and who have conformed their lives to the same degree as others who have "become Christians," but very little changes in their behavior. They are now opposed to abortion and attend church services. But they are still greedy, lustful liars and thieves.

Did Jesus want everyone to repent? Is it possible for everyone to repent? Did Jesus offer forgiveness of sins to everyone; or was it only offered to a few whom God pre-selected? Jesus' lament over Jerusalem reveals the answers. He did not say, "O a few in Jerusalem, a few in Jerusalem....How often I wanted to gather just a few of your children together, unlike a hen gathers her entire brood under her wings, but God has not yet zapped you few chosen ones with some irresistible grace!" (13:34)

Day 150, Luke 14

At more elaborate banquets in Jesus' day, there were always certain "seats of honor," just as there are often head tables at modern banquets. At this particular meal attended by lawyers and Pharisees, the "men of God" were vying to sit in the places of honor. Because of Christianity's influence on Western culture, most of us know that it looks bad to exalt ourselves so obviously. Still, we find more subtle ways to elevate ourselves in the eyes of others. We "casually" mention our job titles or important people we know, make sure those letters that reveal our education are always after our names, or talk about how God has used us so gloriously. The goal is the same—we want people to respect us. Jesus' lesson is still true: If we exalt ourselves, we will be humbled. If we humble ourselves, we will be exalted.

Did you notice that twice in today's reading Jesus mentioned caring for the poor, the crippled, the lame and the blind? He told the banquet host not to invite friends, family, or rich neighbors to his luncheons and dinners because they would reciprocate. (Isn't it true that "wining and dining" is often done for the express purpose of getting something in return? It is a selfish kindness.) Rather, he should invite those who could not repay him, the disadvantaged, and God would repay him in the next life. Imagine God's perspective as He looks down from heaven and sees people "generously" giving their food to their rich friends, at the same time that He sees the poor going hungry.

Jesus also mentioned the same marginalized people in His parable of the wedding feast (14:21), subtly revealing a secret to successful evangelism. That secret is this: People who have money are often not receptive to God's heavenly invitation because they are so devoted to their wealth, whereas the poor and handicapped are much more likely to open their hearts to the good news of the gospel. Notice that two of three excuses that were given by the wealthy for not attending the dinner related to their devotion to their possessions (14:18-20).

Most of the people reading this daily devotional live in countries where there are many government and private social services for the poor and the handicapped. But there are actually quite a few reading this in developing countries where handicapped people must beg on the streets to survive. God cares about them, *and through them, He tests the rest of us.* Forgive me for putting in a little advertisement here for the ministry of *Heaven's Family*, but everything we do is for the sake of the poor around the world. I hope you are involved with us!

Jesus had a mega-church (14:25), but He wasn't thrilled with big crowds! He wanted disciples, that is, committed followers willing to pay a price, and not just tag-alongs. He still wants disciples (Matt. 28:19). What is a disciple? Jesus listed three requirements. We must love Him supremely, more than our family members (14:26). We must deny ourselves and be willing to suffer hardship for His sake (14:27). And, we must love Him more than possessions, and thus obey His commandments regarding stewardship (14:33).

A careful and honest examination of the New Testament makes it very clear that it is only disciples of Christ who are actually believers in Him and true Christians. All others are pseudo-Christians who are "following" someone other than "Bible Jesus." If a person does not meet Jesus' requirements for discipleship he is not really saved. Rather than pressing for quick "decisions for Christ," we ought to instruct people, as did Jesus, to first count the cost of becoming His true follower (14:28-32).

Considering the context, it would seem logical to conclude that Jesus' unsalty salt analogy has something to do with discipleship. *True* salt is salty. *True* disciples are committed to Christ. If salt became tasteless (an actual impossibility), it would be good for nothing and be discarded. Similarly, professing disciples who are uncommitted are good for nothing and will be discarded. There is no such thing, really, as an uncommitted Christian.

Day 151, Luke 15

All three of the parables we've just read were aimed at the Pharisees and scribes who were grumbling that Jesus was spending time with sinners. For that reason, what is commonly referred to as the Parable of the Prodigal Son should really be referred to as the Parable of the Grumbling Older Brother.

Jesus did His best, using three stories, to convey the truth that saving sinners is a high priority on God's list. By expending His efforts to reach lost sinners, Jesus was doing nothing different than the shepherd who leaves ninety-nine sheep to search for one that is lost, or the woman who owns tens coins and focuses all her attention on finding one that was missing. Moreover, His priority was no different than heaven's priority, because there is "more joy in heaven over one sinner who repents than over ninety-nine righteous persons who need no repentance" (15:7). Imagine that! God, of course, loves those who serve Him, but He has more joy over one repentant sinner than over ninety-nine saints!

If we are going to lay hold of Christ-likeness, we also must prioritize reaching out to the yet-unrepentant. How easy it is for churches to become inwardly-focused. It isn't easy for God to bless such churches, and they usually dry up or split up. Don't blame your pastor if your church has no outreach. Outreach is not supposed to be a church program, but a function of every individual member. Dead churches consist of dead members.

Let us not overlook the fact that Jesus did not say that heaven becomes excited over nonbelievers who "accept Jesus as their personal Savior." God is looking for repentance, as repentance opens the door to forgiveness and salvation. Heaven rejoices when sinners *repent* (15:7, 10).

Repentance is what was illustrated by the prodigal son. He "came to his senses" (15:7) and determined to humble himself, journey back to his father, confess his guilt, and ask for a job. Yet I've heard some modern preachers point out the father's "unconditional love" for his son, illustrated by his running to his son when he saw him from far off, and his embracing his son even prior to his confession. Yet I think it is safe to say that any such father, seeing his son returning in the distance, could discern that he was returning in repentance. How do you suppose the father would have reacted if his son had returned with his arms wrapped around two women, holding a bottle of wine in each hand, and saying, "Hey Pop, I've been having a lovely time with your money! Can me and my friends here kill the fattened calf and throw a little party?"

As I mentioned earlier, the third parable is more about the jealous older brother than it is about the prodigal son. Personally, I can kind of relate to that older brother. I'm not always as happy as I should be when God shows mercy to undeserving sinners, except, of course, when I happen to be the undeserving sinner to whom He is showing mercy! My fellow Pharisees and I really needed to hear this parable!

Keep in mind that this parable is imperfect in its analogy, as is every parable. That is, not every detail of the parable has some direct spiritual correlation. The relationship of the father and son does not perfectly and fully correlate to that of the unsaved and God. Before they repent and are born again, they were spiritually children of the devil, not of God. When they repent, they aren't returning to God, since they never served Him in the first place. Yet, when sinners repent, they are indeed showered with mercy and acceptance. Their creator then becomes their Father.

Finally, this story does not discount the fact that sin has its consequences or that God is fair. The younger brother was restored to his father, but his inheritance was gone forever. The father told his older son, "All that is mine is yours" (15:31). That means the older son's unfailing obedience would ultimately pay off as his full inheritance was still waiting for him. *Yeah for fairness!* (Too bad I need so much mercy.)

Day 152, Luke 16

The parable of the unrighteous steward often raises questions because it appears as if Jesus was sanctioning dishonesty and thievery, as exemplified by the swindler in His story. But let us erase that thought from our minds, as it is an impossibility. No swindler will inherit God's kingdom (1 Cor. 6:9-10).

As I have so often said, a parable is simply an expanded metaphor, which is a comparison of two things that are basically dissimilar but that share at least one similarity. The key is not to assign a *similar* classification to what should be understood as *dissimilar*. Jesus wants His followers to imitate the unrighteous steward in only one sense, and that is to prepare for their future by using money to make friends. That is it. He does not want us to imitate the means of the unfaithful steward.

More specifically, Jesus wants us to "make friends for ourselves by means of the mammon of unrighteousness; that when it fails, they may receive us into the eternal dwellings" (16:9). He speaks of money as being "the mammon of unrighteousness" simply because money is intrinsically linked to the world's evil. The money in your wallet has likely been used, before you possessed it, for many things that God hates. It is now your responsibility, however, to use that unrighteous mammon righteously.

The *unrighteous* steward made friends by the *unrighteous* use of his master's money, so that when he lost his income, his friends would take care of him. Like him, we have been entrusted with our Master's money. We, too, should use it to make friends, not in an unscrupulous manner, but rather by meeting pressing needs and caring for the poor. One day, specifically the day we die, we will lose our income, just as did the unrighteous steward. Yet our beneficiaries who have already gone to heaven will be waiting there to receive us, not into temporal, but "eternal dwellings."

We all need to have friends waiting for us there who will testify before God, "I was hungry, and that person was my friend, and he fed me." Jesus solemnly warned, "If therefore you have not been faithful in the use of unrighteous mammon, who will entrust the true riches to you?" (16:11). If we have not been faithful stewards of God's money, we are foolish to think that we will inherit God's kingdom. No greedy person will enter heaven. Jesus emphatically declared, "You cannot serve God and mammon" (16:13). It is one or the other.

The Pharisees, who thought themselves to be lovers of God, actually loved money, and they scoffed when they heard Jesus (16:14). Jesus, ever-patient, told them a story that reveals what happens at death to people who don't "make friends by means of the mammon of unrighteousness." They, like the rich man in His story, find themselves in hell, reaping what they have sown. Just as Lazarus once sat outside the rich man's mansion, longing for the crumbs that fell from his table, the rich man found himself outside of Lazarus' "mansion" as it were, longing for a single drop of water from him. But his request was denied, because hell is a place of perfect justice for those who refused the mercy that God offered through Jesus, continuing in their selfish lives.

Concerning this story, I once heard a well-known evangelist say before a huge crowd, "The rich man didn't go to hell because he was rich any more than Lazarus went to heaven because he was poor!" The crowd roared with approval, because what he said sounded so right. But the fact is, even though Lazarus' poverty had nothing to do with his salvation, the rich man's wealth had a lot to do with his damnation. Abraham explained it quite clearly to the rich man that his treatment of Lazarus was very much related to why he was suffering in hell (16:25). Keep in mind that Abraham was a rich man when he was on the earth, but obviously, he "made friends by the means of the mammon of unrighteousness" when he had the opportunity.

If you are interested, I've written much more extensively on Luke 16 at: www.heavensfamily.org/ss/ttne/ttne_04.

Day 153, Luke 17

Take note that Jesus did not say in 17:3, "If your brother sins against you, forgive him!" No, he said, "If your brother sins, rebuke him, and if he repents, forgive him." So if I have been offended by a brother (or sister) in Christ, I am not to forgive him or her. I am to confront the offending party. Then, *if the offending one repents*, I am commanded to forgive. I've observed Christians who allegedly forgave those who don't repent (something God generally does not do, by the way), and they are often fooling themselves. They (naturally) avoid any contact with the people they've "forgiven" because they remain offended. There is no reconciliation. That is not forgiveness!

Nine times out of ten, if we confront an offending fellow believer, and I'm speaking of a true believer, he or she will repent. Then genuine forgiveness can be granted and reconciliation can occur. But if we don't confront the offending one, we disobey Christ. We hold a grudge, and we haven't even given the offending party an opportunity to repent in order to achieve reconciliation.

What Jesus taught was nothing new. It is an application of loving one's neighbor as oneself. God said in the Law of Moses:

> You shall not hate your fellow countryman in your heart; you may surely reprove your neighbor, but shall not incur sin because of him. You shall not take vengeance, nor bear any grudge against the sons of your people, but you shall love your neighbor as yourself; I am the Lord (Lev. 19:17-18).

When we reprove our offending neighbor, it shows that we value our relationship with him, and thus do what needs to be done to work towards reconciliation. And if a brother or sister offends us seven times in one day and *repents*, we are commanded to forgive (17:4).

Like so many of us, the apostles thought that they possessed some faith and needed more. But according to Jesus, just a little faith goes a long way. A mustard seed is very tiny, but a mustard seed's worth of faith can do what would be otherwise impossible. Perhaps Luke included the story of the ten lepers in this chapter as an illustration of the kind of faith of which Jesus spoke. The lepers begged Him for mercy, obviously believing that He could heal them. He told them to show themselves to the priests, which would require a one- or two-day journey to Jerusalem. The clear implication was that, by the time they arrived, they would be cleansed of their leprosy, and the priests would declare them clean, as required by the Mosaic Law (Lev. 14:1-32). The point is this: they had to act upon their faith. As they did, they were healed.

Faith acts on God's word regardless of other circumstances. Had any of the 10 lepers not acted on their faith, it would have indicated that they had no faith. Had they not believed, they would not have been healed, even though it is obvious from the story that it was Jesus' will that they be healed. This is inescapable truth. Jesus told the Samaritan leper who returned to give thanks, "Your faith has made you well" (17:19).

Why are more of us not healed by our faith? I suspect there are two primary reasons. One is lack of faith. Modern, unbelieving theology regarding divine healing has robbed us of any faith we have. Second, many of us are digging our graves with our teeth, eating foods that have been processed to death and robbed of much of their nutritional value, rather than on foods that God has given to nourish us. We are eating slow poison. I recommend an eye-opening book by Dr. Joel Furhman, M.D. titled, *Fasting and Eating for Health: A Medical Doctor's Program for Conquering Disease*.

The second half of Luke 17 contains Jesus' consistent teaching on His future coming. You may have noticed that He gave no indication that He will be returning twice! No, He is coming back once, and when He does, He will rapture the righteous (17:34-36) and pour out His wrath on the unrighteous (17:26-32).

Day 154, Luke 18

As always, it is important to consider context when we interpret Jesus' parable of the unjust judge. Remember that in Luke 17, Jesus was talking about the end times and His return to judge the earth, a time of great persecution for His followers. They will be longing then for His coming, and wondering why He doesn't return immediately to save them from the injustices that they are suffering. So Jesus told His disciples a parable "to show that at all times they ought to pray and not to lose heart" (18:1).

The parable He told is a perfect illustration of the importance of not assigning spiritual significance to every detail of every parable. The unjust judge is by no means a representation of God, except in the sense that God is a Judge. Unlike the unrighteous judge, however, who granted the persistent widow justice just so he wouldn't be bothered any longer, God is a perfectly righteous judge. He dearly loves His children, and He will "bring about justice for them quickly" (18:8) as they "cry to Him day and night" during those difficult days.

Take note that Jesus was not talking about praying to be saved, baptized with the Holy Spirit, healed, or to have one's temporal needs met. Those requests and others like them do not require continual and multiple requests. This parable does not teach us that we need to bombard heaven with our prayers so that a reluctant God will become weary of them and thus ultimately grant us our requests!

We must also consider context in the next parable, that of the Pharisee and the tax-collector. It was targeted at those "who trusted in themselves that they were righteous, and viewed others with contempt" (18:9). It is no surprise that Jesus used a Pharisee as His example of one who fit that description. The proud Pharisee wrongly thought that he had no need for repentance and God's mercy, believing salvation was something he had earned by his own efforts. Contrasted with him was the sinful tax collector, who realized his need for mercy, asked for it, and received it. The Pharisee was proud, the tax collector was humble. The Pharisee would be humbled in the end and the tax collector would be exalted, having been declared just in heaven's court. Amazing grace!

It is an inescapable fact that Jesus required the rich, young ruler to give up his possessions to inherit eternal life. What Christ said to him was not a unique requirement given only to him, as is often claimed. Jesus did not say, "How hard it is for that one guy to enter the kingdom of God!" Rather, He said, "How hard it is for those who are wealthy to enter the kingdom of God" (18:24). The reason it is so hard for them is because they, like the rich, young ruler, love their money, and will not repent and follow Jesus, who commands them to live more simply and lay up treasure in heaven as they love their neighbors as themselves. They foolishly cling to what they must ultimately relinquish anyway, when they could have transferred all of it to heaven!

Finally, we read another story about someone who was healed, and Jesus again credited his faith (18:42). This story also illustrates a flaw in Calvinistic theology. (You are no doubt surprised to read me commenting about Calvinism!) Calvinists claim that whatever God wants, He gets, because He is sovereign. So, they say, if He desires that someone be saved, that person will be saved. To say otherwise, they claim, is to say that the unsaved person whom God desires to be saved is more powerful than God. This is absurd reasoning. God, who is sovereign, obviously permits people to do many things He desires that they not do. That does not diminish His sovereignty. Had Bartimaeus had no faith, he would not have been healed, even though it was clearly God's will for him to be healed. He could have circumvented God's will by unbelief. Indeed, unbelief is what circumvents God's will that all be saved and come to the knowledge of the truth (1 Tim. 2:4).

Day 155, Luke 19

Did you notice Jesus didn't ask Zaccheus if He could stay at his house? God doesn't need to ask to visit anyone's house. He's God! Here's one more proof of Jesus' deity. If He wasn't God, He was arrogant and intrusive.

Zaccheus may possibly have liquidated all of his wealth if he kept his word to Jesus. Half he was going to give to the poor, leaving a half, or four-eighths. And if he paid back anyone whom he had defrauded four times as much, and if he had gained one-eighth of his income by defrauding people (something for which tax collectors were notorious), that would have left him with nothing. He was unlike the rich, young ruler in this regard, who was unwilling to liquidate his wealth to benefit the poor.

Notice that Jesus did not say to Zaccheus, "Oh no! You don't need to do all that to be saved! That would be salvation by works, not faith! So just accept me as your personal Savior and everything will be alright!" Rather, He commended Zaccheus for repenting of two damning sins: greed and thievery. Previously, he hadn't cared for the poor, and he had gained his wealth, at least in part, by dishonesty in his business of collecting taxes. Because of his public repentance, Jesus said salvation had come to his house. In light of such clear scriptures, it is incredible that anyone within Christendom thinks that he or she can gain eternal life while being dishonest in money matters and ignoring the plight of the poor, especially of poor believers. And why did Zaccheus repent? Because he believed in the Lord Jesus.

Those traveling with Jesus towards Jerusalem naturally thought He was about to establish the long-awaited kingdom of God. He had already told His apostles that He would be scourged and crucified, but His statements were incomprehensible to them. So He told another parable to give them some idea what to expect of Him, and what He expected of them in His absence. Specifically, He expected them, just as He expects us, to be fruitful, making a profit on what He has to entrusted us for His kingdom.

Everyone who produces a spiritual profit will receive a reward, perhaps in the form of being entrusted with some greater responsibility in His future kingdom. Anyone who does not will be considered a "worthless slave" (19:22). In a similar parable that we read in Matthew 25:14-30, the parable of the talents, the unprofitable servant was "cast out...into the outer darkness" where there was "weeping and gnashing of teeth" (Matt. 25:30). All unprofitable servants of Christ will be cast into hell, because even though they professed to be servants of Christ, their unfruitfulness will prove their profession to be bogus.

The Mount of Olives sits directly beside Jerusalem. It was probably from there, looking across the Kidron Valley, that Jesus wept over the city. Picture, for a moment, Jesus sitting on a stationary donkey, weeping over Jerusalem. That will give you a little deeper revelation of the Lord's character. While weeping, Jesus predicted the destruction of Jerusalem, fulfilled 37 years later by a Roman army. God would use the Romans as a tool of His divine judgment.

I've read the ancient historian Josephus' eyewitness account of Jerusalem's fall. The city was besieged by Titus with 80,000 Roman troops during Passover, when Jews were gathered from all over Israel. The siege lasted for months, so that no one could get in or out of the city. Thousands died of starvation while hoping for a messiah to come and rescue them. Jews who went out of the city at night to gather food were caught by the hundreds, and were whipped, tortured and crucified near the city walls. So many were crucified that there weren't enough crosses, so several at a time would be crucified on one cross. Some who deserted the city to surrender to the Roman camp were discovered to have swallowed gold, and consequently thousands of deserters were killed and dissected for the potential find of gold in their stomachs. By the time Jerusalem fell, more than one million Jews had died. No wonder Jesus wept.

Day 156, Luke 20

Isn't it interesting that the common folks in Jesus' day were more spiritually in tune with God than were the Jewish religious leaders—the chief priests, scribes and elders? While the common folks held to the belief that John the Baptist was a prophet sent from God (20:6), the guys who had "studied at seminary for years" did not. That was a sad phenomenon that certainly has its counterpart in modern Christendom. Multitudes of so-called "lay people," who simply read and believe Scripture, are miles ahead of seminary-trained spiritual leaders. The reason for this tragic reality is the same as it was in Jesus' time: the spiritual leaders are not motivated by love of God or others, but love for themselves (20:46-47). Many of them, rather than being called of God, pursue ministry as a career. They love the respectful greetings. They, just like the Pharisees, will "receive greater condemnation" in hell (20:47).

The parable of the vine growers, of which the interpretation is quite obvious (yet missed entirely by the scribes and chief priests), provides another good example of the danger of assigning spiritual significance to every detail of a parable. Consider what the owner of the vineyard (who represents God) said after his servants (who represents God's prophets) had been beaten or killed by the vine-growers (who represent the nation Israel): "What shall I do? I will send my beloved son; perhaps they will respect him." Obviously we should not conclude from reading those words that God did not know how His Son would be received when He came to the earth. So the rule when reading the parables is to make sure we assign spiritual significance only to those details that are obviously intended to have spiritual significance. How do we know which details those are? That answer is found in 1 David 21:7: "The Lord Thy God hath given thee a brain."

Those "smart" and "tricky" religious leaders really hoped to force Jesus to make a public statement against Caesar that could be used to incriminate Him (20:20-22). But it isn't easy to trick God! He's been around the block a few times! And the God who exalted

Caesar to His position as Emperor of the Roman Empire, and who could easily (and did) remove Caesar from his throne, was not afraid of what Caesar might do to Him.

We also learn from Jesus' reply to their loaded question ("Render to Caesar the things that are Caesar's, and to God the things that are God's"), that we should be subject to the ruling authorities. Of course, if the ruling authorities dictate that we should disobey God, then, and only then, is civil disobedience acceptable, and in fact, our duty. Paying taxes, however, is not contrary to God's law. God established human government, and it takes taxes to run a government. Paul wrote to the Roman Christians, "For because of this you also pay taxes, for rulers are servants of God, devoting themselves to this very thing. Render to all what is due to them: tax to whom tax is due; custom to whom custom; fear to whom fear; honor to whom honor" (Rom. 13:6-7).

In a republic or democracy, all citizens have the opportunity to help determine the law of the land to some degree, thus Christians have the responsibility to participate in the process. Since true believers are often the minority, however, and because the majority rule, injustice and ungodly policies often win over what would be in line with the will of God. Still, the godly should not remain silent. We are only endorsing what everyone knows to be true within their own consciences.

For all the church folks who think Christians are obligated to obey the Law of Moses, I wonder how many are committed to obeying Deuteronomy 25:5, mentioned in today's reading:

> If a man's brother dies, having a wife, and he is childless, his brother should marry the wife and raise up children to his brother.

A good reason to pray that your brother's wife has a child soon after they are married, and a good reason to send your brother vitamin supplements to keep him healthy until his first child is born!

Day 157, Luke 21

The little story of the widow who gave her two small copper coins contains a big challenge to us. God measures our sacrifices, not by how much we give, but by how much we still possess after we have given. And by that measure, many who give very little are, in God's eyes, very big givers. That poor widow who gave her two copper coins gave her food money. She would find herself with much more treasure in heaven than all the rich folks who made much larger contributions. This is a truth worthy of our meditation.

Keep in mind, as I have told you in the past, if you make $30,000 per year in 2009, you are in the top 7% of the world's wage earners. If you earn $50,000 per year, you are in the top 1%. Most of us reading this are quite wealthy by the world's standards.

Both Matthew and Mark also recorded Jesus' Olivet discourse. Remember that, according to Matthew, the disciples' questions were not only about the temple's future destruction, but also about the signs of Jesus' coming and the end of the age (Matt. 24:3). They probably didn't imagine that those events would be separated by at least 2,000 years, and what Jesus said didn't help them to imagine such a scenario. In any case, part of what Jesus said in His response obviously applied to the events leading to the temple's destruction, and part of what He said obviously applied to the events leading to His return. The challenge is to sort all of that out (assuming that there is no overlap), and that challenge has given rise to varying interpretations.

In my humble opinion, Luke first focuses on Jesus' response to the disciples' question about the signs preceding His return and the end of the age (21:8-11). He then moves backward in time to focus on the more immediate future beginning in 21:12, starting with the words, "But before all these things..." He then proceeds to inform them of what they can expect over the next few decades. They would be persecuted and delivered to synagogues and prisons. Remember that before the close of Acts 6, all twelve apostles had spent a night in jail and stood trial before the Sanhedrin. Peter and John spent two nights in jail and had been on trial twice. In both cases, just as Jesus promised, the apostles received supernatural utterance and wisdom that none of their opponents could resist or refute (21:15).

Also just as Jesus promised, almost all of the twelve were martyred for their faith. In some cases, they were apparently betrayed by their own friends or families (21:16). All were hated during their ministries (21:17).

In verse 20, Jesus foretells of Jerusalem's siege and destruction. It was in A.D. 66 that Rome sent a general named Cestius to crush a Jewish revolt. He surrounded Jerusalem for six months of siege, and then withdrew for an unknown reason. After Cestius' withdrawal, all the believers, following Jesus' instructions we've just read, fled from Jerusalem and Judea. It was a brief window of opportunity to escape. When Jerusalem fell to Roman general Titus in A.D. 70, no one who obeyed Jesus' instructions in 21:21 perished in the ensuing holocaust, having been forewarned forty years before.

Once Jerusalem fell, just as Jesus foretold, the survivors were "led captive into all the nations" and Jerusalem has been "trampled under foot by the Gentiles" (21:24). Jesus said that would occur "until the times of the Gentiles are fulfilled" (21:2Although many consider Israel's 1947 statehood and its 1967 recapture of Jerusalem's old city as signs that the "times of the Gentiles" are now fulfilled, we should remember that there is still further Gentile trampling of Jerusalem to come when the anti-christ rises to power.

I am persuaded that beginning in 21:25, Jesus then began revealing signs that would occur prior to His return, which would all happen at an undetermined time after the fall of Jerusalem. And in my humble opinion, the generation that will see the "signs in the sun and moon and stars" (21:25) and so on, will see Jesus return (21:32).

Day 158, Luke 22

If there ever was an example of someone serving mammon over God, Judas' betrayal of Jesus is it. Note that Judas took the initiative to secretly visit the chief priests, and "they agreed to give him money" (22:5). He offered them his services for pay, and they ultimately agreed on 30 pieces of silver. That may not sound like very much money, but it was enough to buy a field (Matt. 27:7). Incidentally, if Jesus and His apostles were so wealthy, as is so often claimed by modern prosperity preachers, one would have to wonder why Judas would betray the One who was helping him to get rich in hopes of gaining enough money to buy a field.

Beware of the love of money! Even one who literally lives with Jesus for three years, who witnesses miracles, and who serves in supernatural ministry, is not beyond its lure. Judas had already seared his conscience by pilfering funds from the ministry moneybox, effectively stealing from Jesus, His disciples, and the poor (Jn. 12:6). Selling Christ Himself was the final step in his downward fall. The one who opens the door to greed opens the door to Satan, just as Judas did. When we disobey Christ to give money primacy, we betray Christ as Judas did, only to a lesser degree. Choose serving Christ or serving money! Both cannot be master!

The church's first Lord's Supper was Jesus' last Passover meal, and so we see that both were full meals. That is how the Lord's Supper was practiced by the early church, which is why it is referred to as the Lord's *Supper* (1 Cor. 11:20) rather than the Lord's *Snack*, which is what it has become in modern Christendom. Jesus made it clear that He Himself was the fulfillment of what had been annually practiced by millions of Israelites for centuries. As we chew the bread of the Lord's Supper, it should remind us that Jesus was "crushed for our iniquities" (Is. 53:5), and as we swallow that bread we should remember that the Living Bread had come down from heaven to live inside us (Jn. 6:51)!

Today we read something that is not found in Matthew or Mark's Gospels. Jesus told Peter that Satan had demanded (or, "obtained by asking") permission to sift him like wheat. This reminds us of the story of Job. Satan "obtained by asking" permission to bring trouble into Job's life.

What was Peter's sifting? From the context, it seems it was his experience of denying the Lord three times after publicly declaring his loyalty. Imagine how Peter felt when the cock crowed a third time and his eyes met Jesus' eyes. The Lord had no need to lip the words, "I told you so." The tough fisherman from Galilee wept bitter tears over his failure, and it no doubt continued to trouble him deeply even after the Lord's resurrection. But as He foretold Peter of his betrayal, Jesus also foretold him of his restoration. Peter would "turn again" and be able to "strengthen his brothers" (22:32). Amazing grace!

Luke is the only Gospel-writer who mentions that Jesus' "sweat became like drops of blood, falling upon the ground" (22:44) in the Garden of Gethsemane. Luke was likely describing a rare condition known as *hematidrosis*, when, under extreme emotional stress, tiny blood vessels rupture in a person's sweat glands, producing a mixture of blood and sweat. Jesus was not only anticipating being scourged and crucified, but bearing God's wrath for the sins of the world. No wonder He prayed to escape what He was about to suffer if it were possible. There was no other way, however, to save you and me.

I almost wish that the high priest's slave wouldn't have ducked when he saw Peter's sword swinging in his direction. Had he not, Peter may have cut off his head (as he apparently intended), and Jesus would have performed a greater miracle than just healing a severed ear! What a testimony that man would have had: "I was decapitated by a preacher, but Jesus put my head back on!"

Day 159, Luke 23

The Sanhedrin's charge against Jesus was blasphemy. They found God guilty of claiming to be divine. But their powers were limited by the occupying Roman government, which did not allow them the right of capital punishment. Needing to persuade governor Pilate that Jesus was worthy of death, they accused Him of treason. Pilate tried to pass the responsibility to Herod Antipas, murderer of John the Baptist, but to no avail. Now consider this: eventually all those people—the Sanhedrin, Pilate, Herod, the soldiers who mocked Him, and the crowd who cried for His crucifixion—would all be judged before Jesus' throne.

How is it that the people who cried, "Hosanna!" on Palm Sunday were crying, "Crucify Him!" on Good Friday? We shouldn't conclude that they were the same crowds. Those who called for Jesus' crucifixion were primarily the chief priests and religious leaders according to 23:13. Wanting to avoid a Jewish riot during Passover in Jerusalem, Pilate acquiesced to their request even after declaring Christ's innocence *three* times.

During Passover, Jews from many nations converged on Jerusalem to celebrate the feast. Simon of Cyrene, who had journeyed as many as 800 miles from Libya, became involved with a Passover Lamb on a grander scale than he ever imagined—as he carried Jesus' cross. Some commentators suggest that Simon later became a Christian. Mark's Gospel identifies him as "the father of Alexander and Rufus" (Mark 15:21), two men whom Mark assumed his readers would know. And Paul once sent greetings to a Christian named Rufus in Rome (Rom. 16:13), and so perhaps Simon and his sons did become followers of Christ. What an honor it would have been to have helped Jesus carry His cross!

While anyone else who found themselves in similar circumstances would have been consumed with their own troubles, Jesus amazingly was more concerned for the weeping women along His route to Golgatha than He was for Himself. Their sympathy for Him would not prevent the holocaust that would ultimately befall Jerusalem within forty years. Jesus' quotation from Hosea (23:30) reveals that He also had the earth's final judgment in mind, something that was only foreshadowed by Jerusalem's destruction in AD 70. God takes no delight in the death of the wicked (Ezek. 33:11), which is one reason He forestalls His judgment. Jesus' amazing love shines so brightly in today's reading as it is contrasted with the cruelty of the mocking religious leaders and Roman soldiers.

The repentant thief who hung beside Jesus is a beautiful example of a person who was saved by grace through faith, but through a *living* faith made evident by works. What were those works? First, he openly confessed that he was a sinner, which is the first step toward salvation (23:40-41). Second, he stated his belief that Jesus was innocent and unworthy of death, defending Him before the other thief (23:40-41). Third, without shame he looked to Jesus as the source of salvation and, before a hostile crowd, publicly asked Him for it. His faith was genuine, and Jesus responded to it with an affirmation: "Today you shall be with Me in Paradise" (23:43).

I wonder, however, how Jesus would have responded if that thief had whispered, "Pssst....Jesus! Keep looking straight ahead. Act like we're not talking right now. Hey, I want to tell You that I accept You into my life right now. I've heard that if I do that, things will begin to get better in my life. Now that I've accepted You, I'm expecting my situation to change!"

Jesus hung on the cross for six hours. It was during the second three hours that "darkness fell over the whole land" (23:44). When astronomers attempt to establish the exact date of Jesus' crucifixion by means of past solar eclipses, they run into one problem. That is, Jesus was obviously crucified during the Passover, which always occurs at the time of a full moon, which makes a solar eclipse an impossibility. The darkness that day was a special supernatural sign from God. The Son of God, clothed in flesh, was dying for the sins of the world, the most significant day in all of history.

Day 160, Luke 24

Wow. What an inspiring story! We've read and heard it so many times that we often don't appreciate our privilege of knowing it. Billions of people living on earth have never heard it once. May the Lord help us to change that.

Had Jesus' body not been buried by Joseph of Arimathea, it most likely would have been discarded in a garbage dump along with the bodies of the thieves who had been crucified with Him. In order, however, for His resurrection to be all the more convincing, God arranged that Jesus' body be buried securely in a specific tomb for a specific length of time. If Jesus had been resurrected from a garbage heap, our faith would have to rest on the testimony of His followers who saw Him after His resurrection, a testimony that could be doubted by reason of the potential bias of Jesus' followers. But as it turned out, we have the testimony of the Roman soldiers who stood guard at His tomb and the religious leaders who bribed them to lie, not to mention the fact that a large stone had been moved and Jesus' empty grave clothes were inside. The greatest proof that Jesus is alive, however, is your transformation, the result of His living in you!

I would love to have been there when Jesus gave His Bible lesson to those two disciples on the road to Emmaus, during which he pointed out all the Old Testament scriptures that spoke of Himself. He no doubt referenced Psalm 22 and Isaiah 53, as well as a host of other messianic passages. He may have even pointed out how Jonah's experience of being three days and nights in the fish's belly prefigured the Messiah's three days and nights in the heart of the earth.

Later that day, as Jesus began to break bread with those same two disciples "their eyes were opened" (24:31), while previously "their eyes were prevented from recognizing Him" (24:16). Similarly, later that same evening, when Jesus appeared to the eleven, we read that "He opened their minds to understand the Scriptures" (24:45). Obviously, God can make us perceptive or imperceptive, understanding or ignorant, which is a good reason to humbly pray, "Lord, open my eyes."

Even though Jesus now has a resurrected and glorified body that apparently can walk through walls and digest fish, He still has nail prints on His hands and feet. Thomas, who was not present the first time Jesus appeared to His disciples, declared, "Unless I see in His hands the imprint of the nails, and put my finger into the place of the nails, and put my hand into His side, I will not believe" (John 20:25). About a week later, Jesus appeared to him and said, "Reach here your finger, and see My hands; and reach here your hand, and put it into My side; and be not unbelieving but believing" (John 20:27). It has been rightly said, "The only works of man in heaven are the marks of the cross on Jesus' body."

I've mentioned it several times before, but today we read what I've so often quoted. Just before His ascension, Jesus said to the eleven, "Repentance for forgiveness of sins [should] be proclaimed in [My] name to all the nations" (24:47). Repentance for forgiveness of sins was a familiar theme to the eleven. It is the message they heard Jesus preach from the outset of His ministry, and the message He had instructed them to preach when He had sent them out by twos (Mark 1:15; 6:12). What ever happened to that commission and that message?

This commission, however, was different from the former in one respect. Previously, Jesus sent them to preach throughout the villages and towns of Israel. This time, He was sending them to "all the nations," or more literally, "all the ethnic groups of the world," of which there are thousands. For this reason, more than ever, we should pray, as Jesus instructed, for "the Lord of the harvest to send out laborers into His harvest" (Luke 10:2). Christians who don't care about those who have not heard the gospel are not Christians.

Day 161, Ephesians 1

We're back into our chronological study, now around AD 61, the time when Paul penned his letter to the Ephesian believers while he was incarcerated in Rome (or perhaps Caesarea). Along with Colossians, Philippians and Philemon, the book of Ephesians is one of Paul's so-called "prison epistles," a designation which I consider to be slightly misleading. They are better described as Paul's "house arrest" letters (Acts 28:30-31).

You will recall that Paul was God's human instrument to plant His church in Ephesus, and his Spirit-empowered ministry caused quite a stir during his three-year sojourn there, culminating with a riot of thousands of Ephesians chanting for two hours in the city amphitheater, "Great is Artemis of the Ephesians!" (Acts 19:1-41). Paul wrote this letter about seven years after that event.

This first chapter begins with lots of good information about what God has done for us through Jesus. Take note how many times you can find expressions such as, "in Christ," "in Him," "through Jesus Christ," "in the beloved," and "through His blood." There are quite a few. They are all connected to many "spiritual blessings" that are ours through Jesus.

Those spiritual blessings started long ago. Paul wrote that we were chosen (in Christ) "before the foundation of the world" (1:4). As I have written before in this daily devotional when we've come across scriptures about our being chosen, God's choosing was not arbitrary or "unconditional," but conditional. He chose people based on their faith in Christ. Obviously, possessing foreknowledge, that is something God could do even before we were born. Most importantly, however, notice that God's great intention from before the foundation of the world was that "we would be holy and blameless before Him" (1:4). Paul was surely speaking, not of some kind of alleged "legal" holiness and blamelessness that would be bestowed on us by virtue of Jesus' sacrifice, but rather of a genuine and practical holiness and blamelessness that would characterize our lifestyles, all because of Christ.

Not only were we chosen before the world was created, but we were also predestined to be adopted as God's children through Jesus (1:5-6). Jesus' sacrifice is what made possible our redemption (1:7), a word that speaks of a ransom being paid for the release of a prisoner, and also the forgiveness of our sins (1:8). Every future plan that God has for heaven and earth revolves around Jesus, who will one day rule the whole world, His inheritance, and with whom we will rule and reign, as He shares His inheritance with us (1:9-11)! Finally, through Jesus, God sealed us with the Holy Spirit, His mark upon us, who is not only our helper, but also a down payment from God of our future inheritance (1:14).

Obviously, the church Paul founded in Ephesus had continued to grow numerically over the years, and there would have been many believers in Ephesus who would have never seen his face. Paul, of course, kept abreast of the ongoing revival in Ephesus through his extensive network (1:15), and he continually thanked God for what was happening there, and also prayed that He would grant the believers "a spirit of wisdom and revelation in the knowledge of Christ" (1:17). Paul lists in 1:18-19 three specific prayer requests that he offered to that end. Those are three good prayers to pray for yourself as well as other believers. Note that they all revolved around knowing Jesus better, prayers that are a definite step above, "God please give me a better-paying job so I can afford the payments on my new hot tub!"

In keeping with those prayers for the Ephesian believers to know Jesus better, Paul reminds them of some facts about Jesus to help them know what is most important about Him, namely that *He is absolute Lord*. Jesus is at God's right hand, "far above all rule and authority and power and dominion, and every name that is named, not only in this age but also in the one to come" (1:21). Everything is under His feet, and He is head of the church (1:22). This describes, not American Jesus, but Bible Jesus, *Lord* Jesus!

Day 162, Ephesians 2

It is sometimes argued that, because Paul wrote that we were formerly "dead in our trespasses and sins" (2:1), his statement somehow proves that it would have been impossible for us, even under the drawing of the Spirit, to repent and believe in Jesus. "Dead people can't believe," it is said, thus if they are to believe, it requires a sovereign act of God, and so those who are saved must be those whom God has selected, not those who have selected God by means of their God-given free will.

Isn't it also true, however, that dead people can't eat, breathe or think? So if being "dead in our trespasses and sins" somehow proves that we were unable to believe in Jesus since "dead people can't believe," then it also must be true that we were unable to eat, breathe or think. This exposes the absurdity of such reasoning.

Indeed, unregenerate people are spiritually dead, are under the influence of Satan, "the prince of the power of the air" (2:2), and they "indulge the desires of the flesh" (2:3), but this condition does not make it impossible for them to resist temptation, make moral choices, or repent and believe in Christ under the conviction of the Holy Spirit. This is what Scripture continually affirms. And once we have repented and believed, the Holy Spirit continues His gracious work, regenerating our spirits, what is nothing less than a spiritual resurrection (2:7).

Our response to the Holy Spirit's conviction does not diminish the grace of God in salvation, any more than my accepting a gift from anyone diminishes the grace in their act of kindness. No one has ever accused me of "taking credit for" or "earning" the birthday gifts I've received, just because I actually believed that my friends wanted to give me gifts and I accepted them. Any person of average intelligence can understand this simple truth.

We are saved "by grace through faith" and "not as a result of works" (2:8, 10), but not so that we could then sin with impunity. Rather, the same grace that saves us also transforms us. We are "created in Christ Jesus for good works, which God prepared beforehand so that we would walk in them" (2:19). Workless "Christianity" is worthless Christianity, of which there is no shortage today.

Ever-vigilant against the Jewish teachers who were infiltrating Christian churches and persuading Gentile believers to be circumcised and keep the Mosaic Law, in the second half of today's chapter, Paul fortifies his mostly Gentile readers from being seduced. If they believed what Paul wrote, it would have stopped the Jewish legalists from making any inroads in Ephesus. Although the Gentile believers were not circumcised, Paul reminds them that circumcision is "performed in the flesh by human hands" (2:12), which is of no comparison to the work that the Spirit had performed in their spirits. Thus, they should not be intimidated by the condescending looks of proud Jews. And although they were previously alienated from God and His covenant with Israel, that was no longer true because of Christ, who brought them near through His cross.

Paul is quite forthright in declaring that Jesus abolished "the Law of commandments contained in ordinances" (2:15). He could have only been speaking of the Mosaic Law. The old covenant had been fulfilled by the new covenant, the benefits of which are now available to everyone who will believe, circumcised or uncircumcised. Thus, there is no division between Jews and Gentiles who believe in Christ. They are now one body, or one "holy temple" in Christ (2:21).

Rather than be upset with this, Jews should be thrilled, as the Mosaic Law was "the enmity" that Jesus "put to death" (2:16). The Law did not save them, but only condemned them as they broke its requirements. In light of all that we've read in the New Testament about the end of the Mosaic Law, it is surprising that new covenant Gentiles in our day sometimes put themselves under its curse. We are free from the Mosaic Law, and obligated now to follow the commandments of Christ.

Day 163, Ephesians 3

Paul continues today with his previous theme of the Gentiles' inclusion into God's kingdom, first by making reference to the divine source of his revelation (3:3-4). The Gentile inclusion had previously been a mystery, but not because it was never foretold in the Old Testament, but because the Old Testament clues had not been sufficiently pieced together by anyone. But the Holy Spirit had assembled the puzzle quite sufficiently, not only to Paul, but to other "holy apostles and prophets in the Spirit" (3:5). It was not Paul's unique revelation. Remember that Peter, James and John had all endorsed Paul's gospel to the Gentiles (Gal. 2:9).

Paul was adamant about it: "Gentiles are fellow heirs and fellow members of the body, and fellow partakers of the promise in Christ Jesus through the gospel" (3:6). And this had been God's *eternal* purpose (3:11). Again, the only reason that Paul would be emphasizing this theme is because his old antagonists, the Jewish legalists, must have also been a threat in Ephesus.

I cannot resist mentioning at this point that we once again see that the epistles often addressed church issues of Paul's day that today are not issues at all. How many of us have ever found ourselves debating with a Jew who was trying to persuade us that we need to be circumcised and keep the Mosaic Law in order to be saved?

Paul reminded his readers that he possessed a specific calling to serve the Gentiles with his gospel (3:2-4, 7-8). He obviously had no hidden motive, as he was a literal prisoner due to pursuing his call (3:1, 13). And lest anyone think that he was boasting about his special calling, he made sure his readers understood that he knew that his ministry had been granted to him purely due to God's grace, bestowed upon "the least of all the saints" (3:8). All true ministers who understand their calling can identify with Paul. They know they are nothing special. Proud servants are deceived servants.

I must confess that it is a mystery to me why God would even care to display His manifold wisdom "through the church to the rulers and the authorities in the heavenly places" (3:10), which can only be a reference to the hierarchy of evil spirits who rule the kingdom of darkness under Satan. Perhaps Paul was not saying that God had any such desire, but only that His wisdom being displayed before evil spirits was simply a consequence of His redemption accomplished through Christ. And perhaps Paul wrote about this primarily to assure his Gentile and formerly-pagan readership that they were now serving a very superior God compared to their old gods, who were nothing more than doomed demons.

Paul mentions that he bowed his knees "before the Father, from whom every family in heaven and on earth derives its name" (3:14). This seems to be another shot in the arm for Gentiles. As God has created all the world's families and He is the ultimate Father, Paul bowed his knee to the God of all the Gentile families, and not just the God of the Jews. Paul similarly wrote in his letter to the Romans, "Is God the God of Jews only? Is He not the God of Gentiles also?" (Rom. 3:29).

Thus Paul rightfully prays for Gentiles to enjoy every blessing that has been provided for them through Christ. It seems to me for two reasons that his prayer in 3:16-19 is not for Gentiles who had already received the Lord Jesus Christ, but for those who were still unregenerate. First, note that Paul requested that they would "be strengthened with power through His Spirit in the inner man, so that Christ would dwell in your hearts through faith" (3:16-17). Christ is in all who believe (2 Cor. 13:5). Second, Paul also prayed that Gentiles would "know the love of Christ which surpasses knowledge" that they might "be filled up to all the fullness of God" (3:19). Paul had already written in 1:23 that Jesus, in His body, the church, is "the fullness of Him who fills all in all."

Day 164, Ephesians 4

Generally speaking, this entire chapter is about holiness. God's call to the world to repent and believe is obviously a call to holiness. It is a call to make oneself ready to stand before King Jesus to give an account. It is a call to be prepared for future life in the heavenly kingdom by living in God's earthly kingdom with others who have also responded to the same call. Love is the preeminent goal.

Paul thus implores his Ephesian readers (and us) to "walk in a manner worthy of the calling with which you have been called, with all humility and gentleness, with patience, showing tolerance for one another in love" (4:1-2). Most important is that we preserve "the unity of the Spirit in the bond of peace" (4:3), remembering that there is "one body and one Spirit...one hope of your calling, one Lord, one faith, one baptism" and "one God and Father of all" (4:4-6). Reading such facts, one can't help but wonder why so many little human kingdoms have been carved out of God's kingdom.

Although all of us who believe in Christ have so much in common that should keep us from division, there are special gifts that Jesus has bestowed within His body that differ greatly, and we must guard against allowing those different gifts to divide us. Specifically, Jesus has given the church apostles, prophets, evangelists, pastors and teachers to equip the saints for service (4:11).

This particular passage has been milked by many who pose as apostles, prophets, and so on, in order to prop up the legitimacy of their "ministries." The primary way to discern between those who are genuine and those who are false is to look at their fruit, just as Jesus said (Matt. 7:15-23). Are they "equipping the saints for the work of service"? (4:12). That is, as a result of their "ministries," are their disciples doing good deeds and serving others? Sadly, many modern "ministers" are exposed as being undeniably illegitimate in light of this test.

Genuine ministers of Christ are helping the church understand truth, so it is not misled by false doctrine, and so it becomes spiritually mature, unified, and Christ-like (4:12-14). They do this through teaching by precept and example, just as Paul exhorted his readers to strive for holiness in every aspect of their lives in this very letter (4:20-32) and also lived a life that was above reproach. We need more like Paul today!

Take note of what Paul focused on within his exhortation. They were not things like church attendance, Bible reading, women's apparel (as important as those things may or may not be). Rather, Paul mentions sexual impurity and greed first (4:19), two damning sins according to other scriptures, and then moves on to mention lying, anger, theft, and neglect of the poor (4:25-28), four more damning sins according to other scriptures. Then he mentions sins of the tongue, "unwholesome words" (4:29), as well as bitterness, revenge, slander, malice, and unforgiveness (4:29-32). Putting off these sins is our responsibility, not God's.

Finally, Paul parenthetically tells us that Jesus descended into the "lower parts of the earth" (4:9) and also that He "ascended on high" (4:8), quoting Psalm 68. Some say that the "lower parts of the earth" are a reference to Jesus' body being placed in a tomb. However, a tomb hardly seems like the "lower parts of the earth" to me.

We know that when Jesus died, His spirit did not immediately ascend to heaven, just as He told Mary (John 20:17). Yet Jesus told the repentant thief on the cross beside him, "Today you shall be with Me in Paradise" (Luke 23:43). For these reasons, it is thought by many that Jesus' spirit descended to what is referred to in Luke 16:22 as "Abraham's bosom." That was a paradise in the heart of the earth where the righteous dead dwelt awaiting release to heaven after Jesus' resurrection. It was separated by a "great chasm" (Luke 16:26) from Hades, which was a place of torment for the unrighteous dead. Yet with scant scripture references, it is hard to be dogmatic about these things. Let us rejoice in what is certain!

Day 165, Ephesians 5

Here is yet another chapter that is all about holiness, and which Paul begins by admonishing his readers to imitate God (5:1). There is no better role model. If we do imitate Him, our outstanding character trait will be unselfish love (5:2), of which Jesus, who gave His life for us, is the perfect example. As we start our day today, let us determine to treat others as Jesus would treat them.

There should be no impurity, immorality or any greed even named among us (5:3). Those who are guilty of such sins are idolaters, and they're bound for hell (5:5-6). Paul warned us not to be deceived about this fact (5:6). Sadly, so many are. Most professing Christians possess some degree of conviction regarding sexual immorality, yet it seems so few possess any conviction regarding greed, having relegated it to being nothing more than an attitude of the heart that has no bearing on what one does with his money. But greed is just as damning as adultery. Those who ignore the poor are greedy, and they will be cast into hell according to Jesus (Matt. 25:31-46).

Some professing Christians promote the idea of being "drunk in the Spirit," based on Paul's words in 5:18: "And do not get drunk with wine, for that is dissipation, but be filled with the Spirit." In such circles, one can attend church services where people laugh uproariously, stumble around, shake uncontrollably, fall on the floor and act like fools, all supposedly under the influence of the Holy Spirit! Yet Paul was in no way intimating that Spirit-filled people act like drunks. Rather, he indicated that Spirit-filled people "speak to one another in psalms and hymns and spiritual songs," and that they "sing and make melody with their hearts to the Lord, always giving thanks for all things" (5:19-20). Spirit-filled people are full of the fruit of the Spirit, such as love, joy, peace and so on. As to the idea of acting drunk, Scripture repeatedly instructs believers to act soberly (see Tim. 4:5; 1 Thes. 5:6, 8; 1 Pet. 1:13, 4:7, 5:8).

The call to holiness extends to our treatment of our spouses, concerning which Christ's relationship with the church is the pattern that should be imitated. Although the responsibility of wives to be subject to their husbands "as to the Lord" is certainly endorsed in 5:22, it should be noted that in the verse directly before that, Paul instructs all believers to be subject to each other "in the fear of Christ." That is, we are all supposed to strive to get along and give preference to each other in Christ-like servanthood. Verse 22 literally reads, "Wives, to your own husbands, as to the Lord." The words, "be subject," were added by the translators, to apparently help readers who skipped over verse 21! In any case, no husband has a right to expect from his wife what he does not give to others in the body of Christ (including her). He is commanded to love her as Christ loved the church (5:25). Jesus loves the church so much He died for her! On the other hand, nothing can ruin a marriage relationship more quickly than a wife who is always disagreeable and who does not honor her husband by showing him due respect as the God-ordained head of the family.

Let me emphasize that the husband is the *domestic* head of his wife and family, but he is not the *spiritual* head. Jesus is the head of every member of the church, and so every woman's spiritual head is Christ. If that is not the case, then a woman whose husband is unsaved has an unsaved spiritual head.

Finally, what is the reason that Jesus "gave Himself up for the church" (5:25)? It was to "sanctify her" (5:26), that is, to set her apart for His holy use. He has cleansed us by His word in order that He might "present to Himself the church in all her glory, having no spot or wrinkle or any such thing...holy and blameless" (5:26-27). Jesus died to make us holy! That is why believers are called "saints" in the New Testament.

Day 166, Ephesians 6

Paul quoted one of the Ten Commandments as if he believed it was binding upon new covenant believers, and he also obviously believed that those believers who obeyed it would enjoy the promised blessing (6:1-3). Children who obey their parents will naturally find things going better for them, and they will live longer than they would have otherwise. (I used to tell my kids this when they were young, explaining to them that if they didn't obey me, I'd personally shorten their earthly lives!)

In any case, there is clearly some overlap in the Law of Moses and the law of Christ, and the commandment to obey one's parents is an example. All of the moral laws found in the Mosaic Law, which were already found in the "law of conscience" written on everyone's hearts before the Mosaic Law, are included in the law of Christ.

Fathers should be careful that they don't "exasperate" (as some translations say) their children (6:4), remembering that kids are kids, not adults. That is why God gave them parents—to prepare them, over a couple of decades, for adulthood. When children become exasperated, they quit trying, knowing they'll never measure up to their parents' expectations. In the end they rebel and find others who will accept them as they are, such as their exasperated friends. All children need large doses of love and acceptance from their parents.

Most importantly, children should be brought up "in the discipline and instruction of the Lord" (6:4). Note that this is, according to Paul, the father's responsibility, not the mother's. The reason is because the father is to be the head of the family. Fathers should be teaching their children God's Word.

Also take note that Paul says nothing about Sunday school teachers' responsibilities to instruct the children. In fact, not one word in the entire Bible speaks of Sunday school, and those who have relegated their responsibility to teach their children about the Lord to Sunday school teachers generally regret it. One of the big lies promoted by many modern churches is that their fun and exciting programs for children and youth result in kids that grow up to follow Christ. Yet statistics show just the opposite to be true.

Clearly, there were Christians in Paul's day who had slaves (6:5-9). According to Wayne A. Grudem, a professor at Trinity Evangelical Divinity School, first-century slaves "were generally well treated and were not only unskilled laborers but often managers, overseers, and trained members of various professions (doctors, nurses, teachers, musicians, skilled artisans). There was extensive Roman legislation regulating the treatment of slaves. They were normally paid for their services and could expect eventually to purchase their freedom." Thus, Grudem informs us that, "the word 'employee,' though not conveying the idea of absence of freedom, does reflect the economic status and skill level of these ancient 'slaves' better than either of the words 'servant' or 'slave' today."

The Christian masters to whom Paul wrote, who lived within the framework of the Roman economic system, were very much like modern employers, and their slaves were very much like modern employees who sign legal contracts to work for a specified time period. And certainly it is not wrong to own one's company or farm and employ others, as long as one treats his employees as he would want to be treated, an ethic affirmed by Paul (6:9).

Paul's metaphorical passage about believers' spiritual armor is certainly one that has been overworked and embellished during the past few decades. In summary, Paul was simply saying that by knowing, believing and obeying God's Word, Christians can resist Satan's lies and temptations and remain victorious in spiritual warfare. This was illustrated best by Jesus when He was tempted by Satan (Luke 4:3-13). In every temptation, Jesus quoted and obeyed God's Word.

Although Paul indicates that our spiritual battle is with Satan's hierarchy of evil spirits listed in 6:12, note that he did not encourage the Ephesian believers to "do spiritual warfare by shouting at the demons over Ephesus in order to pull them down from their positions, thus paving the way for revival." That is a modern idea that isn't found in Scripture.

Day 167, Colossians 1

This letter is very much like Paul's letter to the Ephesians—who lived just 100 miles from the Colossians in modern western Turkey. In fact, Paul wrote this letter around the same time that he wrote his Ephesian letter, during his house arrest in Rome. Both letters were carried to their intended recipients by the same man, Tychicus (Eph. 6:21; Col. 4:7), who also carried Paul's letter to Philemon, which is next on our reading list.

This letter was intended to have a limited circulation among the Gentile saints in Colossae and nearby Laodicea (4:16), to whom Paul had also written a letter at the same time, and of which we have no copy. It primarily was intended to counteract false teachings that had infiltrated the Colossian church in the first century, yet it contains truth that can also counteract more modern doctrinal errors.

One of those modern errors is the idea that Jesus suffered for our sins in hell, and thus purchased our redemption after three days of burning in flames. Paul writes, however, that Jesus "made peace through the blood of His cross" (1:20) and "reconciled you in His fleshly body through death" (1:22). When Jesus cried out from the cross, "It is finished" (John 19:30), He meant it. The full penalty for our sins was paid on Calvary.

Another modern doctrinal error debunked in today's reading is what is often referred to as unconditional eternal security, or once-saved-always-saved. Paul wrote to the Colossians:

> He has now reconciled you in His fleshly body through death, in order to present you before Him holy and blameless and beyond reproach—if indeed you continue in the faith firmly established and steadfast, and not moved away from the hope of the gospel that you have heard (1:22-23).

Notice the very conditional "if" in what we just read. We must "continue in the faith firmly established and steadfast" if we expect Christ to present us before God "holy and blameless and beyond reproach." This makes perfect sense, because we are saved through faith. The one who abandons faith in Jesus Christ forfeits his or her salvation, not meeting God's conditions.

Yet another modern doctrinal error that is exposed in today's reading is the dethroning of the Lord Jesus Christ to make Him something less than He is. It seems that within many circles of professing Christians, Jesus is little more than a cosmic vending machine or self-help guru. Bible Jesus' preeminence and all-sufficiency are highlighted by Paul in 1:15-20. Jesus "is the image of the invisible God" (1:15), the one who created the material and spiritual worlds for *Himself*. He existed before everything, and is the supreme head of the church who reconciled us to God. That is an entirely different Jesus than the one so popular today, epitomized in a song sung by the Doobie Brothers in the 1970s hit, "Jesus is Just Alright (with Me)." A speck of dust approves of the Creator of all things! How comforting that must be to God! The real issue is, "Are you just alright with Jesus?"

Amazingly, all-supreme Jesus lives in everyone who believes in Him (by the Holy Spirit), and His indwelling is our "hope of glory" (1:27). That is, because of His glorious presence within us, we have hope of living eternally in His glorious kingdom.

What is the goal of spiritual wisdom and understanding? To enable us to "walk in a manner worthy of the Lord, to please Him in all respects, bearing fruit in every good work" (1:10). Spiritual knowledge that does not result in godly behavior is worthless at best and spiritually damaging at worst if it fosters pride. Paul's goal in teaching was to "present every man complete in Christ" (1:28).

Paul wrote that he was doing his share of filling up that which was lacking in Christ's afflictions (1:24). He was certainly not implying that he was personally finishing the work of Christ's atonement, but simply that the church, Christ's body, always suffers persecution, just as Christ did. When we read of what Paul actually did endure for the sake of the gospel, our sufferings generally pale by comparison. Consequently, so will our rewards.

Day 168, Colossians 2

Paul's greatest concern for the believers in both Colossae and Laodicea was for their spiritual understanding, and rightfully so. False teaching can be potentially damning. Clearly, false teaching had infiltrated the churches in Colassae and Laodicea, apparently converging from two different streams.

First, there were the Jewish legalists with whom we've become so familiar, who were always trying to convince Gentile believers to be circumcised and submit themselves to the Mosaic Law. So Paul reminds the Colossian believers that they have been "circumcised with a circumcision made without hands, in the removal of the body of the flesh by the circumcision of Christ" (2:11). That circumcision is far superior to what the Jewish legalists had to offer. In fact, it could be argued that the circumcision prescribed in the Mosaic Law was simply a foreshadowing of the circumcision that would be experienced by all Christian believers—the cutting off of our old sinful, fleshly nature by Christ.

Second, there was apparently some form of mystic and pagan philosophy that was also making inroads. It was characterized to some degree by asceticism, extreme self-denial that served no worthwhile purpose (2:18, 23).

In light of these doctrinal distractions, Paul pulls his readers back to what they should be focused on—Christ Himself. When we are focused on Him, there is no possibility that we will be enamored by what is really nothing by comparison, what Paul calls "the elementary principles of the world" (2:8). In Christ "all the fullness of the Deity dwells in bodily form" (2:9). Moreover, "in Him [we] have been made complete" (2:10). We don't need to look for fulfillment or truth anywhere else. Additionally, Jesus "is the head over all rule and authority" (2:10). He is higher than any other earthly or spiritual leaders. He's the King of kings and Lord of lords! Compared to Him, everyone and everything is inferior. Thus it would be an insult to Him if we seek after what is lesser.

Beyond these facts about Christ, Paul also points out to his readership (which includes us) that they are united *with* Christ in His death, burial and resurrection (2:12). As a result, we've been spiritually reborn (2:13), our sins have been forgiven, and we're accepted by God (2:14). Jesus defeated the evil spirits that previously held us captive (2:15). In light of these things, how could anyone be enamored with worldly philosophies that are only fit for those who are ignorant of Christ? How could anyone be persuaded to follow old covenant rituals—giving all his or her attention to keeping Jewish festivals, new moons and Sabbaths (2:16), which Paul says are "a mere shadow of what is to come; but the substance belongs to Christ" (2:17)? That is, Jews practiced rituals that were designed to point them to Christ. Yet they missed the point entirely. It was somewhat comparable to a father who lays down a trail of pennies to lead his child to a hidden birthday present. Wouldn't it be tragic if that child stopped following the penny trail and made a religion out of the pennies?

So self-abasement, angel-worship, unbiblical visions, and food regulations, all of which were apparently being promoted in Colossae as containing some "truth," amounted to nothing more than "self-made religion" that was of no real value to make anyone holy (2:23). Only Christ can do that, and He only does it for those who repent and believe in Him.

Finally, I'm afraid the meaning of Paul's metaphorical words about Jesus "disarming the rulers and authorities" has been perverted by certain advocates in the modern spiritual warfare movement. First, note that it is something that Jesus did, so we don't need to. Second, Jesus did it on the cross. Jesus "disarmed the rulers and authorities" by dying for our sins, metaphorically spoken of in the same passage by Paul as the canceling of our debts. By God's righteous permission, Satan has the right to rule transgressors; but those who are in Christ are no longer transgressors but righteous new creations! That is how Jesus' death frees us from sin and Satan. "If therefore the Son shall make you free, you shall be free indeed" (John 8:36).

Day 169, Colossians 3

Following the same pattern of his Ephesian letter, Paul also wrote about all that God has done for us through Christ in the first half of this letter. In the second half, he writes of our appropriate response to what God has done. Notice the word "therefore" in 3:1 and 4. God expects something out of us because He has done some things for us.

It is because we have been raised up with Christ that we should "set our minds on things above," and "not on the things that are on earth" (3:2). Those who criticize others for being "so heavenly-minded that they are no earthly good" are usually those who are so earthly-minded that they are no heavenly good. What percentage of your thoughts are heavenly?

And it is because we have died with Christ that we should consider "the members of [our] earthly body as dead to immorality, impurity, passion, evil desire, and greed, which amount to idolatry" (3:5). I'm sure you've noticed how Paul has in his letters repeatedly identified the sins of immorality, impurity and greed as being particularly grievous to God (1 Cor. 6:9-10; Gal. 5:19-21; Eph. 5:3-5). In fact, Paul often indicates that practicing those sins will exclude one from God's kingdom, and today he warns again that it is because of those very sins that "the wrath of God will come upon the sons of disobedience" (3:6), yet another warning that such sins are exclusionary. Although it is commonly said in Christian circles that "all sins are the same in the eyes of God" because "sin is sin," that is simply not true. All crimes that one might commit are generally grievous to human beings, but all are not equally grievous, as evidenced by the fact that there are varying punishments for varying crimes. With God it is no different. (Thankfully, sleeping during sermons is not listed anywhere in the New Testament as a sin that will exclude us from heaven!)

All of this is to say that we should avoid like the plague any and every form of sexual immorality and greed. Although sexual immorality is generally frowned upon in most Christian circles (as there is always a steady stream of pastors who are caught in affairs to frown upon), there is hardly a mention of greed from most pulpits, much less even a definition of what might constitute greed in God's eyes. More tragic is the fact that the majority of wealthy Christians who live in the world's wealthiest nations think that greed has nothing to do with what they possess, but is only an attitude of the heart. As long as they don't have "greed in their hearts," they can keep *acting* as greedy as they want, ignoring the poor while they live in self-indulgence. Help us, Lord!

Today Paul also hones in on other sins that are very grievous to God, and that he, or another New Testament author elsewhere, warns will exclude one from God's kingdom if practiced. For example, Paul specifically names anger (along with similar sins of wrath, malice, slander and abusive speech), lying and unforgiveness (3:8, 9, 13; see Gal. 5:19-21; Rev. 21:8; Mark 16:15). I'm afraid that multitudes of professing Christians are not aware how important it is to live holy lives. Thankfully, you are not one of them! How many Christians, whose Bibles repeatedly warn of "exclusionary sins," are convinced that they are "safe under grace," to the degree that they would even reject any teacher who intimates that currently-saved people are not guaranteed ultimate salvation apart from holiness?

May I also add that it is obvious that Christ who dwells in us does not live through us without our cooperation; otherwise there would be no need for Paul to admonish his readers to live obediently.

Once again, Paul reminds us that we are "chosen of God" (3:12), as are all who have believed in the Lord Jesus Christ. We are not "unconditionally chosen," as that very phrase is an oxymoron (all choices are conditional), and the idea that phrase expresses actually describes random selection, or chance. God did not choose you by saying, "Eeny, meeny, miny, moe!"

Day 170, Colossians 4

Because today's chapter in Colossians is a little sparse in content compared to the previous chapter, I'd like to begin today by returning to something Paul wrote in chapter 3:

> Let the word of Christ richly dwell within you, with all wisdom teaching and admonishing one another with psalms and hymns and spiritual songs, singing with thankfulness in your hearts to God (3:16).

As I have so often said during our journey through the New Testament, it was not the epistles that were the early church's focus. Most of the Christians of Paul's day, for example, never read his letter to the Colossians, or the majority of his other letters. What we are currently reading was intended to be read only by the Christians in Colassae and Laodicea (4:16). The early church was focused on what we find in the Gospels—the words of Jesus—and so they should have been, because His words were what He said we should focus on (Matt. 28:19-20). Thus the rationale for Paul's admonition to "let the word of Christ richly dwell within you" (3:16).

One reason we are all to "let the word of Christ richly dwell within us" is so that it can then flow out of us to others, and particularly to others in Christ's body. Even the songs we sing when we gather should be full of Jesus' words, so that they teach and admonish all who are present. Sadly, so many modern "worship" songs—in contrast to many great hymns of the past—are light and fluffy, containing very little substance that might teach or admonish anyone. Compare the lyrics of *Holy, Holy, Holy* to the lyrics of *That Guy in the Sky*. (Not actually a song title, but you know what I mean!)

Paul mentions prayer several times in today's reading, and his words help us understand what we should be praying for. He requests that the Colossian believers pray that God would open a door "for the word" so that Paul and his companions might "speak forth the mystery of Christ" (4:3). God is the one who opens doors of opportunity for the gospel, and He often does it through the supernatural power of the Spirit. As we have studied Paul's ministry, we have observed that phenomena repeatedly. And why did God open all those doors for Paul? Obviously, prayer had something to do with it. May I request that you pray for open doors for me to minister God's Word? And why not pray the same thing for yourself while you are at it?!

Paul names Epaphras, who was perhaps the apostolic founder of the church in Colassae, as a man of prayer who always labored earnestly for the Colossian believers, that they might "stand perfect and fully assured in all the will of God" (4:12). There is another valid prayer request.

In both Paul's requests for prayer and Epaphras' prayers, it was the advancement of the kingdom of God that was in view. Compare those prayers with the requests often listed in church bulletins or mentioned at prayer meetings. We should be praying prayers that align with the words, "Thy kingdom come, Thy will be done, on earth as it is in heaven!"

Paul also mentions a man named Onesimus who would be traveling with Tychicus to Colossae to deliver this very letter to them (4:9). According to Paul, Onesimus was a "faithful and beloved brother" (4:9). Don't forget his name, because he is the focus of Paul's letter to Philemon, which is next on our reading list, and which was written at the same time as Paul's letters to the Ephesians, Colossians and Philippians. Onesimus was a runaway slave whom Paul had won to the Lord in Rome, an "open door" during his imprisonment!

A lady named Nympha, who apparently lived in Laodicea, had a church in her house! She is not the only one (see Rom. 16:3-5, 14-15; 1 Cor. 16:19; Philem. 2). As far as we know, most churches met in houses during the first three centuries of the church. Little churches are nothing to be ashamed of! They are great places to make disciples!

Day 171, Philemon

It has always been a mystery to me why this tiny letter of Paul's, written to one person for a very specific reason, has made it into the Bible, while other letters that Paul wrote to entire churches, such as his letter to the Laodiceans (Col. 4:16) or his first letter to the Corinthians (1 Cor. 5:9-11) have not been providentially preserved for us! Paul obviously did not realize that any of his letters would receive world-wide circulation for 2,000 years, but I am sure he would be particularly shocked to learn that his private letter to Philemon has been read by so many for so long!

Paul penned this letter letter during his house arrest in Rome as he waited to stand trial before Nero. It is obvious, as we already knew, that Paul had freedom to share the gospel then, and today we learn that he won a runaway slave named Onesimus to the Lord. It is often wrongly stated that Onesimus was in prison with Paul, but remember that Paul stayed "in his own rented quarters" while he was in Rome (Acts 28:30), and it is unlikely that he rented a jail cell! Paul enjoyed a steady stream of visitors to his place, and he ministered to all who came by (Acts. 28:30-31). Onesimus had been one of those visitors.

Onesimus' master, Philemon, apparently lived in Colossae, where there was a church in his house (v. 2). We don't know how Paul knew him, but he did. It is quite possible that Paul was the one who originally led Philemon to the Lord, as Paul mentions Philemon's "debt" to him (v. 19).

Onesimus, just recently converted to Christ, now faced a crisis of conscience. Should he return to his master, something that he was legally obligated to do? Remember, as I have previously mentioned, many "slaves" within the Roman Empire could be better described as "contract employees." Onesimus was not a slave who had been captured by Philemon and forced to work against his will. His master, or better said, his former employer, was a Christian. If Onesimus was going to do the right thing, he would have to return. Yet he could face legal repercussions for running away, and not only for running away, but for perhaps stealing some of Philemon's money (v. 18). Thus the occasion of this letter, as Paul writes to tell Philemon what has happened to Onesimus, and to intercede on his behalf. This is a wonderful little letter about grace, and perhaps that is why it has been preserved for us in Scripture. God forgave Philemon. God forgave Onesimus. Now it was Philemon's chance to extend the mercy that he enjoyed.

Paul had grown to love Onesimus dearly, calling him "my child" and "my very heart" (vv. 10, 12). He writes that he would have preferred to keep Onesimus in Rome with him in order to benefit from his service on Philemon's behalf, but didn't want to presume upon Philemon's goodness:

> But without your consent I did not want to do anything, so that your goodness would not be, in effect, by compulsion but of your own free will" (v. 14).

Kindness from compulsion, rather than from free will, is really not kindness at all. As I considered these particular words of Paul, my thoughts wandered to the Amish, whom I have always admired for the the love they show to one another. But as I have gotten to know some of them, I've wondered how many are truly born again. It occurred to me that their love does not generally extend outside their own circles. For example, they do nothing to preach the gospel to anyone or to serve the poor around the world (unlike other Anabaptist groups). And if they don't completely conform to what is expected of them, they are shunned by their own families, which is certainly unloving and not something advocated by Scripture. Considering these things, I couldn't help but wonder how much of their goodness is motivated by compulsion rather than free will. It is, of course, more important that we judge ourselves, rather than the Amish, in these things.

Day 172, Philippians 1

Note that Paul addressed this letter to "all the saints...in Philippi, including the overseers and deacons" (1:1). He did not write to the leaders only, or for that matter, to the leaders first. He wrote to every believer in Philippi, and just to make sure that the leaders didn't feel left out, he mentioned them. This helps us to understand how things are supposed to be in the church.

First, leaders aren't supposed to be exalted superstars who lord it over the ignorant peons. They are supposed to be servants. In fact, that is what the word "deacon" found in 1:1 literally means. (Notice, incidentally, that Paul does not mention pastors or elders in 1:1 or anywhere in this letter. The reason is because the word "overseer" is synonymous with the words "pastor" and "elder"; see Acts 20:28; Tit. 1:5-7; 1 Pet. 5:1-2).

Second, those who are not overseers/elders/pastors are not so pea-brained that they can't understand Paul's letters without the assistance of an overseer/elder/pastor. You don't need your pastor's help (or my help) to understand Paul's letter to the Philippians! And since I'm on the subject, Paul would never have dreamed that one day there would be 400-page commentaries that would explore Greek syntax and literary nuances found in this little letter that he likely wrote in less than half an hour!

All of this is to say that the vast spiritual gap between "clergy" and "laity" that exists in the modern church is unbiblical. It is the result of the institutionalizing and commercializing of Christianity. Brotherhood and discipleship have been replaced by a corporate hierarchy and a producer/consumer franchise.

How wonderful it is to know that God is continuing the good work He began in us, and that He is devoted to seeing His work in us perfected (1:6). Paul's prayers for the Philippians indicate that God's goal is for our love to "abound still more and more in real knowledge" (1:9). That is, as we grow in the *true* knowledge of God's will, it motivates us to love others to a greater degree in genuine self-denial. Moral excellence—what can be grasped only by those who abide in the words of Jesus—prepares us to be "sincere and blameless until the day of Christ" (1:10). If what you are feeding on is not motivating you to love more, you are feeding on the wrong spiritual diet.

Just as in our day, in Paul's day there were ministers whose motives were wrong and who were apparently vying for notoriety in the church (1:15-17). Some were apparently happy about Paul's imprisonment, as it hindered him and gave them a chance to "get ahead." Paul certainly adopted a good attitude about those who were motivated by selfish ambition, looking at the positive side. At least they were preaching the true gospel, which is much more than can be said of so many of their modern counterparts.

"For to me, to live is Christ and to die is gain" (1:21). Paul's well-known declaration is the motto of every true Christian, but one that is foreign to false believers. Christ is not our interest, pastime or hobby. He is our life! We are consumed with a passion to please Him! Consequently, death is gain, because it takes us to Him whom we love! We, just like Paul, are torn between earth, where we are privileged to serve Jesus, and heaven, where we are blessed to see Him. Paul knew, of course, that it was not yet his time to depart and be with Christ, because it was God's will for him to stand before Caesar in Rome.

True believers, and only true believers, can relate to Paul's words, "For to you it has been granted for Christ's sake...to suffer for His sake" (1:29). Generally, suffering isn't something that is spoken of as being "granted." But those who love Christ rejoice when they are "considered worthy to suffer...for His name" (Acts 5:41), as it gives them an opportunity to demonstrate their love for Him. Christianity unaccompanied by rejection and persecution is false Christianity. "All who desire to live godly in Christ Jesus will be persecuted" (1 Tim. 3:12). Suffering for Christ's sake? Rejoice!

Day 173, Philippians 2

As we have now read Paul's letters to the Galatians, Thessalonians, Corinthians, Romans, Ephesians, Colossians, Philemon, and now half of Philippians, would you agree that he was supremely interested in the lifestyles and behavior of his readers, who, for the most part, were professing followers of Christ? And what was the single-most important behavioral trait that Paul emphasized continually? If you said, "love," I agree with you. Christians, above all things, are supposed to be people of self-denying love, which should not surprise us, since the first and second greatest commandments are to love God with all one's heart and to love one's neighbor as oneself.

People who love others are humble people, because selfishness stems from pride. Selfish people see themselves as being more important than others, so they are always "looking out for #1." They cling to their money and spend their time on what serves themselves.

Humble people, on the other hand, view others as being more important than themselves, and they are always looking out for the needs of others. They give their time and money in service. And this servant's attitude is exactly what Paul prescribes in 2:3-8, an attitude that was best exemplified by Jesus, who amazingly humbled Himself to become a man, and not just any man, but one who served others in His life and sacrificial death. His example, and God's subsequent exaltation of Him, is a perfect reminder of what we should do to please God—humble ourselves in servanthood. In God's eyes, the greatest among us is the servant (Matt. 23:11). More specifically, the greatest among us gives his time, treasure and talents in service to others.

Because God has exalted Jesus and given Him the highest name, one day every knee in heaven, earth and hell will bow, and every tongue will confess that Jesus is Lord (2:9-11). This is something we should tell the unrepentant to provoke them to consider their ways. They may refuse now to bow their knees willfully and humbly to Christ's lordship, but inevitably and eventually they will bow—although with reluctance—and at a time when there will no longer be any offer of mercy. The wise person would humbly repent now, while only a fool would not. Moreover, only a fool (as the apostle James declares) would imagine that he could have a relationship with Christ by simply believing in Him without obeying Him (Jas. 2:20).

Thus Paul admonishes his readers to obey and "work out" their salvation "with fear and trembling" (2:12). Clearly, the guarantee of ultimate salvation is not something that anyone has "in the bag," but rather, is something we must "work out" with the utmost concern. Salvation can be forfeited, and if not, Paul would have had no reason to admonish his Christian readers to "hold fast the word of life," lest in the end his toil in Philippi proved to be in vain (2:16). The best news in all this is that we are not alone on our journey, as we have God Himself—who certainly wants to find us worthy in the end—working inside us to help us follow His path (2:13). Yet He does not commandeer our free wills.

One way that we can "prove ourselves to be blameless and innocent, children of God above reproach in the midst of a crooked and perverse generation" is to "do all things without grumbling or disputing" (2:14). A grumbler is a rebel at heart, perhaps best exemplified in Scripture by the Israelites who grumbled in the wilderness (1 Cor. 10:10). Take note that in this little letter, the word "rejoice" is found eight times, and the word "joy" is found seven times.

Paul mentions a man named Epaphroditus in 2:25, who brought to him an offering from the Philippians (2:30, 4:18). If Paul was in Rome when he wrote this letter, Epaphroditus journeyed over 500 miles from Philippi, and his long journey had apparently taken its toll on his body. Although he had been deathly ill, "God had mercy on him" (2:27). That means he was healed, and that is another reason to expect that God will have mercy on you as well in your sickness.

Day 174, Philippians 3

Philippi was not off the radar for Paul's old nemeses, the Jewish legalists, who wanted to line up Gentile believers for circumcision and put them under the Mosaic Law. Thus Paul admonished believers in Philippi to "beware of false circumcision," and reminded them that they were the "true circumcision" (3:2-3). The difference between the two groups is that the former had been physically circumcised and trusted in that, along with their physical lineage and limited law-keeping, to make them right before God. They were hopeless, condemned sinners who were making a pathetic attempt to save themselves. The latter, however, had their confidence in Christ, who made them righteous by means of His substitutionary death and a circumcision of their hearts. They had been saved by faith in Him.

Paul was a perfect example of the former who had become the latter. He had all the credentials that the Jewish legalists could boast of and more, yet he considered it all rubbish, or literally "dung," in comparison to what he had gained in Christ (3:7-8). He had tossed aside his reputation, his career, and his social standing within Judaism, all with no regrets. What he had gained compared to what he lost was of no comparison, and the same is true for anything that we have given up to gain Christ. We have found "the treasure hidden in the field" (Matt. 13:44)! Anytime anyone moans about what they have forsaken or lost to become a Christian, it reveals a glaring lack of understanding. They insult Christ by their grumblings—as if what they've gained in Him is hardly worth what they have lost—which is no doubt why God is so offended when His people grumble.

It was not just being made righteous and the hope of heaven that Paul counted as a benefit of salvation by grace through faith. Just as importantly, he recognized the wonderful benefit of knowing Christ, and of identifying with Him in His sufferings, death and resurrection. Believers in Christ are rejected by the world just as Jesus was. They, just like Christ, die to the world and all that previously captivated and held them. And they are reborn, resurrected like Christ, to walk a new path in obedience to God.

This resurrection is an on-going experience. Speaking of it, Paul wrote, "Not that I have already obtained it [the resurrection from the dead] or have already become perfect" (3:12). Figuratively speaking, we are progressively becoming more and more resurrected, as we walk a new life and grow closer to perfection, fully obedient to God. This requires that we, like Paul, "press on," in order that we "may lay hold of that for which [we were] laid hold of by Jesus" (3:12). That is, Jesus laid hold of us to make us holy, and we must cooperate with Him on our journey to that goal. All true believers are following an "upward call" with their eyes on a prize (3:14). I wrote a song about that once that you can listen to at: www.heavensfamily.org/ss/songs/lead_me_higher.

Tragically, some who begin on this journey don't finish it, straying from the path of sanctification. Paul sadly mentions some of them who, having followed Christ at one time, had ultimately become "enemies of the cross...whose end is destruction" (3:18-19). Here we see again that the idea of unconditional eternal security is only a man-made doctrine that contradicts Scripture.

Those who had strayed had allowed the desires of the flesh to dominate their lives once again, and they began to seek after "earthly things" rather than remaining dead to the world. Thus we are well warned to be diligent to seek continually that which is spiritual and heavenly, remembering that we are citizens, not of this world, but of heaven, where our Lord Jesus Christ lives. He will soon return and finish the good work He began in us, giving us glorified bodies and transforming us fully into His image (3:18-21).

The allure of the world and the flesh can be deadly! Don't allow either to pull you away from the path of righteousness! "Set your mind on the things above, not on the things that are on earth" (Col. 3:2).

Day 175, Philippians 4

Anxiety flees from a heart that trusts God. But who among us finds it easy to trust the Lord when our circumstances are tempting us to doubt? So we must do something to overcome our worries and doubts, and Paul offers some great advice in that regard.

First, "Rejoice in the Lord always" (4:4). Regardless of what we're enduring, we always have much for which to rejoice. We're on the road to heaven! Rejoicing is faith in action.

Second, "In everything by prayer and supplication with thanksgiving let your requests be made known to God" (4:6). Thanksgiving is the key. Faith-filled prayers are full of thanksgiving.

Third, monitor your thought life and determine to dwell upon only those things that are true, honorable, right, pure, lovely, of good repute, excellent, and worthy of praise (4:8). Grumpy, negative people are the product of grumpy, negative thoughts! Positive thinking *is* powerful!

Doing those three things is a sure recipe for experiencing "the peace of God, which surpasses all comprehension," which "guards our hearts and minds in Christ Jesus" (4:7). Our journey is supposed to be a joyful, peaceful one.

One other ingredient in Paul's recipe for peace is found in 4:9: "The things you have learned and received and heard and seen in me, practice these things, and the God of peace will be with you." Peace is the possession of those who do the will of God. And isn't it interesting that, while many modern ministers say, "Don't follow me; follow Christ," Paul encouraged everyone to practice what they saw him do? He similarly wrote to the Corinthians, "Be imitators of me, just as I also am of Christ" (1 Cor. 11:1). That is the motto of every disciple-making minister.

As Paul closed his letter, he expressed his gratitude for the offering he had just received from the Philippians via their messenger, Epaphroditus. As those who believed the gospel, the Philippian Christians naturally wanted to help the person whom God used to bring the gospel to them and who was taking the gospel to others. What a privilege it is to "participate in the gospel" (1:5) by supporting God's messengers!

Paul made it clear that, although he "rejoiced in the Lord greatly" when he received their gift, it wasn't because he was in great need (4:11), although he admitted to having an "affliction" (4:14). His joy had more to do with the fact that the Philippians were laying up heavenly treasures, or as he beautifully said it, "Not that I seek the gift itself, but I seek for the profit which increases to your account" (4:17).

Even prior to the arrival of Epaphroditus, Paul was content in his circumstance by the power of Christ (4:11, 13). He had learned to "get along with humble means" as well as "live in prosperity" (4:12).

Of course, when he referred to being periodically prosperous, he did not mean that there were times when he lived in lavish luxury and self-indulgence. That would make him a hypocrite, since he had instructed the Philippians to "do nothing from selfishness" (2:3) and so on. Paul more clearly defined the periodic prosperity he enjoyed in verse 12. When he was prosperous, he was "filled" rather than "hungry." When he was prosperous, he had "abundance," that is, more than he needed, contrasted with when he found himself "suffering need." As a result of the Philippians' offering, he was now again enjoying "abundance" and was "amply supplied" (4:18). Obviously, he did not mean that he could now live in luxury like a modern prosperity preacher, since he was under house arrest when he wrote those words. Yet Paul considered himself prosperous even under such circumstances.

The gift sent by the Philippians was sacrificially given and "well-pleasing to God" (4:18). Because the Philippians had "sought first God's kingdom" (Matt. 6:33), Paul was quite confident that God would keep His promise to supply all their needs "according to His riches in glory" (4:19). The only Christians who can rightfully claim that God will supply all their needs are those who, like the Philippian believers, are givers. I hope you are in that category!

Day 176, 1 Timothy 1

It is commonly thought that Paul wrote this letter to Timothy after his trial before Nero and his subsequent acquittal, which means it was written after the events recorded in the final chapter of Acts. If so, Paul and Timothy would have been closely associated for at least 12 years when Paul wrote this letter to him. (Remember that Paul named Timothy as co-sender of six of his letters: 2 Corinthians, Philippians, Colossians, 1 & 2 Thessalonians and Philemon). Both Paul and Timothy had been ministering once again in Ephesus, but Paul moved on to Macedonia, leaving Timothy behind to tend to the needs of the growing Ephesian church (1:3). How amazed Paul would have been to know that his private letter to Timothy would eventually be printed in hundreds of millions of books in many of the world's languages and read by countless people during the next 2,000 years!

Of greatest concern to Paul was false teaching that was infiltrating the Ephesian church. Like most "strange doctrines" (1:3), this particular strain pulled its pupils away from what was most important, namely, obedience to the commandments of Christ (1:5). Apparently the false teachers' focus was upon "myths and endless genealogies" (1:4), which did nothing to engender what God desired, which is "love from a pure heart and a good conscience and sincere faith" (1:5). How much of modern preaching and teaching engenders what God desires?

The false teachers in Ephesus were apparently taking their texts from the Mosaic Law (1:7), which makes us wonder if Timothy found himself battling the Jewish legalists once again. Paul affirms that the Law is good, yet it was not written for righteous followers of Christ, but instead for rebels, to lead them to repentance (1:8-11). This is just one more indication that true Christians are those who have repented and who are now on the path of holiness. If this were not the case, Paul would not have written that the Law was only relevant to rebels and irrelevant to the righteous.

Along these lines, Paul recalls the time when he himself was a rebel who needed the Law's conviction to lead him to repentance and faith in Christ. He was, in his own estimation, the "foremost" of sinners, being a former "blasphemer and a persecutor and a violent aggressor" (1:13). But the mercy God granted him in Christ was more than sufficient, not only to forgive him for his crimes, but to put him into valuable service. Imagine forgiving your worst enemy and then making him the president of your multi-national company! That is what God did for Paul. And He did so, at least in part, to demonstrate His "perfect patience as an example for those who would believe in Him for eternal life" (1:16). If God would forgive Paul and put him into service, He will also do those things for you. Amazing grace! "Christ Jesus came into the world to save sinners" (1:15).

This amazing grace, however, is not given to us as a veil behind which we can continue sinning out of God's sight. And for this reason Paul admonishes Timothy to "keep faith and a good conscience" (1:19). Others, who at one time had possessed both, had rejected them, and "suffered shipwreck in regard to their faith" (1:19). It is amazing to me that theologians and Bible teachers can read such verses and still cling to the concept of "once-saved-always-saved."

Paul specifically names two men whom Timothy apparently knew, Hymenaeus and Alexander, who were prime examples of the very thing of which Paul was warning against. If one does not "*keep* faith and a good conscience," that means he previously possessed faith and a good conscience. Hymenaeus and Alexander were now apparently blaspheming, and thus deserved to be "handed over to Satan" (1:20). Whatever that means, it also indicates that Hymenaeus and Alexander were previously on the right path, because there would have been no reason for Paul to "hand over to Satan" those who had never escaped Satan's captivity, as is the case of all unregenerate people.

Day 177, 1 Timothy 2

Should we pray for "kings and all who are in authority" (2:1-2) even if they are unbelieving, corrupt politicians? In light of the ungodly character of those in governmental authority in Paul's day—of whom we read about in the book of Acts—the answer must be "yes." The result of our prayers can be "that we may lead a tranquil and quiet life in all godliness and dignity" (2:2). We can not only pray for leaders, we can elect them! Cast your vote for the most righteous candidates, because "When the righteous increase, the people rejoice, but when a wicked man rules, people groan" (Prov. 29:2).

The result of our being able to lead "a tranquil and quiet life" is that the gospel can be spread more freely, which is a good thing, since God "desires all men to be saved and come to the knowledge of the truth" (2:4), and people must hear the gospel to be saved. Hostile governmental authorities are perhaps the greatest hindrance to the gospel around the world. Imagine what would happen, for example, if there was true freedom of religion in the Muslim nations.

Once again we see that Scripture stands in complete contrast to the cardinal Calvinist doctrine that God desires only a few, preselected people be saved. Paul believed that God desires "all men to be saved" (2:4). This verse also stands in complete contrast to the Calvinist theory that, "because God is sovereign, everything He desires, He gets." That is utterly false, and anyone who reads any part of the Bible should realize that when it comes to the free-will decisions of the majority of human beings, God rarely gets what He desires.

Moreover, the cardinal Calvinist doctrine that Jesus died only for a very limited number of people—those allegedly predestined to be saved—is also debunked today. Paul declares that Jesus "gave Himself as ransom for all" (2:6). The "all" of which Paul writes in 2:6 is the same "all" of whom he wrote in 2:4, the "all" whom God desires to be saved and come to the knowledge of the truth. All of this is unmistakably clear.

Is Jesus the only way to heaven, or are there "many ways to God"? Do other religions simply offer a different path to the same God? The answer is that God has provided only "one mediator between God and men" (2:5), the solitary God-man, the only sacrifice for our sins, Jesus Christ. True Christians are very close-minded on this matter, and they can afford to be close-minded, because they are correct!

Paul wrote specific instructions to men and women in this chapter, and his words, "I do not allow a woman to teach or exercise authority over a man" (2:12), have been the subject of controversy. To make his point, Paul appeals to the order of creation (2:13) and the record of fall, during which time Eve, not Adam, was deceived (2:14). Because there is no specific Greek word that is equivalent to the English word *wife*, context must be used to determine if the best translation of the Greek word *gune* should be "woman" or "wife."

In this passage, I think "wife" would be a better translation, because Paul appeals to the relationship between Adam and Eve, a husband and wife, for his reasoning. Additionally, in other passages, both Paul and Peter instruct *wives* to be subject to their *husbands* (Eph. 5:22; Col. 3:18; 1 Pet. 3:1). So is Paul teaching in this passage that *all* women must be submissive to *all* men, and is he forbidding any and all women from teaching any and all men? I don't think so, especially in light of the fact that God has, at times, appointed women to teach or exercise authority over men, as in the cases of Deborah, judge of Israel (Judg. 4:4-24), and Huldah, a prophetess (2 Kings 22:13-20), not to mention Jesus' instructions to the women at His tomb to go and give instructions to the apostles (Mark 16:7). When looking for truth, we must take the whole Bible into consideration, not just one or two verses.

Day 178, 1 Timothy 3

When we read, just a few days ago, the opening sentence of Paul's letter to the Philippians, we learned that the early churches were served by overseers (Greek: *episkopos*) and deacons (Greek: *diakonos*), the latter of which is more literally translated "servants." There were no "deacon boards" in Paul's day who ran the affairs of the church. Deacons served in various capacities, such as in administrating assistance to the poor, while it was the overseers (who are synonymous with *elders* and *pastors*; see, for example, Acts 20:17, 28) who shepherded the flocks under their care. Timothy was apparently selecting men in Ephesus to serve as overseers, and he was selecting men *and* women (3:8-13) to serve as deacons. So Paul listed the qualifications that Timothy should require of potential candidates. Obviously not every believer qualified, which is one more indication that all true Christians have not reached sinless perfection, as some tell us.

Any time I read the qualifications Paul lists for one to be an overseer, I am reminded of how much the church has drifted from its original pattern. Note that the majority of the qualifications Paul listed have to do with the candidate's character, and nothing to do with his education, charisma, or ability to deliver interesting sermons (three things that seem to be essential qualifications for pastors in most churches today). The reason is because a biblical overseer/elder/pastor is a disciple-maker, and he teaches *primarily* by the example that he sets before the members of his little flock. They are all well-acquainted with him and should strive to imitate him (1 Cor. 4:16; 11:1; Eph. 5:1. 1 Thes. 1:6; Heb. 13:7). They likely meet in a house, and in fact, one of the requirements for overseers is that they must manage their own households well (3:4), because managing a church is so similar.

Paul wrote that elders must be "free from the love of money" (3:3), which indicates that love of money is something that can be observed and judged by one's actions, and thus it is not just an attitude of the heart as is so often claimed. To be more specific,

Timothy could, by observing how people gained and used money, righteously judge if they loved it or not. Those who spent all their time working to gain it, or who gained it by unscrupulous means, or who used what they gained to pile up additional earthly treasures rather than lay up treasures in heaven revealed their love of money. If the love of money were only an attitude of the heart, there would have been no way for Timothy to determine if potential candidates for overseers were qualified.

Like overseers, deacons were required to be men and women of holiness, who maintained a "clear conscience" (3:9). Both overseers and deacons should first be tested to make certain they are "beyond reproach" before they were put into their positions of ministry (3:10). Thus we see the repeated emphasis on the necessity of holiness required of those who will minister to the body of Christ. The simple reason is that true Christianity is all about faith in the Lord Jesus Christ and obedience to His commandments. *Without holiness, one is not qualified to serve in ministry.* Many who are called to ministry disqualify themselves because of their character flaws. Those flaws keep some from entering ministry, yet God will still hold them accountable for their calling. And those flaws are often the undoing of those who are already in ministry, and they find themselves expelled from the very thing God called them to. How tragic this is. Yet, if in either case there is repentance, grace can be found and lost opportunity can be regained.

Those who "have served well as deacons obtain for themselves a high standing and great confidence in the faith that is in Christ Jesus" (3:13). As one is established in holiness and bears more fruit, a benefit is that one's assurance of salvation increases. It is those who "ride the fence," dabbling in sin and worldliness, who are always wondering if they are truly saved. Not so for the committed!

Day 179, 1 Timothy 4

Paul's words, "In the later times some will fall away from the faith" (4:1), clearly indicate that it is possible to "fall away from the faith." In order to fall away from the faith, one must first be "in the faith." If I said, "Mr. Smith fell away from his belief in communism," that would indicate that Mr. Smith at one time believed in communism.

Moreover, Paul wrote that the reason some will fall away from the faith is because they pay attention to "deceitful spirits and doctrines of demons" (4:1). Those who were never in the faith in the first place have *always* been paying attention to demonic doctrines.

All this being so, we would be wise to guard ourselves from being influenced by anything that might pull us away from our faith in Christ. In reality, we need not concern ourselves with demons, but with the human agents whom those demons use to attempt to pull us away. Paul described them as hypocritical liars, "seared in their own conscience as with a branding iron" (4:2). They are, foremost, unholy, yet they are also hypocrites, preaching what they don't personally practice. Thus, in order for us to judge them, we must be able to observe and know them, which is essentially impossible in our age of media ministries and mega-churches. So even greater caution is advised! Beware of TV preachers!

Those demonic human agents who deceive the unsuspecting may appear to be quite committed in their devotion to Christ. Paul mentions that some may "forbid marriage and advocate abstaining from foods" (4:3), impressing their followers with the self-denial which they advocate or even practice. Self-denial is, of course, the essence of following Christ. We should beware, however, of those who deny themselves what God intended for us to enjoy, such as food (4:3), yet indulge in that from which God intended us to abstain.

I feel I must mention that when Paul wrote this letter to Timothy, there was basically no such thing as processed food. Sugar and white flour, for example, were unheard of. People ate food that God created in its natural form, not food that man had stripped of its God-given nutrients and then chemically altered. Junk food is not what Paul had in mind when he wrote, "Everything *created by God* is good, and nothing is to be rejected if it is received with gratitude; for it is sanctified by means of the word of God and prayer" (4:4-5). Try praying, "Lord, bless this poison," and see how He answers!

"Discipline yourself for the purpose of godliness" (4:7). Both experience and Scripture teach us that if we want to be godly, self-discipline is required. Holy people are holy because they *want* to be holy, and they take action to reach their goal, just as physically fit people are fit because they *want* to be physically fit, and they take action to reach their goal. Imagine a coach exhorting his team, "This season, we are not going to work out or practice, lest we foolishly try to get in shape in our own strength, and rob God of glory! This season we are simply going to 'Let go and let God!' This isn't about 'works' or self-effort, which would doom us to failure. No, this is all about grace!"

Sounds ludicrous, doesn't it? Yet we've probably all heard sermons about holiness that parallel similar logic.

"But I'm just not a self-disciplined person!" some claim as their excuse. The real problem is with desire. If we want something enough, we will do what it takes to get it. So Paul admonished Timothy to "take pains with these things; be absorbed in them, so that your progress will be evident to all" (4:15).

Jesus "is the Savior of all men, especially of believers" (4:10). Why then do Calvinists claim that Jesus only died for a limited number of people whom God allegedly pre-selected for salvation? If that were true, how is Jesus in any sense, as Paul says, the Savior of unbelievers—for whom He supposedly did not die—those unfortunate folks allegedly destined from eternity for damnation?

Day 180, 1 Timothy 5

You don't have to be putting churches in order to benefit from the wisdom in today's reading. It is always wise to treat those who are older than yourself with due respect, even if you have been given some authority over them. Thus it is foolish to "sharply rebuke an older man" (5:1) and wise to treat "older women as mothers" (5:2). And for single men, like Timothy, it is also wise to treat "younger women as sisters, in all purity" (5:2).

Certain widows were supported by the early church, but keep in mind that the large majority of widows in Paul's day would have been just like those in undeveloped countries today, having no income, savings, or life insurance settlements. Most widows in the modern Western world are living like queens in comparison. In any case, Paul lays down some wise rules regarding which widows should and should not be supported by the church's charity. Again, most modern widows in the wealthy Western world do not meet Paul's requirements.

First, and naturally, if a widow has children or grandchildren, they should be supporting her, not the church (5:4). If they don't, they prove their profession of faith in Christ to be bogus, and they are "worse than unbelievers" (5:8).

Second, only genuine Christian widows whose daily lives and continual prayers validate their faith should be supported (5:5).

Third, only widows sixty years and older are to be helped by the church, presumably because those younger are generally strong enough to earn their own living (5:9).

Fourth, only those widows who have lived a consistent Christian life of service to their husbands, children, strangers and saints, "devoting themselves to every good work," should be supported (5:9-10). They have served the church, and so the church should feel obligated to serve them in return.

Fifth, it appears that these widows were required to make a pledge to remain unmarried so that they could continue to serve the church (5:11-12). For this reason, younger widows were not permitted to be added to the list of those supported by the church, as they might "feel sensual desires in disregard of Christ" and "set aside their previous pledge" when they married once again (5:11-12). Paul is also concerned that younger widows who are receiving the church's support will take advantage of it, and rather than being spiritually productive, they will be enabled to waste their time in ungodly activities, which might ultimately lead to their spiritual destruction (5:13-15). If only our government would be so wise as to not enable irresponsibility by its handouts!

So Paul wants younger widows to be motivated to marry and keep busy in their domestic responsibilities. "Idle hands are the devil's workshop." Incidentally, Paul's somber words about young widows who formerly served Christ, but who "turned aside to follow Satan"(5:15), is one more proof that there is no such thing as unconditional eternal security.

The church also supported the elders who served it, and Paul reminds Timothy that those who serve well in preaching and teaching should be proportionately honored (5:17).

Why did Paul instruct Timothy to "use a little wine for the sake of his stomach and his frequent ailments" (5:23) rather than instruct him to pray for healing? Notice that Paul first said, "No longer drink water exclusively." Obviously, Timothy was breaking the first rule of all traveling missionaries: "Don't drink the water!" Although people generally acquire an immunity to the bacteria in their local water, outsiders will find that their first drink results in some rather unpleasant symptoms. Wine, however, is clear of the local bacteria, and it also provides a medicinal effect upon a sick stomach.

Divine healing does not nullify the need to practice hygiene and the laws of health. If you are a true servant of Christ and you find yourself sick, it is wise to question if you are violating some natural law. It is scientific fact that most of the diseases that kill Americans, for example, are the direct result of their unhealthy eating habits. They are committing slow suicide. I recommend reading *Eat to Live* by Dr. Fuhrman in that regard.

Day 181, 1 Timothy 6

The "double deception" that deludes so many professing Christians is this: First, they believe that they are saved when they actually are not; and second, they believe they can never lose what they actually don't possess. Their doom is doubly sealed, often with the help of their pastor's soothing sermons, and their only hope is if they will listen to what Scripture so plainly teaches. In today's reading, Paul speaks of those who, in the pursuit of wealth, "wandered away from the faith" (6:10); and of those who, because they listened to false doctrine, had "gone astray from the faith" (6:21). Some attempt to persuade us that Paul was speaking of people who had previously been "considering" Christianity but who had never actually believed in Christ. If I said, however, "Joe Smith has wandered away or gone astray from faith in the Mormon church," it would be quite safe to assume that at one time Joe Smith was a practicing Mormon.

Regarding false doctrine that has the potential to lead true Christians away from saving faith, Paul succinctly states two criteria whereby false doctrine can be identified. If teaching does not agree (1) with the words of Jesus, and (2) with the "doctrine conforming to godliness" (6:3), you can be sure it is false. Any teaching, for example, that leads you to think that we can gain heaven apart from holiness is false teaching, because it does not agree with the words of Jesus. Any teaching that leads you to think that it is impossible for you to forfeit your salvation is false teaching, because it does not agree with the words of Jesus.

As I already mentioned, Paul also warns how the love of money has the potential to pull true Christians away from the faith and "plunge men into ruin and destruction" (6:9-10). It was not "financial ruin" or "financial destruction" that Paul had in mind, but spiritual and eternal ruin and destruction. The remedy is to be content even if we only have food and covering (6:8).

Knowing that, we no longer need to wonder where to separate our "needs" from our "wants." All we need is food and covering, and this agrees with the words of our Lord Jesus Christ, who in His Sermon on the Mount defined our needs as being those two things (Matt. 6:25-33), and who also warned that serving God and serving mammon are mutually exclusive of each other (Matt. 6:19-24). That fact alone reveals that it is possible for followers of Christ to forfeit their salvation. Is it possible for someone who is serving God to start serving mammon? If the answer is "yes," then it is possible for a Christian to forfeit his salvation.

May I also add that Paul's words to Timothy, "Take hold of the eternal life to which you were called" (6:12), are additional proof that ultimate salvation is not the guaranteed right of everyone who currently believes in Jesus. Clearly, Timothy, a saved man when Paul wrote to him, had the option to "take hold" or not "take hold" of the eternal life to which he was called. How does one "take hold" of the eternal life to which he was called? By pursuing "righteousness, godliness, faith, love, perseverance and gentleness" (6:11). And, according to Paul, those who have more than they need "take hold of that which is life indeed" by doing good, by being rich in good work, by being generous, and by storing up heavenly treasure (6:18-19).

Finally, may I point out that Paul's words to Timothy to "take hold of the eternal life to which you were called" (6:12) are just one more nail in the coffin of Calvinism, which I'm sure you were hoping I might not mention for at least one day. (My motto, however, is: "A scripture a day keeps Calvinism at bay!") Calvinists claim that God only calls those whom He has pre-selected for salvation, drawing them with an irresistible grace. Thus, everyone who is called by God is supposedly guaranteed to be eternally saved. Timothy, however, was called to eternal life, yet unless he took hold of it, he would not obtain it.

Day 182, Titus 1

It is thought that this letter was written some time after Paul's trial before Nero and his subsequent acquittal, perhaps around AD 66, which would place it after the final chapter of Acts. Paul obviously continued traveling and ministering just as before his imprisonment, and after planting churches in Crete with Titus' help, Paul left him behind to set things in order (1:5). Titus was a longtime, trusted co-worker of Paul's, a Greek man, first mentioned as being with Paul when he journeyed to Jerusalem to submit his gospel to the scrutiny of Peter, James and John (Gal. 2:1-3).

In his very first sentence, Paul declared himself to be "an apostle of Jesus Christ, for the faith of those chosen of God" (1:1). God has chosen to save people who repent and believe in Jesus, yet some would have us believe that He chooses to save people who would never, under any circumstances, repent or believe in Jesus, but whom He zaps against their wills and changes. They go from hating Him to loving Him, not because of yielding their free will under the influence of His drawing (a universal drawing which others resist), but solely because of His sovereign action that is directed only at the few whom He has pre-selected. As you realize by now, this is not what Scripture teaches. If it were true, it would make God unjust. If ten men were on death row for the same crimes, and the state chose to forgive and release one but not the others, they would rightfully accuse the state of injustice. That is what Calvinists claim God does.

Is there anything God *cannot* do? Yes! He cannot lie (1:2). He also cannot be tempted with evil, change, or deny Himself (Jas. 1:13; Mal. 3:6; 2 Tim. 2:13). I would be willing to bet that there are other things that He can't do as well. Can He create another God equal to Himself? No, any created God could not be equal to Him, since He is not created! Can He foreknow the future final scores of football games that are never played? No, because there is nothing to foreknow.

Similarly to what he wrote in 1 Timothy, Paul lists the requirements for elders in today's reading. Note that Paul uses the words *elder* (Greek: *presbuteros*) and *overseer* (Greek: *episkopos*) synonymously (1:5, 7). They identify the same ministry. Paul never mentioned pastors in either Titus or 1 Timothy, yet he told the *elders* (Acts 20:17) of Ephesus, whom he also called *overseers* (20:28) to "*shepherd* the church of God" (20:28). The Greek word translated "shepherd" there is *poimaino*, which is the verb form of the noun *poimen*, which is translated "pastor" only in Ephesians 4:11 and "shepherd" everywhere else it is found in the New Testament. For this reason, among others, it is safe to assume that pastors, elders and overseers are all the same. Thus we could say that Paul listed the requirements to be a pastor in Titus 1:6-9.

One requirement is that an elder/overseer/pastor not be "accused of dissipation," which is defined as "a descent into drunkenness and sexual immorality." Dissipation not only disqualifies one from being a leader of Christians, but also from being a Christian.

Elders/overseers/pastors must also not be "pugnacious," which is defined as "being eager to argue, quarrel or fight." Being pugnacious does not mean, however, that one is not eager to discuss true doctrine and expose what is false, as another requirement for church leaders is that they be able to "refute those who contradict" sound doctrine (1:9). Paul also instructed Titus to "severely reprove" those who accept false teaching (1:13).

False teachers were definitely making inroads into the young church in Crete. Paul refers to them as "rebellious men, empty talkers and deceivers...who must be silenced because they are upsetting whole families, teaching things they should not teach for the sake of sordid gain" (1:10-11). One false teacher, however, Paul agreed with at least in part, whom he quoted as saying, "Cretans are always liars, evil beasts, lazy gluttons." Paul elevated a well-known Cretan named Epimenides from poet to prophet for his accurate assessment of Cretan character!

Day 183, Titus 2

The world is watching to see if there is any difference between us and them. They are watching for two reasons. Some observe us because they are sincerely searching for some meaning to life, and they wonder if we have something that they don't. Their hearts are open. If they observe hypocritical behavior, however, it convinces them that we are no different than anyone else in the world. And their conclusion is accurate.

Others watch us in hopes of discovering hypocrisy so that they can justify their own sin and continue in it. They think to themselves, "I'm better than Christians, because at least I'm not a hypocrite." When professing Christians do what is right, however, it condemns those who watch. So they revel when they discover flaws in professing believers. Our sins are a salve for their guilt. Worse, our sins strengthen them in their sin.

How important it is that we live lives that mirror our profession of faith in the Lord Jesus Christ! The greatest hindrance to the gospel in the earth today is the church, the hypocritical church that is. Paul's instructions regarding the behavior of professing believers is motivated, at least in part, by his concern "that the word of God not be dishonored" (2:5), and so that "the opponent will be put to shame, having nothing bad to say about us" (2:8).

For this reason, we should make it our goal to shame Christ-rejectors by our deeds. Twice in today's chapter, and three times in the next chapter (2:7, 14; 3:1, 8, 14), Paul stresses how important it is that we be engaged in "good deeds." In fact, Paul declares that the reason Jesus gave Himself for us was to "redeem us from every *lawless deed*, and to purify for Himself a people for His own possession, zealous for *good deeds*" (2:14). God's intention in the gospel was not just to forgive us, but to make us holy.

Holiness is indeed the major theme in today's reading, and Paul hones in on specific behavior that is expected of older men, older women, young women, young men, Titus himself, and bondslaves (2:1-10). It is not that God has different standards for each of these groups, but that these groups each tend to face unique temptations because of their cultural roles. It is older women with time on their hands, for example, who are most likely to fall into the sin of gossip (2:3). Paul admonishes them to make use of their time by discipling younger women who can learn from their experience and wisdom.

How some women bristle when they read Paul's words in 2:4, where he encourages younger women to "love their husbands, to love their children, to be sensible, pure, workers at home, kind, being subject to their own husbands." Such women have been brainwashed (or better said, "brain-dirtied") by the world into thinking that being a devoted wife and mother is ignoble. It is, however, a very honorable career, requiring the greatest virtue, servanthood. Keep in mind that in Paul's day, there were no day-care centers at which mothers could drop off their children while they hurried off to earn a paycheck. The result was that mothers exerted great influence over their young children by virtue of their time together, and their children did not experience the negative socialization that comes from spending their days with groups of miniature cannibals!

Remember, "A scripture a day keeps Calvinism at bay," and Paul does not disappoint us today. He wrote, "For the grace of God has appeared, bringing salvation to all men" (2:11). God's offer of saving mercy is offered to all, not just a selected few. Paul was not a Calvinist.

And is the grace that God is offering to all a grace that gives them license to sin? Is it so they can continue on their self-willed path while hiding behind the blood of Christ? No, Paul wrote that God's grace instructs us "to deny ungodliness and worldly desires and to live sensibly, righteously and godly in the present age" (2:12). That may not be the grace being proffered from many churches, but it is the only grace being offered from heaven!

Day 184, Titus 3

Once we've been walking with the Lord for a while it is easy to forget that we were once walking in darkness and enslaved to sin, and our forgetfulness breeds disrespect for those who are living as we once did. We should, however, guard ourselves against such pride and show "every consideration for all men" (3:2). The reason we aren't caught in the same trap of sin as they are is because of the grace of God. And we certainly aren't going to attract sinners if they detect that we think we're superior. So Paul reminds us, "For we also once were foolish ourselves, disobedient, deceived, enslaved to various lusts and pleasures, spending our life in malice and envy, hateful, hating one another" (3:3). Remember those days?

This same verse indicates, like so many others, that true believers are no longer characterized by sin. We are no longer "enslaved to various lust and pleasures, spending our lives in malice and envy, hating one another." If we are, we have not been truly born again or we've backslidden.

The salvation that God is offering everyone includes so much more than just forgiveness of sins or entering heaven one day. It includes "washing of regeneration and renewing by the Holy Spirit whom He poured out upon us richly through Jesus Christ our Savior" (3:5-6). We've been *divinely* transformed! This is not something we deserved, but something that was granted to us because of God's mercy and grace (3:5, 7). What a deal!

But notice that Paul wrote, "...so that being justified by His grace we would be made heirs according to the *hope* of eternal life" (3:7). Eternal life is our "hope," which means eternal life is not our guarantee, which is why Paul writes directly after that, "This is a trustworthy statement; and concerning these things I want you to speak confidently, *so that those who have believed God will be careful to engage in good deeds*" (3:8). Paul believed what Jesus plainly taught, namely that God's unprofitable servants will ultimately be cast into hell (Matt. 24:42-51; 25:14-30). So we all should be "careful to engage in good deeds" (3:8).

This is so important that Paul mentions the importance of good deeds three times in today's chapter (3:1, 8, 14). What kind of good deeds? Going to church? Voting for pro-life candidates? Refraining from smoking cigarettes?

As important (or unimportant) as those things might be, Paul had none of those things in mind. His words in 3:14 provide the clue we need: "Our people must also learn to engage in good deeds *to meet pressing needs*, so that they will not be unfruitful." Paul knew that everyone would one day hear Jesus say one of two things, either, "I was hungry, thirsty, naked, homeless, sick and incarcerated, and you sacrificed to meet those pressing needs" or, "I was hungry, thirsty, naked, homeless, sick and incarcerated, and you didn't do anything to meet those pressing needs." Those in the latter category will be cast into hell no matter how many times they attended church, no matter how many pro-life candidates they helped elect, and no matter how many cigarettes they didn't smoke.

Again, Paul knew well the danger of being unfruitful. Jesus clearly warned in His Parable of the Vine and Branches that any unfruitful branches that are "in Him" will be taken away (John 15:2). Only those who "abide in Him" bear fruit, and the branch that does not abide in Him "is thrown away...and dries up; and they gather them, and cast them into the fire and they are burned" (John 15:6). If all professing Christians took these very scriptural truths to heart, it would result in worldwide revival.

Our "scripture a day to keep Calvinism away" is—you guessed it—Titus 3:4: "When the kindness of God our Savior and *His love for mankind* appeared..." God our Savior loves all of mankind, and this is revealed in the gospel, which offers salvation to all through Christ who died for all. Glory be to God!

Day 185, 1 Peter 1

Scholars often place the date of Peter's writing his first epistle between AD 60 and 64, the latter of which is the assumed time of his martyrdom. Peter wrote to persecuted believers who were scattered across modern Turkey, and he reminded them from the outset of his letter that they were "aliens," an apt description of all Christians. We're strangers to this world, a family whose citizenship is in heaven. Of course those who hate God hate us.

We're also "chosen according to the foreknowledge of God" (1:1-2). God foreknows everyone intimately, and thus He can choose people before they are born. But did He flip a coin to determine who would be saved and who would not be saved? Or did He have some reason for choosing some and not others? Obviously, in light of the entire revelation of Scripture, the answer is that God chose all whom He foreknew would repent and believe in Jesus. And clearly, as Peter states, God not only chose us, but planned that we would be sanctified, or set apart for holy use by the Holy Spirit, that we might "obey Jesus and be sprinkled with His blood" (1:2). God's original intention went beyond forgiveness to transformation. It is part of the package!

It is that transformation that attracts persecution from the world. Obviously, if Christians were no different than unbelievers, the world would have no reason to hate and persecute us. Thus, persecution serves a positive spiritual end; namely, it identifies believers. And when we persevere under persecution, it proves the genuineness of our faith. So Peter writes of "the *proof of your faith*, being more precious than gold which is perishable, even though tested by fire, may be found to result in praise and glory and honor at the revelation of Jesus Christ" (1:7). We should rejoice when we are hated, just as Jesus instructed us:

> Blessed are you when men hate you, and ostracize you, and insult you, and scorn your name as evil, for the sake of the Son of Man. Be glad in that day and leap for joy, for behold, your reward is great in

heaven. For in the same way their fathers used to treat the prophets (Luke 6:22-23).

Jesus, however, also spoke of those who "fall away...when affliction or persecution arises because of the word." They "have no firm root in themselves, but are only temporary" (Mark 4:17). And this is why we are so often admonished in Scripture to "continue in the faith" and "hold fast" to what we have (Acts 14:22; Col. 1:23; 1 Cor. 15:2; Heb. 3:6, 14, 4:14, 10:23; Rev. 2:25, 3:11).

These verses are often ignored by preachers who realize that people would rather hear scriptures that seem to guarantee eternal security for everyone who verbalizes faith in Christ. But those scriptures which guarantee *God's* faithfulness (some of which are found in today's reading) do not guarantee *our* faithfulness. There is a difference! And this is the reason Peter so strongly admonishes all of us who "address as Father the One who impartially judges according to each one's work" to "conduct ourselves in fear during the time of our stay on earth" (1:17).

All of us must stand before the impartial Judge one day, and if that judgment was nothing more than a passing out of rewards as some claim, then there would be no reason to fear. In fact, if the worst consequence of that judgment was a little verbal reprimand, there would still be no reason to fear. Peter was concerned that his readers might, like the goats in Jesus' foretelling of the judgment of the sheep and goats, be shocked to find themselves condemned because they did not possess "the holiness without which no one will see the Lord" (Heb. 12:14).

As free moral agents, we can choose to obey or disobey. So it makes perfect sense that Peter wrote to born-again believers, "Like the Holy One who called you, be holy yourselves also in all your behavior" (1:15). Who is holy? Those who want to be holy. It is that simple!

Day 186, 1 Peter 2

Today's chapter continues Peter's emphasis on holiness. Obviously, believers are capable of committing the sins of malice, deceit, hypocrisy, envy and slander, otherwise Peter would not have felt a need to admonish his readers to put them all aside (2:1). Of course, lying, hypocrisy, jealousy and envy are all mentioned elsewhere as being damning sins (Rev. 21:8; Matt. 24:51; Gal. 5:20-21). Peter's admonitions are more than just "helpful hints for self improvement."

Peter paints a few metaphorical pictures to help us to progress in Christ. We are to be "like newborn babes" who "long for the pure milk of the word, so that by it we may grow in respect to salvation" (2:2). We all know how much babies desire their mother's milk. Without that nourishment, they'll die. Likewise, we need to feed regularly on God's Word. A little snack once a week on Sundays is not enough. Babies need their mother's milk every few hours. We literally can't get too much of God's Word. He told the Israelites:

> These words, which I am commanding you today, shall be on your heart; and you shall teach them diligently to your sons and shall talk of them when you sit in your house and when you walk by the way and when you lie down and when you rise up. And you shall bind them as a sign on your hand and they shall be as frontals on your forehead. And you shall write them on the doorposts of your house and on your gates (Deut. 6:5-9).

Peter not only wants us to see ourselves as hungry babies, but also as "living stones" that are being used to construct a holy temple, of which Jesus is the cornerstone. Together, we "offer up spiritual sacrifices," that is, worship through our acts of obedience (2:5).

Peter also describes us as "a chosen race, a royal priesthood, a holy nation, a people for God's own possession" (2:9). These are not metaphorical descriptions, but actual realities. If we see ourselves as God does, we are more motivated to "abstain from fleshly lusts which wage war against the soul" (2:11). All of us face those inward battles. Seeing ourselves as royal priests and a holy nation helps us to win that battle. When faced with temptation, we should remind ourselves, "Because of who I am, I don't stoop to that sort of behavior."

Unjust suffering is certainly not something from which Christians are exempt. In fact, Peter seems to imply that it is our destiny (2:21). Remembering Christ's example can help us to endure. Truly, there has never been a greater example of unjust suffering than when Jesus, sinless and pure, was persecuted and crucified. Yet He patiently and quietly endured, and "kept entrusting Himself to Him who judges righteously" (2:23). He knew that one day, everyone who reviled Him would have to stand before His Father and give an account. So we can also rest in God's ultimate justice. Our calm and non-retaliatory confidence is liable to make them wonder, just as Jesus' silence astonished Pilate (Matt 27:14). Perhaps it will lead to their repentance.

Peter sums up the gospel beautifully in today's final two verses. Jesus "bore our sins in His body on the cross" (2:24). His reason? That "we might die to sin and live to righteousness" (2:24). So the fifth verse of the American abolitionist song, *The Battle Hymn of the Republic*, rings true:

> In the beauty of the lilies Christ was born across the sea,
> With a glory in His bosom *that transfigures you and me*:
> As *He died to make men holy*, let us die to make men free,
> While God is marching on.

Both the repentance required and the transformation offered in the gospel are rooted in the Old Testament, indicated by Peter as he alludes to Isaiah 53. "All of us like sheep have gone astray," wrote both Isaiah and Peter (2:25), but "now we have returned to the Shepherd and Guardian of our souls" (2:25). That is repentance. And "by Jesus' wounds," both Isaiah and Peter wrote, "we were healed" (2:24). That is transformation.

Day 187, 1 Peter 3

There is just no getting around it. The New Testament teaches wives to be submissive to their husbands. We read it today from Peter and we've read it before in Paul's writings (1 Pet. 3:1-6; Eph. 5:22-24; Col 3:18). Of course, both Peter and Paul have instructions about how husbands should treat their wives, and so some Christian wives have adopted an attitude that declares, "I will gladly submit to a husband who loves me like Christ loves the church," implying that they are only responsible to be submissive if their husbands first love them rightly. Peter, however, quashes that position, instructing wives to be submissive to their own husbands even if their husbands are "disobedient to the word" (3:1), that is, unsaved.

Of course, God does not expect any wife to submit to her husband's demands if by doing so she must disobey the Lord. Rather, her "chaste and respectful behavior" will hopefully win her husband to the Lord. So when Peter or Paul instruct wives to be submissive to their husbands, they are not advocating blind subservience; nor are they giving husbands a blank check to dominate their wives. The husband who points his finger and yells at his wife, "You'd better do what I say, because the Bible says I'm the head," is indeed a head—a pinhead! In the simple instructions of Peter and Paul, we find the remedy for most marital disharmony and our soaring divorce rate. If wives will be submissive, and if husbands will honor their wives "as fellow heirs of the grace of life" (3:7), marriage will become the enjoyable blessing that God intended. Otherwise, it can be hell on earth, as many can testify.

Husbands, take note that by not showing your wife the honor she deserves, your prayers may be hindered (3:7). There is a definite correlation between our obedience and the blessings that God bestows upon us. This is true not only within the context of marriage, but in every other area of life. If we want to "love life and see good days," here is Peter's recipe (quoting David in Psalm 34):

He must keep his tongue from evil and his lips from speaking deceit. He must turn away from evil and do good; he must seek peace and pursue it. For the eyes of the Lord are toward the righteous, and His ears attend to their prayer, but the face of the Lord is against those who do evil" (3:10-12).

That is a wonderful motto for daily life.

It is interesting that the early Christians were never told in the New Testament epistles to invite their unsaved friends to church, to go witnessing door to door, or to preach the gospel in the marketplaces. The early church considered the preaching of the gospel to be the responsibility of those who were supernaturally equipped to do so, namely apostles and evangelists. Yet this is not to say that average Christians had no responsibility in regards to spreading the gospel. They were to support those who were called to travel and proclaim the gospel. And they were to live holy lives before a watching world, and be "ready to make a defense to everyone who asked them to give an account for the hope that was in them" (3:15).

Our lives are to be like lights shining in the darkness, demonstrating such a contrast that people notice that we're different. When they ask us why we live as we do, that is our opportunity to tell them about Jesus.

Who were the "spirits now in prison" whom Jesus preached to after His crucifixion, who "once were disobedient...in the days of Noah" (3:19-20)? It sounds as if they were the spirits of people who died physically in Noah's flood, who are now in hell awaiting final judgment. Some claim, however, that Peter was actually saying that back in the days of Noah, Jesus preached "in spirit" to sinners, and those unrepentant people are *now* "in prison." That seems to be stretching the text in my opinion. Yet I have no idea what Jesus would have had to say to people in hell after His crucifixion and before His resurrection. Stumped again!

Day 188, 1 Peter 4

Who wants to suffer? Not me! Who may want me to suffer? God!

Why is that? He wants me to be holy, and "he who has suffered in the flesh has ceased from sin, so as to live the rest of the time in the flesh no longer for the lusts of men, but for the will of God" (4:1-2). Pain, when it is associated with sin, has a way of motivating us to stop sinning—to escape the pain. That is why spanking disobedient children is a smart idea. And God is certainly that smart. "Those whom the Lord loves He disciplines, and He scourges every son whom He receives" (Heb. 12:6).

God often disciplined wayward Israel by means of their enemies. He permitted various nations to persecute His people in order to bring them back to Him. And the New Testament teaches that God sometimes permits persecution in order to discipline His wayward children as well. I would not, however, jump to the conclusion that persecution is always an indication of God's discipline. God may also permit persecution as a test. Peter affirmed this when he wrote, "Do not be surprised at the fiery ordeal among you, which comes upon you for your testing, as though some strange thing were happening to you" (4:12). The intended recipients of his letter were being maligned and reviled for their holy lifestyles and love for Christ (4:4, 14). But Peter wrote that they should count themselves blessed, because their sufferings were proof that "the Spirit of glory and of God" rested upon them (4:14).

This was not, of course, Peter's original thought. Jesus told His followers that they were blessed when they were persecuted for the sake of righteousness, as it was a sure indication that they were on the way to heaven, where their reward would be great. When we arrive in heaven and see the rewards that are given to those who suffered the most, I suspect we will wish that we had suffered more persecution on earth. So it makes sense to follow Peter's admonition, "To the degree that you share the sufferings of Christ, keep on rejoicing, so that also at the revelation of His glory you may rejoice with exultation" (4:13).

What did Peter mean when he wrote that the gospel has "been preached even to those who are dead" (4:6)? I don't think he meant that the gospel had been preached to people after they died physically, as there is no other scripture that would support such an idea. So the only other possibility is that Peter was speaking of the fact that the gospel had been preached to people who are *spiritually* dead. Peter did say that the reason for this was that "they may live in the spirit according to the will of God" (4:6), indicating that it was spiritual death and life that he had in mind. Yet his writing in that particular verse is admittedly not as clear as we would like it to be.

Praise God for everyone who has received some special gift from God that has been graciously given to them to benefit the body of Christ. Those who have gifts should never forget that a stewardship has been entrusted to them and that they will have to give an account. Peter first lists those who have been given speaking gifts. They should, he said, not speak their own ideas or theories, but "the utterances of God" (4:11). How many sermons meet that condition?

This chapter ends with sobering words: "For it is time for judgment to begin with the household of God; and if it begins with us first, what will be the outcome for those who do not obey the gospel of God?" (4:17). God was examining all those who claimed to be His own, and He was disciplining those who were falling short of His expectations in order to purify them to ensure their ultimate salvation. According to Peter, people who are unrighteous don't have a chance of being saved, because "it is with difficulty that the righteous are saved" (4:18). So let us trust God as He works to make us holy.

Day 189, 1 Peter 5

Some modern biblical scholars debate if Peter is actually the author of this epistle. They doubt that an unlearned fisherman could write in such an urbane, cultured style of Greek. They seem to forget that Peter retired as a fisherman about 35 years earlier to embark in a career of public speaking! Is it possible that Peter learned some things about communication during 35 years of practice? May I also mention that even from the outset of Peter's new career, learned men were amazed at his speaking ability since he was "uneducated and untrained" (Acts 4:13). The Holy Spirit is a good helper!

Incidentally, if Peter didn't write this epistle, then we ought to rip it from our Bibles, as the person who did write it was a liar who claimed to be the same Peter who witnessed Christ's sufferings.

Today's chapter begins with instructions to *elders* regarding their *shepherding* responsibilities (5:1-2), so they are instructions to pastors/elders/overseers. Remember that there wasn't a single pastor/elder/overseer to whom Peter wrote whose ministry was like that of most modern pastors. Those whom Peter addressed did not prepare weekly sermons or conduct services in special church buildings. They did not direct worship teams or Sunday school teachers, or oversee a staff consisting of assistant pastors, youth pastors and children's ministers, and so on. They simply discipled little flocks that met in houses for participatory and interactive meetings. Therefore, such pastors could actually be "examples to the flock" (5:3), something that is impossible for most modern pastors, whose interaction with their congregations usually amounts to nothing more than standing in front of them for an hour on Sundays and shaking their hands as they exit the sanctuary. Only those pastors with little flocks have the potential to teach their flocks by their example.

Heavy-handed "pastors" who manipulate their flocks for their own selfish ends, beware! You will stand before the Chief Shepherd one day, who laid down His life to serve the sheep whom you "lord it over" (5:3). Genuine pastors who serve their flocks will "receive the unfading crown of glory" (5:4). God bless all the good pastors around the world! They deserve their future crowns!

How wonderful it is to know that God cares for us (5:7). That simple fact fills our hearts with peace. There is no good reason that we have to worry about anything, so we are wise to follow Peter's instruction to cast all our cares upon the Lord (5:7). Worrywarts, repent! Worries are like prayers that say, "God, I know you can't be trusted!"

Peter paints a picture of Satan as a "roaring lion" who "prowls around...seeking someone to devour" (5:8). His prowling about to devour someone was, in Peter's mind, connected to the persecution that his readers were suffering (5:9). If Satan "devours" a believer by means of persecution through unbelievers, what is the outcome? It would seem quite logical to think that Peter was speaking once again of the danger of believers falling away from the faith, especially since Peter admonishes them in the same passage to resist the devil, "firm in their faith" (5:9). That is, suffering believers must hold fast in faith to the Lord Jesus Christ, even though they are tempted to abandon their faith to escape the fires of persecution.

It is also good to remember that God is always in control even when He permits His people to suffer under persecution, and that He is working all things together for our good (Rom. 8:28). He uses our trials, according to Peter, to "perfect, confirm, strengthen and establish" us (5:10). If you will look back at your spiritual life, you will probably notice that your times of greatest spiritual growth were those times when everything wasn't easy. It could well be said: "No spiritual pain; no spiritual gain!"

Peter closed this epistle with the admonition, "Greet one another with the kiss of love" (5:13). Have you kissed a Christian today?

Day 190, Jude

When Jude wrote this short epistle—assumed to be some time between AD 66 and 90—he was quite alarmed over a certain heresy that was creeping into the churches. The very gospel itself was being subverted by false teaching, and so Jude wrote an appeal to all true believers to "contend earnestly for the faith which was once for all handed down to the saints" (1:3).

More specifically, false teachers who had "crept in unnoticed," were "turning the grace of God into licentiousness," and "denying our only Master and Lord, Jesus Christ" (1:4). Because they had "crept in unnoticed," it seems unlikely that they were publicly and verbally denying the Lord. Rather, their false teaching about God's grace—which turned it into a license to sin—was tantamount to denying the Lord and Master. Obviously, the titles of *Lord* and *Master* denote a person of authority who should be obeyed.

This same heresy, of course, has crept in unnoticed in our day as well. God's grace, which Scripture says instructs us to "deny ungodliness and worldly desires and to live sensibly, righteously and godly in the present age" (Titus 2:12), has been turned into a license for sin. When preachers tell us that holiness is not part of the salvation equation, or that any teaching about obedience is legalism, or that it is impossible for a true believer to forfeit his salvation for any behavioral reason, we should be greatly alarmed. God's grace is being turned into licentiousness.

In quick succession, Jude lists some biblical examples that illustrate the necessity of holiness. Even though God delivered the Israelites from Egypt, most never entered the Promised Land because of sin (1:5). And there are angels who once resided in heaven who are now "kept in eternal bonds under darkness" (1:6). So one's current favor with God is no guarantee of one's future favor if one abandons obedience.

Jude also cites the people of Sodom and Gomorrah, sexual perverts upon whom God reigned fire and brimstone; Cain, whom God judged for hatred and murder of his brother; Balaam, whose god was money; and the rebellious men of Korah, who, when the ground opened, were swallowed. All illustrate God's hatred of sin and the necessity of holiness if one is to have a relationship with Him.

The false teachers and their disciples could be, just as Jesus said, "known by their fruits" (Matt. 7:15-21). According to Jude, they were characterized by sexual immorality, rejecting authority, reviling angelic majesties, grumbling, fault-finding, following their own lusts, speaking arrogantly, flattering people for the sake of gaining an advantage, mocking and causing divisions (1:7-8, 16, 18-19). Yet they were within the church, "hidden reefs in your love feasts," love feasts being shared meals among the believers (1:12).

Interestingly, Jude quoted two apocryphal books—that is, books that have not been accepted as being inspired by the Holy Spirit and thus were not included in the Bible. The first quotation is found in 1:9, where Jude referred to the devil having a dispute about the body of Moses. According to the writings of some early church fathers, that incident was recorded in a book titled *The Assumption of Moses*, and in it the devil tried to claim Moses' dead body because he had once killed an Egyptian. Remember that, according to the record in Deuteronomy, no one knew where Moses' body was buried because God performed the funeral (Deut. 34:6). Perhaps arch angel Michael did the actual burying of Moses' body.

The other apocryphal quotation is found in 1:14-15, taken from *The Book of Enoch*. Enoch was the pre-flood man who "walked with God; and he was not, for God took him" (Gen. 5:24). He prophesied in the book of his name concerning the return of the Lord to earth to execute judgment on the ungodly.

So why did Jude use information from books that are uninspired? Jude was not endorsing those apocryphal books as being inspired by God, but was simply endorsing two passages as being historically accurate. Just because something is true doesn't mean it is inspired by God.

The main message today? Be holy.

Day 191, 2 Peter 1

Praise God that "grace and peace" (1:2) as well as "everything pertaining to life and godliness" (1:3) are ours by means of "the true knowledge of Him who called us by His own glory and excellence" (1:3). Note that Peter stresses not just knowledge about God, but *true* knowledge about Him. A false knowledge does not result in grace, peace, eternal life or godliness. And by these criteria we can ascertain if our knowledge about God is true or false. If what we know is not producing godliness in our lives, for example, we do not possess true knowledge about God.

Peter essentially repeats that same concept yet a third time but by using different words in 1:4, where he writes that it is by means of God's "precious and magnificent promises" that we have become "partakers of the divine nature, having escaped the corruption that is in the world." He is obviously writing about the holiness we possess due to our accurate understanding of God and His Son. Again we see that those who truly know God are transformed people. As John wrote, "By this we know that we have come to know Him, if we keep His commandments" (1 John 2:3).

Yet our transformation is not something that occurs without our cooperation; nor do we reach perfection instantly. Peter admonishes us to diligently apply ourselves to personal sanctification. Verses 5-7 are not a list of steps to take one at a time, but are a checklist of virtues towards which we should already be applying ourselves. Peter did not say, "Now that you've got faith (the first step), start working on the second step, moral excellence. And once you've achieved that, go to the third step," and so on. Rather, he said, "In your faith supply moral excellence, and in your moral excellence, knowledge," and so on. Moral excellence is born out of our faith, and the same is true for knowledge, self-control, perseverance, godliness, brotherly kindness and Christian love.

Every true believer possesses all those traits to some extent and should be increasing in them: "For if these qualities are yours and are increasing, they render you neither useless nor unfruitful in the true knowledge of our Lord Jesus Christ" (1:8). Yet Peter describes the one who lacks those qualities as being "blind or short-sighted" (1:9), that is, lacking true knowledge, even though he may at one time have possessed it. He has, according to Peter, "forgotten his purification from his former sins," and as I'm sure you know by now, he has put himself in a very dangerous spiritual condition, because he will stand before God "useless and unfruitful" (1:8).

That is precisely why Peter then admonishes us to "be all the more diligent to make certain about His calling and choosing" us (1:10). Those who lack the qualities Peter listed have good reason to question if they are among those chosen by God, because He chooses those who have faith in the Lord Jesus and whose lives demonstrate that faith. Only those whose lives make evident their profession of faith have a genuine assurance of salvation, as Peter writes, "As long as you practice these things, you will never stumble, for in this way the entrance into the eternal kingdom of our Lord and Savior Jesus Christ will be abundantly supplied to you" (1:10-11). Again we see that heaven belongs to the holy. This is not salvation by works, but salvation by a faith that works.

Peter knew that "the laying aside of his earthly dwelling was imminent" (1:14), and he was concerned that once he died, some might give up hope that Jesus would ever return, since He had not returned in Peter's lifetime. Thus Peter affirmed his confidence that, even though he would not live to see Christ's return, Christ *would* return. He then recounted the time some 30 years earlier when he, along with James and John, saw Jesus transfigured and heard God's voice (Matt. 16:27 - 17:8). That experience only confirmed what the prophets had been foretelling for centuries: God will one day come to earth and establish His kingdom. Everyone needs to be ready for that day!

Day 192, 2 Peter 2

If Peter wrote his second epistle near the same time as Jude wrote his epistle, then there is little doubt that Peter would have been equally horrified over the heresy that was infiltrating the church then, a heresy that "turned the grace of God into licentiousness" (Jude 4). Peter also describes the false teachers who were responsible for spreading this heresy, and his words are so similar with some of Jude's words that it seems safe to assume that one borrowed from another. Preachers take note: It is OK to borrow material from other preachers, as long as what you are borrowing is biblical!

The false teachers whom Peter warned against would "secretly introduce destructive heresies, even denying the Master who bought them" (2:1), indicating a subtlety in their methodology. Naturally, they were not publicly teaching, "We deny the Master, the Lord Jesus Christ," or else they would have been easily identified and shunned by every believer. Rather, their teaching undermined the necessity of holiness while their lifestyles were characterized by sensuality and greed (2:2-3), which is why Peter wrote that they denied the *Master*, a title which emphasizes Jesus' rightful role as Lord and our obligation to obey Him.

Notice Peter believed that Jesus had "bought" the false teachers, which indicates that Jesus died for their sins, paying the price for their redemption. Using the identical Greek word that Peter used that is translated "bought" (*agarazo*), Paul wrote to the Corinthian believers, "You have been *bought* with a price: therefore glorify God in your body" (1 Cor. 6:20). So, undeniably, Jesus died for the sins of the false teachers who were "bringing swift destruction upon themselves" (2:1). This exposes the error of the Calvinistic idea that Jesus only died for those whom God allegedly predestined to be saved.

Because it is impossible to circumvent Peter's plain declaration that Jesus bought the false teachers, some Calvinists resort to claiming that the "swift destruction" that those false teachers would experience was only speaking of their imminent physical deaths, after which time they would be welcomed into heaven, secure in God's grace. That is, however, a worse heresy than the one being promoted by the false teachers. If it were true, then we are to think that adulterers and greedy people (2:2-3, 14), whom Scripture repeatedly warns will *not* inherit eternal life (1 Cor. 6:9-10; Gal. 5:19-21; Eph. 5:3-5), *will* inherit eternal life. Moreover, the three groups whom Peter immediately cites to illustrate what happens to those like the false teachers, namely, the angels who rebelled and were cast into hell, the ancient world whom God judged with a flood, and the perverts in Sodom and Gomorrah upon whom God reigned fire and brimstone (2:4-6), are not very good examples of people who were ultimately welcomed into heaven!

Take note that the false teachers whom Peter condemned were formerly in good standing with God, having at one time "known the way of righteousness," they had "escaped the defilements of the world by the knowledge of the Lord and Savior Jesus Christ" (2:20-21). Peter used a similar expression in 1:4, where he wrote of believers who have "escaped the corruption that is in the world" through knowledge of Jesus. There is no doubt that the false teachers had at one time been delivered from their sins through Christ. Yet they, like all of us, were still free moral agents, and they became "again entangled in [their sins] and were overcome," so that "the last state had become worse for them than the first" (2:20).

This passage clearly debunks the cardinal doctrine of Calvinism that maintains that all true believers will persevere in their faith. It also debunks the widely-held notion among evangelicals that those who believe in Jesus for any amount of time, no matter how limited, can never forfeit their salvation.

It is also interesting that all Calvinists adamantly maintain that no person can escape his sins without the divine help of the Holy Spirit (which is absolutely true), yet some Calvinists want us to believe that the false teachers of whom Peter wrote were never actually saved, but had only experienced false conversions. Yet they had been delivered from their sins.

Day 193, 2 Peter 3

When reading the New Testament epistles, I am often struck by the stark contrast between what was emphasized by Peter, Paul, James, John and Jude, and what is emphasized in contemporary "Christian" culture, specifically in churches, "Christian" bookstores, and on "Christian" television. These are often at polar opposites from Scripture, making them not just sub-Christian but anti-Christian.

Today I find myself thinking about that contrast once again. Clearly, Peter's greatest concern was that his readers be holy and ready for the coming of the Lord. He was also concerned that they be on their guard "lest, being carried away by the error of unprincipled men" they "fall from [their] own steadfastness" (3:17). Yet so many teachers in the modern church do not share Peter's concern, convinced that it is impossible for the saved to forfeit eternal life for any reason. In fact, rather than warning their flocks of this danger of which Scripture speaks repeatedly, they assure them that such a thing could never occur. Worse, holiness is equated to legalism and contrary to the gospel of grace! May God help us!

Peter was also concerned that after he and the other apostles had died, believers who remained would begin to wonder if they had been hoaxed, especially as mockers questioned why Jesus still had not returned (3:2-4). So Peter reminds us that it was God who created everything long ago, and it was God who once destroyed the world by a flood.

Some speculate that Peter, when writing of the earth that "was formed out of water and by water" (3:5), was not speaking of the time of Noah's flood, but of an earlier flood in which God's judgment was poured out upon an pre-Adamic creation, the aftermath of which is described in Genesis 1:2:

> And the earth was formless and void, and darkness was over the surface of the deep; and the Spirit of God was moving over the surface of the waters.

This view is embraced by those who theorize that there is a gap of perhaps millions of years between Genesis 1:1 and 1:2, which then makes allowance for an earth that is much older than a few thousand years, which is what one might conclude from the more standard reading of the book of Genesis.

Regardless of which interpretation is correct, God has historically demonstrated His wrath against the entire world in the past, and He has also historically demonstrated His mercy with a new beginning for the world. That same wrath and mercy will be demonstrated once again, yet with one difference. The next time, "the heavens will pass away with a roar and the elements will be destroyed with intense heat, and the earth and its works will be burned up" (3:10). Afterwards, however, true to historical precedent, God will renew what He has destroyed. There will be "new heavens and a new earth in which righteousness dwells" (3:12).

Knowing this, according to Peter, should motivate us to be holy (3:11). In fact, he even states that we can hasten "the coming of the day of God" (3:12), implying that our obedience can affect the timing of Christ's return. Contrasted with this, Peter tells us that one reason Jesus has been so slow to return is because He is "not wishing for any to perish but for all to come to repentance" (3:9). So the reason it has taken Jesus so long to return is not because He is slow, but because He is lovingly patient, giving rebels more time to repent before their doom is forever sealed.

According to Peter, even in his day people were twisting Paul's writings (3:16), so it shouldn't surprise us to witness the same thing today. Some who distort Paul's words do it "to their own destruction" (3:16), and Peter warns his readers to guard themselves against such teachers, lest they "fall from [their] own steadfastness" (3:17). Giving heed to false teaching can be spiritually deadly. Beware of the multitudes of pastors and teachers today who distort Paul's writings about salvation by grace, all to their own destruction and the destruction of their hearers. Paul's gospel was a call to repentance and holiness.

Day 194, 2 Timothy 1

Paul's second letter to Timothy could be considered his last words, as he knew that "the time of [his] departure had come" (4:6). He wrote from Rome during his final imprisonment there, apparently during a second trial before Nero. Church tradition tells us that Paul was beheaded just outside Rome in AD 67, around the same time that Peter was executed by being crucified upside down. When Paul wrote this letter to his "beloved son" in the faith, Timothy had been his close and trusted companion for about 15 years. Paul longed to see Timothy before leaving this world and requested that he come to Rome (1:4; 4:9, 21).

Times were very hard for Christians when Paul wrote this letter. Because Nero was being blamed for the burning of Rome in AD 64, he fastened blame on the Christians, whom he consequently violently persecuted. Roman historian Tacitus reported:

> Mockery of every sort was added to their deaths. Covered with the skins of beasts, they were torn by dogs and perished, or were nailed to crosses, or were doomed to the flames and burnt, to serve as a nightly illumination, when daylight had expired.

It would have been dangerous for anyone to associate with Paul, and concerning this, Paul writes near the end of this letter, "At my first defense no one supported me, but all deserted me; may it not be counted against them" (4:16). And although Paul also reports that "all who were in Asia" had turned away from him (1:15), thankfully, Luke had faithfully stood by him (4:11) as well as a disciple by the name of Onesiphorus, who was not ashamed of Paul's chains or afraid to visit him (1:16-18). Thank God for faithful friends who stick with you in your trials! Proverbs 17:17 says, "A friend loves at all times, and a brother is born for adversity."

The current wave of persecution had apparently affected Timothy as well, which is why Paul reminded him that "God has not given us a spirit of timidity, but of power and love and discipline," and also admonished him, "Do not be ashamed of the testimony of our Lord or of me His prisoner, but join me in suffering for the gospel" (1:7-8). God has not given any of us a spirit of timidity, but like Timothy, we can yield to the temptation to be fearful of man. When we do, the remedy is to "kindle afresh the gift of God which is in us" (1:6), namely, the Holy Spirit who can make us bold. Paul's analogy is excellent. A fire is a supernatural thing that none of us can create, but that any of us can start with a spark. The spark that ignites boldness is faith. Step out of your comfort zone by faith and then stand amazed at the fire that burns! You can do all things through Christ who strengthens you! (Phil. 4:13).

Although Timothy knew well the fundamentals of the faith, Paul wisely reiterates them to him, knowing that there is nothing comparable that can motivate us to action than the simple knowledge of the gospel. God has "saved us and called us with a holy calling, not according to our works, but according to His own purpose and grace which was granted us in Christ Jesus from all eternity" (1:10). For this, we live, and for this, Paul "was appointed a preacher and an apostle and teacher" (1:11). For this, he also suffered without shame, knowing that in the end he would be vindicated and rewarded.

Anyone who truly follows Christ will be persecuted to some degree. At bare minimum, we will find ourselves mocked by those who are in darkness. So we would be wise to follow Paul's admonition to "guard, through the Holy Spirit who dwells in us, the treasure which has been entrusted" to us (1:14). That treasure is eternal life and the new birth, and if those need to be guarded, then they can potentially be forfeited. Jesus warned that when persecution and affliction arise, some fall away (Matt. 13:21). Paul was not one of them. Make sure you are counted with him!

Day 195, 2 Timothy 2

The biblical principle of discipleship is well illustrated at the beginning of today's reading, as Paul writes to Timothy:

> The things which you have heard from me in the presence of many witnesses, entrust these to faithful men who will be able to teach others also (2 Tim. 2:2).

This principle is violated every time ministers entrust truth to unfaithful pew sitters who have no intention of obeying it, much less teach it to others. The successful minister seeks "faithful men" whom he can instruct, knowing that they will teach others what they have learned. Dear pastor, look for disciples who are comparable to good soldiers who are willing to suffer hardship, athletes who compete according to the rules, and hard-working farmers who enjoy the fruit of their labors (2:3-6).

Paul was certainly one who was willing to suffer hardship as a good soldier. As he penned this letter to Timothy, he was imprisoned for the sake of the gospel, and he would soon pay the ultimate price. He wrote, "For this reason I endure all things for the sake of those who are chosen, so that they also may obtain the salvation which is in Christ Jesus and with it eternal glory" (2:10).

Paul clearly believed the possibility existed that "those who are chosen" might not "obtain the salvation which is in Christ Jesus and with it eternal glory." If their being chosen was unconditional—an arbitrary act of God's sovereign choice—then there would be absolutely no possibility that those chosen ones would not "obtain the salvation which is in Christ Jesus and with it eternal glory." This being so, Paul must have believed that those who are chosen of God are *conditionally* chosen, and thus there exists the possibility that they may not meet His conditions in the end, falling away from the faith. Being one of God's chosen at the present is not a guarantee that one will be among God's chosen in the future since God's choosing is conditional.

In the very next verses, Paul underscores this very fact. His words are undeniably addressed to believers, and he writes, "For if we died with Him, we will also live with Him; *if we endure*, we will also reign with Him; *if we deny Him, He also will deny us* [just as Jesus promised in Matt. 10:33] (2:11-12). Notice all the conditional "ifs."

Those who reject the gospel invite God's curse upon them, not only when they die, but immediately upon their rejection of the gospel. This is one reason why Jesus told His disciples to shake the dust off their sandals as they departed from any city that rejected their message. Scripture is clear that those who harden themselves against the truth stand in danger of having God Himself harden their hearts or darken their understanding to a greater degree. Paul wrote to the Thessalonians of this form of God's judgment:

> For this reason God will send upon them a deluding influence so that they will believe what is false, in order that they all may be judged who did not believe the truth, but took pleasure in wickedness (2 Thes. 2:11-12).

But is there no hope at all for those who initially reject the truth? Is their doom sealed? No, as long as they are breathing there is hope that God might be merciful, which is why Paul wrote to Timothy:

> The Lord's bond-servant must not be quarrelsome, but be kind to all, able to teach, patient when wronged, with gentleness correcting those who are in opposition, if perhaps God may grant them repentance leading to the knowledge of the truth, and they may come to their senses and escape from the snare of the devil, having been held captive by him to do his will (2:25-26).

Again, if people's repentance was purely God's decision, with individuals themselves playing no part at all (as some try to make Paul say here) there would be no reason for the Lord's servants to gently correct "those who are in opposition" (2:15). Gentleness can help soften hard hearts. So let's be gentle, "kind to all," and "patient when wronged" (2:24). We might help someone obtain eternal life.

Day 196, 2 Timothy 3

Although Paul apparently believed that he would not live to see what he refers to as "the last days," he obviously believed that Timothy might live to see them. Therefore, he wanted him to be ready for the difficult times ahead (3:1).

Although sin has always characterized the human race, humanity's ever-increasing rebellion will surge in the last days, which one would suspect, since the last days culminate with God's wrath being poured out on the world. It would seem strange for the Lord to return to pour out His wrath upon a world making moral progress. I admit that I've never understood the "Kingdom-Now" and "Dominion" theologians who try to persuade us that Christians will increasingly take charge of the world's institutions and improve life for everyone. Nor have I understood those who tell us that a world-wide revival is on the horizon.

Naturally, as the world approaches its apex of rebellion, things will become worse for everyone on the planet, as sin carries with it its own inherent judgment. Times will become uniquely difficult for Christians, whose holy lives will contrast even more starkly against the backdrop of the world's wickedness. Persecution against the righteous will also reach its zenith, and they "will be hated by all nations" as Jesus Himself foretold (Matt. 24:9). There will be a world-wide political movement against Christians under the rule of the antichrist.

After Paul lists some of the specific sins that will characterize the ungodly in the last times, it is interesting that he mentions that they will hold "to a form of godliness" yet "deny its power" (3:5). It is hard to imagine how the extremely wicked people whom he has just described could also be characterized as "holding to a form of godliness." I can only think that he meant that people will be religious but not righteous, maintaining a facade of morality that hides their rotten core. It is also interesting that Paul instructs Timothy to "avoid such men as these" (3:5). To share the gospel with these kinds of people is to cast one's pearls before swine

(Matt. 7:6). They are "men of depraved mind, rejected in regard to the faith" (3:8). Tragically, their judgment is already sealed.

Never forget, "All who desire to live godly in Christ Jesus will be persecuted" (3:12). That's one promise that you don't need to claim by faith for it to come to pass! Paul mentioned the sufferings he endured at Antioch, Iconium and Lystra, out of which God delivered him every time (3:11). As you may recall, in Antioch, Paul was run out of town. In Iconium, he barely escaped being stoned. At Lystra, Jews from Antioch and Iconium succeeded in stoning him, leaving him for dead. But the Lord raised him up (Acts 13:14 - 14:20).

So why didn't God deliver Paul from being executed shortly after he penned this letter? Because, as we'll read tomorrow, he had fulfilled his ministry and his time of departure had arrived (4:6-7, 17). Paul viewed his death as a "drink offering" (4:6)—an act of worship whereby he could once more prove his devotion to the Lord.

"All Scripture is inspired by God" (3:16). The words "inspired by God" literally mean "God-breathed." God's words fulfill a fivefold purpose in our lives: they teach, reprove, correct, train and equip us (3:16-17). Don't downplay the reproving and correcting aspect. I've met professing Christians who aren't open to any teaching that reproves or corrects them because they've found out they're "the righteousness of God in Christ," and thus they no longer "receive any condemnation." Such an attitude is a perversion of scriptural truth.

Notice also that *Scripture* is what Paul said makes the man of God "adequate, equipped for every good work" (3:17). The primary job of ministers is to communicate biblical truth. So the best thing anyone can do to prepare for ministry is read the Bible. Every Christian, and ministers especially, should "be diligent to present [themselves] approved to God as [workmen who do] not need to be ashamed, accurately handling the word of truth" (2:15).

Day 197, 2 Timothy 4

It is difficult not to think that we are living in the time that Paul describes in this chapter, when those within the church "will not endure sound doctrine; but wanting to have their ears tickled, they will accumulate for themselves teachers in accordance to their own desires, and will turn away their ears from the truth" (4:3-4). When so many embrace a false gospel that is nothing more than a license to sin, or think that they are safe in God's grace without holiness, or believe that there is nothing they could ever do to forfeit their salvation, or trust that there is no possibility that they will have to endure tribulation, or expect Jesus to return twice, or flock to preachers who tell them that God wants them to be even wealthier than they already are, or believe that God has sovereignly predestined some to be saved and some to be damned, or think that Jesus did not die for the sins of everyone in the world, then surely we are living in the time that Paul foretold.

This sad state of things is not reason for us to put our heads in the sand, but reason to continue to boldly "preach the word" and to "reprove, rebuke [and] exhort, with great patience and instruction" (4:2), just as Paul solemnly charged Timothy to do. Paul knew that if Timothy did those things he would suffer hardship. He would also, however, fulfill his ministry and be ready to stand before the Lord (4:1, 5). Paul set an excellent example for Timothy to follow, describing his own ministry as the "good fight" and as a race that he had run. Fulfilling his own calling required great determination and perseverance. But in the end, he knew a prize awaited him, "the crown of righteousness" (4:8). That same crown awaits all "who have loved Christ's appearing" (4:8), which would of course be all true believers. All of us, like Paul, must "not grow weary and lose heart" (Heb. 12:3).

Note that Paul declared that he had "kept the faith" (4:7), which means that it would have been possible for him *not* to have "kept the faith." This is one more nail in the coffin of the idea that once a person is saved he is guaranteed to always be saved.

Additionally, Paul makes reference to a man named Demas, who at one time was his traveling companion and a servant of Christ whom he mentioned in other epistles (Col. 4:14; Philem 24). Demas, however, had recently deserted Paul, "having loved this present world" (4:10). John wrote, "If anyone loves the world, the love of the Father is not in him" (1 John 2:15). Tragically, Demas had been lured back to that from which he had been delivered.

I can't imagine that Timothy was not moved to tears as he read Paul's words, "The time of my departure has come" (4:6). From reading his story in the books of Acts, we know that Paul proved to have had an accurate foreknowledge of major future events in his life. Timothy was certainly well aware of Paul's accuracy in foretelling his own future, so he knew that his long-time friend and mentor would soon be "going home." Paul, however, did not believe that his death was just days away, as he requested that Timothy visit him as soon as possible and that he "make every effort to come before winter" (4:21). Timothy would be bringing Paul's cloak that he left in Troas, which we assume he needed for warmth in the winter months (4:13).

Paul's trial in Rome had already begun, and he had made his "first defense" (4:16), at which those whom he hoped would bravely testify in his favor sadly deserted him. Apparently, however, Paul felt that his first defense had gone well, as he was "rescued out of the lion's mouth" (4:17). We don't know if that expression was meant to be taken figuratively or literally. We do know, however, that the Romans sometimes entertained themselves by executing criminals by means of confining them with wild dogs, bears, boars and lions. Regardless, Paul has been in heaven for almost 2,000 years enjoying his reward!

Day 198, John 1

The other three Gospels were probably all in circulation by the time that the apostle John wrote his account. Most scholars suggest a date of sometime between AD 90-100. John would have been an elderly man by then, and Peter and Paul would have been in heaven for at least 20 years.

Ninety percent of the information found in John's Gospel can't be found in any of the other three, so it is thought that his purpose was to "fill in the gaps." Church father Clement of Alexandria (AD 150-215) stated that John wrote to supplement the accounts found in the other Gospels. John was writing to a readership whom he assumed already had a fair knowledge of the Lord (1:16).

Clearly, "the Word" in 1:1 and 14 refers to Jesus, who certainly was a message, or word, from God to the world. But Jesus was much more than that. He existed eternally with God. He created everything. He was God (1:1-3). Beware of anyone who teaches that Jesus was anything less.

The priests and Levites from Jerusalem who visited John the Baptist wanted to know if he was the Christ, or Elijah or "the Prophet" (1:25). They were looking for one or all of those based on Old Testament promises.

Of course, "the Christ" was foretold throughout the Old Testament, and every Jew was expecting His appearance eventually. "The Prophet" whom they were also expecting was mentioned by Moses in Deuteronomy 18:15: "The Lord your God shall raise up for you a prophet like me from among you, from your countrymen, you shall listen to him." Jesus, of course, was that Prophet (Acts 3:22, 7:37). Concerning their anticipation of "Elijah" coming, God had promised in the last few verses of Malachi that He would send Elijah before the coming of the "great and terrible day of the Lord" (Mal. 4:5). John the Baptist actually fulfilled that prophecy in part, although he apparently didn't realize it. All he knew was that he was fulfilling some verses in Isaiah, a voice crying in the wilderness, preparing the way for the ministry of the Lord Jesus (1:23).

Most importantly, John the Baptist knew that Jesus was "the Lamb of God who takes away the sin of the world" (1:25). Taken at face value, any reasonable person would interpret that phrase to mean that Jesus, God's sacrificial Lamb, made atonement for the sins of the whole world, and not just for a limited few (as Calvinists claim). In the book of Revelation, also written by the apostle John, Jesus is referred to as "the Lamb" 28 times, a continual reminder of His sacrificial death for our sins, foreshadowed by every other sacrificial lamb. *His sacrifice for us deserves our sacrifice for Him.*

It is interesting that John knew that he was Christ's forerunner, and he personally knew Jesus (who was his relative through their mothers), but he didn't know that Jesus was the Christ until he saw the Spirit descend upon Him at His baptism (1:33). Yet you may recall that when Jesus came to John to be baptized by him, John objected, saying, ""I have need to be baptized by You, and do You come to me?" (Matt. 3:14). John's objection was not based on the fact that he knew that Jesus was the Christ, but that he knew how holy Jesus was. Remember, Jesus never sinned. Everyone who knew Him knew He was perfect. On that basis, John the Baptist considered himself unworthy to baptize Jesus. As holy as *he* was, he knew Jesus was holier.

Before Andrew became a disciple of Jesus, he was a disciple of John the Baptist. This reveals Andrew's spiritual hunger, and it gives us some insight into why Jesus ultimately called him to be one of the twelve. Like anyone else who has ever truly believed in Christ, Andrew wanted to immediately introduce his family members to Him, and he started with his now-famous brother, Simon Peter. Over the course of the next three years, Simon, which means "reed," a tall grass with a hollow stalk, would become known as Peter, which means "rock." Jesus is changing you too!

Day 199, John 2

John's Gospel consists of twenty-one chapters, of which the first eleven cover about three years of Jesus' earthly ministry, while the last ten cover just the final week of His life. So John's Gospel is heavily focused on what was the most significant aspect of Jesus' life and ministry, that is, His sacrificial death. Even in chapter one we see that focus, as John recorded John the Baptist's declaration that Jesus was the Lamb of God who takes away the sins of the world. He was looking towards the cross. Today's reading continues with that same focus as John recounts the story of Jesus' first miracle.

Note that when Mary informed Jesus that the wedding feast wine had run out, He replied, "Woman, what does that have to do with us? My hour has not yet come" (2:4). That phrase, "My hour has not yet come," is repeatedly found in John's Gospel. As we progress through it, it will become crystal clear that every time Jesus used that phrase, He was making a reference to His future crucifixion and death. The "wine" people truly needed would not be available until Jesus' "hour," the time when He would pour out His blood. When Mary informed Jesus of what appeared to her to be an urgent matter, in Jesus' eyes it was trivial by comparison to everyone's more significant spiritual need, the need to have His blood applied to their sins.

Nevertheless, Jesus met everyone's temporal need for wine in a foreshadowing of what He would do for everyone's spiritual needs on the cross. And may I add that the wine He created that day wasn't made for just a select few, but for everyone who wanted to drink. If each of those six stone water pots held thirty gallons (2:6), Jesus provided enough wine for 2,880 people to each enjoy an eight-ounce glass. There was plenty for everyone, praise God! The former wine was so good that the entire supply was quickly exhausted in spite of the certain planning for that not to occur. But the wine that Jesus made was even better according to the testimony of someone who was well-qualified to make that judgment (2:10).

Incidentally, the wine in Jesus' day was often diluted with water and so low in alcoholic content that it wouldn't even be considered an alcoholic beverage by modern standards. For a person to get drunk on wine, he had to consume a very large quantity. Scripture tells us that drunkenness is a sin, and one that can be damning (1 Cor. 6:9-10). A sure way to avoid ever becoming intoxicated is to avoid drinking any alcohol.

The Passover cleansing of the temple which we read about today was not the same incident recorded in the other three Gospels. This cleansing occurred at the beginning of Jesus' ministry, while the other occurred close to the end of His life.

Why didn't anyone attempt to restrain Him? Possibly Jesus was anointed with a Samson-like strength and no one dared get in His way. Or possibly everyone knew in their consciences that what they had been doing was very wrong, which weakened their wills to resist. Three years later when Jesus cleansed the temple again, He accused the sellers of making God's temple into a den of thieves. So we assume it was not just the money exchanging and selling of animals that bothered Him, but also the fact that people were being cheated in the process. They were taking advantage of sincere seekers of God in order to make a dishonest gain. TV prosperity preachers, take note!

Again we see John's focus on Jesus' journey to the cross, as he recorded Jesus' reply to those who questioned His authority to cleanse the temple. Jesus said, "Destroy this temple, and in three days I will raise it up" (2:19). His statement foreshadowed His death (at the hands of the Jews) and His resurrection.

Jesus "was not entrusting Himself" to "many who believed in His name." Why so? Because "He Himself knew what was in a man" (2:23-25). Jesus knows that, generally speaking, people are deceptive. He knows that many who claim to believe in Him are phony.

Day 200, John 3

Generally speaking, the Gospel writers portray the Pharisees of Christ's time as hard-hearted hypocrites. So it is nice to read about one whose heart was soft. Nicodemus, a prominent Jewish teacher, visited Jesus secretly, and humbly confessed his certainty that Jesus was sent by God. Jesus' miracles demonstrated God's endorsement (3:2). Jesus replied that only those who are born again can "see the kingdom of God" (3:3). All others are blind to it. Jesus also said that only those who are born again will *enter* God's kingdom. He then made it clear to Nicodemus that He wasn't speaking of a physical rebirth, but a spiritual one, something that was done by the Holy Spirit.

Note that Jesus didn't say to Nicodemus, "Of course, none of this has any application until after I've been resurrected." Rather, He seemed to be telling Nicodemus that, even at that present time, only those who were born again could enter heaven. This makes me (and others) suspect that the new birth was available under the old covenant. That is, old covenant people who believed and were forgiven also had their spirits regenerated by the Holy Spirit, even though they were not indwelled by the Holy Spirit as we are under the new covenant. If that was not the case, then those who were saved prior to Jesus' death and resurrection were left spiritually dead in their sins.

Speaking of sinners under the old covenant, Jesus indicated that Moses' lifting of the serpent in the wilderness was analogous to His own "lifting." He was speaking of either His lifting on the cross or His ascension to heaven, or perhaps both.

According to the original story found in Numbers 21, those who had been bitten by a deadly serpent—the consequence of God's wrath upon their sin—could be healed by looking up at a bronze serpent that Moses had attached to a pole. The modern medical emblem of a snake curled around an upright post finds its origin in that very story.

Just as "whoever" among the Israelites looked at the bronze serpent on the pole were saved from death, "whosoever" (3:15 & 16) believes in Jesus "shall not perish, but have eternal life" (3:16). This is based on the wonderful truth that God loves *the world*, which is what Jesus declared, in contrast to what modern Calvinists teach. If "the world" in John 3:16 means "those few who were preselected for salvation" as Calvinists maintain, Jesus was very confused, offering eternal life to "whosoever will believe."

This particular passage is also an excellent illustration of the imperfection of any comparison, including every comparison found in the Bible, and how dangerous it could be if spiritual significance is assigned to every detail of an imperfect comparison. Obviously, a serpent is not a perfect illustration of Jesus. The bronze serpent that Moses lifted is, however, a good representation of Jesus in one sense: all who were dying, but in faith looked to it, lived. And that is where the similarities end. Jesus did not become a spiritual child of Satan on the cross, as some teach based upon this passage. Jesus cried out to His Father with His last breath (Luke 23:46).

John the Baptist, the greatest man who had ever lived according to Jesus (Matt. 11:11), demonstrated an attitude that God hopes to see in all those who serve Him. John's goal was not to build a ministry or become "the foremost evangelist" of his day. He wanted everyone to be less focused on himself and more focused on Jesus (3:30). Praise God.

The inseparable correlation between faith and obedience is affirmed by John the Baptist's statement found in 3:36: "He who *believes* in the Son has eternal life; but he who does not *obey* the Son shall not see life, but the wrath of God abides on him." John used the words *believe* and *obey* synonymously. Those who believe, obey. You can't see the wind, but you can see the effects of it (3:8). Similarly, the effects of our inward rebirth show up on the outside. If the leaves aren't rustling, the wind isn't blowing!

Day 201, John 4

We are apt to picture John the Baptist delivering fiery, convicting messages of righteousness, but picture Jesus quietly teaching small groups of disciples. That picture, however, is unbalanced. Jesus' message was identical to John's: "Repent, for the kingdom of heaven is at hand!" (Matt. 3:2, 4:17). Once Jesus began His ministry, the crowds of people streaming to John to be baptized diminished because so many were streaming to Jesus to be baptized. Jesus' preaching ministry was all about repentance and baptizing the repentant (4:1-2). His ministry was very similar to John's.

In Jesus' day, most Jews hated Samaritans (and vice versa). The Samaritans were a mixed race, part Jew and part Gentile, a product of the Assyrian captivity of the 10 northern tribes of Israel some 700 years earlier. Because the Jews forbade the Samaritans to worship at the temple in Jerusalem, they established their own temple and religious services on Mount Gerizim.

Jesus, not one to follow culture's lead, took time for a woman who was hated by other Jews, had suffered the rejection of divorce five times (and who was very possibly despised among her own people because of it), and was now living in an immoral relationship. What a lesson we can learn from Jesus' love from this story of "the Bad Samaritan!" The church should reach out to foreigners and have no bigotry. The church should oppose divorce but love divorced people, and hate immorality but love immoral people.

We can also learn something about sharing the gospel from observing Jesus in this story. He first caught the Samaritan woman's attention by His love. She was shocked that He, a Jew, would even speak to her. Who would be shocked if you spoke to them?

Second, He used her current circumstance to create a bridge to a spiritual conversation. She was interested in drawing some water. Jesus was also interested in a drink, and asked for water from her. Yet He knew that He possessed some "water" that she needed, and He told her. That got the ball rolling.

She probably considered Him to be a little crazy at that point, and just to humor Him, asked for some of the living water that He was offering so that she would no longer be thirsty or have to draw water from a well. But her patronizing attitude quickly changed when He mentioned her five former husbands and her live-in boyfriend. This is the third point for us to remember: Before people will repent, they must be brought under conviction for their sin.

Once under conviction, the woman quickly turned religious and tried to divert the conversation away from herself to a contemporary theological difference between Jews and Samaritans about the proper place to worship. Jesus briefly addressed the issue and used it to bring the conversation back to what was important, revealing Himself as the Messiah. She left her water pot and hurried back into the city to tell others about Him. Missionary Jesus had crossed a culture, and a foreign revival had begun.

Notice that, during the old covenant, Jesus was offering someone "living water," and a "well of water springing up to eternal life" (4:14), water which may well represent the Holy Spirit according to 7:38-39. That makes me wonder once again if the new birth was available under the old covenant.

When Jesus told the nobleman to go his way because his son lived, the Bible says that he "believed the word that Jesus spoke to him and started off" (4:50). If we examine the story closely, we see more evidence of his faith. He probably could have returned that same day to Capernaum, because it was only about one o'clock in the afternoon, and Capernaum was only about sixteen miles from Cana. But he rested in his faith. There was no need to rush home to see how his son was doing. He believed, so he took his time and arrived home the next day.

If we're trusting God, we also don't need to be in a hurry or check to see "if" God's promise is coming to pass. Faith is a rest. Are you resting today?

Day 202, John 5

Obviously people were genuinely being healed when an angel periodically troubled the waters of the Pool of Bethesda: Otherwise there would not have been so many sick people waiting for the waters to move. I am of the persuasion that God, who periodically sent the angel, had more in mind than the occasional healing of one person. Israel's covenant with God included divine healing. He promised that if they would serve Him, He would "remove sickness" from their midst (Ex. 15:26, 23:25; Deut. 7:15). But, as Jesus lamented in 4:48, "Unless you people see signs and wonders, you simply will not believe." So God mercifully performs signs to provoke people to believe, and He sometimes heals people who have no faith. Those kinds of healings fall under the category of "gifts of healings" which operate as the Spirit wills (1 Cor. 12:1-11).

Those who lost the periodic race to the troubled waters of Bethesda should have been encouraged by every demonstration of God's healing power that occurred before their eyes. They should have wondered, "Is God trying to convey to us that He delights in periodically making all of us compete in a sickening race in which the majority of us come out as losers? Or is He trying to encourage us to believe that He is still in the healing business?"

One day, the God who periodically sent an angel to the Bethesda Pool showed up Himself in the form of Jesus—and healed one man. Should we conclude from this that it was not God's will for the others at the pool to be healed? That would be an unwarranted assumption in light of the many stories we've already read in the Gospels in which Jesus credited the faith of those He healed as being the reason for their miracle. Had they not had faith, they would not have been healed, even though it was God's will for them to be healed, as proved by the fact that He did heal them. All of this is to say that, if someone else is healed by God, it should encourage, not discourage, those of us who still need healing. If God forgives one person, is it right to conclude that the reason is because God singled out that person for forgiveness at the exclusion of others? Certainly not.

Another spiritual lesson from today's reading is that sin can open the door to God's judgment in the form of sickness. Jesus told the crippled man whom He had healed, "Do not sin anymore, so that nothing worse happens to you" (5:14). The implication is that his former sickness was the consequence of his sin, and if he didn't repent, he might find himself suffering something even worse.

The ultimate lesson that everyone should learn from all those whom Jesus healed (and even raised from the dead) is that Jesus is the one who will one day heal everyone of whatever killed them when He resurrects their dead bodies. This is not just true for believers, but for unbelievers as well, as Jesus declared in today's reading. Note that those who will experience a "resurrection of life" will be those who did "good deeds" (5:29). Those who experience a "resurrection of judgment" will be those who committed "evil deeds" (5:29). We are saved by faith, but those who believe are characterized by good deeds.

Other scriptures teach us that not everyone will be resurrected at the same time. At the rapture of the church, all those who have died in Christ will be resurrected and given glorified bodies, as Christ has now. It won't be until the end of the millennial reign of Christ that the unrighteous will be resurrected to stand at the final judgment (Rev. 20:5).

How tragic was the blindness of the Jews who debated with Jesus and rejected Him, refusing to accept the testimony of Moses (5:45-47), John the Baptist (5:33-35), and the greatest testimony of all, that of God the Father, who endorsed Christ through His many miracles (5:36-37). The rejection of Him was due to their loving men's approval more than God's approval (5:44). May we never forget who is on the throne!

Day 203, John 6

Jesus' words are not always easy to understand, and today's reading is proof. What we want to be careful of is that we don't take any of His words and extract a doctrine that contradicts the rest of Scripture. Those who are always attempting to persuade others of their aberrant doctrines rely heavily on Jesus' difficult-to-understand or vague statements as their "proof-texts."

John 6 is a favorite of Calvinists, for example, because they find a few verses that seemingly support a few of their five cardinal doctrines. But they must exalt those verses at the expense of many other verses in which Christ is quoted saying things that contradict Calvinist doctrine.

An example of this would be John 3:37. There Jesus said, "All that the Father gives Me will come to Me." "See," Calvinists say, "God chooses people for salvation before they are saved, and those whom He chooses He gives to Jesus, and then they come to Jesus." Calvinists read so much more into Jesus' words than what He said. If I said, "All the new employees whom the boss gives to me will come to me," does that prove that the new employees had nothing to do with the fact that they work for the boss? Of course not. The boss can only give to me those new employees who first applied for a job! What Jesus said in 3:37 does not nullify individual free will in salvation.

Within the context of John 6, it is obvious that Jesus was offering salvation to everyone in the crowd that day. He said to them, "Do not work for the food which perishes, but for the food which endures to *eternal life, which the Son of Man will give to you*" (6:27). Jesus undeniably offered eternal life to all of them.

In His very next sentence, Jesus told them that the means to eternal life was faith in Him (6:29), again implying His universal offer. But, quite amazingly, the same people who had eaten a miraculous meal the day before then asked Him for a sign in order to believe in Him! And they mentioned how Moses had provided manna in the wilderness. They wanted more food!

Jesus reminded them that it was not Moses who provided them bread the day before, but it was His Father who gave them "the true bread out of heaven" (6:32). Clearly, that "true bread" was Himself, and take note that Jesus said to the unbelieving crowd that His Father was giving *them* that true bread (6:32). The Father was giving Jesus to all of them so that they could have eternal life by believing in Him. In fact, Jesus declared that He was the true bread who came from heaven to "give life," not just to them, but "to the *world*" (6:33). That's everyone.

The crowd then asked Jesus for that true bread, not understanding that it was Him (6:34). So Jesus explained Himself again: "*I* am the bread of life; he who comes to *Me* will not hunger, and he who believes in *Me* will never thirst" (6:35). Again, His universal offer of salvation is implied. Then He said, "But I said to you that you have seen Me, and yet do not believe" (6:36). Clearly, He expected them to believe in Him. But they didn't, and He found fault with them for it. This sure doesn't sound like Calvinism!

Finally, in the very next verse, He said what Calvinists rip from its context: "All that the Father gives Me will come to Me, and the one who comes to Me I will certainly not cast out" (6:37). Was Jesus contracting everything He had just said? No. Obviously, those whom the Father gives to Jesus are those who believe in Him. He only grants *believers* the privilege of coming to Jesus (6:65). That anyone can believe in Him is underscored even more in the verses that follow (6:40, 47, 50-51, 54, 58).

No unregenerate person can come to Jesus unless the Father draws him (6:44). That does not prove that God only draws a few. Jesus later said, "If I am lifted up from the earth, will draw all men to Myself" (John 12:32).

Day 204, John 7

For a second time in John's Gospel we read of Jesus making reference to the fact that His time, or hour (as in 2:4), had not yet come (7:6, 8). He obviously didn't mean that His time hadn't come to attend the Feast of Booths, because He ultimately did attend it. Rather, He was once again speaking of the hour of His atoning sacrifice. Jesus knew that the Jewish leaders in Jerusalem "were seeking to kill Him" (7:1), but it wasn't time for Him to die, so it was prudent for Him to go to the feast secretly.

When we read the third reference in John's Gospel to Jesus' hour which "had not yet come" (7:30), it becomes even more clear that it was a reference to the time of His crucifixion. John wrote, "They were seeking therefore to seize Him; and no man laid his hand on Him, because His hour had not yet come" (7:30).

Each day during the Feast of Booths, the priest would gather water from the Pool of Siloam in Jerusalem and pour it out at the altar of the temple. It was with this ceremony as a backdrop that Jesus cried out, "If any man is thirsty, let him come to Me and drink. He who believes in Me, as the Scripture said, 'From his innermost being shall flow rivers of living water'" (7:37-38). This was yet *another* obvious universal invitation to everyone who is spiritually thirsty.

John said that the water Jesus spoke of was representative of the Holy Spirit (7:39). It would seem safe to think that the "living water," of which Jesus spoke to the woman at the well of Samaria (4:4-29), and which He said would become "a well of water springing up to eternal life" (4:14) within whomever He gave it, also represented the Holy Spirit.

Believing this is so, some thus deduce that these two "water scriptures" illustrate a comparison between being born of the Spirit and being filled with (or baptized in) the Spirit. When a person is born again, the Holy Spirit indwells him, becoming "a well of water springing up to eternal life" (4:14). But when a believer is baptized in the Spirit, the waters of the Holy Spirit do not just reside within him, but flow from him. He is "clothed with power from on high" (Luke 24:49) and empowered to be Christ's witness.

Others think that the second "water scripture" is also a reference to being born again, as Jesus offered the "rivers of living water" to "anyone [who] is thirsty" and to anyone who believes in Him (7:37-38). Also, we know that the fruit of the Spirit flows from every person who is truly born again.

Regardless of which interpretation is correct, I am persuaded that every person who is born of the Spirit can also be baptized in the Holy Spirit simply by asking the Lord with faith. Based on Jesus' promise in Mark 16:17 and the historical record in the book of Acts (Acts 2:4; 10:44-46; 19:2-6), the initial evidence of that baptism is speaking in other tongues. This is not something just for Pentecostal or charismatic Christians, but for all who believe in Jesus, and it has been experienced and enjoyed by millions. That being said, those believers who have not enjoyed the experience are not lesser Christians in any sense.

We gather from our reading today that Jesus was the center of controversy in Jerusalem. Bible Jesus *is* controversial, whereas American Jesus gets along so well with everyone. Just today I read an article in our local newspaper about a man who walked into a fitness club just a few miles from where I live, turned out the lights in a women's aerobic class, and then indiscriminately started shooting two handguns. He killed three women and himself. He wanted to kill many more. His pastor was quoted as saying that he was sure the murderer was in heaven because he once professed faith in Christ, and the Bible teaches that once a person is saved, he is always saved. There's American Jesus for you. He even gets along quite well with mass murderers.

Day 205, John 8

It seems that the naked partner of the woman who was caught in the act of adultery "somehow" got away from the scribes and Pharisees. I wonder how? I also wonder what Jesus wrote with his finger in the dust before that crowd of hypocrites. Some speculate that it was the names of the Pharisees' girlfriends or the women in their fantasies!

Speaking of the fantasies of Pharisees, they were certain that they had laid a trap for Jesus that would force Him to contradict the Mosaic Law, thus proving that He was not from God. Jesus, however, laid a trap within their trap, which exposed their own hypocrisy. And He left all of us with an unforgettable object lesson about guilty people who condemn others. Jesus once said that the sin of lust is equivalent to adultery within one's heart, and so it is fairly safe to assume that a group of adulterers were condemning a woman for adultery.

Beyond those things, Jesus played the part of God perfectly in this incident (as you might expect). The mercy He showed to the adulterous woman is the same mercy that God shows to all sinners. He does not immediately condemn them for their sin—even though He would have every right to do so. Rather, He mercifully warns them to repent and gives them time to do it. Take note that if that adulterous woman did not heed Jesus' admonition, He did condemn her when she ultimately stood before Him after her death. His Word promises that no adulterer will inherit God's kingdom (1 Cor. 6:9-10). That is why He told her, "Go and sin no more."

Incidentally, what was true in about AD 30 was also true from the time the Mosaic Law was given. Although God's Law legislated the stoning of adulterers, no adulterers or adulterers-at-heart ever had the right to stone an adulterer. And is it possible that such a brutal means of capital punishment was mandated in the Mosaic Law to reveal God's repulsion regarding the sin of adultery as well as His love for those whose spouses are unfaithful, and to motivate everyone—those caught and uncaught—to repent?

During the Feast of Tabernacles, which had just ended the day before, four great candelabrum were lit at dusk representing the pillar of fire that led Israel through the wilderness. It was with this backdrop that Jesus declared, "I am the Light of the world; he who follows Me will not walk in the darkness, but will have the Light of life" (8:12). How it must have grieved Him to observe those who were engrossed over some giant candelabrum while He, the Light of the world, stood in their midst. Notice once again His clear *universal* invitation to salvation.

John wrote that, as Jesus taught in the temple, "many came to believe in Him" (8:30). Jesus then said "to those Jews who had believed Him, 'If you continue in My word, then you are truly disciples of Mine; and you will know the truth, and the truth will make you free'" (8:31-32). This indicates that, in Jesus' mind, true believers are disciples, and there are not two separate classes of Christians consisting of believers and more-highly-committed believers called disciples, as is often taught today. If one is a true believer, one is a disciple of Christ. If one is not a disciple of Christ, one is not a true believer in Christ.

Notice also from this same passage that Jesus did not assume that everyone who professed to believe in Him actually did believe in Him. The test was their repentance. If they continued "in His word" they would be progressively set free from sin, and that would prove that they were truly His disciples. By this criteria, it is obvious that many people who profess to believe in Jesus are fooling themselves.

Finally, there is no doubt from today's reading that Jesus believed He was God's eternal and divine Son. He said, "Before Abraham was born, I am" (8:58). "I AM" was a name God told Moses to call Him (Ex. 3:14). The Jews recognized this and consequently tried to stone Jesus right then.

Day 206, John 9

Did God preordain that this man of whom we read today be born blind so that Jesus could one day heal him? That seems to be what the text is saying in 9:3-4.

There is, however, one other possible interpretation. There were no capital letters and periods in the original Greek that would indicate where sentences started and ended. So translators do their best when adding them. Notice also that the words "it was" in 9:3 are italicized (in the NASB), which indicates that they were not in the original text and were also added by the translators. Thus 9:3-4 could be translated, "It was neither that this man sinned, nor his parents. But, in order that the works of God might be displayed in him, we must work the works of Him who sent as long as it is day."

If this translation is correct, then it could be said that Jesus fully answered His disciples' question. They asked if the man or his parents' sin was responsible for the birth defect. Jesus said it was neither. Then, He implied that it was not the work of God that the man was born blind, saying, "But, in order that *the works of God might be displayed in him...*" The idea is that healing blindness is God's work, and making people blind is not His work.

If it was not the work of God that the man was born blind, then we could pin it on the devil, as many would like to do. That does not, however, alleviate every struggle we might have with this passage, as it still begs the questions, "If Satan is responsible for birth defects, why doesn't God stop him?" And, "If Satan does possess that ability, why does he afflict some and not others?" Ultimately, we all struggle with why some children are born with birth defects, just as Jesus' disciples. They had narrowed down the potential explanations to two, of which both, according to Jesus, were wrong. If the man's own sins were the reason he was born blind, then he would have sinned while still in his mother's womb. And if his parents were the reason, then God was punishing a child for his parents' sins, something He forbade Israel to do and something He said He does not do (Deut. 24:16; Ezek. 18:20).

God once said to Moses, "Who has made man's mouth? Or who makes him dumb or deaf, or seeing or blind? Is it not I, the Lord?" (Ex. 4:11). Yet God did not explain to Moses why He made some deaf or blind. So we are still left wondering. I have wondered if God makes some deaf or blind to test the compassion of those of us who can hear and see. Jesus said, "When you give a reception, invite the poor, the crippled, the lame, the blind, and you will be blessed, since they do not have the means to repay you; for you will be repaid at the resurrection of the righteous" (Luke 14:13-14). For this reason, the ministry of *Heaven's Family* has a special fund that exists just to serve very poor and handicapped believers in developing nations.

Although we don't have all the answers, we can rejoice that Jesus healed this man who was born blind. It resulted in his salvation. We can also rejoice in the many others whom Jesus healed during His earthly ministry and throughout the last 2,000 years, and we can rejoice for His many promises regarding healing found in Scripture. The Bible says that Jesus bore everyone's sicknesses and diseases (Is. 53:4-5; Matt. 8:17).

What an interesting contrast we observe between the former blind beggar and the spiritually blind Pharisees. The simple understanding of average people often trumps the educated reasonings of the spiritual elite. I love his short sermon to the Pharisees:

> Well, here is an amazing thing, that you do not know where He is from, and yet He opened my eyes. We know that God does not hear sinners; but if anyone is God-fearing, and does His will, He hears him....If this man were not from God, He could do nothing." (9:30-34).

Day 207, John 10

Jesus' shepherd and sheep analogy was much more understandable to His contemporary audience than to those of us who are unfamiliar with shepherding in general, and particularly to shepherding in Israel 2,000 years ago. So here is a little help:

First, when several flocks are grazing in one area or are sharing a corral, it might appear that the shepherds would never be able to sort out which sheep belong to which shepherd. All the shepherds need to do, however, is call their sheep, and the flocks immediately divide and follow their respective shepherds. Sheep know their shepherd's voice. If a stranger calls them, they will not follow him. Jesus' simple point was that those who belong to Him follow Him. Those who don't follow Him are not His sheep.

Second, shepherds kept their flocks safe at night by gathering them into corrals built of stone fences. There were no gates at the openings of those corrals, and so one shepherd would lie down across his corral's opening for the night, thus actually becoming "the door" of the sheepfold. That shepherd was the "doorkeeper" of 10:3. Jesus' point was that the only way anyone can gain entrance to salvation and to the sheepfold is through Him, "the door."

Moreover, those who attempted to gain access to the sheepfold by not going through the "door," obviously had ulterior motives. They were sheep thieves. So anyone who tries to infiltrate God's flock by some means other than through Jesus is selfishly motivated. Obviously, false teachers are in that category.

Third, a good shepherd sincerely cared for his sheep. At times he had to protect them from wolves. A temporary or hireling shepherd, however, would run at the first sign of trouble. The "hirelings" in Jesus' analogy were representative of the scribes and Pharisees, who had no real concern for the people. But Jesus gave His life for His sheep!

As with all of Jesus' metaphorical words, His shepherd/sheep analogy has been exploited by those who hope to find biblical justification for their doctrines that contradict so many other scriptures.

For example, Jesus' promise that no one will be able to snatch His sheep out of His Father's hand (10:28) is a favorite of those who promote the idea of unconditional eternal security. Notice, however, that Jesus defined His sheep in the preceding verse as those who follow Him (10:27). Certainly no man can steal the salvation of a sheep who follows Jesus, but any of us can stop following Jesus if we desire to no longer be one of His sheep.

Remember that every analogy is imperfect. In the analogy we just read, Jesus is both the door and the good shepherd. We must be careful that we don't read more into any parable or analogy than what was intended by the speaker.

Calvinists often cite Jesus' words to the unbelieving Jews, "But you do not believe because you are not of My sheep" (10:26), in order to buttress their idea that people don't believe because they haven't been preselected for salvation by God. This is grasping at straws. Jesus was simply communicating that His sheep are characterized by their belief in Him. If I said to a group of people, "You don't believe I can bench press 500 pounds because you are not on my team," does that prove that I didn't want them on my team? No, I was simply expressing that those on my team believe.

Another phrase in Jesus' sheep/shepherd analogy in which the greater context is ignored is that about the thief who "comes only to steal and kill and destroy" (10:10). This is not a reference to Satan, but to false spiritual leaders (10:1, 8). This phrase is often quoted to prove that anything that kills or destroys is of Satan and not of God. There are, however, numerous scriptures that attribute destroying and killing to God. One is James 4:12: "There is only one Lawgiver and Judge, the One who is able to save and to destroy" See also Gen. 38:7; Ex. 13:15; 1 Sam. 2:6; 1 Cor. 3:17; 2 Pet. 3:10-12; Jude 5. Let's stay balanced!

Day 208, John 11

It is interesting that when John first mentions Mary in today's reading, he identifies her as "the Mary who anointed the Lord with ointment, and wiped His feet with her hair" (11:2), an incident that hasn't occurred yet in the chronology of John's Gospel (12:1-3). John assumed that his readers already knew of that incident. It was *that* Mary, not any of the other three women named Mary mentioned in the Gospels—Jesus' mother, Mary Magdalene, and the mother of James—whose brother Lazarus, was sick.

Concerning Lazarus' sickness, Jesus said that it was "not unto death, but for the glory of God" (11:4). Obviously, Jesus was not saying that God was glorified by Lazarus' sickness, but rather, that God would be glorified by Lazarus' healing and resurrection. I mention this only because we occasionally hear a sick Christian claim that his or her sickness is like Lazarus' sickness, one that glorifies God. God is not glorified by sickness, but by healing.

Notice that even though Jesus loved Lazarus (11:3, 5), He didn't prevent Lazarus from becoming sick. By the same token, there is no reason to think that sickness is an indication that Jesus doesn't love you. Your sickness could, perhaps, be permitted by Him as a test of your faith. In that case, your sickness could also then be said to be "for the glory of God," if you, like Lazarus, are ultimately healed. So trust God!

Speaking of tests of faith, Mary and Martha certainly had their faith tested. Jesus deliberately delayed His coming to them when He received their news of Lazarus' sickness. It is more difficult to believe that someone is going to come back to life after being dead four days than it is to believe that someone who is ill will recover. Martha, however, certainly expressed faith that Jesus' arrival was not too late (11:21-22).

Mary and Martha both had their faith tested again when Jesus ordered that the stone across Lazarus' tomb be removed. Martha reacted with concern that Lazarus' body would stink. Jesus reassured her that if God could raise her dead brother, He could also take care of little things like bad odors! (My paraphrase.)

I would love to see a video of this entire incident, but just imagining it tickles my brain. When Jesus commanded Lazarus to "come forth," a mummy appeared at the cave's entrance. Lazarus was "bound hand and foot with wrappings" and even "his face was wrapped around with a cloth" (11:44). There is a good possibility that his legs were wrapped together, meaning that he crawled or perhaps supernaturally floated to the cave's entrance. Imagine the reaction of the multitude (12:17) who were there! If the entire Bible consisted of just this single chapter in John, it would be enough to convince any open-minded person that Jesus is the Son of God who is offering eternal life to everyone who will believe in Him. Yet, amazingly, some who witnessed what was perhaps the greatest miracle of all human history up until that time ran to deliver a negative report to Jesus' greatest antagonists, the Pharisees (11:46). More amazing, however, is the fact that this miracle is nothing compared to what is coming in the future, when Jesus will call forth *every* dead body in the world from their tombs (5:28-29). Jesus was just warming up at Lazarus' tomb!

If you aren't good at memorizing Bible verses, you are in luck today if you still would like to give it a try by memorizing John 11:35: "Jesus wept." That is the Bible's shortest verse.

Why did Jesus weep if He knew Lazarus would be raised from the dead? I wonder about that. Since Jesus was the most compassionate person to ever walk the face of the earth, perhaps He wept simply because He was among other weeping people. Paul wrote that we should "weep with those who weep" (Rom. 12:15). Or perhaps Jesus wept for Lazarus because He knew he was going to have to return to this sinful world after spending four glorious days in paradise. Going from earth to heaven is quite a joy. I understand the return trip, however, can be quite depressing!

Day 209, John 12

Jesus lived about 33 years on the earth, yet almost half of John's Gospel focuses on His final week. In John's thinking, that week was the most significant week of Christ's life and of human history. It began with Jesus and His disciples coming out of their wilderness hideaway to make their way towards Jerusalem. They would have been journeying with tens of thousands of other Jews who were streaming there for the Passover, a perfect cover. Two miles outside of Jerusalem, they stopped and enjoyed a meal in the home of Mary, Martha and Lazarus (whom had recently been resurrected).

When we compare the specific details of Mary's anointing of Jesus with similar incidents mentioned in all three Synoptic Gospels involving unnamed women, we must conclude that they are not all the same incident (Matt. 26:6-13; Mark 14:3-9; Luke 7:37-39). John's account highlights Judas' hypocritical and deceptive complaint. Jesus' reply to him—"The poor you always have with you, but you do not always have Me (12:8)—could only be considered to be words of an incredible egotist, *unless* Jesus were not God in the flesh. It is, of course, impossible for God to be proud, as He could never think more highly of Himself than He should.

Judas was a perfect example of a person who outwardly appeared righteous but who was inwardly corrupt. If we didn't know the whole story, some might say, "Now that Judas, he's the kind of man we'd like to have as our pastor. He's a person of convictions, and isn't afraid to challenge even the denomination's top man in his concern for social justice!" Things aren't always as they appear to be. Judas was a lover of money, and for that reason he betrayed Jesus.

Did you notice two more of Jesus' "hour statements" in today's reading (12:23, 27)? In one of them, Jesus revealed that the ultimate purpose of His life was to die, saying, "For this purpose I came to this hour" (12:27). He compared His death to the planting of a dead grain, from which a new plant grows and produces more grains. Jesus' death, burial and resurrection would result in the spiritual rebirth of many people. Moreover, His death and resurrection would serve as an object lesson for all who desire eternal life. They, too, must die, dying to their love of the world (12:25). John later wrote in his first epistle: "If anyone loves the world, the love of the Father is not in him" (1 John 2:15).

Jesus' sacrificial death would also result in "the ruler of this world" being "cast out" (12:31). Obviously, Satan has been given permission by God to rule over all human rebels. He is a subordinate instrument of God's wrath against them. By virtue of Jesus' atoning sacrifice, however, God's wrath was propitiated, and thus Satan's dominion is broken over everyone who repents and believes. Satan will ultimately be fully "cast out" from the earth when it suits God's purpose. That, too, will be due to Jesus' atonement on the cross, whereby God can righteously pardon sinners.

We read previously Jesus' statement that no one could come to Him unless the Father drew him (6:44). We read today His promise to draw all people to Himself if He would be lifted up on the cross (12:32). Obviously, if people are being *drawn* then they are not being forced, and they can obviously resist His *drawing*.

Just as Paul, in his letter to the Romans, indicated that God had hardened the hearts of the Jews, so John reiterates the same idea in 12:39-40 quoting Isaiah. By themselves, these few verses could lead someone to believe that God didn't want those Jews whom He hardened to be saved. Yet there are 31,215 other verses in the Bible to balance our understanding, and some are found in this very chapter! God is not *arbitrarily* hardening some hearts and softening others. Jesus came to "save the world" (12:47), and the same sun that melts wax, hardens clay. By His act of drawing all, God softens some and hardens others.

Day 210, John 13

Jesus said that the greatest person is the servant of all (Matt. 23:11), and so we should expect that Jesus, who is the greatest, would also be the greatest servant. Today's story of Him washing His disciples' feet certainly confirms that. However, Jesus' greatest act of servitude was His death for us on the cross: "The Son of Man did not come to be served, but to serve, and to give His life a ransom for many" (Matt. 20:28).

Also being the greatest teacher who ever lived, Jesus knew that the best lesson is not a lecture but an example. It boggles our minds that the Lord of heaven would humble Himself to wash the feet of 12 men, but we must not forget that He did it not only to serve them, but to illustrate what He expected of them. Jesus wants all of His followers to serve each other, but I think that it is significant that He specifically commanded the future *leaders* of His church to wash one another's feet. The reason that the church is so divided today is because its leaders are so divided. How much good might come out of monthly meetings of pastors who gathered just to wash each other's feet?

Of course, foot washing was a cultural practice in Israel in Jesus' time, because people wore sandals and traveled on dusty roads used by both animals and people. Washing a guest's feet was a common courtesy, usually done by servants. I am not persuaded that Jesus expects Christians of all times and cultures to literally wash each other's feet, but I'm sure He wants us to humbly serve one another. Literal foot washing, however, certainly can't hurt to that end! If you've been involved in a foot washing, you know that is true. Jesus promised, "If you know these things, you are blessed if you do them" (13:17).

I once heard of a church that, tragically, split over the issue of foot washing. Some believed that foot washing should be literally practiced, and some thought that they should humbly serve one another in other practical and culturally-relevant ways. They couldn't agree on how to love each other, so they split, demonstrating to the world how they hated each other.

Like Peter, if the Lord doesn't wash us, we have no part with Him (13:8). Only He can forgive us and clean us up! And also like Peter, once we've experienced the Lord's initial full washing, thereafter we still need Him to wash us at times. That is the sanctification process, and that is the reason we can pray every day, "Forgive us our debts," as Jesus taught us (Matt. 6:12).

I wonder what was going through Jesus' mind as He washed Judas' feet? Probably the same thing that goes through His mind every day as He shows His love for those all over the world who hate Him. Incidentally, isn't it amazing that when Jesus announced to His disciples that one of them would betray Him, none of them suspected Judas (13:22)? He played the part of a follower of Christ quite well for more than three years. He was, apparently, not one who could be "known by his fruits," at least, not until his act of betrayal.

Although the devil put into Judas' heart the idea to betray Jesus (13:2), Judas was a free moral agent acting on his own volition. This is proven by the fact that he, by his own free will, decided to follow Jesus for over three years, did not betray Him earlier, and felt remorse afterwards to the point of committing suicide. Satan presented the temptation to betray Christ for profit, Judas weighed it, wrestled with it, yielded to it, and ultimately regretted it. Judas was neither God's or Satan's robot.

We've already read the self-denying requirements for one to be a true disciple of Jesus in Luke 14:25-33. Today we learn that the mark that distinguishes the true disciple before the world is his love for other disciples. Thus we should all ask ourselves, "As the world looks at me, do they see me as a person who loves those who love Jesus?"

Day 211, John 14

The eleven were naturally fearful of what was about to happen and confused. Those of us who know the end of the story can hardly appreciate the tension of the moment. The disciples only knew that Jesus was about to depart from them, which was cause for hearts to be troubled. So with words that comfort us 2,000 years later, Jesus reassured them that everything was going to be OK. He was going to His Father to prepare a place for them, and He would ultimately return to personally escort them there (14:3). In the interim, He would send a marvelous helper and teacher to live in them, the Holy Spirit, who would be equivalent to having both the Father and Son living in them (14:16-17, 23).

Beyond those things, Jesus granted the eleven His supernatural peace, the peace that Paul wrote "surpasses all comprehension" (Phil 4:7). But their faith was a factor, and so He exhorted them: "Believe in God, believe also in Me" (14:3). He meant more than just to believe that He or God existed. It was an exhortation to trust both the Father and Jesus that everything was under their control.

Jesus told the eleven that He was in the Father and the Father was in Him (14:10-11). He also stated that if we've seen Him, we've seen the Father (14:9). Notice, however, that He didn't say that He *was* the Father. The Father and Son are two distinct persons, but are so much alike that if you know one, you know the other. For that reason, when you hear a preacher say that many Christians know Jesus but don't know the Father, you know that he hasn't done his homework.

What did Jesus mean when He said that those who believe in Him would do the same works as He did and greater works (14:12)? Some think Jesus was referring to the entire body of Christ corporately doing the same and greater works than He did. Some think it means every believer should be doing the same and greater works than Jesus, yet I've noticed those who say that aren't coming anywhere close to doing the same works Jesus did. In fact, even the original apostles never performed certain miracles that Jesus did, much less greater miracles.

Most of the miracles recorded in the book of Acts were done by apostles or evangelists, not ordinary believers. For this reason, I suspect that the promise of believers doing greater works will have its complete fulfillment in the future world. We know that the nine gifts of the Spirit are referred to in Scripture as "the powers of *the age to come*" (Heb. 6:5). Through Isaiah, Jesus prophetically spoke of believers during His millennial reign, saying, "I and the children whom the Lord has given me are for *signs and wonders* in Israel from the Lord of hosts who dwells on Mount Zion" (Is. 8:18; compare with Heb. 2:11-13).

This is not to say that miracles and gifts of the Spirit are not for today, but that not all believers should expect to walk on water, raise the dead and multiply food.

Three times in today's reading Jesus reinforced the connection between loving and obeying Him.

> If you love Me, you will keep My commandments.... He who has My commandments and keeps them, it is he who loves Me; and he who loves Me shall be loved by My Father, and I will love him, and will disclose Myself to him....If anyone loves Me, he will keep My word; and My Father will love him, and We will come to him, and make Our abode with him (14:15, 21, 23).

How often we list excuses for not obeying Jesus, yet how many of us will simply admit that the major cause is our lack of love for Him?

Notice also that Jesus only promised that He and the Father would come to live in those who love Him and keep His word (14:23). So there must be an initial repentance to even begin a relationship with the Lord. The idea that we can "accept Jesus as Savior" yet reject Him as Lord has no biblical foundation.

Day 212, John 15

As with all analogies, Jesus' analogy of the vine and branches is imperfect, as grape vines and vinedressers are not wholly analogous to a believer's relationship with Jesus and the Father. Yet Jesus obviously saw some characteristics of grape vines and vinedressers that served well to illustrate some important spiritual truths. We only need to be cautious that we don't "push the parable too far."

It seems safe to assume that only believers are comparable to branches in Jesus' vine, as only those "in Christ" can bear fruit that stems from "abiding in the vine." Jesus, of course, was not speaking to unbelievers, but to His closest disciples, telling them that they were the branches.

Just like a vinedresser, the Father wants to see fruit on the branches. Those that are bearing fruit, He prunes, cutting away what is undesirable to Him in order that the branch might bear more fruit. That is God at work in the process of sanctification.

Those that are not bearing fruit, He cuts off. Because this is a metaphor, we can't be entirely sure if this "cutting off" speaks of the judgment of physical death in which a believer still maintains his eternal salvation, or if it speaks of a forfeiture of salvation all together. Of course, Jesus exhorted His closest disciples to "abide in [Him]" (15:4) that they might bear fruit, and then went on to warn them, "If anyone does not abide in Me, he is thrown away as a branch, and dries up; and they gather them, and cast them into the fire, and they are burned" (15:6). This certainly sounds like a warning of hell, and if the branch that removes itself becomes fruitless and is cast into hell, it would seem odd that a fruitless branch that is removed by the Father would inherit eternal life.

In any case, after reading John 15, no one can argue that our bearing fruit is a trivial matter to God. The reason He chose and appointed us was so that we could "bear fruit," and so our "fruit would remain" (15:16).

Take note of the role of prayer in the matter of bearing fruit. Jesus promised:

> If you abide in Me, and My words abide in you, ask whatever you wish, and it shall be done for you. By this is My Father glorified, that you bear much fruit, and so prove to be My disciples" (15:7-8; see also 15:16).

When Jesus encouraged His disciples to "ask whatever they wished," He wasn't thinking that they would be asking for material treasures to lay up on earth, as that would indicate that they were not abiding in Him and His words were not abiding in them. Jesus was thinking that their supreme desire would be holiness, and so His encouragement to "ask whatever they wished" was supposed to encourage them to pray for what would make them more fruitful. God *always* answers those kinds of prayers!

Jesus' words, "If you keep My commandments, you will abide in My love," does not sounds like a promise of "unconditional love" that is so often touted in Christian circles, but of *conditional* love, and so it is. God loves everyone conditionally. We are Jesus' friends *if* we do what He commands us (15:14). If God loved everyone unconditionally, then no one would be ultimately cast into hell. What many refer to as "God's unconditional love," would be better termed, "God's temporary mercy." God loves everyone with a merciful love, but that is temporary for those who don't repent.

True Christians are loved and hated—loved by each other and hated by the world. How strange and confusing it can be to find yourself hated by "Christians!" Take comfort knowing that Christians who hate Christians aren't Christians. (You can quote me on that.) "Christians" who hate Christians are every bit as deceived as the scribes and Pharisees of Jesus' day who professed to love God but hated Jesus (15:23-24). This was also greatly emphasized in John's first epistle, where he repeatedly told his readers that love for each other is a litmus test of genuine faith in Jesus. Heaven is for lovers!

Day 213, John 16

Once again, it is difficult for those of us who know how the story ends to appreciate the disciples' confusion over what was about to occur. They were full of sorrow (16:6, 20) when they should have been rejoicing, believing that Jesus was going to His Father (John 14:28), and trusting that they would soon see Him again as He promised. Moreover, Jesus told them it was to their advantage that He go; otherwise the Holy Spirit would not come to them (16:7). His encouraging words apparently had little effect on their disposition, yet He was still certain that their sorrow would be turned to joy (16:20, 22). God is in the business of giving "beauty for ashes, the oil of joy for mourning, [and] the garment of praise for the spirit of heaviness" (Is. 61:3). How often we are like the eleven, weeping when we should be dancing!

Jesus promised that when the Holy Spirit came, He would "convict the world" of three things, "sin and righteousness and judgment" (16:8). Has the Holy Spirit been doing those things or not? I believe He has, which makes Him the greatest evangelist on our planet. Because of the conviction of the Holy Spirit, everyone in the world innately knows they are sinners who are called to live righteously and who will one day stand judgment before God. Of course, people deceive themselves in this matter, filling their minds with lies that suppress the truth in their hearts, but they will have no excuse before God. We are wise to pray for God to lead us to those who are yielding to rather than resisting the Spirit's conviction.

The coming Holy Spirit's ministry would not be limited to convicting the world of certain essential truths, but also of guiding the church into truth (16:13), which begs the question, "Why then is the church so divided regarding doctrine?" The answer is that much of the "church" is not the true church of Christ, but rather an unholy religious conglomeration of unregenerate leaders and followers, the "blind leading the blind." Second, God does not override the free wills of His children, and He does not force them to believe truth or to stop listening to those who twist Scripture to their own liking. Thus, even true believers can be deceived. And third, much of the doctrinal differences between genuine believers revolve around non-essentials. They agree, however, on the essentials.

Jesus' promise to His disciples, "Truly, truly, I say to you, if you ask the Father for anything in My name, He will give it to you" (16:23), was not, as it is sometimes taken, a blank check that we can use to acquire material luxuries from God. Note that Jesus' made this promise within the context of the disciples' confusion about God's plan, and His promise of the Holy Spirit's leading them into truth.

Note also that the sentence directly before His promise in 16:23 reads, "In that day you will not question Me about anything." *Then* He said, "If you ask the Father for anything in My name, He will give it to you" (16:23). Jesus was encouraging the eleven to ask for understanding and insight. It is within that context that He promised in His very next sentence, "Until now you have asked for nothing in My name; ask and you will receive, *so that your joy may be made full*" (16:24). Again, He was not implying that they should ask for material luxuries to make them happier, but to ask for understanding, so that their current sorrow could be turned into joy. This blessing is not limited to 11 disciples who lived 2,000 years ago. It is the privilege of all believers today as well. James wrote:

> If any of you lacks wisdom, let him ask of God, who gives to all men generously and without reproach, and it will be given to him. But let him ask in faith without any doubting (Jas. 1:5-6).

May we be unlike the eleven in this regard, who apparently didn't take advantage of Jesus' wonderful promise that would have filled them with joy in the midst of their sorrow!

Day 214, John 17

Jesus' High Priestly Prayer, as it is often referred to, is Jesus' longest recorded prayer in Scripture. All of His other prayers found in the Gospels are very short, and it is interesting to me that this longest of His prayers is also quite short, requiring no more than a couple of minutes to pray. I point this out because it seems that the devil has duped many of us into thinking that if we don't have at least a half hour to pray, we don't have enough time, so we should just skip it. "Praying without ceasing," which is what Paul prescribed (1 Thes. 5:17), necessitates lots of short prayers throughout our day.

It is also interesting that Jesus apparently prayed this special prayer with His eyes open, lifted towards heaven (17:1). There is, of course, nothing wrong and everything appropriate about bowing our heads in humility and closing our eyes to distractions when we pray. Yet there is nothing wrong with lifting our eyes to heaven either.

It is most important to remember that Jesus prayed this prayer a short time before He was arrested in the Garden of Gethsemane, and thus the evening before His crucifixion. He begins by saying, "Father, the hour has come" (17:1). That is the eighth and final time that John recorded Jesus making reference to His "hour" (or "time"), an obvious reference to the culminating event of His life and ministry, His death on the cross (2:4; 7:8, 30; 8:20; 12:23, 27; 13:1). John has portrayed Jesus' life and ministry as a journey to the cross. The "hour" had finally arrived.

Jesus declared that He would give eternal life to all whom the Father gives to Him (17:2). Notice that Jesus said nothing about how the Father decides whom to give to Jesus. We know from reading hundreds of other verses in Scripture that they can only be those who believe. Jesus was not, of course, contradicting what He Himself said so many other times; nor was He revealing "the real truth" about how people are actually saved in contradiction to the rest of the New Testament. He was not endorsing the Calvinistic idea of unconditional election. John 17:2 must be harmonized with the 31,217 other verses in the Bible.

It is clear from Jesus' prayer that He was supremely interested in bringing glory to His Father, and it is also very obvious that it was important to Him that His disciples know and believe that He had come from the Father. Additionally, He wanted them to be unified, just as He and the Father are unified, and He mentioned it within four verses of His prayer (17:11, 21, 22, 23). Our unity, according to Jesus, has some bearing on the world believing that God sent Him. Jesus said so twice in this prayer (17:21, 23). Obviously, a "church" that demonstrates hypocrisy to the world is not going to influence people to believe in Jesus. It would, in fact, have the opposite effect. Disunity among believers sends a message to the watching world that we are no different than anyone else. Why should they believe in our God when we can't get along with each other?

This truth, so clearly stated by Jesus, is one more indication of the fallacy of the idea that God has sovereignly pre-selected some to be saved and some to be damned. If the world's coming to faith is dependent on our unity, which it is according to Jesus, then obviously God has created people as free moral agents, and He gives them the choice to believe or disbelieve. Otherwise, our actions and influence would have no effect on who believes and is saved.

So much of what Jesus prayed in this prayer is beyond my understanding. I wish I grasped it better! One part of His prayer that I think I do understand fairly well is found in 17:24: "Father, I desire that they also, whom You have given Me, be with Me where I am, so that they may see My glory which You have given Me." I'm so glad Jesus wants us in heaven, where we will see Him in His glory. That's easy-to-understand theology!

Day 215, John 18

Only John records the fact that Jesus' captors fell backwards onto the ground when Jesus identified Himself by saying, "I am *He*" (18:6). Note that in many translations that word *He* is italicized, indicating it was not part of the original text. So Jesus literally said, "I am," and then everyone fell to the ground. You may recall that "I AM" was a name by which God revealed Himself to Moses:

> God said to Moses, "I AM WHO I AM"; and He said, "Thus you shall say to the sons of Israel, 'I AM has sent me to you'" (Ex. 3:14).

In this same vein, John is the only Gospel-writer who recorded all of Jesus' "I ams." He declared: "I am the bread of life" (6:35); "I am the light of the world" (8:12); "I am the door of the sheep" (10:7); "I am the good shepherd" (10:11); "I am the Son of God" (10:36); "I am the resurrection and the life" (11:25); "I am the way, and the truth, and the life" (14:6); and "I am the true vine" (15:1). When people say that they believe that Jesus was "just a good man," or "a great moral teacher," it shows they haven't done their homework. Those who are only good men or great moral teachers don't claim to be the Son of God and the way, the truth and life.

Every time I read about one of Peter's antics, it makes me feel better about myself. He was full of zeal but empty of understanding, and for that reason, he sliced off the ear of the high priest's slave attempting to defend Jesus. It would seem more likely that Peter was aiming for the slave's head or neck. Incidentally, only Luke, a physician (Col. 4:14), mentions in his Gospel that Jesus immediately healed the slave's ear (Luke 22:51). Within the space of a minute or two, all those who came to arrest Jesus witnessed two undeniable miracles: the healing just mentioned and the entire crowd falling to the ground when Jesus revealed Himself. God was still trying to reach their hardened hearts. Amazing grace!

By the time John penned his Gospel, Peter's denial of Christ had been recorded in all three of the other Gospels. We may have thought that John would have excluded it, just out of courtesy to Peter, or to his memory, as he was likely in heaven by the time John wrote his Gospel. Yet John did include it, and I can only think the Holy Spirit inspired him to do so in order to showcase God's amazing grace one more time—as it was extended to Peter.

I've met people who argue vehemently that if Peter had died after he denied Christ, he would have gone to hell, since Jesus promised that He will deny before His Father those who deny Him before men (Matt. 10:32-33). That seems to be an unnecessary debate, as Peter didn't die until many years after he was long forgiven by Jesus and reconciled to Him. Who holds the power of life and death in His hands? Regardless of Peter's spiritual standing after he denied Christ (and wept bitter tears I must add), God kept him alive long enough to restore him and ultimately bring him into heaven. That is the grace of God. Professing Christians who are so happy to have God immediately cut off those who fall reveal how far their hearts are from God's heart. God is in the redemption business.

How ironic it was that the chief priests and Pharisees would not enter Pilate's Praetorium lest they be defiled from eating the Passover (18:28), yet they were there to condemn and kill the Lamb of God, the true Passover Lamb (1 Cor. 5:7). That is a picture of religion.

Under Roman law, the Jews could punish lawbreakers, but they were forbidden to execute anyone. Had the priests and Pharisees executed Jesus themselves, they would have done it by stoning Him. So according to 18:32 (and to 12:32-33 as well), Jesus was accurate in His foretelling that He would die by hanging on a cross, the Roman method of capital punishment. Jesus is never wrong.

Day 216, John 19

Pilate declared Jesus' innocence three times (18:38; 19:4, 6), yet he caved under the pressure of the Jewish leaders. He hoped after seeing Jesus scourged they would be satisfied that He had suffered enough. Still they insisted on His crucifixion, and Pilate wilted under their threat of reporting him to Caesar if he released a man who claimed to be a king, which would make him appear to be an accomplice to a conspiracy (19:12). He gained some redress by having the sign placed on Jesus' cross that read, "The King of the Jews"—a humiliation to them but ironically the absolute truth. Jesus was their King who will some day rule the world from the very city in which He was crucified.

Although it appeared, from a human standpoint, that Pilate was master over Jesus, holding His fate in his hands, the truth was that Jesus was master over Pilate and held his *eternal* fate in His hands. The only reason that Pilate had any temporal authority was because it had been given to him by God (19:11). This is true of anyone who has any authority over others, as all authority is ultimately granted by God (Rom. 13:1). Therefore, anyone who has authority over others will have to answer to God if they misuse it. The rule for those in authority to follow is: "Treat others just as you want to be treated." That goes for political leaders, judges, police and all employers.

Jesus, of course, never abuses His authority, and always judges righteously. It is astounding that, under the circumstances, He told Pilate, "...he who delivered Me to you has the greater sin" (19:11). That is, Jesus knew that Pilate was in a hard place and was facing a situation that he would have preferred to avoid. That did not, however, exonerate him of responsibility to do the right thing. He still sinned, but not as grievously as Judas and the chief priests.

Apparently, at some point in Jesus' life, his stepfather Joseph had died, which would seem to be the only logical reason why Jesus, during His final moments on earth, assigned John (whom we assume is "the disciple whom Jesus loved") to take care of His mother, Mary (19:26-27). It was Jesus' final act of "honoring His parents," and it teaches us something about our responsibility to take care of our adult parents in the event that they need our help. It also once again demonstrates the incredible love of Jesus, who, in the deepest agony of the cross, was more concerned about someone other than Himself.

When Jesus cried out with His final breath, "It is finished!" He meant more than just the fact that His life on earth had ended. Unknown to anyone who watched Him die, He had accomplished the work for which He had been sent, paying the full price for the sins of humanity. The New Testament teaches us that our redemption was completed on the cross (Col. 1:22).

When the Roman soldier pierced Jesus' side with his spear, John tells us that "there came out blood and water" (19:34). According to medical authorities, this reveals that Jesus most likely died from a ruptured heart.

Pilate was surprised to discover that Jesus was dead after being on the cross only six hours (Mark 15:44-45). Many survived for days. Jesus, however, was half dead before He arrived at Golgotha.

Not wanting anyone to be hanging on a cross during the Sabbath, which would begin at sunset, the Jews requested of Pilate that the legs of the two thieves be broken to speed their deaths by asphyxiation (19:31-33). To remain alive on the cross, a condemned person had to push himself up by the nails in his feet in order to fill his collapsing lungs with air. Broken legs made that impossible. Because Jesus was already dead, His legs were not broken, fulfilling Psalm 34:20, "He keeps all his bones, not one of them is broken," and making Him a more perfect fulfillment of a Passover lamb, of which it was commanded of Israel, "They shall leave none of it until morning, nor break a bone of it" (Num 9:12).

Day 217, John 20

When Peter and John arrived at Jesus' tomb, it was light enough for them to see inside, unlike Mary's first visit. Remember that Nicodemus and Joseph of Arimathea had wrapped Jesus' body in linen cloths along with myrrh and aloes weighing about 100 pounds (19:39). Jesus' body was wrapped like a mummy. When Peter and John later peered into the tomb on that first Easter morning, all they would have seen was the collapsed shell of the linen wrappings. They had no doubt that Jesus was alive. If His body had been stolen, the wrappings would have been unwrapped or missing. So they "saw and believed" (20:8).

By His own testimony to Mary (20:17), Jesus had not yet ascended to His Father since His death and resurrection. So where was His spirit while His body was lying in the tomb? Jesus told the repentant thief on a cross beside Him, "Today you shall be with Me in Paradise" (Luke 23:43). If Jesus had not yet ascended to His Father, but went to Paradise, it seems that there must have been a place of paradise that was not heaven. We also know that Scripture states that after His death, Jesus descended "into the lower parts of the earth" (Eph. 4:9). Jesus also declared that He would spend "three days and three nights in the heart of the earth" (Matt. 12:40). In the story of the Rich Man and Lazarus (Luke 16:19-31), Jesus spoke of a place that seems as if it might be a paradise in the heart of earth, adjacent to Hades, where the righteous lived after death. I only wish we had a few more verses of Scripture that gave us certain insight into this!

During His first appearance to His disciples on the evening of His resurrection, Jesus breathed on them and said, "Receive the Holy Spirit" (20:22). Some say this is when the disciples were born again (even though they were already "saved" in the sense of being forgiven). Others say it was a foreshadowing of their being baptized in the Holy Spirit, the fulfillment of which was about 50 days later on the day of Pentecost.

Jesus also told them, "If you forgive the sins of any, their sins have been forgiven them; if you retain the sins of any, they have been retained" (20:23). It is difficult to believe that Jesus was giving them the authority to decide who would be forgiven and who would not, as it would seem as if that would be stepping into God's sole domain. Thus I think Jesus likely meant that they were to carry the message of forgiveness to everyone. Whoever accepted it would be forgiven, and whoever didn't would not. This interpretation certainly harmonizes with the rest of the New Testament.

Personally, I'm glad Thomas doubted, as his being persuaded that Jesus had been resurrected bolsters my own faith. To trust the report of naive people is risky, but when a skeptic does his investigation and is convinced, that gives us more reason to believe. Although most of us have not seen Jesus since He was resurrected, it is good to know that at least 500 eye-witnesses did see Him alive not long after His resurrection (1 Cor. 15:6). And, as Jesus said, blessed are we who have not seen Him, "yet believed" (20:29).

What a frustration it is to read 20:23: "Therefore many other signs Jesus also performed in the presence of the disciples, which are not written in this book." How I wish John had recorded them! John felt, however, that he had mentioned a sufficient number of Jesus' signs in order to achieve his purpose: "But these have been written so that you may believe that Jesus is the Christ, the Son of God; and that believing you may have life in His name" (20:31). Incidentally, that is one more verse that indicates God's universal offer of salvation. John believed that any and all of his readers, current and future, could believe in Jesus and receive eternal life. (I'll bet you were hoping we could go one day without my refuting Calvinism! So sorry! I just couldn't resist!)

Day 218, John 21

Peter was obviously full of regret that he had let the Lord down, having denied Him three times. Jesus did not hate him for it or end their relationship permanently, but loved him, and gently confronted him to ultimately encourage and restore him. It began with another fish miracle that was similar to the one Peter witnessed when he first repented. Could Jesus' intention have been to reveal His love in the same fashion in order to remind Peter that His love for him had not waned? God loves sinners who sin, and so of course He still loves His children when they sin. Both need to repent.

Jesus, ever gentle, didn't immediately raise the subject, but first served Peter, fixing him breakfast, a task not below the resurrected Son of God who loves to serve. Then, taking Peter apart from the others, Jesus asked him a probing question: "Do you love Me more than these?" (21:15). Remember that Peter had boasted that his love for Jesus was greater than the other apostles. He had said, "Even though all may fall away because of You, I will never fall away" (26:33). Shortly after his claim, he denied the Lord three times. Jesus now gave him three opportunities to reaffirm his love.

In most translations it appears that Jesus asked Peter the same question three times, but actually He didn't. The first two times, Jesus asked Peter if he loved Him using the Greek verb *agapeo*, which each time is translated "love." The final time, He used the Greek verb *phileo*, which is also translated "love." *Agape* is a self-denying, sacrificial love, whereas *phileo* is a lesser love based on common interests and mutual benefits.

Interestingly, when Jesus first asked Peter if he loved Him with an *agape* love, Peter replied, "Yes, Lord, You know I *phileo* You." It was probably said with a sigh of regret, and meant, "Yes, Lord, You are well aware from my actions that my love for You falls short of *agape* love." Jesus repeated His question a second time, and Peter responded with the same answer.

The third time, however, Jesus said to him, "Peter, do you love me with *phileo* love?" That is why Scripture says that Peter was so grieved at the third question. I don't think Jesus asked him this because He Himself didn't know the answer, but because He wanted Peter to affirm it to help lift him from his despondency. Sometimes when we fail, we give up, which is a greater failure. Failures should make us more determined to do better, thankful for God's grace. Peter replied, "Lord, You know all things; You know that I *phileo* You" (21:17).

Most importantly, notice that after each of Peter's three replies, Jesus gave him a commandment: "Tend My lambs...Shepherd My sheep...Tend My sheep" (21:15-17). Surely this was intended to encourage Peter. Even though he had failed the Lord, Jesus had not given up on him, and there would be plenty of future opportunity to prove his love for Jesus. That is probably why Jesus also told Peter, "When you grow old, you will stretch out your hands and someone else will gird you, and bring you where you do not wish to go" (21:18). John knew that this was a reference to Peter's future martyrdom, perhaps because Peter had already been crucified by the time John wrote his gospel. In any case, we might wonder why Jesus foretold Peter about his future martyrdom. I think it was meant to encourage him. Peter was so disappointed in himself. He had shown by his actions that he was not willing to die for Jesus. Jesus assured him that would change. He would glorify God in martyrdom. Tradition tells us that Peter requested to be crucified upside down, considering himself unworthy to die in the same position as Christ.

I can relate very much to this story, and I'll bet you can, too. When we let the Lord down, He doesn't hate us, and we make a huge mistake if we give up. He is there to encourage and restore us, just as a father with his child. Thank God for His amazing grace!

Day 219, Hebrews 1

As we read through the book of Hebrews, it becomes clear that it was written to fortify Jewish Christians who were under fire from Jewish non-Christians. Not only were these Jewish believers being assailed with arguments designed to persuade them to revert to Judaism, they were also being intensely persecuted at times. They needed truth that would strengthen and encourage them, and this letter provided it.

No one knows who wrote this letter, but whoever it was, he was a close acquaintance of Timothy (13:23), and he was very knowledgeable of the Old Testament. Some say the author was Paul, while others suggest Apollos, Barnabas, Luke or even Priscilla (who is mentioned three times in Acts).

No one knows when this letter was written, and suggested dates vary from AD 60 to 100. So we are making an assumption by reading it at this point in our chronological journey through the New Testament.

The general theme of Hebrews is the superiority of Christ. Keep in mind that any knowledgeable Jew could convincingly argue for the truth that is found in Judaism since Judaism is founded upon divinely-given truth. We know, of course, that Christianity is built upon Judaism's foundation. The promised Messiah of Judaism is the Christ of Christianity. So the author begins this letter by showing the superiority of a revelation delivered by God's own Son over one that was revealed through prophets and angels (1:1-2; Gal. 3:19; Acts 7:28, 53; Heb. 2:2). Using Old Testament scriptures, he shows that Jesus, unlike any angel, is God's Son (1:5). Angels worship Jesus by God's command (1:6). He is heir of all things and will rule over His kingdom forever (1:8). He created the world (1:10). He is sitting at the right hand of God the Father (1:13). He's God (1:8)!

Angels, on the other hand, are simply "ministering spirits" who work on our behalf (1:14). Their ministry to us is invaluable, but they're still no comparison to Jesus our Lord and Savior. He created them, and they do His bidding. Jews could argue that the truth they clung to was sent to them via anointed prophets and angels; Christians can respond that the truth they cling to was sent to them via God's own Son!

It is interesting to take a closer look at the Old Testament scriptures which the author quotes that refer to Jesus. One is found in Psalm 2: "Thou art My Son, today I have begotten Thee" (1:5). Psalm 2 is a messianic Psalm that speaks of the time when the inhabitants of the earth will rebel near the end of Christ's (future) 1,000-year reign. In that light, we see that Jesus truly is "heir of all things" (1:2) because Psalm 2 informs us that God has given Him the nations as His inheritance (Ps. 2:8). You might want to read all of Psalm 2 if you have the time.

The author also quotes from 2 Samuel 7:14, where God, referring to one of David's descendants, promised, "I will be a Father to Him, and He shall be a Son to Me." God's promise to David was somewhat fulfilled in his son, Solomon, but ultimately it was fulfilled in Christ.

We have sure proof that Psalms 45, 102 and 110, all quoted by the author of Hebrews in 1:8-13, are at least partially messianic. It would be worth your while to read each of those psalms in their entirety as well, looking especially for the portions quoted in the first chapter of Hebrews.

Take note that Jesus is "the exact representation of [God's] nature" (1:3), which is another way of saying that if you know Jesus, you know the Father. Jesus spoke, acted, reacted, and so on, identically to how the Father would have, had He come to earth in human form instead of Jesus. That is nice to know. Jesus perfectly revealed God to us, because He is God. Anyone's conception of God that differs from Jesus is a wrong conception.

Day 220, Hebrews 2

Today we are introduced to the author's primary concern for his Hebrew Christian readers. He did not want them to "drift away" (2:1) from the truth they had embraced about Jesus. So he returns to his comparison of the old and new covenants, endorsing both but emphasizing the superiority of the latter, reminding his readers that the consequences were dire for those who ignored God's old covenant revelation delivered by angels. Thus how much more true would that be for those who ignored God's new covenant revelation delivered by His own Son, to whom, unlike angels, He has exalted to rule "the world to come" (2:5-8)? To stress its importance, God confirmed that same message through apostles anointed with signs and wonders (2:3-4). It was not meant to be ignored!

The author again appeals to old covenant scripture to make his new covenant point, citing Psalm 8, where David spoke prophetically of Christ's incarnation, a time when He was made "a little lower than the angels" and of His subsequent exaltation and still-future reign over the world. He declares that Jesus "tasted death for *everyone*" (2:9). (I'm sure you noticed that he wrote, "everyone," and not "the alleged pre-selected few," so I won't mention it!)

When the author writes that Jesus was perfected through sufferings, he does not mean that Jesus had any need to become morally perfect, but that He became the perfect substitute and Savior through His sufferings. It was by that act that He met the requirements of God's justice. His sufferings and death were credited to our account, and the end result will be His "bringing many sons to glory" (2:10). Now we have become members of His family, and we share His Father! He not only provided our forgiveness, but He now works in us to sanctify us (2:11). We're spiritual brothers of the Son of God (2:11-13)! No wonder the author refers to all of this as "so great a salvation" (2:3). It is amazingly, incredibly wonderful. To drift away from it would be criminal.

What was one of the reasons that Jesus became a man? "Since then the children [that is, we who believe] share in flesh and blood [we have physical bodies], He Himself likewise also partook of the same [a physical body], that through death He might render powerless him who had the power of death, that is, the devil" (2:14). In order to render Satan powerless by His death, Jesus had to have a physical body that could die, because God can't die.

How has Satan been rendered powerless over us by Jesus' death? Satan has the God-given right to rule all those who are not submitted to God. He serves as a subordinate instrument of God's wrath upon rebels. By Jesus' death for our sins, however, we've been set free from God's wrath and thus also from Satan's power, which the author refers to as "the power of death" (2:14). The spiritual death that resides within every unsaved person is Satan's very nature (see Eph. 2:2). We could almost say that anyone who is not born again is mildly devil-possessed, but when he believes in Jesus he undergoes an immediate exorcism. Satan's nature is eradicated from his inner man!

Another reason that the Son of God became a man was so He could become our high priest (2:17). The Hebrew Christians could certainly understand that analogy, because it was only through the mediation of the high priest and the blood sacrifice that their sins could be covered under the old covenant. It was through the sacrifice of Himself that Jesus made "propitiation for the sins of the people" (2:17). To propitiate means to "turn away wrath," and that's what Jesus did for us. He turned away God's righteous wrath by bearing the penalty we deserved.

Jesus is a *compassionate* high priest, because He knows from experience what it's like to be tempted as a human being, and "He is able to come to the aid of those who are tempted" (2:18). To the persecuted Hebrew Christians who were being tempted to drift away from Christ and revert to Judaism, that would have been especially encouraging news.

Day 221, Hebrews 3

Moses was and is, of course, revered among Jews, as he is the human agent whom God used to deliver Israel from Egypt and to convey the old covenant Law. So you can imagine what non-believing Jews would say to Christian Jews who had abandoned the ritualistic and ceremonial aspects of the Mosaic Law: "We know that what we have is from God! We cannot forget all that He did to deliver to us His holy revelation!"

That argument is quite valid, of course, yet someone greater than Moses has appeared, bringing additional revelation that harmonized with and fulfilled Moses' revelation. In fact, that Greater Person is the One who made Moses so great! So naturally, the Greater Person is worthy of more glory (3:3-4). The author compares Moses' ministry to Christ's with an analogy that contrasts a servant in a household to a son over that same household. Moses was a faithful servant "in" God's "house" (3:5), but Jesus was a faithful Son, not "in" God's house, but "over" God's house (3:6), a big difference!

All who believe in Jesus are blessed to be in God's house over which His Son presides, but our *remaining* in His house is not guaranteed. This is so clear from what we have read today that only a theologian could miss it. The author of Hebrews writes, "Christ was faithful as a Son over His house—whose house we are, *if we hold fast our confidence and the boast of our hope firm until the end* (3:6). Notice the conditional "if."

So we must continue in faith if we expect to remain in God's house. And only those who are *currently in a house* could be in any danger of *not remaining in that house*. Thus, the author is not writing to "potential believers who were considering Christ," regardless of what some theologians tell us in a desperate attempt to preserve their man-made doctrines.

So the author admonishes his Jewish Christian readership—using Old Testament scriptures—to beware of hardening their hearts as did those under Moses' leadership, which resulted in their not entering the rest God had promised them. The lesson is obvious and it becomes even more obvious as we keep reading. Although the Israelites were chosen by God, delivered from Egyptian bondage, received special care from God, and were led to a land of promise, most failed to enter that promised land because of their unbelief (3:19). Theirs was not an example we want to follow.

The evidence is overwhelming that the author of Hebrews was writing to Christian believers. Yet, because of the many admonitions and warnings it contains against falling away and forfeiting salvation, those who promote the doctrine of unconditional security go to great lengths to persuade us that the author was writing to Jews who were only considering Christ. Yet any child can understand this:

> Take care, brethren, that there not be in any one of you an evil, unbelieving heart that falls away from the living God. But encourage one another day after day, as long as it is still called "Today," so that none of you will be hardened by the deceitfulness of sin (3:12-13).

Note that the warning is addressed to "brethren." The author was not addressing "Jewish brethren," but "holy brethren" according to 3:1, those who were "partakers of a heavenly calling" and who considered Jesus to be their Apostle and High Priest. They are admonished to be cautious that none have an "evil, unbelieving heart" that would lead them to "fall away from the living God" (3:12). How can those who are alienated from God, as are all unbelievers, "fall away" from Him? Moreover, why would the author admonish unbelievers, who all possess unbelieving hearts, to "take care that there be not in any one of you an evil, unbelieving heart"? Why would he admonish unbelievers, who are all slaves of sin, to "encourage one another" so that none will become "hardened by the deceitfulness of sin"?

So, we are indeed "partakers of Christ, *if* we hold fast the beginning of our assurance firm until the end" (3:14). That's what I'm planning on doing! How about you?

Day 222, Hebrews 4

Citing truth from the old covenant Scriptures, the author of Hebrews once again focuses on his greatest concern—that his readers might ultimately fall short of "entering God's rest." As in the previous chapter, he again references Psalm 95:7-11, where God said:

> Today if you hear His voice, do not harden your hearts as when they provoked Me, as in the day of trial in the wilderness, where your fathers tried Me by testing Me, and saw My works for forty years. Therefore I was angry with this generation, and said, "They always go astray in their heart; and they did not know My ways"; as I swore in My wrath, "They shall not enter My rest" (Heb. 3:7-11).

Psalm 95 was written hundreds of years after Israel's conquest of Canaan, and so the author argues that it speaks of a different "rest" than that which was enjoyed by the generation of Israelites who entered the Promised Land under Joshua's leadership (4:8). He also points out that God speaks in Psalm 95 of entering *His own* rest, which can only be the rest that He took on the seventh day of creation, as there is mention of no other rest by God in Scripture. Thus we have in Psalm 95 a promise that remains for us to enter "God's rest," of which some Israelites enjoyed only as a foreshadow in Canaan. But just as in the case of their rest in Canaan, God's rest is only enjoyed by those who "do not harden their hearts," and who believe the good news. The Israelites in Joshua's day who did not believe failed to enter Canaan's land. So those who refuse to believe the gospel fail to enter God's rest now.

The author takes his analogy one step further by mentioning that on the seventh day of creation, Scripture says that God rested from all His works. So he writes that those who enter into God's rest have also rested from their works (4:10), an obvious reference to the attempt of so many Jews to gain righteousness and eternal life by their limited keeping of the ceremonial and ritualistic aspects of the Mosaic Law. The author could not have been endorsing the idea that those who believe have rested from making any attempt to keep the moral teachings of the Mosaic Law, as those same moral teachings are contained in the Law of Christ, and the author later wrote in this same letter, "Pursue peace with all men, and the sanctification [or "holiness"] without which no one will see the Lord" (12:14).

So we are admonished to "be diligent to enter that rest," and clearly obedience is part of the package, as the author goes on to say, "...lest anyone fall through following the same example of disobedience" (4:11). Moreover, he continues in the very next two verses writing that God's Word is sharper than any sword, as it pierces deep inside us and judges our thoughts and motives. We can hide nothing from the Lord.

Again we plainly see that the author was not writing to Jews who were considering becoming Christians, but to Jews who had already professed faith in Christ. If that was not the case, he would not have written, "Let us hold fast our confession" (4:14). His readers had already made their confession of faith in Christ, and now needed only to "hold fast" to it. The only reason any commentator on the book of Hebrews would maintain that the author was writing to Jews who were not yet Christians is to prevent the false doctrine of unconditional eternal security, also known as "once-saved-always-saved," from crashing down. If saved people can't forfeit salvation under any circumstances, that begs the question, "Why did the author of Hebrews so often warn his Christian readership of the danger of ultimately forfeiting salvation?" So they go to great lengths to prove that the intended readers were not yet believers.

Believing Jews no longer needed an earthly high priest, as they had a superior, new and heavenly high priest who is full of compassion and grace. More on that in the next chapter.

Day 223, Hebrews 5

The priestly ministry was woven into the fabric of Jewish culture, as it was the God-ordained means under the old covenant for obtaining forgiveness of sins through animal sacrifice. Jewish believers who stopped participating in priestly rituals naturally came under fire from practicing Jews. How could they abandon the means God had given Israel to find forgiveness?

The answer, of course, is that God had appointed a superior and perpetual high priest of the new covenant, His very own Son, of whom all the previous priests only served to prefigure. The author of Hebrews points out why Jesus is fully qualified to serve as a high priest and why Jesus is superior to any before Him.

Every previous high priest was "beset with weakness," and each was "obligated to offer sacrifices for sins, as for the people, so also for himself" (5:3). Jesus, of course, had no such need to offer any sacrifice for Himself, as He was sinless. He was not only the perfect and superior high priest, but He was also the perfect and superior sacrifice. He offered up, not an animal, but Himself for our sins.

The author makes reference to verses in Psalms 2 and 110, both universally recognized by all Jews as messianic psalms that make reference to the Lord's future reign over the entire world. Both contain quotations of God speaking to God. In Psalm 2, the Father speaks to the Son—during the time when the Father will have installed His Son to rule the earth from Mt. Zion—saying, "Thou are My Son, today I have begotten Thee." In Psalm 110, the Father is again speaking to the One whom He has installed on Mt. Zion to rule the world. It begins with David prophetically saying, "The Lord says to my Lord" (110:1), and goes on to quote what God says to God, part of which is, "The Lord has sworn and will not change His mind, 'You are a priest forever according to the order of Melchizedek'" (110:4).

So it is indisputable that God revealed in the Old Testament that He would one day appoint the Messiah—the One who would rule over the world—to be a priest *forever*. Moreover, he would not be a priest after the order of Aaron, as were all previous priests, but after the order of a mysterious Old Testament man named Melchizedek, of whom we will read more about in chapter 7.

That Messiah and High Priest of whom Scripture foretold had been revealed, and so everyone in relationship with Him had obviously not lost anything relative to the benefits of a priesthood. And they would be foolish to go back to an inferior priestly system, one that was actually designed to point them to Christ.

When did Jesus offer up "both prayers and supplications with loud crying and tears to the One able to save Him from death" (5:7)? It must have either been when He prayed in the garden or from the cross, where we know that our great High Priest and holy sacrifice cried out with a loud voice, "My God, My God, why have You forsaken Me?" (Matt. 27:46). The author writes that Jesus "was heard because of His piety" (5:7). Perhaps this is a reference to Him being "saved from death" (5:7) by means of His resurrection. Our High Priest receives what He prays for, which should fill us with confidence.

If Jesus was sinless, why did the author write that Jesus "learned obedience from the things which He suffered" (5:8)? The author could not have meant that Jesus learned to become obedient by suffering the consequences of disobedience, but rather that He learned from experience the cost that is paid by those who are obedient to God. It cost Jesus His life. But His sufferings resulted in His complete perfection, not making Him morally perfect (since He already was), but making Him the perfect Savior and High Priest.

Finally, notice that Jesus "became to all those who obey Him the source of eternal salvation" (5:9). This is just one more indication that there is a correlation between holiness and heaven because there is a correlation between belief and behavior.

Day 224, Hebrews 6

We gather from the last four verses of chapter 5 that the author of Hebrews was not pleased with the slow spiritual progress of most of his readers. They had become "dull of hearing" and should have been teachers by that time, but they had need for someone to teach them again "the elementary principles of the oracles of God" (5:11-12). Six of those "elementary principles" he lists, the first of which are "repentance from dead works" and "faith toward God" (6:1). How tragic it is that many evangelical ministers today are lacking understanding of these most basic of the "elementary teachings about the Christ" (6:1), having redefined faith so that works are not a component and having removed repentance from the gospel. "Dead works," by the way, are religious works that do not stem from a living faith in Christ, but instead from ingrained tradition.

"Instruction about washings" could be translated "instruction about baptisms," of which the New Testament speaks of three: the believer's baptism into the body of Christ, baptism by immersion in water, and baptism in the Holy Spirit.

By means of the "laying on of hands," another "elementary principle," healing power or an anointing of the Holy Spirit is transferred or bestowed (Matt. 19:13-15; Mark 5:23; 8:23; 10:16; 16:18; Luke 4:40; Acts 8:17-18; 9:12-17; 1 Tim. 4:14; 5:22; 2 Tim. 1:6). The baptism in the Holy Spirit is often administered through laying on of hands.

"The resurrection of the dead" refers to the foundational truth that every person, righteous and unrighteous, will one day be bodily-resurrected.

Finally, "eternal judgment" is the fundamental Christian belief that all persons will stand before God, and the results of each person's judgment will be eternal, something that seems to be rarely mentioned from many pulpits these days.

Taken at face value, 6:4-8 proves once again that it is possible for saved people to forfeit their salvation, which was, of course, one of the primary concerns of the author of Hebrews for his contemporary readers. It is in fact impossible, he wrote, for believers who have fallen away from the faith and who fit the five criteria listed in these verses to regain what they lost.

One who cannot regain the salvation that he lost first must be "enlightened" (6:4), which means he recognized his sinful condition and need for a Savior. Second, he must have "tasted of the heavenly gift" (6:4), that is, received the gift of eternal life. Third, he must have been born of and baptized in the Holy Spirit. Fourth, he must have "tasted the good word of God" (6:5), indicating more than just a beginner's understanding of God's Word. He grew beyond the "milk stage" into the "meat stage," no longer a baby Christian. Fifth, he must have tasted "the powers of the age to come" (6:5). That must mean that he had some experience with the gifts of the Holy Spirit.

If a person has reached that level in his Christian walk and then falls away, "it is impossible to renew [him] again to repentance" (6:6). He's compared to ground that was formerly fruitful but which now produces only thorns and thistles, reminding us of one of the soils in Jesus' well-known parable by the same name. Such a backslider, in effect, re-crucifies Christ and thus inherits a curse which will result in hellfire (6:6-8). It is incredible that any commentator would claim that those five criteria can be met by a person who is only considering becoming a Christian, yet many do in order to protect the false doctrine of unconditional eternal security.

Clearly, the author of this letter wanted to prevent the Hebrew Christians from the consequences of falling away from Christ. Their love for the saints, manifested in practical ways, proved their current genuine faith, and provided assurance of their salvation (6:9-12). Yet ultimate salvation was not "in the bag." It is through faith and patience that we ultimately inherit what God has promised us, as proven by Abraham, whose patient faith ultimately paid off. Similarly, our faith will be rewarded if we persevere. It is impossible for God to lie, and His promise is an anchor for our souls (6:18-19)!

Day 225, Hebrews 7

Melchizedek is mentioned only twice in the Old Testament, within just four verses (Gen. 14:18-20; Psalm 110:4). Yet what is contained in those four verses emboldened the author of Hebrews to declare the end of the Levitical priesthood, a thousand-year-old institution founded by Moses in obedience to God. The author's ultimate intention was to assure his wavering Hebrew readers that they were in sync with God's plan. They had lost nothing by believing in Jesus, and had rather gained the benefit of a superior high priest.

Melchizedek was the "king of Salem," an ancient name for Jerusalem. "Salem" is derived from the Hebrew word "Shalom." Thus Melchizedek's title means "king of peace" (7:2). Jesus, the "Prince of Peace" (Isa. 9:6) will of course one day rule from Jerusalem.

Melchizedek's name means "king of righteousness," which also reminds us of Jesus, "the Holy and Righteous One" (Acts 3:14). Melchizedek was a king and a "priest of the Most High God," as Jesus is also.

And there is more about Melchizedek that makes him resemble Christ. There is no information in Scripture about his genealogy, his birth or death. So like Christ, he seems to have no beginning or end. Some suspect that Melchizedek actually was Christ in a pre-incarnate form. But the Bible doesn't say so.

We've already learned that, according to Psalm 110:4, the Messiah was appointed by God to be an eternal priest after the order of Melchizedek. So the author of Hebrews first shows how the Melchizedekian order was superior to the Levitical order as a means to prove Christ's superior priesthood. He points out that Abraham paid tithes to Melchizedek. By this act, writes the author, Levi, a future descendant of Abraham "in the loins of his father," in effect paid tithes to Melchizedek (7:9). Moreover, when Abraham paid his tithes, Melchizedek blessed him, and "without any dispute the lesser is blessed by the greater" (7:7). So Melchizedek was greater than both Abraham and his descendant, Levi, and thus his priestly order was superior to that of Levi's. All of this is to say that Jesus is a superior high priest.

The author also argues that, if the Levitical priesthood had been sufficient, God would never have announced a plan to install an eternal priest of a different order who was not a descendant of Levi. But God did make such an announcement in Psalm 110, and it was *after* He had established the Levitical priesthood. Jesus, who was so much like Melchizedek, was obviously the promised priest of Psalm 110.

But there is more to be gleaned from Psalm 110 that points to Christ's superiority. The eternal priesthood of Jesus came by an oath from God the Father Himself, which was not true of any other priest before Him (7:20-22). And unlike Christ's priesthood, God never promised that the old covenant priesthood would go on forever.

Under the old covenant, there were many high priests. Prevented from continuing in their service by limited life spans, they followed one another successively from generation to generation. But Jesus is the only high priest of the new covenant, as He is alive forever. Consequently, He can offer us eternal salvation, because He will always live to ensure our covenant with God (7:25).

The old covenant priests had to make daily sacrifices for their own sins and the sins of the people. But Jesus was sinless, and no sacrifice was required for Him. And as the perfect, sinless sacrifice, He needed to offer Himself only once for our sins (7:27). By His sacrifice He atoned for every sin once and for all.

Finally, Jesus was a superior priest because He was not just a man, but also the Son of God (7:28).

The message to Hebrew Christians was clear: There was no sound reason to revert to the Levitical system of the old covenant now that the promised, long-awaited, superior, eternal, heavenly, sinless, God-appointed, perfect high priest had been revealed to the world. In fact, if you suspect that the entire Levitical system was designed by God to ultimately point to the priestly ministry of Christ, you are correct. Stay tuned!

Day 226, Hebrews 8

The promise of Psalm 110 that God was going to appoint a perpetual high priest after the order of Melchizedek rather than Levi (highlighted in the previous chapter) implied the ultimate abolishment of the Levitical priesthood. This, in turn, implied that a significant part of the Mosaic Law that had anything to do with the Levitical priesthood would become obsolete. Thus one could easily see how the arrival of the promised perpetual high priest would necessitate a complete changing of the Law of Moses. We read in 7:12: "For when the priesthood is changed, of necessity there takes place a change of law also." That change was nothing less than the end of the old covenant and the beginning of the new. Jews who were (and are) in sync with God's plan have made that transition.

This reality becomes even more obvious when we realize that the priestly ministry under the old covenant was simply a foreshadowing of Christ's priestly ministry. In this chapter of Hebrews, the author declares that the earthly tabernacle, for which Moses was given detailed construction plans by God, was a copy of a tabernacle in heaven (8:5; 9:23-24). Jesus was "a minister in the sanctuary and in the true tabernacle, which the Lord pitched, not man" (8:2). Thus, not only is Jesus personally superior in His priestly office as compared to any former priest, but He also has a superior ministry to any former priests as well. The high priests of the old covenant performed their ministry in an earthly, man-made tabernacle. They stood before a symbol of God's throne in the earthly Holy of Holies to present the blood of animals. Jesus, however, presented His own blood before God's throne in the heavenly Holy of Holies.

And it was that superior act in a superior place by a superior priest—foreshadowed thousands of times by inferior acts in inferior places by inferior priests—that inaugurated a superior new covenant. That superior new covenant, just like that superior high priest, had also been promised in the Old Testament. The author of

Hebrews cites such a promise from Jeremiah 31:33-34, arguing that "if that first covenant had been faultless, there would have been no occasion sought for a second" (8:7). Because God promised a second covenant, that implied the fact that He found fault with the first, and naturally anyone who remained under the old covenant when the new covenant was inaugurated would be missing the mark.

The new covenant has made the old covenant obsolete (8:13). And we are now obligated to obey the law of Christ and not the Law of Moses. Any Christian, Jew or Gentile, who is trying to live under the old covenant is going backwards 2,000 years with God. Those who teach that Christians are obligated to keep the Mosaic Law might just as well start sacrificing animals to receive forgiveness of their sins!

Hundreds of years before the inauguration of the new covenant, God foretold through Jeremiah a few of the benefits that would be enjoyed by those who would partake of its promises. It would be superior to the old covenant because God would write His laws on hearts and minds, an inward work that would result in holy lives. Everyone who experienced that inward work would "know the Lord" (8:11), because knowing Him is revealed by a lifestyle of obedience to Him. So we see that hundreds of years before Jesus' incarnation, God was already revealing the true nature of our salvation and exposing the false grace that is so often being peddled today, a grace that doesn't change anyone's behavior.

The apostle John similarly wrote, "By this we know that we have come to know Him, if we keep His commandments" (1 John 2:3). Knowing the Lord is synonymous with following His commandments, which was true even under the old covenant. The Lord also once said through Jeremiah:

> Did not your father eat and drink and do justice and righteousness? Then it was well with him. He pled the cause of the afflicted and needy; then it was well. Is not that what it means to know Me? declares the Lord (Jer. 22:15-16).

Day 227, Hebrews 9

Without any doubt, the old covenant tabernacle and its furniture, coupled with the continual ministry of the priests, all served to reveal important spiritual truths. But the most significant truths they revealed, namely, concerning the ministry of Christ, have been missed by most Jews.

The author of Hebrews points out that priests were continually serving in the outer tabernacle, but into the inner tabernacle, the Holy of Holies, only the high priest entered once a year to sprinkle blood on the mercy seat of the ark of the covenant, which represented the throne of God. Obviously, all that was done in the tabernacle under the regulations of divine worship did nothing to make it possible for the average person to enter the Holy of Holies. Even after the high priest performed the annual rituals of the Day of Atonement, it still was not permissible or even possible for anyone to enter the Holy of Holies, including the high priest himself, unless he came one year later, and under the required great precautions.

So what occurred continually for hundreds of years, first in the tabernacle and later in the temple, only foreshadowed what Jesus, our high priest, would one day accomplish. He would enter heaven before God's actual throne, presenting His own blood as testimony to His suffering and death for the sins of the world, "having obtained eternal redemption" (9:12). Surely if the presenting of the blood of animals in an earthly tabernacle provided some cleansing benefit to worshippers, the blood of the sinless Son of God presented before God's throne provides a much greater benefit. The author writes that it cleansed our consciences "from dead works to serve the living God" (9:14), another reference to the inward work of the Holy Spirit that results in sincere holiness stemming from a changed nature.

Remember that when Jesus cried out from the cross, "It is finished!" the veil in the temple was ripped in half (Matt. 27:51). We now have confidence to enter the holy place by the blood of Jesus, as we'll read in the next chapter (10:19). If we could be transported back to Moses' time, we could walk into the Holy of Holies without fear!

Doubtless, many Jews objected to the concept of a Messiah who was crucified. But the author points out that ancient covenants were often agreements made between two parties that had bearing only upon their descendants after they died. Some ancient covenants that included immediate benefits for covenanting parties were ratified by the death of an animal, perhaps symbolic of the deaths of both parties, and indicative of the finality and unchangeableness of the covenant's conditions. This was what occurred at the inauguration of the old covenant. Thus the new covenant is revealed as superior again, because it was ratified, not by the symbolic death of an animal, but by the actual death of one of the covenanting parties, amazingly, God Himself.

Moreover, God has clearly and repeatedly demonstrated under the old covenant that "without shedding of blood there is no forgiveness" (9:22). The old covenant was inaugurated with blood, and so it makes perfect sense that the new covenant would follow suit, and this also explains why Christ had to die.

Take note that the author believed that Christ did not just die for sins committed after His death, but also for sins committed under the old covenant (9:15). The fact is, no one in the history of humanity has had his sins forgiven apart from Christ's death. Just as His death 2,000 years ago paid for sins that had not yet been committed, so it paid for sins committed by people who died long before Jesus lived, whether they realized it or not. Salvation has always been by grace through faith, made possible by Jesus' future or past sacrifice.

Christ's superior sacrifice of Himself was necessary only once (9:25-28). Under the old covenant, when the high priest exited the Holy of Holies to appear before the people, they knew it was just another year before they would witness another atonement. But when Jesus appears again, He'll be coming "without reference to sin, to those who eagerly await Him" (9:28). Praise God!

Day 228, Hebrews 10

God may have accepted the death of animals as a token means of atonement, but something much more was needed to ransom us forever, not only from the penalty of sin, but from sin itself. No animal's death ever atoned for every sin that a person may have committed, nor effected an inward, supernatural change in someone, making him righteous both legally and practically. But Jesus' once-and-for-all sacrifice makes us holy and will ultimately result in our perfection (10:1, 14). So we see that the sacrificial system of the old covenant was "only a shadow of the good things to come" (10:1).

The author of Hebrews boldly declares, "It is impossible for the blood of bulls and goats to take away sins" (10:4). When you compare the relative value of animals to that of human beings who are created in God's image, it would seem there is little comparison. So how could an animal possibly atone for the sins of a human being? When you compare, however, the relative value of Jesus to that of human beings, He is of infinitely greater value, and thus it is easy to see how He could atone for the sins of everyone.

Pointing his readers back once again to the old covenant Scriptures, the author shows how they foretold of Christ's atoning sacrifice that would bring an end to the old covenant system of animal sacrifice (10:5-7). He attributes the words found in Psalm 40:6-7 to Christ, spoken to His Father when He first entered the world. Those words show the deficiency of the old covenant sacrificial system, surprisingly revealing that God actually took no pleasure in animal sacrifices, and indicating that something that Jesus would do in His incarnation would make up for that displeasure. We know, of course, what it was that Jesus did!

And unlike the old covenant priests who needed to offer sacrifices continually for sins year after year, Jesus' one sacrifice atoned "for sins for all time" (10:12). So He "sat down at the right hand of God, waiting from that time onward until His enemies be made a footstool for His feet"—another reference to Psalm 110—because His work was completed.

All these wonderful truths about Jesus' once-and-for-all sacrifice and His high priestly ministry gave first-century Jewish believers reason to continue following Jesus, even under persecution. So the author admonishes his Jewish readers to "hold fast," which, incidentally, indicates that the possibility existed of their not holding fast. We also gain a glimpse of the degree of persecution that his readers had already endured for the sake of Christ. They had "accepted joyfully the seizure of [their] property," knowing that they had "a better possession and a lasting one" in heaven (10:34). Some had been imprisoned. Their faith was genuine, and it would be rewarded (which is the theme of the next chapter).

Perhaps more than any other chapter in Hebrews, this one ends the debate on whether or not a true believer can forfeit his salvation. The author writes of the terrifying ends of those who have been sanctified by Christ's blood, but who then "trample under foot the Son of God" (10:28-31). He warns of the dire consequences of those who are righteous but who don't persevere in faith, who "shrink back to destruction" (10:36-39). It couldn't be more clear to those who are honest with language.

May I stir up a little trouble? Thank you.

Pastors are often apt to quote Hebrews 10:25, reminding their flocks that the Bible says we should "not forsake our own assembling together, as is the habit of some." Yet when the flock assembles, many pastors ignore what the immediate context of Hebrews 10:25 teaches, namely, what is supposed to happen when we assemble. We are to "stimulate one another to love and good deeds" and "encourage one another" (10:24-25). When we come together, we all have something to offer from the Spirit, and gatherings are supposed to be participatory, not a one-man show:

> When you assemble, each one has a psalm, has a teaching, has a revelation, has a tongue, has an interpretation (1 Cor. 14:26).

OK, I got that off my chest!

Day 229, Hebrews 11

Only after reading the first 10 chapters of Hebrews are we properly prepared to read Hebrews 11. Now we understand its important context. The author's intent was to encourage persecuted Jewish believers, who were being tempted to waver, to imitate the example of familiar Old Testament characters who held fast in their faith and were ultimately rewarded.

We learn today something that the Old Testament does not reveal: God accepted Abel's animal sacrifice because of his faith (11:4). Abel had a basis for his faith, namely, God's clothing of Adam and Eve with animal skins after their sin. Cain, on the other hand, had no basis to believe that God would accept his offering of "the fruit of the ground," and he represents the one who comes to God on the basis of dead works that do not stem from faith.

Noah acted in faith, trusting that God would keep His promise to flood the earth, and he was saved from God's wrath (11:7), serving as an example to the readers of Hebrews. Like Noah, believers are now safely in God's ark, Jesus, as judgment is about to fall on the earth again.

Abraham and Sarah trusted God to give them an inheritance in a land where they lived as aliens. The Hebrew believers could relate, living as aliens on the earth, believing that they would one day inherit it from God.

Many of the "faith heroes" mentioned all "died in faith, without receiving the promises, but having seen them and having welcomed them from a distance" (11:13). That is, they had some foresight of the promised blessings of the gospel, insight that was tragically being missed by unbelieving Jews. It seems those ancient saints must have had more knowledge of the future plan of God than we might suppose from reading the Old Testament. Abraham, for example, "was looking for the city which has foundations, whose architect and builder is God" (11:10). He knew about the New Jerusalem which is described to us in the book of Revelation (see also Heb. 13:14). We're looking forward to that same city.

Abraham's faith was tested, as was the faith of the Hebrew believers. He believed that God was able to resurrect his son from the dead, just as the author's readers were required to believe that God resurrected His Son from the dead (11:17-19).

The life of Moses was also exemplary to Jewish believers. He decided to follow God, even though it meant denying himself worldly stature and pleasures. He paid a high price, but his faith was rewarded (11:24-28).

It took faith for all the children of Israel to keep the first Passover, sacrificing lambs and sprinkling the blood over their doors (11:28). What seemed completely foolish to the Egyptians paid off for the Israelites when the destroying angel killed all the firstborn who weren't "under the blood." Their faith in the blood saved them, just as our faith in the blood of the Lamb of God saves us.

It took faith to circle Jericho silently for seven days within earshot of the mocking Jerichoites, but those walls came tumblin' down (11:30).

Rahab, the harlot, found that salvation comes by faith, as she and her family were the only inhabitants of Jericho to survive the Israelite onslaught. She trusted the spies' "gospel" and acted accordingly, tying a scarlet thread in her window, which some say is a symbol of Jesus' blood flowing down His cross (11:31).

And there are many more excellent Old Testament examples of those who persevered in faith and whom God rewarded. It was Daniel, of course, who "shut the mouths of lions" by his faith (11:33). His three friends "quenched the power of fire" (11:34). The widow of Zarephath (1 Kings 17:17-24) and the Shunammite woman (2 Kings 4:17-35) "received back their dead by resurrection" (11:35).

Tradition says that it was Isaiah who was sawn in half for his faith (11:37). Jeremiah was imprisoned for his, and Zechariah was stoned. This is good to remember in an age when faith is often being promoted as a means to wealth, success and victory. The truth is, faith generally precipitates suffering, but it always ends in blessing. God is a rewarder of those who seek Him (11:6).

Day 230, Hebrews 12

Our earthly spiritual journey is comparable to a runner's long-distance race. We're being cheered on from the grandstands of heaven, as it were, by those who have run before us, the heroes of faith (12:1). Knowing that spurs us on. Moreover, Jesus is standing at the finish line, and so we should "fix our eyes on Him." Being with Him forever is our goal, and endurance is the key. Runners have greater endurance if they carry less weight, and similarly, we should "lay aside every encumbrance and the sin which so easily entangles us" if we want to cross the finish line in heaven.

Notice that the author mentions both sins and encumbrances that might slow us down. Encumbrances, although they may not be sinful, can be anything that slows down our spiritual progress. What we do with our time can certainly fall into this category. Wasting time, our most precious commodity, in meaningless relationships or mindless entertainment, is something that weighs down many believers in their spiritual progress. Long-distance runners don't cross any finish line accidentally. They cross the finish line because that is what they set their hearts on, and they expect to suffer on the way to their goal.

The greatest example of enduring faith in the midst of suffering is Jesus, of course. He endured the cross because of the "joy set before Him" (12:2). He believed. The Hebrew Christians were also suffering "hostility by sinners," but their sufferings were minor by comparison to His (as are ours). They had not yet shed their blood (12:4).

Some may have wondered why their loving Father, the all-powerful God, did not stop their persecutors. The author explains that, in His divine plan, God uses our sufferings to discipline us, that "we may share His holiness" (12:10). He "scourges every son whom He receives," and the reason is because He loves them all (12:6). So He permits His own children to suffer, at least at times, to call them to repentance. If we "are without discipline" that reveals that we are not truly God's children.

There are two wrong reactions to God's discipline. We can "regard it lightly" (12:5), that is, essentially ignore it, or we can "faint when we are reproved" (12:5), that is, give up in exasperation (as the Hebrew believers were being tempted to do). The fact is, when many believers are rebuking Satan in their trials, they might consider rebuking themselves for behavior that has invited God's discipline.

No one enjoys discipline, and that is the point. We learn to avoid sin in order to avoid the consequences. We associate disobedience with pain, just as do disobedient children who are spanked. God disciplines us and it trains us, which yields "the peaceful fruit of righteousness" (12:11). This is no small thing, because without holiness "no one will see the Lord" (12:14). God is training us for heaven, where holiness reigns.

The author uses Esau as a poor example to follow, since he "sold his own birthright for a single meal" (12:16). That is, he didn't rightly value his birthright, and gave it up under temptation during a temporary trial. Later, when he deeply regretted his decision, the consequences of his foolishness could not be reversed (12:17). The message was clear to the Hebrew Christians and to all those who have reached a place of maturity in Christ. To abandon faith at this point is an irreversible decision (remember 6:4-6).

Finally, the author paints a picture that compares the awesome scene witnessed by the children of Israel at the giving of the Mosaic Law with the much more awesome future scene that will be witnessed by all believers who enter the New Jerusalem. Unbelieving Jews likely pointed to the former to attempt to persuade Hebrew Christians to revert to Judaism. But the Hebrew Christians need not be persuaded. God had a more awesome scene prepared for them! At the giving of the Mosaic Law, God's voice shook a mountain, but one day it will shake the earth, and all that will remain are those things that cannot be shaken, namely, what belongs to His eternal, unshakable kingdom. Believers, keep on believing, and you will be unshakable!

Day 231, Hebrews 13

The final admonitions of this letter are just as applicable to us as they were to the Hebrew Christians of the first century. First and foremost, "love of the brethren" should characterize our lives (13:1). That love is the defining mark of true believers. If we love Jesus, we will love His family, and it seems the author of Hebrews had in his mind Jesus' foretelling of the judgment of the sheep and goats (Matt. 25:31-46) as he wrote this final chapter.

He first mentions showing "hospitality to strangers" (13:2), reminiscent of Jesus' words to the sheep, "I was a stranger, and you invited Me in" (Matt. 25:35). He then mentions prisoners and the persecuted (the ill-treated), reminiscent of Jesus' words, "I was in prison, and you came to Me" (Matt. 25:36). Although many of us are not living in nations where Christians are being significantly persecuted or serving time in prison because of their faith, this does not mean that there is nothing we can do for persecuted and imprisoned Christians around the world. There are a number of excellent ministries that focus on serving the persecuted, such as *Voice of the Martyrs*, *Christian Solidarity Worldwide*, and *Open Doors* that can keep you informed of specific believers around the world who can use our prayers and to whom you can write to encourage. *Heaven's Family* also has a Persecuted Christians Fund which is used to meet the pressing needs of persecuted believers and their families.

The author mentions other "holiness essentials," reminding his readers (as Paul often did, which makes me suspect that he is the author) that God will judge fornicators and adulterers (13:4). He also warns against the love of money, often expressed by Paul using the words *greed* and *covetousness*, which he also frequently listed as sins that will keep one out of heaven. The author defines the love of money as "not being content with what you have," a heart attitude that would of course be manifested by actions. As long as we know that the Lord will never forsake us, we never need to fear suffering the lack of what we need (13:5-6).

Although the old covenant sacrificial system has been abolished, there are still sacrifices that new covenant believers can offer up to God. They are "sacrifices of praise" which the author says we should continually offer up (13:15). God is also pleased when we sacrifice our time, talents and treasures, "doing good and sharing" (13:16).

We are instructed to "obey [our] leaders and submit to them," but the author defines the kind of leaders who are worthy of such submission as being leaders "who keep watch over your souls as those who will give an account" (13:17). Genuine pastors are, above everything else, concerned for the spiritual health of their flocks. So they lead their sheep on the path of righteousness and make sure that they stay on that path, knowing that they themselves will give an account to the "great Shepherd" one day (13:20).

With this in mind, it is easy to see how far short so many fall who claim to be pastors, who in our age, very rarely even do so much as preach on biblical holiness, much less "keep watch over the souls" of anyone. It is also easy to see that it is only the pastor who oversees a small group who can possibly "keep watch over the souls" of his flock. A pastor must have a personal and close relationship with those in his flock if he is to know how they are living their lives. Discipleship is relational.

Although this letter has been packed with analogies drawn from the Old Testament, it seems the author couldn't resist sharing at least one more. Just as the bodies of the animals whose blood was brought into the holy place were burned outside the camp, so Jesus was crucified outside the walls of Jerusalem (13:11-12). The Hebrew Christians should not think it strange that they were being ostracized from Jewish society, because Christ was also. They may not have been welcome in Jerusalem, but they were gaining an eternal city, the New Jerusalem (13:13-14).

Day 232, 1 John 1

This letter is thought to have been written around AD 85 or 90, making it one of the final New Testament epistles to be penned. Most, if not all, of the original apostles had been martyred, with the exception of the aged apostle John, who reportedly spent the last years of his ministry in Ephesus before being banished to the Isle of Patmos.

To what group of Christians was John writing? That's uncertain, but he obviously wrote to protect them from heresies that were spreading. From certain historical sources, we know that there were those who were teaching a concept of the complete, separate distinction between the physical (impure) and the spiritual (pure). Therefore, it made no difference what a person did with his body, as long as his spirit was clean. This kind of logic led some to claim that they had never sinned. Moreover, it was being contended that one could become a Christian without his behavior being affected. An additional heresy existed that claimed Jesus had only come in the spirit, not in the flesh.

Right from the start of his letter, John addressed the latter of those heresies. In the first three verses, he stated that he and others heard, saw and touched Jesus, whom he calls "the Word of Life" (1:1; see also 4:2). Jesus came in the flesh and was not just a spirit.

John then introduces three erroneous conceptions, beginning each one with the words, "If we say that" (1:6,8,10). Obviously, there were some who were making certain erroneous statements.

First, some were claiming to be in fellowship with God yet at the same time practicing sin, a heresy that continues to this day. John will address that heresy so often throughout this first epistle that we could say that the primary theme of this letter is: "How one can know if he has been truly born again by God's Spirit." John will repeatedly list three tests in that regard, the first being the test of obedience:

> God is Light, and in Him there is no darkness at all. If we say that we have fellowship with Him and yet walk in the darkness, we lie and do not practice the truth... (1:5-6).

"Walking in darkness" is synonymous with living in disobedience to Jesus' commandments, as Jesus is the Truth (John 14:6). Everyone is either walking in darkness, following Satan and his lies, or walking in light, following Jesus and His commandments.

It will become clear as we continue to read John's letter that the phrase, "being in fellowship with God," is an equivalent expression to "being saved" or "being a child of God." The word *walk* in the same verse implies an ongoing practice. Thus we could paraphrase 1:6 to read, "If we claim that we are saved but practice sin, we are lying."

Lest anyone think that John was advocating that all true Christians are perfectly obedient, he quickly offers further clarification and corrects another erroneous conception:

> If we say that we have no sin, we are deceiving ourselves and the truth is not in us. If we confess our sins, He is faithful and righteous to forgive us our sins and to cleanse us from all unrighteousness (1:8-9).

So believers aren't perfect, but they are striving for perfection. When they fall short, which they all do, they confess their sins and receive God's forgiveness and cleansing. That is the pruning and sanctification process that all believers experience.

Finally, some were apparently claiming *never* to have sinned (1:10). That is heretical because it contradicts Scripture and eliminates the need for salvation and a Savior, making Jesus' death meaningless.

If we "walk in the light...we have fellowship with one another" (1:7). When John wrote of having "fellowship with one another," he was not thinking of people standing around after church drinking coffee in the "fellowship hall." The Greek word translated "fellowship" is *koinonia*, which denotes a sacrificial sharing with others. We read in Acts, "Those who had believed...had all things in common," or "in *koinos*" (Acts 2:44). Those who "walk in the light" love each other. Holiness is primarily characterized by servanthood. Does the word "servanthood" describe your lifestyle?

1 John

Day 233, 1 John 2

Throughout his first epistle, John repeatedly returns to three different tests that validate authentic conversion. The first is moral: Are you practicing righteousness and keeping God's commandments? The second is social: Do you demonstrate unselfish love for fellow believers? The third is theological: Do you believe that Jesus Christ is the Son of God who has come in the flesh? In today's reading we encounter the first two tests.

John indicates that true Christians shouldn't sin and don't practice sin, but sometimes do commit sins. Those sins should be confessed, and when they are, they are forgiven (1:9). We can take heart knowing that we "have an Advocate with the Father, Jesus Christ the righteous" (2:1). As our attorney before God's throne, Jesus never pleads our innocence or presents extenuating circumstances. Rather, He offers His sufferings as the ground for our acquittal. Jesus is "the propitiation for our sins" (2:2). That means He's the One who has appeased God's wrath against us.

Notice also that Jesus is the propitiation, not only for our sins, "but also for those of the whole world" (2:2). The word "our" obviously refers to those to whom John was writing, which, according to him was "you that believe on the name of the Son of God" (5:13). So Jesus not only died for the sins of believers, but "for those of the whole world," which must include unbelievers. John uses the word "world" over 20 times in this short letter, and every time it either refers to everyone in the world or everyone in the kingdom of darkness. Thus 1 John 2:2 is the final nail in the coffin of the Calvinist idea that Jesus died only for the sins of those allegedly predestined to be saved.

Although John's style sometimes seems confusing, it helps to take note that he often uses synonymous phrases in the same sentences or passages. For example, in 2:3-6, "knowing Jesus," "being in Him," and "abiding in Him" are synonymous. "Keeping His commandments," "keeping His word," and "walking as He walked" are also synonymous. If we know Jesus, are in Him, and abide in Him, it is revealed by the fact that we keep His commandments, keep His word and walk as He walked. That is the moral test, and John repeats it several times in this chapter: "The one who does the will of God lives forever" (2:17) and, "Everyone also who practices righteousness is born of Him" (2:29).

John's first mention of the social test is found in 2:9-11. True Christians, that is, people who are "in the light," love each other, just as Jesus said, "By this all men will know that you are My disciples, if you have love for one another" (John 13:35). The one who hates his brother is not really a brother and is still in darkness.

Apparently, some among those to whom John wrote had broken fellowship from the body (2:19). John calls them "antichrists" because those who are against the body of Christ are against Christ. They revealed that they were not true believers and were likely guilty of at least some of the doctrinal errors that John addresses, perhaps even denying that Jesus was the Christ (2:22). They were attempting to draw others away to join them in their heresies. But John reminded his readers that they had an inward anointing from the Holy Spirit that would lead them into truth and away from false doctrine.

Lest John's readers think he was doubting the authenticity of their salvation, he wrote to assure them. Although each individual reader fell into one of three different categories of spiritual maturity—children, young men or fathers—their sins had been forgiven, they knew God, and they had overcome Satan through faith in Jesus (2:12-14).

What are "the lust [*desire*] of the flesh and the lust [*desire*] of the eyes and the boastful pride of life" (2:16)? Some suggest that they speak of the world's preoccupation with sex, money and power, sometimes more crudely expressed as "girls, gold and glory." According to Paul, however, the desires of the flesh lead to deeds that include not only illicit sex, but idolatry, strife, drunkenness and more (Gal. 5:16-21).

Day 234, 1 John 3

John continues to focus in this chapter, first on the moral test, and then on the social test of authentic conversion. The application of both these tests disqualify multitudes who claim to be born again.

John begins by reminding his readers that those who have a hope of seeing God purify themselves, knowing that He is pure. That is logical, and that is the moral test. If I expected to have an audience with the Queen of England today (I happen to be in England as I'm writing this), I would be preparing myself, wouldn't I? I wouldn't be driving towards Windsor Castle in my pajamas.

But do true believers never stumble into sin? Are they perfect? No, notice that John uses the word "practice" seven times within the space of seven verses (3:4-10). To "practice sin" indicates some degree of habitual repetition. Thus, to extract, as some do, a single verse from this chapter, such as 3:6, which says, "No one who abides in Him sins; no one who sins has seen Him or knows Him," to prove that true Christians never sin, is to ignore context.

Be that as it may, let us not miss John's clear message. In their behavior, true Christians stand out in contrast among non-Christians. John writes that by both the moral and social tests, the children of God and the children of the devil are *obvious* (3:10). How that contradicts what we so often hear about not being able to judge if people are Christians because "only God knows what is in their hearts." John indicates that "God's seed" which abides in us, which must be a reference to the Holy Spirit, prevents us from sinning.

Next, on to the social test. "We know that we have passed out of death into life because we love the brethren" (3:14). "Christians" who hate Christians are not Christians. And there is basically one reason why non-Christians hate Christians. It is because their deeds are evil and *true* Christians are righteous in their behavior, and that is certainly an evil reason to hate someone. Perhaps that is why John writes that "everyone who hates his brother is a murderer" (3:15). Granted, there are things to legitimately hate about wicked people. But to hate someone whose deeds are righteous is to reveal one's utter depravity.

I'm afraid that the significance of 3:17—"Whoever has the world's goods, and sees his brother in need and closes his heart against him, how does the love of God abide in him?"—is missed by most of us living in wealthy Western nations. We rarely encounter a fellow Christian who is truly "in need" by biblical standards, this is, lacking essentials such as food and covering. Yet there are multitudes of such Christians around the world. As I suspect that you already know, the primary goal of the ministry of *Heaven's Family* is to link Christians like us, who have "the world's goods" (3:17), with Christians who are suffering very pressing needs. If we close our hearts against them, we show that the love of God does not abide in us. But when we, in obedience to God, make sacrifices on their behalf, we "assure our heart before Him in whatever our heart condemns us" (3:19-20). That is, when our hearts condemn us for not making those sacrifices for our spiritual family in need, our repentance restores the assurance that we are genuine believers and "of the truth" (3:19).

How tragic it is when Christians are taught that guilt is from the devil, and that they should rebuke it in Jesus' name. According to John, it is quite possible for a true believer to possess a heart that condemns him, and for good reason.

The great blessing of having a non-condemning heart (due to sacrificial obedience) is that "we have confidence before God; and whatever we ask we receive from Him" (3:21-22). Obviously, there is a correlation between obedience and answered prayer. Proverbs 21:13 says, "He who shuts his ear to the cry of the poor will also cry himself and not be answered." That's a promise of unanswered prayer!

Day 235, 1 John 4

John centers today on the theological and social tests of authentic conversion. With a warning about false prophets, he begins this chapter with the theological test: Any person who denies that Jesus came in the flesh is not from God (4:2-3). Apparently, that particular heresy was prevalent in John's time.

You may have noticed that John referred to the testing of *spirits* rather than the testing of *prophets* (4:1). The two are related, however, because at least some false prophets are motivated by demonic spirits that empower them with a degree of convincing (and deceptive) supernatural power. There are, of course, "lesser" false prophets who just prophesy from their own imaginations with no accompanying supernatural manifestations, of which there are hoards today.

It would seem to be impossible to test a spirit directly, because spirits are invisible, inaudible beings that exist in the spiritual realm. It may be possible, however, to test the spirit that is motivating or inspiring a person by asking that person if Jesus came in the flesh. If he responds in the negative, that would be a telling sign. I suspect, however, that there are many false teachers and prophets who would readily confess that Jesus came in the flesh yet who deny other essential truths about Him. So I would not make this one doctrinal position the only litmus test for determining if someone is a false or true prophet.

The only time when it might be possible to test a spirit directly would be when that spirit is in manifestation in the physical realm. For example, if a person began to prophesy under the inspiration of a demon spirit, it could perhaps then be questioned. I have heard of such instances, but have never experienced any myself. It seems that the Corinthian church faced a similar problem during their assemblies in trying to determine who was speaking under the influence of the Holy Spirit and who was speaking under the influence of a demon spirit. Paul told them that no one who was speaking under the influence of the Holy Spirit could say "Jesus is accursed." However, no one under the influence of a demon could say "Jesus is Lord" (1 Cor. 12:2-3).

In any case, we can be thankful that we have nothing to fear when it comes to demon spirits, because we've overcome their former dominion over us through Christ. We are no longer listening to their lies as everyone else is, because we've believed the truth. Greater is He who is in us (the Holy Spirit) than he who is in the world (the devil and evil spirits) (4:4).

Beginning with 4:7, John returns once more to the social test of authentic conversion. Because God has regenerated our spirits, we now possess His unselfish nature within us, and it gives us the capacity to love as He does, unselfishly. That unselfish love verifies that we've been "born of God" and "know God" (4:7), two synonymous expressions. True Christians are the "love people."

Is it true that whoever simply "confesses that Jesus is the Son of God, God abides in him, and he in God" (4:15)? It is true if a person's confession is more than just a *verbal* confession, and one that is lived out in his daily life so that he not only passes John's doctrinal test, but also his moral and social tests. Lots of people these days claim to believe that Jesus is the Son of God but deny their profession by their actions.

John's words, "Perfect love casts out fear," have been misconstrued by some to mean, "If we really understand how much God loves us, then we would never fear being punished." The truth is, however, that God loves the worst of sinners, and those who haven't repented should certainly fear the punishment that is waiting for them. John means that those who grow perfect in their love for others, obeying God and thus assuring their hearts before Him, find that fear of punishment fades away. John wrote that the one who fears punishment is "not perfected" or "complete" in love (4:18). If that speaks of you, then the solution is obvious: Love more!

Day 236, 1 John 5

Today's chapter begins with yet another restatement of the three tests of authentic conversion. God's true children believe that Jesus is the Christ; they love God's other children; and they obey the commandments of their Father (5:1-2). John reminds us that God's commandments are not burdensome due to the fact that we've "overcome the world" (5:4). That is, because we've been spiritually reborn, we've been delivered from our addiction to the world's sinful system and possess a God-given ability to obey.

What did John mean when he stated that Jesus "came by water and blood...not with the water only, but with the water and with the blood" (5:6)? Historical sources indicate that in John's day, there were those who taught that Jesus was born a mere man, but that Christ descended on Him at His baptism and then departed from Him just before He went to the cross. John refuted this heresy by affirming that Jesus was the divine Son of God when He submitted Himself to baptism (through water) and when He died on the cross (through blood). Jesus and Christ were not two separate persons; notice how John referred to Him as "Jesus Christ" directly in the middle of the verse under consideration. He was from birth to death and forevermore both the man Jesus and the Christ of God.

Years ago I used to quote 1 John 5:13 to every person who came forward to "receive Christ" in the church I pastored in order to "give them assurance of their salvation:"

> These things I have written to you who believe in
> the name of the Son of God, so that you may know
> that you have eternal life.

I would ask each new convert, "Do you believe in Jesus, the Son of God?" When they replied affirmatively, I would say, "Then the Bible says you have eternal life." However, I began to wonder if I was making false affirmations when I noticed that so many new "converts" never returned to my church, indicating that they had no interest in learning how to follow the Jesus in whom they supposedly believed.

I realize now, of course, that John was saying in 5:13 that he had written his *entire* letter, which repeatedly listed the three tests of authentic conversion, so that his readers who passed those three tests would know that they have eternal life.

Passing the three tests not only gives us assurance of salvation, but also gives us assurance in prayer, as long as we ask for what is according to God's will (5:14). John cites two examples of prayer requests, one of which can be prayed with assurance and the other which can't. We can pray confidently for a brother whom we've seen commit a sin "not leading to death" and God "will for him give life" (5:16). But in regard to a brother committing a "sin leading to death" (5:16), we cannot pray confidently.

So what is "the sin leading to death"? Some (particularly those in the unconditional eternal security camp) think John was referring to a sin that would result in God's discipline in the form of *physical* death, but I don't know how we could discern if a certain sin was about to invite God's discipline in the form of physical death. And if we *assumed* that a sick Christian was being disciplined by God with sickness, how would we know if the ill person had committed a sin that ultimately would or would *not* lead to physical death?

It seems to me that the greater context indicates that it was spiritual death that John had in mind. So what is a sin that a believer can commit that leads to spiritual death? Remember that we read in the book of Hebrews that "it is impossible to renew to repentance" those believers who have "fallen away" after having reached a certain level of knowledge and spiritual maturity (Heb. 6:4-6). Certainly we would be able to discern if a fellow believer commits apostasy, and there is no sense praying for his impossible restoration. How I wish that this, and many other things in John's epistle, were more clear!

Day 237, 2 John

This short letter, obviously penned by the elderly apostle John, was cryptically addressed to "the chosen lady and her children" (1:1), which was either a Christian woman and her spiritual children or more likely a church and its members. "Your chosen sister" (1:13), mentioned at the end of this letter, would then be the church in Ephesus where John was serving, and her "children" would be the individual members. It is thought that John may have written ambiguously for the safety of his letter's recipients if they were in danger of persecution.

The letter obviously carries the same themes as John's first epistle, as he mentions the importance of loving the brethren, obeying God's commandments, and he warns against false teachers who denied that Jesus came in the flesh. In apostolic times, Christian teachers who journeyed from church to church were always extended the Christian hospitality of food and lodging, as the inns of that day were notorious for being little more than brothels. Disguising themselves as Christian missionaries, however, false teachers were on their way to promote their heresies among John's readers, and he therefore warned against showing them hospitality or even giving them a greeting (1:10-11).

John's instructions challenge the common thought that, as Christians, we're always supposed to be kind and welcoming to everyone. Although that is generally true, it is not so in the case of false teachers. They are to be shunned. If John's instructions were fully obeyed, many churches would be empty this Sunday!

Day 238, 3 John

John's final epistle is addressed to Gaius, probably a leading member of a local church and one of John's own converts, as he referred to Gaius as his own child (1:4). Just as in his second letter, John mentions the treatment of itinerant teachers, only this time in reference to true Christian missionaries as opposed to false teachers. Christians ought to show hospitality to the former group while shunning the latter group.

A first-century church manual known as the *Didache* indicates that early Christian hospitality was sometimes abused. It stated that anyone claiming to be an apostle who stayed longer than two days or who asked for money was a false apostle! True prophets had a right to stay and be supported, but ordinary Christian travelers were not to be entertained for free for more than two or three days. Those who wanted to settle for longer periods should work to support themselves, otherwise they were "trading on Christ."

John commended Gaius for his hospitality towards traveling ministers, stating that we ought to be involved in supporting such men that we may be "fellow workers with the truth" (1:8). Not all of us can take the gospel to foreign places, but all of us can help those who can. (You can support your own native missionary, by the way, through *Heaven's Family's* Native Missionary program!)

Contrasted with Gaius is a man by the name of Diotrephes who obviously held considerable influence in the church. He was marked by John as a self-seeking slanderer who had not "received the brethren" as Gaius had, and he even excommunicated those who did receive them. John would publicly expose Diotrephes when he arrived (1:10). Sometimes, in the interests of the entire church, hypocrisy must be exposed. This is particularly true when the sinning individual is in a position of leadership in the church. Covering such a person's sins under the guise of "walking in love" is not walking in love toward the people he leads and influences.

Verse 2 of this short letter is often used by prosperity preachers to prove to their greedy audiences that God wants them to become even wealthier than they already are. In light of what we recently read in John's first epistle, however, it would be incredibly foolish for us to conclude that John hoped Gaius would become rich so he could live in luxury and self-indulgence. The only reason John wanted Gaius to prosper would be so he would have more to share. Gaius was a loving servant of the brethren, a financial supporter of traveling missionaries (1:5-8), and if he prospered (and enjoyed good health, John's other desire) he could serve and give all the more.

All of this being so, certainly it should be our desire that every Christian who is seeking first God's kingdom will prosper, because more good would be done by their obedience to Christ and their love for the brethren. 100% of their prosperity can be used to do more good. But to teach that 3 John 2 proves that God wants those of us who are already so wealthy by the world's standard to increase our luxury and self-indulgence—as exemplified by modern prosperity preachers—is entirely unwarranted.

Day 239, Revelation 1

I tend to greet with skepticism anyone who claims to understand everything written in the book of Revelation. So please don't expect me to unravel every mystery about it over the next four weeks. My fundamental premise is that if God wants something to be clear, He can make it clear. The reason Revelation is sometimes vague is because God intended it to be vague. He wants us to wonder, and so that's what we'll do! And we'll be blessed as we read, just as John promised in 1:3, but *only* if we "heed the things which are written" (1:3). This book will motivate any soft heart towards holiness and purity.

Revelation can be divided into three sections. The first part, which we've read today, is the introduction. The second part, chapters 2-3, contains messages to seven actual churches that existed in Asia Minor in John's day. The third part, from chapter 4 to the end, contains foresight into future events. These three divisions were established by Jesus in His instructions to John: "Write therefore the things which you have seen, and the things which are, and the things which shall take place after these things" (1:19).

Some think that much of what John wrote of the future was fulfilled within a few years of his writing about them, namely by the time of the destruction of Jerusalem in AD 70. Others, like myself, believe that most of the future events which John foresaw are still yet to be fulfilled during a time of world-wide tribulation—when the antichrist will rise to power.

In his final years, John had been banished by the Roman emperor, Domitian, to the isle of Patmos in the Aegean Sea. It was there that he experienced his incredible vision, first seeing Jesus in His glorified state. Pay attention to John's description, as that is how He will appear when we see Him! Jesus was glorious and John was mortified.

In John's vision, Jesus was standing in the midst of seven golden lampstands and holding seven stars in His right hand. We are informed that the lampstands represent the seven churches to whom John was writing, and the seven stars represent the seven angels (or "messengers") over those churches (1:20). We would not have known this had it not been explained, so we see that God can make clear anything He wants to make clear, and keep mysterious anything He wants to keep mysterious.

I think it is safe to assume that there is a reason that Jesus chose to use lampstands to symbolize churches. Churches are supposed to be spreading the light of the truth in the midst of darkness. I'm afraid that many churches today would be best symbolized by black boxes.

If we understand nothing else in this wonderful book, there is one fact that couldn't be more clear, and that is the certainty of the second coming of Christ. Loosely quoting from the Old Testament books of Daniel and Zechariah, John writes in his introduction:

> Behold, He is coming with the clouds, and every eye will see Him, even those who pierced Him; and all the tribes of the earth will mourn over Him (1:7).

Everything we will read in this book leads up to that solemn and cataclysmic event that is highlighted in the 19th chapter. Jesus is He "who is and who was and who is to come" (stated twice in this chapter, in 1:4, 8). So many people are focused on Him "who was" while too few are focused on Him "who is to come."

Jesus claimed to possess "the keys of death and of Hades" (1:18). This was obviously a metaphorical expression. Keys unlock what is locked. Through His sacrificial death and resurrection, Jesus provided a means whereby people can escape the sentence of spiritual and eternal death and hell. Praise God that He "released us from our sins by His blood" (1:5), and He has "made us kings and priests unto God" (1:6; KJV). So from one king to another, have a great day!

Day 240, Revelation 2

What a hair-raising chapter! Jesus, the Great Judge, speaks from heaven, directly addressing four churches in modern Turkey. Did you ever wonder what Jesus would say to your church? Pondering that some years ago changed the entire direction of my life and ministry and marked the beginning of *Heaven's Family*.

Jesus had commendation, correction and encouragement for all four of the churches we read about today. His example is a good one to follow. Every correction should be preceded by a compliment and followed with encouragement. A spoonful of sugar helps the medicine go down. Another spoonful of sugar washes away any aftertaste!

Jesus promised rewards to those in every church who would "overcome." They would, for example, "eat of the tree of life" and would not "be hurt by the second death" (2:7, 11). Obviously, those who *don't* overcome *will not* eat of the tree of life, which is something mentioned near the end of Revelation as being the privilege of all saved persons (22:14, 19). Moreover, those who *don't* overcome *will* be hurt by the second death, something mentioned near the end of the book of Revelation as being the fate of all unbelievers (21:8). Thus, to "overcome" is to continue in obedient faith until the end so that one is ultimately saved. Jesus' promises to overcomers are one more indication that unconditional eternal security is a myth.

Just because one is currently a believer does not mean that in the end one will be considered an overcomer. One must "keep Christ's deeds until the end" (2:26). Indeed, Jesus warned the entire church at Ephesus that if they did not repent and do the deeds that they did at first, returning to their first love, He would remove their lampstand out of its place, which doesn't sound like a good thing. We must "hold fast" (2:25) until Jesus comes.

Some of Jesus' other promises to overcomers seem somewhat cryptic, such as His promises of "hidden manna" and "a new name" written on a "white stone" and "the morning star" (2:17, 27-28). Whatever those things signify, you can be sure they are good!

The church in Smyrna could have benefitted by a visit from some modern prosperity preachers since Jesus said they were impoverished, but rich (2:9). Obviously Jesus meant that they were materially poor but spiritually rich. If they could have only learned "their right to wealth as King's kids" and "activated prosperity principles" they could have become materially rich and spiritually poor, just like modern prosperity preachers. Too bad they lived before the time Jesus revealed those "prosperity principles" to the church. Worse, Jesus told them they were about to suffer tribulation for 10 days (2:10). If only they had known how to "exercise their authority in Christ," they could have experienced victory and blessing and avoided all that suffering! What a shame.

False teaching had infiltrated the churches in Pergamum and Thyatira, and it was as if they were being influenced by Balaam and Jezebel of Old Testament fame. Jesus was greatly concerned because His people were being led astray to "commit acts of immorality and eat things sacrificed to idols" (2:20; see also 2:14). We know that sexual immorality is a sin which excludes one from heaven (1 Cor. 6:9-10), yet Paul taught that there was nothing wrong with eating meats sacrificed to idols. Perhaps "eating things sacrificed to idols" was simply a reference to idolatry. We know that Paul equated immorality and greed to idolatry (Col. 3:5).

Regardless, Jesus promised to judge a certain woman whom He referred to as Jezebel, who was posing as a prophetess in Thyatira and leading the saints astray. He had mercifully given her time to repent, but she would soon find herself "on a bed of sickness" (2:22). Those who committed adultery with her would also suffer tribulation and Jesus would "kill her children with pestilence" (2:23). I assume that He was referring to her spiritual children, her disciples. His judgment upon them would serve as an object lesson to the churches that God repays everyone according to their deeds (2:23). Sobering stuff! We're certainly not reading about American Jesus today!

Day 241, Revelation 3

Why did Jesus address just seven specific churches in Asia, among hundreds that could have been addressed at that time in the ancient world? Some speculate that these seven churches represent seven consecutive ages in church history, and that we are now in the "Laodicean" or "lukewarm" age of the church. That is, of course, pure speculation, and the truth is that there have always been lukewarm churches since John's day (obviously) and there have always been on-fire churches as well. I think it is obvious, however, that at least six of the seven churches addressed by Jesus in these two chapters were in significant spiritual danger and needed warned.

Except for a small remnant, the majority of professing Christians in Sardis were certainly in deep spiritual trouble. Jesus described most of them as being dead, having incomplete deeds, being unready for His return, unworthy, in need of repentance, and wearing, not white, but soiled garments. They were in danger of having their names erased from the book of life and finding themselves denied by Jesus before His Father and His angels (3:1-5). But there was still hope—if they would repent. Overcomers, and only overcomers, have assurance of salvation (3:5).

Incidentally, isn't it amazing that anyone would cling to the theory of once-saved-always-saved in light of verses like 3:5? If Jesus promises not to erase the names of overcomers from the book of life, then the possibility of having one's name erased from that book exists for non-overcomers. That means people whose names are currently in the book of life are not guaranteed that their names will be found there when they stand before Christ. They must overcome. We are told at the end of Revelation that those whose names are not found in the book of life will be thrown into the lake of fire (20:15).

Take note that within chapters 2 and 3, Jesus uses the word *deeds* 17 times. To five of the seven churches He says, "I know your deeds" (2:2, 19; 3:1, 8, 15). God knows our deeds as well, and we ought not justify bad deeds with the excuse, "God knows my heart." Our deeds reveal what is in our hearts, and God promises to give to each one of us according to our deeds, not according to what is in our hearts.

Of the seven churches, the only one that Jesus did not find fault with was the church in Philadelphia (3:7-13). Still He admonished them to "hold fast" to what they had lest they forfeit their crown (3:11).

Did Jesus' promise come to pass quickly to make the antagonistic Jews from "the synagogue of Satan" (3:9) come and bow down at the feet of the Philadelphian believers? I suspect that was a promise that would be fulfilled in the afterlife. Can you imagine being released from hell for just a short time in order to bow before the feet of those whom you once persecuted?

The lukewarm Laodiceans were entirely blind to their spiritual condition. Jesus' view of them was the exact opposite of their view of themselves. They considered themselves rich—and they likely were *materially* rich—but He considered them "wretched and miserable and poor and blind and naked" (3:17). He thus advised them to repent and spend their wealth to buy gold from *Him* that had been refined by fire. I can only think that He was referring to laying up treasure in heaven rather than on earth. He also advised them to use their wealth in such a way that it would result in their being holy and spiritually perceptive. Wealth can be wonderful when it is used for what brings glory to God, but it can become a terrible snare otherwise. Let all buyers beware!

The very well-known painting of Jesus knocking at the door illustrates Revelation 3:20 beautifully. The artist did not paint a door handle on Christ's side of the door. It can only be opened by the person inside. I suppose that if the artist had been a Calvinist, he would have painted Jesus breaking down the door with a sledgehammer, illustrating His "irresistible grace!" (Couldn't resist!)

Day 242, Revelation 4

This chapter begins the third of three natural divisions in the book of Revelation—when John begins to record what will take place "after these things" (compare 4:1 with 1:19). He was apparently transported to heaven to witness the scene around God's throne. If this chapter doesn't put the fear of God into you, nothing will.

More theories and speculation have been extracted from this book than perhaps any other. For example, from this chapter, some find support for the idea that the church will be raptured *before* the world-wide tribulation simply because John heard a trumpet sound just before he was transported to heaven, and Scripture tells us that the church will be raptured at "the last trumpet" (1 Cor. 15:52)! And because John was in heaven *before* he experienced his visions of the earth's tribulations, this is presented as proof that the church will be in heaven before the earth's tribulations. The truth is, the only thing that is proven by John hearing a trumpet and being transported to heaven before he had his visions of the earth's tribulation is that John heard a trumpet, was transported to heaven, and then had visions of the earth's tribulation.

Some point out that, although the church is mentioned many times in the first three chapters of Revelation, it is not mentioned again until chapter 22, supposedly proving that the church is in heaven during the time of earth's tribulation. The truth is, however, that believers are mentioned in Revelation as being on the earth during its tribulations (6:1; 7:3-17; 9:4; 11:3-7; 12:14-17), and if there are believers there, the church is there as well, even if John didn't use the word "church" to describe them. Granted, many believers will suffer martyrdom during the time of the tribulation, and so they will be transported from earth to heaven due to their deaths.

John did his best to describe the scene around the throne of God, a sight that was almost indescribable by earthly standards. Can you imagine a primitive man from the jungles of Borneo visiting New York City and then trying to describe what he saw when he returned to his friends? That was John's problem. It was interesting that the four living creatures whom John saw—each with six wings and full of eyes—were very similar to the four-winged cherubim Ezekiel saw (Ezek. 1, 10), and the six-winged seraphim that Isaiah saw (Is. 6). John wrote of those creatures:

> And the first creature was like a lion, and the second creature like a calf, and the third creature had a face like that of a man, and the fourth creature was like a flying eagle (4:7).

Ezekiel similarly wrote of the creatures that he saw:

> As for the form of their faces, each had the face of a man; all four had the face of a lion on the right and the face of a bull on the left, and all four had the face of an eagle (Ezek. 1:10).

Imagine all that if you can!

Both John and Ezekiel described a rainbow over God's throne (Ezek. 1:28; Rev. 4:4).

John also saw "seven lamps of fire burning before the throne," explaining that they were the "seven Spirits of God" (4:5). This is certainly a mystery. Some commentators suggest those seven fires represent the sevenfold nature of the Holy Spirit listed in Isaiah 11:1-6: "And the Spirit of the Lord will rest on Him, the spirit of wisdom and understanding, the spirit of counsel and strength, the spirit of knowledge and the fear of the Lord." Again, that is speculation that doesn't convince me.

Rather than trying to comprehend every mystery of this chapter (as well as other mysteries in the book of Revelation), it is better to simply allow what we read to fill us with awe and wonder. May it inspire us to worship our awesome God whom we'll someday see in heaven as John did, and bow before Him!

Day 243, Revelation 5

As I mentioned yesterday, it is generally better to simply be awed by the glorious scenes which John describes in the book of Revelation rather than attempt to comprehend everything that he mentions in those scenes. In today's reading, John witnessed what all believers can look forward to participating in one day—worship in heaven. There, Jesus is the central focus, and He is worshipped for who He is and what He did. I think our worship today should follow that same pattern. There is no "fluff" in the songs that are sung in heaven!

Clearly, some of what John describes in this chapter should not be taken literally, but symbolically. We are told that the smoke that arises from the incense bowls of the twenty-four elders and four living creatures represents "the prayers of the saints" (5:8). The Lamb who is worthy to open the seven-sealed book is obviously symbolic of Jesus (5:6). The seven eyes on that symbolic Lamb represent "the seven Spirits of God, sent out into all the earth" (5:6), whatever that might mean!

These three symbols in chapter five make me wonder what else might be symbolic there that is not explained to us as such. For lack of knowing any better, I tend to take everything else in this chapter as being literal, including the seven-sealed scroll. That sacred book apparently contained God's predestined plans concerning the events of the tribulation, events of which we'll be reading as the unsealing of that scroll is described in the next few chapters.

Why these future events were written in a sealed scroll, and why only someone as worthy as Christ is qualified to break the seals, is a mystery. Perhaps the scroll itself is also simply symbolic. If nothing else, we are impressed with the fact that there is no one like Jesus anywhere in the universe, and the future destiny of the world is in His hands.

Although there is certainly a chronological element to this book, it is not always consistent, which adds to its mystery. For example, this worshipful chapter culminates with *every* created thing, not only in heaven and hell, but also on earth, worshipping Jesus (5:11-13). It doesn't seem likely that such a scene will occur anytime prior to or during the coming tribulation, or before Christ's second coming. It is almost as if the scene of pre-tribulational heavenly worship that John was witnessing suddenly leaps forward in time to after the tribulation. This being so, it is always good to be cautious before assigning slots on a timeline to any event of which we read in this book.

You may recall that God promised Abraham that through His seed "all the families of the earth [would] be blessed" (Gen. 12:3). According to Paul, that seed of Abraham who brought blessing to all the earth's families was Christ (Gal. 3:16), the one who told us to makes disciples of all the nations, or more literally, all the ethnic families of the world (Matt. 28:19) and the one who died for the sins of everyone in the world (1 John 2:2). We learn today that God's ancient promise to Abraham will be fulfilled, because "men from every tribe and tongue and people and nation" will be among those who will reign upon the earth, purchased by Christ's blood (5:9-10). Yet those who study such things tell us that there are still thousands of ethnic groups in the world today who have no disciples of Christ among them. So it seems that there is still work to be done. And there is still a harvest waiting for those who will set their eyes on the fields.

I was once inspired to write a song after reading this particular chapter. It is titled, *Worthy is the Lamb,* and if you have a few extra minutes, you can listen to it at: www.shepherdserve.org/songs/mp3/worthy_isthe_lamb.mp3. Please excuse the poor lead vocal and pray that the Brooklyn Tabernacle Choir will record it one day!

Worthy is the Lamb "Song"

Day 244, Revelation 6

Although this chapter is full of mystery regarding the specific details, the overriding message is clear: perilous days precede the time of Christ's return. It seems this chapter contains a general overview of those times, and as each seal of the scroll is broken by Jesus, a divine judgment is revealed that afflicts the earth.

If there is any chronological order implied in today's reading, then the earth's major woes begin with the revelation of the antichrist. He is symbolized by the first of four "horsemen of the apocalypse." Note that he rides a white horse, just as Jesus does when He returns (see 19:11-14). He thus portrays himself not only as a "good guy," but as the Messiah. The world will be deceived by him, ultimately believing he is God.

We are told that the antichrist will go "out conquering, and to conquer" (6:2). According to the prophet Daniel, the antichrist is a man of war who will rise from a ten-nation confederacy and subdue three of those nations (Dan. 7:8, 20-24). Take note that his rising is by divine decree, a sovereign judgment from God. You may remember that we read in 2 Thessalonians:

> Then that lawless one will be revealed whom the Lord will slay with the breath of His mouth and bring to an end by the appearance of His coming; that is, the one whose coming is in accord with the activity of Satan, with all power and signs and false wonders, and with all the deception of wickedness for those who perish, because they did not receive the love of the truth so as to be saved. For this reason God will send upon them a deluding influence so that they will believe what is false, in order that they all may be judged who did not believe the truth, but took pleasure in wickedness (2 Thes. 2:8-12).

The earth will be plagued by war during the antichrist's time (also symbolized by the *second* horseman of the apocalypse), and famine with its accompanying skyrocketing food costs (6:6), as well as widespread death and disease, respectively symbolized by the third and forth horsemen. Apparently, one-fourth of the world's inhabitants will either live in regions that will suffer these judgments, or one-fourth of the world's inhabitants will perish in these judgments (6:8).

Remember that Jesus also foretold of false messiahs, wars and famines that will plague the world during the end times. He warned, "For many will come in My name, saying, 'I am the Christ,' and will mislead many. And you will be hearing of wars and rumors of wars...for nation will rise against nation...and in various places there will be famines and earthquakes" (Matt. 24:5-7).

The end times will also mean martyrdom for many believers, as revealed by the breaking of the fifth seal. Note that those martyrs have a complaint that they make before God: "How long, O Lord, holy and true, will You refrain from judging and avenging our blood on those who dwell on the earth?" (6:10). They are told to wait until after even more martyrs are made. Note that they had not forgiven those who murdered them; nor were they told to forgive them. As we have learned repeatedly on our journey through the New Testament, we are obligated to love our enemies, but that doesn't mean we are obligated to forgive them. God loves the wicked but He doesn't forgive them—unless they repent.

This chapter's overview of the final days ends with a description of what Jesus said would occur just before His return (Matt. 24:29-30). There will be a great earthquake, the sun will be darkened, the moon will become blood red, and the stars will fall from the sky (meteorites?). Every mountain and island will be moved from its place (6:14). All the earth will cower in terror from the wrath of the Lamb and Him who sits on the throne (6:15-16).

Where will believers be then? They will be either protected on earth, or safe in heaven by virtue of martyrdom or the rapture. "God has not destined us for wrath, but for obtaining salvation through our Lord Jesus Christ" (1 Thes. 5:9). Praise God!

Day 245, Revelation 7

This seventh-chapter interlude in the "seal judgments" is a prelude to chapter eight, in which the seventh and final seal of the sacred scroll is broken by Christ, which introduces seven successive "trumpet judgments." Prior to those judgments, it is apparently important to mark "the bond-servants of God" on their foreheads so that they will not suffer the judgments that are about to fall upon the world. In chapter nine, for example, we will read about stinging locusts that will torment only those who do not have "the seal of God on their foreheads" (9:4).

We are later told in Revelation that the mark on the foreheads of these 144,000 bond-servants is the name of the Lamb and the name of His Father (14:1). We are also later told that *all* of the bond-servants of God will have His name on their foreheads (22:3-4). For that reason, we may be jumping to a wrong conclusion if we think that *only* 144,000 descendants of Israel receive that mark at the time it is mentioned in this chapter. It is certainly possible that there will be more than 144,000 bond-servants of God on the earth then, and if so, it is certainly possible that all of them will be marked, but that 144,000 who are descended from Israel among them are specifically mentioned for some reason. Some theorize that they are called as evangelists, but that is speculation. They are mentioned again in 14:1-5, but by that time they are found in heaven worshipping before God's throne, either by virtue of martyrdom or rapture. So many mysteries!

How will it be possible to single out 12,000 descendants from each of the 12 tribes of Israel when there has been so much intermixing of those tribes over the past 2,000 years? Obviously, if we are to take the twelve-thousand number literally, then those who are marked won't necessarily possess a pure lineage from just one tribe, but each could have a dominant lineage from one tribe. God knows everyone's genetics. It has also been suggested that the 144,000, unlike other bond-servants who are sealed on their foreheads at that time, are ancient believing Jews who are already in heaven, and who thus may all possess pure lineages. On the other hand, there would seem to be no reason to mark those who are already in heaven. Again, we have more questions than answers.

Some suggest that it is during this interlude between the sixth and seventh seal judgments that believers will be raptured from the earth due to the fact that, in this chapter, John sees a multitude of redeemed people in heaven who are described as "the ones who have come out of the great tribulation" (7:14). Yet we will read in chapter nine, as I have already mentioned, of the release of stinging locusts that will torment only those who do not have the seal of God on their foreheads, implying that there will be people on earth at that time who do possess God's mark. On the other hand, we may be wrong to assume that what we read in chapter nine follows chronologically what we're reading today in chapter seven! It is also possible that the great multitude whom John saw is a multitude of martyrs rather than of "rapturees!" I don't know!

In any case, we can be certain that, although believers who are alive during the tribulation may not be spared from suffering under the antichrist's political system, they will certainly not be the objects of God's wrath as He pours it out upon the earth. There are only three possibilities. They will either be martyred, raptured or protected. God has not destined us for wrath (1 Thes. 5:9).

Rather than worry ourselves with what might lie ahead in our temporary future, let's rejoice in what lies ahead in our eternal future. As the angel told John, God will "spread His tabernacle" over us (7:15) and "wipe every tear" from our eyes (7:17). In the "ages to come," He will be showing us "the surpassing riches of His grace in kindness toward us in Christ Jesus" (Eph. 2:7). Praise God!

Day 246, Revelation 8

Today's reading reminds me of an old joke about a Presbyterian and a Baptist. The Presbyterian makes the claim that Presbyterians will be the first to be taken up in the rapture. "Does not Scripture say, 'There was silence in heaven for about a half an hour'? (8:1). That must be when God's frozen people, the Presbyterians, arrive!" His Baptist friend counters, "Oh no, Baptists will be in heaven first. The Bible says, 'The dead in Christ will rise first'!" (1 Thes. 4:16).

I suspect, contrary to that joke, that the reason for the half-hour of silence in heaven is not due to the arrival of the Presbyterians, but because of the solemnity of the judgments that are about to occur on earth at the breaking of the seventh seal. This begins the seven "trumpet judgments," the first four of which all affect one-third of the earth in various catastrophic ways.

You probably noticed that the seven trumpet judgments are preceded by mention of "the prayers of all the saints" (8:3), symbolized by the smoke of incense that arises from an angel's golden censer before God's throne (8:4). The judgments that follow are clearly related to those prayers, as we read that the angel fills the censer with fire from the altar and then throws it to the earth, which results in thunder, lightning and an earthquake. It seems that the martyrs' prayers for vengeance, of which we read in 6:9-10, are finally being answered after an initial delay. Remember that the Lord initially promised that He would avenge their deaths once additional martyrs suffered their fates. If the multitude before God's throne of whom we read in the final part of chapter 7—who came "out of the great tribulation"—were those additional martyrs, then perhaps chapter 8 begins to describe the answers to the prayers of the initial martyrs.

Surely, if any followers of Christ remain on the earth during those first four trumpet judgments, they will be protected from God's wrath. Some speculate that the repeated mentioning of the afflictions that plague one-third of the earth indicate a *geographical* third of the earth. That is, when we read that "a third of the trees were burned up," John doesn't mean that one-third of all the trees across the entire planet will be burned, but that in one geographical third of the earth, all the trees will be burned. This principle would seem to be true regarding the second trumpet judgment when "a third of the sea became blood" (8:8). Still, it isn't clear enough to make a confident assertion either way.

To those who are inclined to believe that the trumpet judgments should not be taken literally, it is helpful to remember that much of what John describes of earth's future judgment is similar to the judgments that the Egyptians experienced prior to Israel's exodus. Moreover, Jesus spoke of similar future judgments in literal terms: "And there will be signs in sun and moon and stars, and upon the earth dismay among nations, in perplexity at the roaring of the sea and the waves, men fainting from fear and the expectation of the things which are coming upon the world; for the powers of the heavens will be shaken" (Luke 21:25-26).

Revelation offers a true revelation of God's holy wrath, and those who say that the God of the New Testament is different from the God of the Old haven't read Revelation too closely. Aren't you glad that you've been saved from the wrath of God through Jesus?

Day 247, Revelation 9

I have more questions than answers regarding the fifth and sixth trumpet judgments. But rather than be frustrated over what is a mystery, let us be glad that the general themes are crystal clear. No one who reads this chapter debates the fact that God's ever-increasing end-time judgments will result in much misery for the earth's inhabitants, and when the sixth trumpet judgment is completed, the world's population will have decreased by a third. Still, those who survive will not fear God, as evidenced by the fact that they don't repent of their idolatry, murder, sorcery, immorality and thievery (9:20-21).

Regarding the stinging locusts who are released to torment earth's inhabitants for five months, it seems reasonable to believe that they are demonic spirits rather than a new species of physical insects. They are released by an angel from the "bottomless pit," and their leader is a fallen angel named Abaddon/Apollyon. The fact that John describes them as resembling war horses with crowned human faces that have women's hair, lions' teeth, locusts' wings, and the tail of a scorpion, seems to also support the idea that they are demonic spirits. I suppose that if they are invisible that will make their stinging torment all the worse. John writes that people will wish for death then. Pharmaceutical companies will be working overtime to come up with a pill for those afflicted with "sudden sting syndrome."

Take note that the stinging locusts are not permitted to harm those "who have the seal of God on their foreheads" (9:4), a reference to those in chapter seven who were specially marked, which included 144,000 descendants of Israel (and perhaps others). So God will differentiate between the righteous and the wicked, a comforting thought. And if only 144,000 descendants of Israel do possess the seal of God on their foreheads, then this passage seems to strongly suggest that all other believers will have been martyred or raptured by the time of the fifth trumpet judgment.

The sixth trumpet judgment also seems to be a release of demonic spirits—200 million of them—by means of the release of four fallen angels who for some unexplained reason are bound "at the great river Euphrates" (9:14). The Euphrates begins in Turkey, and flows across Syria and through Iraq, emptying into the Persian Gulf, so it is not too difficult to imagine a few demons in that region of the world!

Some commentators suggest that John was not describing demons, but an army of 200 million men accompanied by tanks and artillery, something John had never seen in his day, and thus he described as having "mouths" from which "proceed fire and smoke and brimstone" (9:17). I wonder, however, why John would describe tanks and artillery as having horses with heads like lions, and why he would refer to gun barrels as the mouths of those "horses," which, incidentally, had riders whose breastplates were "the color of fire and of hyacinth and of brimstone" (9:17). I also wonder about those horses' tails which "are like serpents and have heads" and which also do harm (9:19). That hardly sounds like a description of army tanks to me. I am more inclined to think that John witnessed yet another release of tormenting demonic spirits.

Obviously, God will hope that the two-thirds of the earth's inhabitants who survived the sixth trumpet judgment will be motivated to repent; otherwise He would have had no mercy on them and killed them all. His mercy will be spurned, however. Take note that God foreknows that His mercy will be spurned by the survivors, but He only foreknows it because He allows them to survive and He observes their reaction, a reaction which can then be known as well as foreknown! God cannot foreknow the reactions of free moral agents unless those free moral agents are tested in the realm of time. So foreknowledge is not quite all it is cracked up to be!

Day 248, Revelation 10

The eleven short verses of chapter ten are parenthetical between the sixth and seventh trumpet judgments. It begins with an angel who is apparently quite large, as he places "his right foot on the sea and his left on the land" (10:2), who cries out with a loud voice. At the same time, John hears "seven peals of thunder" (10:4) which communicate something that John is forbidden to record. So *there* is a sure example of something God does not want us to understand.

Apparently, however, that particular event signals the end of a long delay to the finishing of the "mystery of God...as He preached to His servants the prophets" (10:6-7). That must be reference to all that was foretold in the Old Testament about "the day of the Lord." Although the final pouring out of God's wrath upon the earth had been delayed for a long time, nothing will be able to stop it when the seventh angel sounds. This is the beginning of the end.

The book that John then ate was symbolic of the words he would prophesy concerning all that would occur after the seventh angel sounded his trumpet, what we will be reading in the remainder of Revelation. Although that book was sweet in his mouth, it was bitter in his stomach, perhaps symbolizing the bittersweet quality of the message. We're all looking forward to the inevitable end of things, but who is looking forward to the final judgments that precede Jesus' wonderful return? And once He has returned, there will never be another opportunity for mercy and repentance, which is why, according to Peter, Jesus has delayed His return for so long:

> The Lord is not slow about His promise, as some count slowness, but is patient toward you, not wishing for any to perish but for all to come to repentance. But the day of the Lord will come like a thief, in which the heavens will pass away with a roar and the elements will be destroyed with

intense heat, and the earth and its works will be burned up (2 Pet. 3:9-10).

I'm glad the Lord was patient with me!

Day 249, Revelation 11

During the final days of the final days, Jerusalem, referenced in this chapter as "the holy city" and "Sodom and Egypt" (11:2, 8), will be trodden underfoot by the nations for forty-two months, or exactly three-and-a-half years (11:2). Due to a prophecy in the ninth chapter of Daniel that leads many to believe that the end times' tribulation lasts seven years, the three-and-a-half years mentioned by John is often thought to be the last half of seven years of tribulation. But no one really knows for sure.

We are introduced today to "two witnesses," prophets whom John wrote will prophesy for exactly 1,260 days in Jerusalem, clothed in sackcloth (11:3). If we divide 1,260 by the number of days in a Jewish year—360—we discover that 1,260 days is exactly 3 ½ years also. We don't know, however, if the 3 ½ years in which Jerusalem is trodden underfoot by the nations is the same 3 ½ years that the two witnesses prophesy there.

We are also not told the identities of those two prophets. Some speculate that they are Enoch and Elijah, two Old Testament prophets who never died. Yet nothing is said about the two reincarnated witnesses being Old Testament men. I happen to be flying home from Texas as I write these words, and while I was there I met a man who believes that he is Elijah and that he is one of those two witnesses. I was not convinced, however.

God refers to those witnesses as the "two olive trees and two lampstands that stand before the Lord of the earth" (11:4). That doesn't help us much! We find something similar in the fourth chapter of the Old Testament book written by the prophet Zechariah, who saw (about six-hundred and fifty years before John's vision) his own vision of two olive trees and a lampstand (Zech. 4:1-4, 11-14). Zechariah was told that the two "olive branches" were "two anointed ones who are standing by the Lord of the whole earth" (Zech. 4:14).

Regardless of what we don't understand about them, it is quite clear that God will grant those prophets incredible powers by which they will be able to kill those who oppose them and make life even more miserable for everyone on the earth. They will surely call the world to repentance, but their preaching will apparently be fruitless. After three-and-a-half years of ministry, they will be slain by a "beast that comes up out of the abyss" (11:7), who will later be revealed to us as the antichrist.

The demise of those two prophets will make world headlines, and everyone will celebrate, thinking that their problems are finally over. The party, however, will last for just three-and-a-half days, because the dead bodies of those two prophets will be resurrected as they lie on Jerusalem streets and then be taken up to heaven. That event will doubtlessly be broadcast around the globe as well. Yet there will be no revival. Rather, there will be an earthquake in Jerusalem that will kill 7,000 people.

When God removes those two prophets, it would seem that all hope of mercy on the earth departs with them. The seventh angel sounds his ominous trumpet, over which there is reason to rejoice in heaven, for the inhabitants there know that God will soon judge the dead, rewarding the righteous and destroying the unrighteous (11:18). And then He will reign over all the earth.

These future events are sure to come, and they could occur within your lifetime if you eat healthy!

Day 250, Revelation 12

This chapter could be called "a short history of the devil in relationship to Israel." What we've just read certainly doesn't fit well into any assumed chronological order within the book of Revelation, as it begins with a vision of the birth of Jesus.

The unnamed woman to whom we are first introduced, and from whom Christ comes, can only represent Israel, and the 12 stars on her head must represent Israel's 12 tribes. Her child is portrayed in 12:5 as the One who will "rule all the nations with a rod of iron," who is unquestionably Christ (Ps. 2:9; Rev. 2:27; 19:15). He is also seen as being caught up to the throne of God, which is what happened at Christ's ascension. Satan is unquestionably portrayed as a dragon, who attempts to kill Jesus at His birth, which we know he attempted through Herod's slaughter of the Bethlehem babes. Satan is also portrayed as "the accuser of the brethren" (12:10) and as a persecutor of Israel (12:13, 17).

The dragon's seven heads and ten horns must represent endtimes governments and political leaders over whom he will hold sway. His tail sweeping away a third of the stars in heaven and throwing them to earth may represent a third of the angels joining Satan's original rebellion against God. This is, however, speculative.

We also read today of Satan being expelled from heaven and cast down to earth, and it can't be a reference to his original expulsion because he is spoken of being cast down as "the accuser of the brethren." There were no brethren to accuse when he was originally expelled. Additionally, when Satan finds himself on the earth, he persecutes the descendants of Israel, which also didn't exist when he was originally cast out of heaven. Also take note that when Satan is cast down to the earth, we are told that he has "great wrath, knowing that he has only a short time" (12:12), one more indication that we are reading about a future expulsion. It seems safe to conclude that Satan has had some access to heaven even after his pre-Adamic rebellion and expulsion according to certain scriptures (Job 1:6, 2:2; Zech. 3:1-2; Luke 22:31-32). Satan's accusing of the brethren before God "night and day" (12:10) also points to his current access to heaven.

The devil has certainly persecuted the descendants of Israel down through the centuries, and after his future expulsion from heaven he will apparently specifically target them again (12:13). However, twice in this chapter we learn that at least some of Israel's descendants will be given divine assistance to "flee to the wilderness," where they will find safe haven for 1,260 days, a span of time that is also described by John in today's reading as "a time and times and half a time" (12:6, 14). That identical expression is found in Daniel 7:25 and 12:7, and Daniel was told that it was the length of time that the saints would be given into the hands of the antichrist. So we can say with certainty that "a time and times and half a time" is one year, two years, and half a year, or a total of three-and-a-half years, which is the identical length of time that Jerusalem will be trodden underfoot by the nations (11:2) and the length of the two witnesses' prophetic ministry in Jerusalem (11:3). Interesting stuff!

Perhaps Israel's fleeing to the wilderness corresponds to Jesus' warning to His followers that they should "flee to the mountains" when they see the "abomination of desolation" standing in the holy place, that is, when the antichrist sets himself up in the temple as being God (Matt. 24:15-18). Jesus said that event would mark the beginning of a "great tribulation" (Matt. 24:21).

Will there be believers on the earth during Satan's end times persecution of Israel? There will definitely be *believing* Jews then, as some are spoken of as "the rest of [the woman's] children, who keep the commandments and hold to the testimony of Jesus" (12:17).

Day 251, Revelation 13

A few chapters from now, we'll read an angel's explanation to John of what this first beast, to whom we are introduced today, represents. His seven heads represent seven mountains and seven kings (17:9-10), and his ten horns also represent ten kings "who give their power and authority to the beast" (17:12-13). John is also told that the beast himself is an eighth king and is "one of the seven" (17:11). Although this is not as clear as we might desire, it is clear enough for us to be certain that the first beast is no less than the antichrist—who will one day captivate and dominate the world—through his ten-nation confederacy. Note that he has the same number of heads (seven) and horns (ten) as the dragon (Satan) whom we met in the previous chapter (12:3). Indeed, it is Satan who gives the beast his "power and his throne and great authority" (13:2).

John also notes that the first beast has characteristics of a leopard, bear and lion. The prophet Daniel also had a vision in which he saw four beasts come out of the sea, the first three of which successively looked like a lion, bear and leopard. The fourth beast Daniel saw also had ten horns, and he was told that each one represented a king who would come under the domination of the future antichrist (Dan. 7:1-28).

John saw one of the heads of the first beast receive a fatal wound that was then healed, causing the world to be amazed and worship both Satan and the beast (13:3-4). The antichrist may well use his miraculous resurrection to validate his messiahship. He will truly be a false messiah, an impostor of Christ.

John also describes the beast as "speaking arrogant words and blasphemies" (13:5) just as did the "little horn" in Daniel's vision which I previously mentioned, a horn which clearly represented the antichrist (Dan. 7:8, 19-26). Also, the little horn in Daniel's vision "makes war with the saints" (Dan. 7:21) just as does John's first beast (13:7). John wrote that he will have authority to act for

42 months—exactly three-and-a-half years (13:5), a number with which you should be quite familiar by now.

The second beast to whom we are introduced today is called "the false prophet" in 16:13 and 19:20. Aided by miraculous signs, he will be the leader of the new religion of beast worshippers. Jesus, of course, foretold that "false christs and false prophets will arise and will show great signs and wonders, so as to mislead, if possible, even the elect" (Matt. 24:24).

That false prophet will tell "those who dwell on the earth to make an image of the [first] beast" (13:14), which he will somehow animate so that it speaks and even kills those that don't worship it. Obviously, some will *not* worship it. Could John have seen some kind of interactive television? Can you imagine having a TV set that has a tiny camera on it, that when an image of the antichrist is broadcast, it monitors who is and is not bowing before it? I'm writing this right now on a laptop that has a tiny built-in camera, so the scenario I've just described is not so far-fetched!

The false prophet will force everyone to take a mark on their hands or foreheads, without which they will not be able to buy or sell. Some speculate that the mark will be an implanted microchip that contains individual data, something already being done in both animals and humans. There would be no need for cash and no worry about stolen credit cards, because everyone's financial information would be contained within his implanted chip, and his bank account could be automatically adjusted at each transaction. This interpretation, however, has its opponents, because John said that the mark would be the name or number of the beast, indicating the mark would perhaps only symbolize allegiance to the beast. Whatever it is, that is a mark you don't want to take if you're ever given the opportunity.

Regarding the number 666, many speculate, but I don't have a clue!

Day 252, Revelation 14

Interpreting the book of Revelation certainly isn't getting any easier with this chapter. Yet if we remain content understanding general themes, it isn't so bad. God is holy. He offers mercy. When His mercy ends, His judgment begins.

At first it seems as if Jesus, the Lamb of 14:1, and the 144,000, are on the earth, standing on Mt. Zion in Israel. But as we continue reading, we discover that the scene is actually in heaven (14:2-3). Is there a Mt. Zion in heaven? According to the author of the book of Hebrews, it seems there is. In Hebrews 12, he contrasts the ancient Israelites standing before Mt. Sinai at the giving of the Mosaic Law with the church of the redeemed, standing before a heavenly Mt. Zion:

> But you have come to Mount Zion and to the city of the living God, the heavenly Jerusalem, and to myriads of angels, to the general assembly and church of the firstborn who are enrolled in heaven, and to God, the Judge of all, and to the spirits of the righteous made perfect (Heb. 12:22-23).

So it seems that chapter 14 begins with the 144,000 worshipping in heaven, but we are not told how they got there!

Next, we encounter three angels flying through mid-heaven. The first preaches the gospel and admonishes the earth-dwellers to worship God (14:6-7). I wonder if his ministry to earth's inhabitants is the fulfillment of Jesus' promise that in the end times: "This gospel of the kingdom shall be preached in the whole world as a testimony to all the nations, and then the end will come."

The second angel announces the fall of "Babylon the great," which "has made all the nations drink of the wine of the passion of her immorality" (14:8). This is the first mention of Babylon in Revelation, and we will read more about it in chapters 16, 17 and 18. Babylon is an ancient empire and an ancient city, located in modern Iraq, which has been in ruins since before John's time. Unless that city (or empire) will be re-established and once again rise to world-wide prominence, then Revelation's Babylon must be symbolic of a very wicked city that likely exists now, or a future evil empire. In chapter 17 Babylon is referred to as being "the mother of harlots and of the abominations of the earth" and in 18:10 and 21 it is called a city. We'll consider this more when we read about Babylon in those chapters.

The third angel who flies through mid-heaven warns the earth's people of the consequences that will befall those who worship the beast or his image, or take his mark: They will be tormented with fire and brimstone, and as much as we may not want to accept it, it appears to be a punishment that will last forever (14:11). Thus it is important that the saints persevere in faith and obedience, as John declares in 14:12, lest they suffer that awful fate (John did not believe in "once-saved-always-saved"). It is better to die than to take the beast's mark, which is likely why a voice then told John to write, "Blessed are the dead who die in the Lord from now on!" (14:13).

The reaping and pressing of the grapes, depicted in 14:18-20, is obviously symbolic for God's gathering of the wicked and their subsequent judgment. I suspect it's a description of the battle of Armageddon, when Jesus returns to wage war with the armies of the antichrist. The carnage will apparently be immense, described by John as being so great that blood will flow for 200 miles to the depth of horses' bridles (14:20). This is hard to imagine, making me suspect that John's description is part of the overall symbolism of the passage. But who knows?

The prophet Zechariah described God's future destruction of a great horde of the wicked, perhaps seeing what John also foresaw. Zechariah wrote, "Now this will be the plague with which the Lord will strike all the peoples who have gone to war against Jerusalem; their flesh will rot while they stand on their feet, and their eyes will rot in their sockets, and their tongue will rot in their mouth" (Zech. 14:12). Yikes!

Day 253, Revelation 15

After reading about the seven "seal judgments" and then the seven "trumpet judgments," this chapter prepares us for the "bowl judgments." John does give us some hint of their chronological sequence, informing us that these are the final plagues. We will discover in the next chapter that those seven plagues culminate with the battle of Armageddon.

By this time, those who refused to worship the antichrist or his image, and who refused to take his mark, are found worshipping in heaven (15:2-4). Whether they are there as a result of martyrdom or a rapture, we are not told. In any case, no one can argue against the fact that they were on the earth during the rise of the antichrist and his persecution of believers. And nothing is said about them being Jews who were born again during the tribulation, as some who believe in a pre-tribulation rapture of the church like to think. For this and other reasons, I think believers are much safer if they don't count on being raptured before the antichrist "wages war against the saints," something which God foretold Daniel (Dan. 7:21; 13:7). Better to be prepared for the worst.

Will there be any believers still on the earth during the final seven plagues of the bowl judgments? We will read in chapter 16 that when the first bowl is poured out, the result will be "loathsome and malignant" sores "on the people who had the mark of the beast and who worshipped his image" (16:2), perhaps indicating that some on the earth at that time will not have the antichrist's mark or have worshipped his image. Moreover, after the sixth bowl judgment, which results in the gathering of kings for the battle of Armageddon, Jesus is then quoted as saying, "Behold, I am coming like a thief. Blessed is the one who stays awake and keeps his clothes, so that he will not walk about naked and men will not see his shame" (16:15). If every believer was in heaven by this time, there would seem to be no need for such admonitions for people to remain ready for Jesus' coming.

On the other hand, as we read through the seven bowl judgments, it is difficult to understand how some of them will not affect everyone who is still alive on planet earth. So, once again, we're left scratching our heads!

Day 254, Revelation 16

The seven "bowl judgments," which are God's final judgments upon the earth, will surpass the seal and trumpet judgments in their severity. It is difficult to believe that there will be any believers on the earth then, as the judgments seem to be world-wide. However, as I mentioned in the previous commentary, John does specify that the first bowl judgment affects those "who had the mark of the beast" (16:2), perhaps implying that there will be some on earth without that mark. Additionally, between the sixth and seventh bowl judgments, and not long before Jesus' return, He reminds his readers that He is coming like a thief, and states that those who stay awake and keep their clothes are blessed, as they will not be found naked and shamed when He comes (16:15). It would seem odd that He would warn people to remain ready for His coming if no one who believes in Him will be on the earth when He comes.

Although these bowl judgments seem quite severe, God is just in pouring them out, because they will afflict those who will have served the antichrist in the martyrdom of perhaps millions of followers of Christ. Because they "poured out the blood of saints and prophets" (16:6), God will give them blood to drink by turning the water of the sea, rivers and springs into blood. An angel declares, "They deserve it" (16:6).

Twice we read today the report that those who suffer the bowl judgments will not repent of their deeds (16:9, 11), which indicates that they will possess the capacity to repent. They will, however, blaspheme God and seal their doom.

During the fifth bowl judgment, darkness will cover the beast's kingdom, and its citizens will experience great pain to the degree that they will gnaw their tongues in anguish (16:10). Amos, Nahum and Zephaniah all foretold the time of darkness during the "day of the Lord." If you have the time, you might want to read Amos 5:18, Nahum 1:6, 8, and Zephaniah 1:15.

The sixth bowl judgment will result in the drying up of the Euphrates River "that the way might be prepared for the kings from the east" (16:12). This will be a preparation for the battle of Armageddon, when, through the divinely-permitted deception of evil spirits, nations will gather for one final battle in the valley of Megiddo, located in central Israel. When the 1,780-mile Euphrates River is dried up, it will give easier access for any nation east or north of Israel to invade.

When the final bowl judgment is poured out, it will result in the greatest earthquake in human history, so that "the cities of the nations" fall (16:19). Imagine all the world's cities crumbling at the same moment. Zechariah, Haggai, Joel and Isaiah all spoke of a great earthquake during the time of God's future wrath (Zech. 14:4-5; Hag. 2:6-7; Joel 3:1-16; Is. 24:18-20). John specifically mentions "the great city" being split into three parts as a result of that earthquake, which is apparently "Babylon the Great," mentioned in the very next sentence as being "remembered before God, to give her the cup of the wine of His fierce wrath" (16:19). It will become even more clear as we read the next two chapters that Babylon is a reference to a very wicked city, the capital of an empire. Which city might it be? Stay tuned!

Day 255, Revelation 17

This chapter has provided more fodder for speculation than perhaps any other in the Bible! What or whom does the great harlot represent? The final verse of this chapter identifies her as "the great city, which reigns over the kings of the earth" (17:18). So, she is a politically-significant, globally-dominant city, at least in her time.

John tells us that she has a mysterious name written on her forehead that reads, "Babylon the great, the mother of harlots and of the abominations of the earth" (17:5). So she is clearly associated with the Babylon of which we've already read in earlier chapters. Babylon is also mentioned in Revelation as being a "great city" in 16:19; 18:10, 16, 18-19, 21. For this reason, many consider the great harlot to be one and the same with Babylon.

The name across her forehead also reveals that she will possess unsurpassed evil influence around the world. John writes that she will commit acts of immorality with the earth's kings (17:2). So she will have a harlot-like relationship with world leaders (17:2), perhaps meaning that she performs her wicked services for their pleasure and pay. John also writes that the world will be "made drunk with the wine of her immorality" (17:2), indicating that she will seduce them to love her.

If the beast she rides is the same beast that was introduced in chapter 13 (it also possessed seven heads and ten horns; see 13:1), it would indicate that she has very close ties to the antichrist and his empire. Moreover, she is also very wealthy, "adorned with gold and precious stones and pearls" (17:4). Most significantly, John sees her as "drunk with the blood of the saints" (17:6). The great harlot is a "martyr-making machine."

Protestants often identify her as representing the city of Rome, seat of the Roman Catholic Church—a church which abandoned her first love and is thus guilty of spiritual adultery, possesses great wealth and world-wide political influence, is rooted in pagan Babylonian customs, has led multitudes astray by means of unbiblical doctrines, and which has been responsible for the martyrdom of millions of Christ's followers through the centuries. Historically, Rome has been known as "the city of seven hills," and we note that in John's vision, she is seen sitting on the seven heads of the beast, which are explained to him as being seven mountains and seven kings (17:9-10). Yet I think we should leave room for the possibility of another city arising to prominence in the future that may better fit Revelation's description of the great harlot.

We read near the end of today's chapter that the antichrist and his political allies will ultimately turn against the great harlot, strip her of her wealth and destroy her, unwittingly executing God's purpose upon her (17:16-17). The reason for their hatred, however, is not explained.

The beast that the harlot rides possesses ten horns, which are explained to John as being ten kings who give their power and authority to the beast for "one hour" (17:12). Those ten horns may well correspond to the ten toes on the famous statue that Babylonian king Nebuchadnezzar once saw in a dream that held endtimes significance (Dan. 2:31-45), and they may also correspond to the ten horns on the indescribable beast which Daniel once saw in a vision that depicted the antichrist's empire (Dan. 7:7, 20-24).

The seven heads of the beast also represent seven kings, of which John is told that "five have fallen, one is, the other has not yet come; and when he comes, he must remain a little while" (17:10). I've read scores of speculations in an equal number of commentaries, but none satisfy me.

I'm so glad that the most important thing for us to understand is quite clear: the antichrist and his allies are definitely doomed for destruction, and Jesus will defeat their armies at His coming (17:14). I suspect that all the other details which have been the subject of speculation for so long will become more clear as they occur.

Day 256, Revelation 18

Today we read a further indication that the great harlot of chapter 17, on whose forehead is written, "Babylon the great, the mother of harlots and of the abominations of the earth" (17:5), is one and the same as the "Babylon" of which we read today. Concerning the great harlot, an angel describes her as "the great harlot who sits on many waters, with whom the kings of the earth committed acts of immorality, and those who dwell on the earth were made drunk with the wine of her immorality" (17:1-2). In our reading today, an angel describes Babylon by declaring, "For all the nations have drunk of the wine of the passion of her immorality, and the kings of the earth have committed acts of immorality with her" (18:3). Sounds the same, doesn't it? And as I mentioned in our previous study, both the harlot and Babylon are called great cities, and both will be destroyed. Both are also said to be responsible for the martyrdom of multitudes of believers (17:6; 18:24).

It is also clear that Babylon will be a very wealthy center for global commerce, and for this reason, some suspect that Babylon represents New York City, which is also a place where world leaders often gather (at the United Nations), qualifying it to be a place where "the kings of the earth have committed immorality" (18:3) literally and more figuratively. It can hardly be said, however, at least at the current time, that New York City is full of "the blood of prophets and of saints and of all who have been slain on the earth" (18:24). The destruction of Babylon will be due, at least in part, to God's vengeance on behalf of His "saints and apostles and prophets" (18:20; 19:2).

Unlike New York City, Rome, of course, has a reputation for making martyrs, including apostolic martyrs such as Peter and Paul. Millions of Christians were martyred by Roman decree in the first three centuries. Papal decrees from Rome resulted in martyrdom of millions more through the centuries.

Babylon must represent a coastal city, as we are told that the smoke of its destruction will be seen by "every shipmaster and every passenger and sailor" (18:17) as they lament its demise. New York City meets that qualification. In John's day, the city of Rome was the center of the world's commerce. Although it was not a coastal city, it was (and is) not far from the Mediterranean Sea, connected to it by the Tiber River.

Addressing the never-ending question of whether or not there will be believers on the earth during earth's future tribulation, we note that at this point in the chronology of Revelation, God calls His people to come out of Babylon that they may not "participate in her sins and receive of her plagues" (18:4). It would seem odd for God to call His people to come out from Babylon if all of them were in heaven.

In any case, the righteous will rejoice when God finally brings an end to what will apparently be the capital of the world's wickedness during the antichrist's time. In fact, the saints are told to rejoice over its judgment (18:20). In the next chapter, the rejoicing really starts!

Day 257, Revelation 19

We have just read about the battle of Armageddon, where Jesus makes very short work of the great harlot, the beast, the false prophet, and the armies that foolishly gather to do battle against Him at His return. They are truly deluded by the devil to even hope that they might win such a war, and their fate is sealed before the war begins. The birds that will feast on their flesh are summoned in advance (19:17-18).

We are told in today's reading that, after her judgment, the smoke of the great harlot will ascend "forever and ever" (19:3), one more indication that she represents a wicked city. Keep in mind that the previous chapter ended with a scene of the smoke of Babylon rising (18:18), while this chapter begins with a scene of the smoke of the destroyed great harlot rising, once again leading us to believe that the great harlot and Babylon are one and the same.

We are also told that the kings of the earth and the armies that will gather to battle Christ as He returns will be killed by a sharp sword which comes from His mouth. This, I assume, is symbolic of the fact that He will kill them with just a word. Paul wrote concerning the antichrist: "And then that lawless one will be revealed whom the Lord will slay *with the breath of His mouth* and bring to an end by the appearance of His coming" (2 Thes. 2:8). After the antichrist is slain, he will be cast into the lake of fire along with the false prophet. We will read in the next chapter that they will be "tormented day and night forever and ever" (20:10) along with the devil himself.

It seems quite possible that when Jesus returns to earth riding a white horse, you might also be riding a white horse along with the army that returns with Him! That army does not seem to consist of angels, but of the redeemed, as they are described as being "clothed in fine linen, white and clean" (19:14), and we are told in an earlier verse that those who are invited to the marriage supper of the Lamb will be given clothing of "fine linen, bright and clean" (19:8). I suspect that there will be no casualties among that army at the battle of Armageddon. And with all this in mind, we may have a better idea what Paul meant when he wrote to the Corinthians, "We are ready to punish all disobedience, whenever your obedience is complete" (2 Cor. 10:6).

The marriage supper of the Lamb will apparently occur sometime within this same time frame, and we note that the church is the Lamb's bride. She will be pure and holy, cleansed by His blood, and the fine linen that she will wear will symbolize the "righteous acts of the saints" (19:8). So she will be more than "legally righteous," but also "practically righteous." It is possible that it was this supper that Isaiah foresaw when he wrote: "The Lord of hosts will prepare a lavish banquet for all peoples on this mountain; a banquet of aged wine, choice pieces with marrow" (Is. 25:6). Won't that be a wonderful occasion?

Day 258, Revelation 20

It will require only one angel to subdue and incarcerate Satan for 1,000 years, giving us insight into how much more powerful God is than the devil. God could easily immobilize Satan right now if it were His will. The devil, however, serves a purpose in God's eternal plan, namely, as the alternate choice set before free moral agents whom God is testing. This becomes even more obvious when we learn that the devil will be released for a short time at the end of the Millennium, at which time he will deceive the nations into foolishly attacking Jerusalem, from where Christ rules. God will use Satan to reveal those who are inwardly rebellious against Him, and then He'll judge them with fire from heaven. Keep in mind that Satan will be able to deceive only those who are rebels at heart. Until they are deceived by him, they would never entertain the absurd idea of attempting to overthrow Christ's global government.

It does seem amazing that anyone would not be happy with Jesus reigning over the world. When you think about it, however, it is amazing that there is anyone who wouldn't want Jesus reigning over his or her life right now. Most people, however, want nothing to do with Him. And just as it will be with those whom Satan deceives at the end of the Millennium, those whom he has presently deceived are those who want to believe his lies and who refuse to believe the truth. It all comes down to the condition of people's hearts.

Scripture promises that those who endure in faith will one day reign with Christ (2 Tim. 2:12), and today's reading affirms that overcomers will "reign with Him for a thousand years" (20:6). Our positions of authority then will be based on our faithfulness now, as Jesus' Parable of the Nobleman reveals (Luke 19:11-27). It is quite possible that the "thrones" (plural) of which we read in 20:4 are thrones on which we will sit. Paul wrote that we will judge angels (1 Cor. 6:3)!

Note that John refers to the resurrection of those who had been martyred under the reign of the antichrist as "the first resurrection" (20:5). One wonders how that resurrection—which obviously occurs after believers have been martyred by the antichrist—could be the "first resurrection" if there was another mass resurrection that occurred globally just *before* the time of the antichrist at the "pre-tribulational rapture" of the church, as so many believe. If, however, the rapture of the church and the resurrection of the dead in Christ—of which Paul wrote in 1 Cor. 15:51-55 and 1 Thes. 4:15-17—occurs when Christ returns at the end of the tribulation period, then it is obvious why that resurrection would be called "the first resurrection."

The bodies of the unsaved dead will not be resurrected until after the Millennium (20:5). The spirits that previously resided in those dead bodies, however, will be very much alive all during those 1,000 years, as disembodied spirits in hell (literally, "Hades"). The only thing they will have to look forward to is their physical resurrection, after which they will stand before the "great white throne" (20:11) of judgment, and then be cast into the lake of fire, which John refers to as "the second death" (20:14).

Words can hardly describe the solemnity of the scene when the book of life is opened and those who stand before the throne of God wait as it is searched for their names. Any hopes of salvation will be crushed. Other books, which describe the deeds of their lives, will be searched as well. Although we are saved through faith in Christ, our deeds reveal our faith or lack of faith. The unsaved will have no defense before God, as their deeds will testify to the unbelief in their hearts.

It seems quite obvious that the most important issue that everyone should resolve is the issue of whether or not one's name is recorded in the book of life. Everything else is insignificant by comparison. How tragic it is that most people spend their lives playing a daily version of *Trivial Pursuit*.

Day 259, Revelation 21

Peter wrote in his second epistle that one day "the heavens will pass away with a roar and the elements will be destroyed with intense heat, and the earth and its works will be burned up" (2 Pet. 3:10). Jesus also foretold that "heaven and earth will pass away" (Matt. 24:35). Obviously, the righteous will be far away from earth then, safe from harm. John was blessed to see the new heaven and earth that God will create, and he noted that there will be no sea. Surely there will be lakes and rivers though! (I hope!)

John was also blessed to see the New Jerusalem coming down from heaven to earth, which leads us to believe that the New Jerusalem is currently in heaven. It is quite a large city—1,500 miles by 1,500 miles. It would stretch halfway across the United States. Because it is also 1,500 miles in height, some imagine it to be a pyramid in shape (rather than a cube), with God dwelling at the pinnacle. The entire city shines with His brilliant glory.

The walls of the city are over 200 feet high, and they will appear somewhat like a grand encircling rainbow, being constructed with layers of precious stones (21:17-20).

John tells us that "the city was pure gold, like clear glass" (21:18). How gold can be transparent is impossible for us to comprehend, so we'll have to wait to see it for ourselves. But if the entire city is transparent, God's glory will penetrate every corner. John tells us that "the city has no need of the sun or of the moon to shine on it, for the glory of God has illumined it, and its lamp is the Lamb" (21:23). That doesn't mean that there will be no sun or moon, but that they will both be unnecessary for illumination.

The New Jerusalem will be the eternal capital of the world, and from there God will rule over the nations. It will be a city that is full of joy, void of death, crying or pain (21:4). Everyone will continually sense the love of God.

Most importantly, it will be a holy city. It is promised only to those who "overcome" (21:7) which are those who persevere in obedient faith, "those whose names are written in the Lamb's book of life" (21:27). God solemnly declared to John:

> The cowardly and unbelieving and abominable and murderers and immoral persons and sorcerers and idolaters and all liars, their part will be in the lake that burns with fire and brimstone, which is the second death (21:8).

How tragic it is that so many modern preachers assure their carnal audiences that "carnal Christians" (an oxymoron if there ever was one) are safe under God's grace, and that it is impossible for any saved person to ever forfeit salvation. John would disagree with both of those lies. Is it possible for a saved person to become an unbeliever, a murderer, immoral, an idolater or a liar? If yes, then it is possible for a saved person to forfeit his salvation. Heaven is not for the unholy, and that message sounds forth strongly, right to the final pages of the Bible (even through the final chapter, which is all that remains for us to read together)!

Day 260, Revelation 22

The river of the water of life mentioned in this chapter is similar to what Ezekiel and Zechariah saw hundreds of years before the apostle John lived (Ezek. 47:1-12; Zech. 14:8). Ezekiel also mentioned seeing the tree of life along that amazing river:

> And by the river on its bank, on one side and on the other, will grow all kinds of trees for food. Their leaves will not wither, and their fruit will not fail. They will bear every month because their water flows from the sanctuary, and their fruit will be for food and their leaves for healing (Ezek. 47:12).

Notice how similar that is to what John wrote:

> On either side of the river was the tree of life, bearing twelve kinds of fruit, yielding its fruit every month; and the leaves of the tree were for the healing of the nations (22:2).

How leaves will heal, and why nations will need healing, we are not told. In any case, it is interesting that the tree of life is found in the very beginning of the Bible (Gen. 2:9), and at the very end. Someday, when we're permitted to eat from it, we'll understand it better (22:14).

Amazingly, believers will someday see the face of God, something that God once told Moses that no man could do without forfeiting his life (Ex. 33:20). Our glorified bodies will apparently be able to handle what our old, physical bodies could not.

It also seems that our new bodies may not need to sleep. If they do, we'll have to sleep in the daytime, as there will no longer be any night in the city that is illuminated by God's glory (22:5).

It is interesting that the apostle John, perhaps the most spiritual person on earth during his day, twice made the error of worshipping angels during his visions (19:10; 22:8-9). This makes me feel better about my blunders. John was obviously overcome with what he was experiencing. In both instances, the angels told him, "Worship God."

In light of the fact that it has been almost 2,000 years since John had his vision, it is also interesting that an angel told him that the things which he saw in his visions "must soon take place" (22:6), and that "the time is near" (22:10). We know, of course, that 1,000 years to us is like one day to God (2 Pet. 3:8), so from His eternal standpoint, the things which John saw would take place shortly. It has, however, seemed like a long time to us.

One would expect that the final chapter of the Bible would emphasize the most important themes, and so it is. For the final time we hear that God is holy, yet He freely extends His mercy. In His mercy He offers to all, not a license to sin, but an opportunity to repent of sin, receive forgiveness, continue in obedience, and be rewarded eternally.

> Blessed are those who wash their robes, so that they may have the right to the tree of life, and may enter by the gates into the city. Outside are the dogs and the sorcerers and the immoral persons and the murderers and the idolaters, and everyone who loves and practices lying (Rev. 22:14-15).

These truths should guide the affairs of our lives and chart the course of our remaining years on earth.

Although this ends our journey through the New Testament, I don't have room to share my closing thoughts within my 700-word restricted allotment. So you'll hear from me one more time in your inbox! Thanks for reading with me over the past year!

Day 261, Congratulations! And some final words.

First of all—congratulations for reading through the entire New Testament—chronologically, no less—over the past twelve months. I hope that you've been as blessed as I have as we've studied the most important part of the most important book ever written. A lovely journey for both of us!

When I first committed myself to this project, I was probably biting off more than I should. I found myself waking up by 5 AM most mornings—without an alarm clock—motivated in my mind to complete one day's writing before I headed off to work at the offices of *Heaven's Family*. During that year's worth of writing, *Heaven's Family* grew from four employees to ten, and we moved our offices from my home's sunporch to rented commercial office space. I also traveled during those twelve months on ministry trips to Peru, Bolivia, Ecuador, England, the Dominican Republic, Canada, Kenya, Burundi, and twice to Myanmar. It was a very full year, to say the least.

In any case, my goal was your and my spiritual growth, and so I hope I've succeeded in challenging you to serve the Lord with deeper devotion and greater zeal.

If you haven't done so already, please visit the website of the ministry that I direct, *Heaven's Family*, at HeavensFamily.org. There you can find many teaching articles and video teachings, and learn how you can become involved in loving Jesus by loving "the least of these" among His family around the globe.

Again, congratulations on reaching your goal. I recommend treating yourself to something good and healthy! Personally, I'm treating myself to a strawberry and banana smoothie with a dash of honey! — David

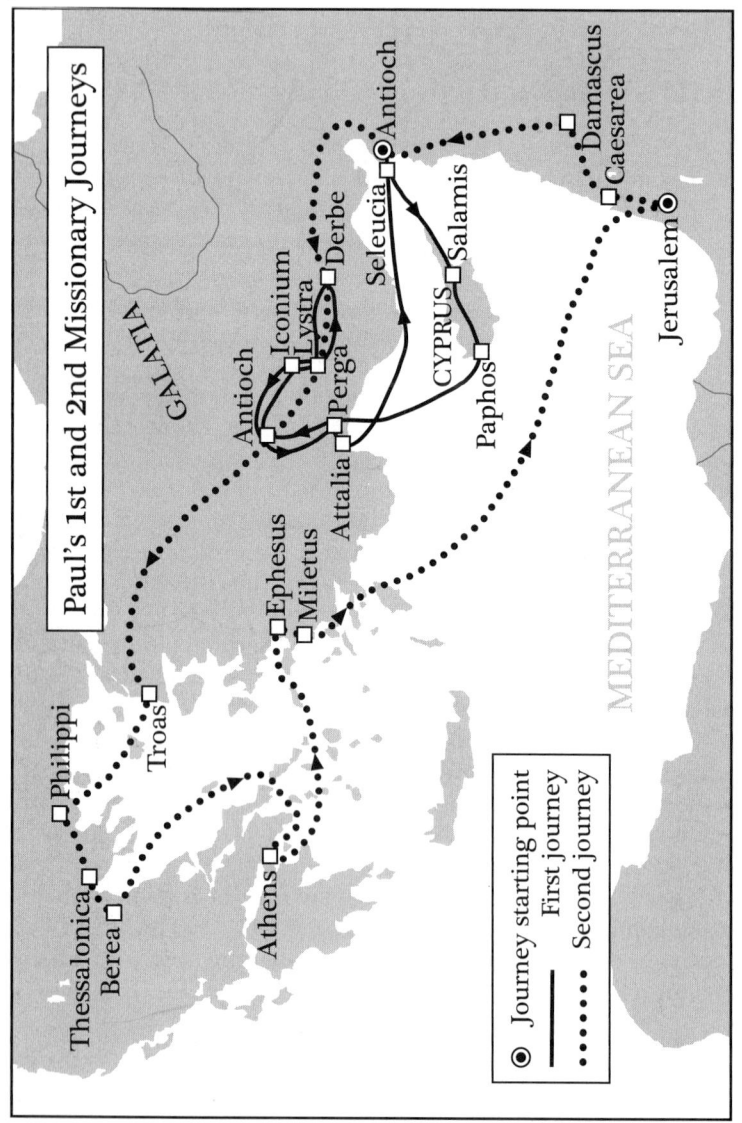

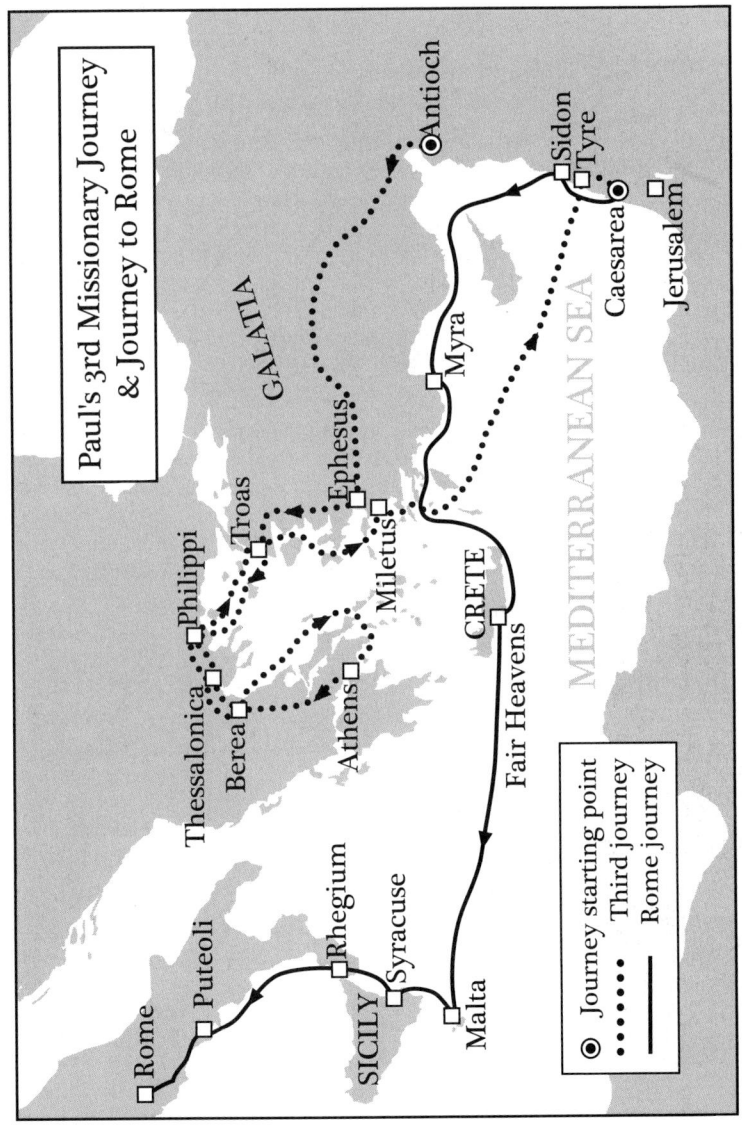

Also by David Servant...

Through the Needle's Eye
An Impossible Journey Made Possible by God

In this book, David Servant considers everything that Jesus, as well as every author of the Old and New Testaments, taught in regard to stewardship. His conclusions are not easy to disregard. Although impossible by pure human effort, the journey through the needle's eye is possible with God! (ISBN 096-296-2592) 269 pages, Paperback, $17.95)

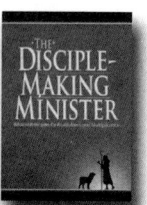

The Disciple-Making Minister
Biblical Principles for Fruitfulness and Multiplication

David Servant has been ministering to Christian leaders in conferences around the world for over two decades. From his experience of speaking to tens of thousands of pastors in over forty countries, he has compiled biblical teaching in this book that addresses the most important issues that Christian leaders are facing today. (ISBN 096-296-2585) 489 pages, Paperback, $19.95)

Forgive Me for Waiting So Long to Tell You This

Searching for a respectful way to share the gospel with a friend or loved one? Give them a copy of this book. In an easy-to-understand style, David Servant presents a convincing and biblical viewpoint that provokes readers to look at themselves, Jesus Christ, and their eternal destiny. (ISBN 096-296-2503, 132 pages, Paperback, $6.95)

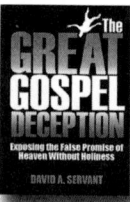

The Great Gospel Deception
Exposing the False Promise of Heaven Without Holiness

In this eye-opening book, David Servant takes a close look at what the New Testament actually teaches about saving faith, God's transforming grace, and "the holiness without which no one will see the Lord" (Hebrews 12:14).
(ISBN 096-296-2578) 240 pages, Paperback, $17.95)